JOAN OF ARC
AND SACRIFICIAL AUTHORSHIP

JOAN OF ARC
AND SACRIFICIAL AUTHORSHIP

ANN W. ASTELL

UNIVERSITY OF NOTRE DAME PRESS
Notre Dame, Indiana

Interior Design by Wendy McMillen
Set in 10.6/13 Minion by Four Star Books
Printed in the U. S. A. by The Maple Press Company

Library of Congress Cataloging-in-Publication Data
Astell, Ann W.
Joan of Arc and sacrificial authorship / Ann W. Astell.
p.   cm.
Includes bibliographical references and index.
ISBN 0-268-03259-9 (alk. paper)
ISBN 0-268-03260-2 (pbk. : alk. paper)
1. Joan, of Arc, Saint, 1412–1431—In literature.   2. Literature,
Modern—History and criticism.   3. Authorship—Psychological aspects.
I. Title.
PN57.J4 A84   2003
809'.93351—dc21

                                                            2002151554

∞ *This book is printed on acid-free paper.*

To My Colleagues in the Department of English
At Purdue University (Wonderful Comrades in Arms)

And to All the Saints
Who Have Helped Me Stay
In the Company of Saint Joan

CONTENTS

ACKNOWLEDGMENTS

One can never point precisely to the first beginnings of a book. Perhaps this one was already conceived when I was in ninth grade, cut my hair short, and declaimed a speech of Saint Joan of Arc before the student body in the auditorium at Jefferson Junior High. Perhaps it was already within me at Marquette University when I, as a master's student, wrote a Joan of Arc poem for *Saints in Soliloquy*.

The immediate starting point was a variable-title, 400–level course in literature and history that I taught at Purdue University in the spring semester of 1997. That course was dedicated to the study of different versions of the story of Joan of Arc in literature and film, from Shakespeare to Sackville-West. I discovered that biographical criticism worked well to explain the multiple mirrors of Joan and that it spoke to the propensity of undergraduates to identify with the youthful battle leader, saint, and martyr. To my students in that course and to Christine Neulieb, another student of Joan, I wish to express my gratitude.

Teaching that course in 1997 led to a TEAMS session on pedagogical approaches to Joan of Arc in honor of the historian Charles Wood at the International Medieval Congress in Kalamazoo, Michigan, in

May 1998. The paper I gave at that session has since been published in *SMART*. Shortly thereafter Bonnie Wheeler, the organizer of that session, founded the International Joan of Arc Society, to which I am happy to belong.

In spring 1998 I participated as an auditor in Dino Felluga's wonderful graduate seminar on nineteenth-century medievalism and wrote a first draft of the essay on Robert Southey's *Joan of Arc* that appears in this book as chapter 1. In February 2000 I gave a paper on Mark Twain's *Personal Recollections of Joan of Arc* at the meeting of the Illinois Medieval Association and received much encouragement from Allen Frantzen, who has also been working lately on medievalist topics and thinking and writing about sacrifice from a Girardian perspective. In June 2001 I was able to present my reflections on Schiller's *Maid of Orléans* in Antwerp, Belgium, at the international meeting of the Colloquium on Violence and Religion.

Thanks to a fellowship in the Center for Research in the Humanities at Purdue University in spring 2001, I could devote myself to work on this book. For that fellowship, I wish to express my sincere gratitude to the dean of the School of Liberal Arts and to Barbara Newman and Bonnie Wheeler, who wrote on my behalf.

This chronological account only begins to suggest the extent of my indebtedness. I have dedicated this book to my colleagues in the Department of English at Purdue University not only as a general sign of my love, respect, and thankfulness after a fourteen-year tenure in their midst but also because so many of them have offered me practical help and shown personal interest in this project.

Thomas Ohlgren and Shaun F. D. Hughes, my fellow medievalists, have been warmly supportive from the start. Justin Jackson and James Palmer read and responded to the rough draft of my introduction. Paul Whitfield White and Katharine Goodland pointed me to scholarship on Shakespeare's Joan. Geraldine Friedman, Paula Leverage, and Jean-Pierre Hérubel have coached me at different times in my pronunciation of French proper names. Charles S. Ross encouraged my research on Southey and Spenser. Marshall Deutelbaum and Richard Dienst helped me in my study of Joan of Arc movies. Dino Felluga, Geri Friedman, and Michael Yetman shared my interest in the British Romantics. Robert Paul Lamb read my chapter on Mark Twain and commented generously on it, making valuable suggestions for revision.

Arkady Plotnitsky encouraged my reading of Schiller's writings on aesthetics. Margaret Moan Rowe, Dorothy Deering, and Anne Fernald cheered me in my work on Sackville-West and Woolf. Elizabeth Thompson, Stephen Pierson, Shaun Hughes, Graham Smart, and Katie Goodland were fans of my inclusion of Leonard Cohen. Patricia Henley, Patsy Schweickart, and Ellen Kelly modeled for me political activism inspired by a Joanlike spirituality. Thomas P. Adler and Wendy S. Flory were my spiritual companions as I read Brecht, Shaw, Gordon, Hellman, and Ehn. No one was more generous and thoughtful than Tom Adler and Marshall Deutelbaum in putting Joan of Arc articles and newspaper clippings in my mailbox.

My greatest mentors in developing a theoretical approach to the materials presented here were Leonard Neufeldt, who first suggested the relevance of Harold Bloom's *Anxiety of Influence* to Shaw's "Preface" to *Saint Joan;* Dino Felluga, who spurred my reflections on medievalism and suggested the importance of Benjamin to this project; Thomas Ryba, who guided my reading of Marx; Geri Friedman, who braved my approach to Freud; and, most especially, Sandor Goodhart, who first introduced me to the person and the work of René Girard. This book as a whole and the concluding chapter, "The Catholic and the Jewish Joan," in particular would have been impossible without Sandy's beneficent influence.

I thank my good friend and colleague Ingeborg Hinderschiedt for translating Friedrich Schiller's "Das Mädchen von Orleans" for inclusion in this volume. I acknowledge gratefully the permissions granted by the Johns Hopkins University Press to quote from Erik Ehn's *Wholly Joan's;* by Sony/ATV Music Publishing to quote from Leonard Cohen's "Last Year's Man"; by the Continuum International Publishing Group to quote from Schiller's translated *Essays;* by Little, Brown, and Company to quote from Lillian Hellman's *The Lark* and *Scoundrel Time;* by Curtis Brown Group Ltd., London, on behalf of the Estate of Vita Sackville-West, to quote from Vita Sackville-West's *Saint Joan of Arc;* by Grove/Atlantic, Inc., to quote from Alan Sheridan's translation of Michel Tournier's *Gilles et Jeanne;* and by the University of North Carolina Press to quote from *The Maiden of Orléans* by Friedrich Schiller, No. 24 in the University of North Carolina Studies in Germanic Languages and Literatures, translated by John T. Krumpelmann (copyright © 1959). Figures 1 through 8, as well as the image on the cover, are selected from among the illustrations by Frank Du Mond, published in the first edition of Mark Twain's *Personal Recollections of Joan of Arc* (New York: Harper and Brothers, 1896).

Nadia Margolis and Robert Snyder read my manuscript, and they provided wonderful suggestions and much encouragement. Because of their generous and careful response, the book is better. To Barbara Hanrahan, director of the University of Notre Dame Press; to Sheila Berg, for her expert copyediting; to Christina Catanzarite; and to others at the press, I owe and offer my sincere thanks.

I hesitate to canonize in a list of names those saints who have increased my love for Saint Joan (although I have already done so, in part, in the preceding acknowledgments), but I do want to mention gratefully a holy priest who went on pilgrimage in my stead in France in the footsteps of Saint Joan; my parents and all those who went on pilgrimage with me in June 2000 to the Schoenstatt Shrine and to the Joan of Arc Chapel at Marquette University; and the many holy Schoenstatt Sisters of Mary who are striving, like Joan of Arc, to lead their "king," Fr. Joseph Kentenich (1885–1968), founder of the International Schoenstatt Movement, to his canonization as a saint through their lives of prayer and dedicated service. Jhesus Maria!

Modern historical renditions of the story of Joan of Arc (1412–1431) often depart from the historical record. For those unfamiliar with the history of Saint Joan, I offer a brief chronological sketch.

Joan was born in 1412, perhaps on January 6, the Feast of Epiphany, to Isabella and Jacques d'Arc and baptized in the church at Domremy. She was a pious child and participated in the work, religious devotions, and traditional festivities that belonged to the life of the village. At age thirteen she began to hear "Voices" of instruction from God and the saints — in particular, Saints Michael, Margaret, Catherine, and sometimes Gabriel (as she later testified). She kept these communications secret for five years. Her father, sensing something, had a troubling dream in which Joan ran off with soldiers.

In 1428 and 1429, with the somewhat reluctant assistance of her uncle, Joan made repeated petitions to Robert de Baudricourt at his stronghold in Vaucouleurs, asking him in the name of God to provide her with a horse, an armed escort, and authorization for an audience with the Dauphin, Charles VII. She claimed that God had chosen her as his instrument to lead the armies of France to victory over the

English invaders and to secure the ascendancy of Charles to the throne. Joan eventually won Baudricourt's cooperation. Dressed in the clothes of a soldier, Joan made a dangerous, eleven-day journey on horseback from Vaucouleurs to Chinon, accompanied by Jean de Metz, Bertrand de Poulengy, and their attendants.

Arriving at Chinon on March 4, 1429, Joan recognized the disguised Dauphin and disclosed a secret to him, thus winning his confidence in her prophetic powers. Her arrival in the desperate circumstances of the war seemed to many the fulfillment of several well-known prophecies. Joan's claim of divine guidance in the form of voices and visions required, however, serious discernment on the part of ecclesiastical authorities. An examination of Joan, in which leading prelates participated, ensued at Poitiers. No record of the proceedings at Poitiers has survived, but the content of the interrogation can be reconstructed, as Deborah Fraioli has shown. At Poitiers Joan was questioned about her male attire and her Voices and pressed to give a sign that she was truly sent by God. The theologians brought to bear on her case various biblical texts and examples. In the end, Joan's moral character, physical virginity, and personal piety were approved, and her judges accepted as a conditional sign the predicted victory at Orléans. While still at Poitiers, Joan dictated the first of her letters, a strongly worded ultimatum to the king of England.

Equipped with symbolic accoutrements—a miraculously discovered sword, white armor, a ring, a standard, and a pennon—Joan joined the royal army on its way to the besieged city of Orléans, which she entered on April 29, 1429. Galvanized by the presence of the Maid ("la Pucelle"), who exhorted them to prayer and penitence, the French troops stormed the English fortresses surrounding Orléans and took them, one by one, until the siege ended in English defeat on May 8.

The victory at Orléans was followed by a rapid succession of victories in the Loire valley and in Champagne, the most famous of which occurred at Patay on June 18. Joan wept over the dead and wounded, French and English alike, and called repeatedly for peaceful submission to Charles. As city after city yielded to the Maid, in accord with her prophecies, the way opened for Charles to proceed to Rheims, where he was anointed and crowned king by the presiding archbishop on July 17, 1429.

His succession to the throne secured, Charles began to vacillate in his support of Joan's martial efforts for a complete expulsion of the English army from France. In September he ordered the cessation of Joan's attack on Paris and the disbanding of the army. In winter 1429 and spring 1430, Joan no longer enjoyed the sure guidance of her Voices. She participated with mixed success in various military expeditions.

On May 23, 1430, Joan was captured outside of Compiègne and then held prisoner for months in a high tower at Beaurevoir, from which she attempted to escape. In early November her Burgundian captor, John of Luxembourg, accepted a valuable payment (10,000 livres) for her from the English, who had imposed a tax for that purpose on the people of Normandy. Charles VII made no offer of ransom or to exchange prisoners. He thus effectively abandoned Joan to her English enemies.

On December 23, 1430, Joan arrived at Rouen. Her trial began on January 9, 1431. Chained and guarded day and night by English soldiers, Joan was charged with heresy and tried by an ecclesiastical court, over which Pierre Cauchon, bishop of Beauvais, presided. She had no advocate, and her appeal to the pope went unheeded by her jurors. The trial records show that the judges repeatedly questioned her about her wearing of male clothes and about her visions and Voices. The interrogation sought to validate charges of heresy, immorality, sedition, idolatry, and witchcraft. Joan's Voices counseled her to answer her judges boldly. The Voices also spoke of her martyrdom and of a great victory.

Abused by her guards and threatened with torture and death at the stake, an exhausted Joan publicly signed on May 24 an abjuration that was read to her, listing the charges against her. She agreed to wear women's dress in the expectation that she would be transferred to a Church prison and allowed to receive the sacraments. Forcibly returned instead to the English prison, she endured a rape attempt there and resumed men's clothes, thus incurring the charge of a relapse into heresy. On May 28 she declared that she had been wrong to deny her Voices by signing the abjuration.

On May 30, 1431, after receiving the Eucharist, Joan was handed over to the executioner and burned alive in the presence of a large crowd, including an estimated eight hundred English soldiers and several dignitaries, among them, the earl of Warwick. She fixed her gaze upon a cross; her dying cry was "Jesus!" The crowd was moved to tears, and an Anglo-Burgundian soldier declared, "We have burned a saint!"

Joan's heart remained unburned and was found, still full of blood, among the ashes of her body, which were tossed into the Seine.

Tried once at Poitiers and a second time at Rouen, with opposite results, Joan then became the subject of two posthumous trials. As Joan had predicted, the Hundred Years' War ended in English defeat. In 1449, at the urging of Joan's mother, Charles VII requested Pope Nicholas V to authorize a new investigation. Inquests were held in Domremy, Orléans, and Rouen, during which 115 witnesses provided testimony to discredit the earlier proceedings at Rouen and to exonerate Joan of the crimes for which she had been condemned. Judges convened on November 17, 1455, in Paris. On July 7, 1456, they declared the trial of 1431 a mistrial and nullified its verdict against Joan—a ruling that both vindicated Joan and removed the taint of instrumental heresy and witchcraft from Charles's kingship.

The second posthumous trial, namely, the process of Joan's beatification and canonization, began in 1869 at the instigation of Félix Dupanloup, bishop of Orléans. Found to have possessed heroic virtue, Joan was beatified by Pope Pius X on April 11, 1909. On May 9, 1920, Pope Benedict XV declared Joan of Arc a saint, numbering the Maid of Orléans among the holy virgins of the Church.

JOAN OF ARC
AND SACRIFICIAL AUTHORSHIP

*From an anthropological viewpoint, the author-writer is
an excluded figure integrated by his very exclusion,
a remote descendant of the accursed.*
—ROLAND BARTHES

The writing (and reading) of poems is a sacrificial process.
—HAROLD BLOOM

*Dying in the same way as Jesus did, for the same reasons as he did,
the martyrs multiply the revelation of the founding violence.*
—RENÉ GIRARD

INTRODUCTION

What could Joan of Arc (1412–1431), an illiterate girl from the small
French village of Domremy, have to do with authorship? The opening
scene of the dramatic oratorio, *Jeanne d'Arc au bûcher* (1938) poses the
question well. The libretto, written by the poet Paul Claudel and scored
by Arthur Honegger, places Joan in an afterlife conversation with Saint
Dominic, who approaches her, carrying a book from Heaven. Joan is
troubled by the book, which she cannot read and which she associates not only with the record of her fifteenth-century trial for heresy
but also with countless, subsequent, authorial retellings of her story.
"Dominic, brother Dominic," she complains, "through all these years—
through all these years till now I have seen myriad pens at work with
me for theme": "Dominique, frère Dominique, tous ces temps, tous
ces temps que voici, / J'ai vu beaucoup de plumes à l'œuvre autour de

moi."[1] She cringes in remembrance of her trial: "That voice of dread that ever questioned me, all those unceasing pens with me for theme, all of those pens upon the parchment grating—all that did make a book. All that did make a book, and me, I cannot read": "Cette voix terrible qui me quéstionnait / et toutes ces plumes sans relâche autour de moi! / Toutes ces plumes sur le parchemin qui grincent, / tout cela a fait un livre. / Tout cela a fait un livre—et moi, je ne sais pas lire."[2]

Claudel's Joan points to the records of her trial for heresy as the first authorial "book" about her, but already before her capture by the Burgundians and the beginning of the interrogations in Rouen (1430–1431), Joan of Arc was associated with authorship in the poetry of Christine de Pizan, who penned the last of her poems, *Le Ditié de Jehanne d'Arc*, in praise of the Maid on July 31, 1429—only two weeks after the coronation of Charles VII at Rheims. Christine sees in Joan's triumph the return of springtime to France and the rejuvenation of her own powers as a writer: "I, Christine, who have wept for eleven years in a walled abbey, . . . now, for the very first time, begin to laugh": "Je, Christine, qui ay plouré / XI ans en abbaye close, / . . . / Ore à prime me prens a rire."[3]

In the seventh stanza Christine calls upon God's inspiration to write about a historical matter, something that is usually the prerogative of male clerks and chroniclers, and in so doing makes a historical intervention with her pen ("no matter who may be displeased": "a qui que desplace") that is, in its own way, comparable to Joan's own miraculous entry into the chronicles of France and England with her banner and sword. Joan's coming was foreseen, Christine affirms, by Merlin, the Sibyl, and Bede (Stanza 31, line 241)—prophetic writers whose power of prophecy Joan herself demonstrates and in whose inspiration Christine herself shares, as she too envisions in poetry Joan's past and future victories: "Oh! What honor for the female sex!": "Hee! Quel honneur au femenin / Sexe!" (Stanza 34, lines 265–266).

Moved by Joan and incorporating her spirit, Christine speaks as another Joan, admonishing the newly crowned king to be worthy of the divine favor shown to him and exhorting the people of Paris to surrender to him. In this way, Kevin Brownlee observes, the *Ditié* becomes "an act of *collaboration* between Christine, the woman poet, and Joan, the woman hero, for the poem that celebrates Joan's career in history is also meant to advance that career."[4] Skillfully tracing aspects of Christine's argument on behalf of Joan back to the clerical debate concerning her at Poitiers, Deborah Fraioli sees the *Ditié* as a response to those who would deny Joan's divine mission. The poem thus evinces a "crosscurrent of unease," an anxious awareness of a viewpoint opposed to Christine's own that was soon to gain expression in charges of heresy levied against Joan by Parisian theologians and in her trial and execution at Rouen.[5]

Christine ends her poem in a way that anticipates the rejection of her message by some members of her intended audience: "But I believe that some people will be displeased by its contents, for a person whose head is bowed and whose eyes are heavy cannot look at the light": "Mais j'entens / Qu' aucuns se tendront mal contens / De ce qu'il contient, car qui chiere / A embrunche, et les yeux pesans, / Ne puet regarder la lumiere" (Stanza 61, lines 484–488). The "very beautiful poem composed by Christine" ("ung tresbel Ditié fait par Christine") will be rejected, and her anticipated fate as author thus shares, already before Joan's arrest, in the saint's own martyrdom.

After Christine de Pizan's fifteenth-century *Ditié de Jehanne d'Arc,* there was no similar literary representation of Joan as a figure of the artist until 1796, when a youthful Robert Southey, working in collaboration with Samuel Taylor Coleridge, retold her story in the form of an epic poem. Southey's blank verse epic was the first English-language depiction of Joan, England's historical enemy, as a literary heroine. Appearing almost four hundred years after the *Ditié,* Southey's *Joan of Arc* bears an uncanny resemblance to Christine's "beautiful poem," insofar as both works offer a mirrored image of the poet in the portrayal of the saint and use the narrative of Joan's life in part as an occasion for reflection on the artistic process. Southey represents Joan as a republican zealot, whose political ideals accord with his own support for the Jacobin revolution in France and whose source of inspiration in nature curiously matches that of the fledgling circle of Lake District poets, whom we know as the Romantics.

Southey's *Joan of Arc* (1796) was but the first in a series of imaginative retellings of Joan's story in the postclassical period, many of which are discussed in this book: Friedrich Schiller's *Die Jungfrau von Orleans* (1801), Jules Michelet's *Jeanne d'Arc* (1841), Thomas De Quincey's "Joan of Arc" (1847), Mark Twain's *Personal Recollections of Joan of Arc* (1896), Charles Péguy's *Mystère de la charité de Jeanne d'Arc* (1910, *Mystery of the Charity of Joan of Arc*), George Bernard Shaw's *Saint Joan: A Chronicle Play* (1924), Bertolt Brecht's *Die heilige Johanna der*

Schlachthöfe (1929–1930, *Saint Joan of the Stockyards*), Georges Bernanos's "Jeanne, relapse et sainte" (1929, "Joan, Heretic and Saint"),
Vita Sackville-West's *Saint Joan of Arc* (1936), Paul Claudel's *Jeanne
d'Arc au bûcher* (1938, *Joan of Arc at the Stake*), Brecht's *Die Gesichte der
Simone Machard* (1941–1942, *Visions of Simone Machard*), Lillian Hellman's 1956 adaptation of Jean Anouilh's *L'Alouette* (1953, *The Lark*),
Leonard Cohen's "Joan of Arc" (1966), Michel Tournier's *Gilles et Jeanne*
(1983), and Erik Ehn's *Wholly Joan's* (1988). What is striking about
them, when considered as a group, is the clearly evident, recurrent use
of the life, death, and afterlife of a medieval saint in order to comment
analogously on—and thus construct, control, and direct—the fate of
the modern author.[6] They forge remarkable structures of identity—
idealizing, anxious, and ambivalent—between authorial autobiography and hagiography, sanctity and art.

The beginnings of this pattern of authorial identification with Joan
of Arc coincide (as confirmed by the date of Southey's epic) with the
crisis of authorship that theorists generally (albeit variously) associate
with the revolutionary period, the rise of democracy, and the emergence of the mass market. Responding to Michel Foucault's "vague"
definition of authorship,[7] Molly Nesbitt observes that authorship first
received a legal definition at that time: "French copyright law dates
from the Revolution; the landmark law on author's rights was enacted
in 1793."[8] The "essential crudeness" of the law's definition distinguished
"a particular kind of labor from another, the cultural from the indus-
trial."[9] The *droits d'auteur* applied to any work done in the "designated
media: writing, music composition, painting, drawing, and engraving,"
regardless of its artistic merit.[10] The law "covered kitsch, avant-garde,
low-, high-, and middlebrow work with equal justice. Authors were
not necessarily artists."[11] All that mattered from a legal perspective
was "the material used and . . . the imprint of the author's personality
which would follow from working in this material."[12]

The law leveled the cultural sphere, according rights of "authorship" to artists and journalists alike, even as it separated culture from
industry, but that very leveling promoted division between and among
the users of language, some of whom looked back to older models of
authorship in order to define themselves in the much different socio-
political settings of a capitalist modernity. Pointing to the time of the
Revolution, Roland Barthes distinguishes between "writers" and "authors": "The author participates in the priest's role, the writer in the

clerk's."[13] Substituting for the priest, whom the Revolution persecuted and rejected, the secular author was asked to fulfill an analogous function in society. Barthes analyzes that authorial function as follows: "From an anthropological viewpoint, the author-writer is an excluded figure, integrated by his very exclusion, a remote descendant of the accursed: his function in society as a whole is perhaps related to the one Lévi-Strauss attributes to the witch doctor[,] . . . both witch doctor and intellectual in a sense stabilizing a disease which is necessary to the collective economy of health."[14]

Paul Bénichou reaches a similar conclusion in his monumental study, *Le Sacre de l'écrivain* (*The Consecration of the Writer, 1750–1830*). There he traces the transmission of spiritual powers during the revolutionary period from the dispossessed clergy to the newly privileged and socially promoted class of authors, secular men of letters who "constitute themselves vis-à-vis society as a humiliated and distant clergy," assuming "the role of a spiritual guide for society, in competition with the old church."[15] Expected to fulfill the priestly function of arbitrating ethical and moral values and uniting society as a whole, authors found themselves simultaneously elevated and humiliated by the new social order, for they realized that an "age, which knows where the real priests are and no longer counts much on them for its salvation, is not ready to grant to newcomers a kind of authority that it denies to their predecessors. Indeed, it goes so far as to wonder whether a writer or poet is qualified to guide human beings. . . . It was precisely because there was no longer room in the spiritual domain for authority properly so called that the writer and poet were promoted."[16]

Authors during the postrevolutionary, modern period have sought to enhance their authority in various, interrelated ways: through an ambivalent, sacrificial relationship with canonical authors of the past; through a competitive collaboration with the contemporary writers who are their brothers and sisters; and by drawing on material and spiritual resources endowed with what Walter Benjamin calls "aura."[17] None of these strategies, as this study demonstrates, are nonsacrificial, but some are sacrificial in their surrender to sacred violence, and others are antisacrificial in their conscious resistance to the real and symbolic killing of victims, for which Joan of Arc stands as a preeminent example. Placed in an ever marginal position as the mediators of spiritual power, modern authors seek to avoid being scapegoated themselves either by sacrificing others or by modeling a refusal of sacrifice.

By looking back to their literary fathers, modern writers sought to secure their claim to authorship; at the same time, however, they sought to disavow or reduce that dependence on tradition by creative manipulations of inherited material. In *The Anxiety of Influence* Harold Bloom famously analyzes such revisions by later poets of the works of their literary precursors as psychological "defense mechanisms," symptomatic of the "poetic misprision" or creative misreading of authors with whom they identify as poets but whose priority in time poses a threat to their own individuality, originality, and authority.[18] Likening the relations between poets to a Freudian Family Romance, Bloom emphasizes the anxieties of influence that "are embedded in the agonistic basis of all imaginative literature."[19] According to Bloom, later poets almost always sacrifice their "fathers" by means of one or more of six possible revisionary ratios: by reducing and correcting them (the "swerving" that Bloom, echoing Lucretius, calls *clinamen*); by complementing them and supplying what they lack (the "linkage" that Bloom, borrowing from the lexicon of ancient mystery cults, names *tessera*); by breaking from them (through the self-emptying of *kenosis* or the mortification of *askesis*); by surpassing them in a return to their own sources of inspiration (*daemonization*); or by conjuring them up as ghosts on the very ground they once inhabited (through *aprophrades*).

Through these ritual acts of sacrifice, poets endeavor to achieve an authorship for themselves that is free from the disease of influence, but they usually fail in their "wrestling with their ghostly fathers."[20] "The writing (and reading) of poems is a sacrificial process," Bloom avers, but rather than serve to renew human vitality, it frequently diminishes it; more often than not, "poetic misprision" is "a purgation that drains more than it replenishes."[21] As a result, "poetry in our tradition, when it dies, will be self-slain, murdered by its own past strength."[22]

When *The Anxiety of Influence* first appeared in 1967, Bloom, "still intoxicated by the High Romantic poets, . . . tried to confine the phenomenon [of influence anxiety] to post-Enlightenment writers."[23] He argued that Dante and Shakespeare belong "to the great age before the flood, before the anxiety of influence became central to poetic consciousness."[24] Since then, Bloom has changed his mind, extending his theory to intrapoetic relations in every age. While Bloom is certainly right in this extension, I would argue that his first impulse was not altogether mistaken. Authorial anxiety of influence increases significantly in an antiauthoritarian age. It was one thing for Chaucer, writing at a time when the place of the classical poets was secure in the curriculum, to misread and to swerve away from Virgil and Ovid (departing from Dante in the process); it was quite another thing for the Romantics, writing in the age of the novel, to sacrifice their "father," Spenser. Why? Because the "death" of Chaucer's *auctores* carried with it the assurance of their resurrection by other readers and imitators, whereas the "death" of Spenser, in a Philistine literary marketplace, might be final, and the Romantics knew it. Much more was at stake for them.

In the post-Enlightenment Jehannine fictions treated in this book, we find modern authors using the history of Joan of Arc's martyrdom and rehabilitation to accomplish a twofold goal: the creative sacrifice of their precursors and their (and their own) literary canonization. Southey's "Original Sin" in *Joan of Arc* is his misprision of Edmund Spenser's allegorical *Faerie Queene*, a fault he corrects in the second edition through the ascetic purging of Spenserian (and Coleridgean) passages from the text. Schiller's *Die Jungfrau von Orleans* deliberately and emphatically swerves away from Shakespeare's *I Henry VI*, on the one hand, and Goethe's *Iphigenia in Tauris*, on the other. Twain's *Personal Recollections of Joan of Arc* puts to death not only the Maid but also the Machine (in particular, the Paige typesetter), and with it the disturbing influence of the archinventor, Thomas Edison. Shaw's *Saint Joan* exorcises Schiller's *Jungfrau*. Hellman's *The Lark* not only adapts but also corrects Anouilh's *L'Alouette*, and Hellman and Brecht both reply to Shaw. Claudel offers atonement to Péguy. The *Joan* of Sackville-West answers to Woolf's *Orlando*, while Tournier's *Gilles et Jeanne* wrestles with the influence of Jean Genet.

René Girard traces the origins of mimetic rivalry to acquisitive mimesis, the "rivalry . . . provoked by an object"[25] that more than one person desires, in part because the other desires it. Joining Girard's analysis to Bloom's, we may understand the agony of artists to be precisely a struggle over "priority" as an object—that is, over originality, over "coming first," not only in time, but also in creativity. This struggle refashions the "father" into a "brother," a double of one's self, as the later poet endeavors to tell the same story that his precursor has told but in a different and better way. The literary mimesis or imitation of poetry thus doubles the psychological rivalry between and among the poets themselves, in a spreading and escalating pattern of contagion.

Such a guilty strife, which sets the later poets against the earlier poets whom they most love and with whom they identify most closely, can only be resolved through sacrifice, the ritual slaughter of an innocent victim, an outsider, that paradoxically belongs to both, and to neither, of them. Killing the victim as a surrogate for both the precursor and one's own self puts a temporary end to the guilt engendered by intra-poetic strife, but it also burdens the later poet with the guilt of a mur-derous sacrifice. For this guilt, the poet atones by honoring the victim with the monument of art and the immortality it promises to the vic-tim and the poet alike.

In the Jehannine fictions, Joan of Arc—an illiterate outsider to the world of letters, an inspired hearer of voices rather than a reader of texts—stands as this victim of intrapoetic rivalry, a victim that joins in her person the foes that struggle over her and are united through her.[26] At the same time that the authorial precursor is put to death in and through Joan by the later poet, the author too dies with her, as the victim of a society incapable of appreciating genius. The author thus both kills and dies, sacrifices and is sacrificed, through the mediation of the martyr.

What is striking about the Jehannine fictions is the way Joan's portrayal varies from work to work, each time mirroring the life and "death" of the author. To the extent that Joan is made to resemble the author who re-creates her, she attests to the importance of biographi-cal criticism and to the thought of the poets, playwrights, essayists, and novelists who conceived of her in an imaginative relationship to themselves, identifying with her. The author (as Barthes bears witness) "still reigns" and lives "in histories of literature, biographies of writers, interviews, magazines, *as in the very consciousness of men of letters anx-ious to unite their person and work* through diaries and memoirs."[27] That same living and reigning author, however, also thinks about, anticipates, fears, and experiences his own death in the writing (and reading) process. Barthes explains: "The author enters into his own death, writing begins. The sense of this phenomenon, however, has varied; in ethnographic societies the responsibility for a narrative is never assumed by a person but by a mediator, shaman, or relator whose 'performance'—the mastery of the narrative code—may possibly be admired, but never his 'genius.'"[28]

In the Jehannine fictions, the distinction between the life and the death of the author is blurred through an exploration of Joan of Arc's inspiring Voices, which offer her counsel but also speak through her, so that her authoritative pronouncements are always a multiple voicing of self and Others. Joan's voice is God's and that of the people for whom she serves as advocate. Similarly, her death at the stake is a real death, a cruel execution accomplished by her enemies, but it is also very much a part of her real and continuous life, for she embraces her own dying and triumphs over it and through it.

In the theoretical quarrels over issues of authorship, Seán Burke has focused attention on the ethics of signature, which, like the signature on legal documents, "set[s] up a structure of resummons whereby the author may be recalled to his or her text" and charged with responsibility for it.[29] "An act of signature," Burke maintains, "binds the text respectively to the still-living author, to the legacy and legatees of the dead author, to whatever traditions might have been established *in nomine auctoris* and to the posthumous reconstructions of authorial intention, biography and any system of oeuvre effects that might enhance the ethical rereading of the text in question."[30]

From the perspective of the ethics of signature, the historical case of Joan of Arc remains richly relevant to reflections on authorship, because she affixed her signature to a confession of guilt, marked it with a cross, and later recanted. In the Jehannine fictions, this episode in the life of Jeanne d'Arc provokes reflection on the validity of confessions given after torture; on the different forms of coercion that can induce a signing; on the accountability of one who signs a document that she or he cannot read or fully understand; on the responsibility of someone who claims authorship, confesses to a crime, or bears witness to a vision; on the motives for confession and recanting; on the possibility of an encoded denial of the signature in the form of the cross and hence of other forms of authorial self-denial, such as irony, pseudonymity, double-coding, and the use of personae.[31]

These and other features of Joan's story allow for an infinite adaptation to the lives of individual authors. Southey's Maid, for example, suffers for political beliefs and ideals that Southey also held. Schiller's Jungfrau is an outcast and a scapegoat, even as the young Schiller endured exile from his homeland for the sake of his art. Twain's Joan is, by his own admission, modeled on his daughter Susy. Péguy's Jeanette is the saint of a political mysticism. Sackville-West's Joan is a female cross-dresser. Woolf's Joan is a madwoman. Brecht's latter-day Joans are a Communist striker and a French Resistance fighter, respectively.

Hellman's Joan answers her inquisitors with words Hellman herself spoke during her hearing before the House Committee on Un-American Activities.

The multiple parallels discussed in this book between Joan's story and that of her authors suggest not only, as Bloom insists, that the author's biography (in comparison with history and literary criticism) is "always the prior mode"[32] but also, and more important, the opposite truth: hagiography—the saint's legendary biography—precedes the author's life and enables his or her self-understanding and self-fashioning out of the matter of a *vita* that is simultaneously preexistent and prophetic. Told in "the imperative mood," a saint's life is always, as Edith Wyschogrod has argued, "lived forward" into the lives of others, who are exhorted "to 'make the movements' of the saint's existence after her/him."[33]

Joan already was what the author has been, is, and will be. Condemned as a heretic and rehabilitated as a saint, Joan of Arc is a figure eminently suitable for appropriation by artists in a capitalist society where art is viewed as useless and guilt-ridden but also—and for that same reason—as possessing a secular transcendence ("art for art's sake"). Interpreted retrospectively, Joan's life may be described (in the words Wyschogrod applies to the legend of the penitent saint, Mary of Egypt) "as always already sinful and always already redeemed, a life making and unmaking itself."[34]

The "reproduction" of a saint's life is, however (as the obvious ambivalence and unease of these Jehannine artists tacitly acknowledge), simply not the same as "imitation" in the sense of *imitatio Christi*. Whereas a Pauline *imitatio* allows for, indeed requires, a succession of unique, authentic embodiments of a Christian life that is (as Wyschogrod insists) "inherently refractory to representation,"[35] the modern, artistic reproduction of a saint's life divorces the saint from his or her own time, place, and tradition, to bring him or her "closer" to an audience of consumers. It substitutes cult for spectacle, and it places art unashamedly in the service of economics and politics.

In the case of Joan of Arc, the saint's own legend seems to provide the authorization for such substitutions. The public spectacles of triumph and degradation alike—whether we consider the splendor of Charles VII's coronation in the cathedral at Rheims or the cruelty of Joan's burning in the marketplace at Rouen—led from religious devotion and ritual to exhibition. A prisoner of the Burgundians, from whom the French failed to ransom her, Joan was bought by the English. In her brief life as a battle leader, the pious Joan advanced the Dauphin's politics; in her death at the stake as a heretic, the steadfast Joan served (at least temporarily) the interests of the English. If Joan was so used during her earthly life, should she not continue to imbue not only art but also politics, both on the Right and on the Left, with her aura?

Identifying their inspirations by the poetic muse with Joan's visions and Voices, on the one hand, and their sufferings at the hands of Philistine contemporaries with Joan of Arc's martyrdom, on the other, the modern authors whose works this book discusses clearly sought to surround their own persons and their writings with the aura possessed by the saint. The very word *aura* joins together the semantic fields of authorship and sanctity, the saint's halo and the poet's laureate crown. As Walter Benjamin has explained in a justly famous essay, the aura of premodern art, like that of objects of natural beauty, consists in "the unique phenomenon of a distance," which is associated with "cult value" and "ritual use."[36] This distance, according to Benjamin, derives from the uniqueness of art in the age before mechanical reproduction—an "authentic," original, and unrepeatable uniqueness defined by each work's existence in a particular time, place, and tradition.[37] Mechanical reproduction through typesetting, photography, and filmmaking (among other technological means) inevitably leads to a loss of distance, the decay of aura, the commodification of art, and the substitution of exhibition value for cult value.

Making Joan's story their own, modern authors sought to revitalize the aura of their art—its distance, transcendence, and uniqueness—and to restore the purity of its cult value. Drawing both on her exalted status as a seeress and a royalist and on her democratic appeal as a leader of the downtrodden masses, they sought to overcome through Joan's influence the challenge to traditional authorship posed by the mass market, reconciling the two. Even as they did so, however, they contributed to the decay of the saint's aura through the multiple retellings, reproductions, and reenactments of her singular, mysterious history. As we shall see, every representation somehow reduces Joan, renders her up for public consumption, in a way that approaches blasphemy and that evokes detectable pangs of guilt in the authors themselves—a guilt frequently covered by the alibi of devotion to her.

The guiltiness of modern artists, as suggested earlier, derives from several sources. Their production lacks the use and cult value that belonged to artwork in premodern societies. They have been assigned a place and function traditionally held and fulfilled by the clergy but without possessing a priest's divine authority and efficacy. They are put in the position of having to sell their work, giving it an exchange value and allowing it to possess a symbolic value that serves impure, political, and economic purposes.[38] If a concern for originality and artistic preeminence leads them to sacrifice their literary precursors or their contemporary rivals and collaborators, they incur the guilt of a symbolic homicide. If they seek to enhance their authority, gain a wide audience, profit financially, or secure literary canonization by using and consuming as their subject matter something or someone holy— such as Joan of Arc—they run the risk of sacrilege or idolatry.

This very guiltiness often becomes, however, another ground for authorial identification with Joan of Arc, who was, after all, burned at the stake as a whore, seditious traitor, murderer, heretic, witch, blasphemer, and idolater.[39] Joan's mythic guilt, as a projection of their own, justifies in turn their fictive execution of her in work after work as a scapegoat. The guilt attributed by Jehannine artists to Joan of Arc, despite her historical rehabilitation in 1456, the nullification of the trial that condemned her to death, and her canonization as a saint in 1920, is, in fact, one of the hallmarks of the sacrificial authorship studied in this book. Southey, for example, represents her as despairing and suicidal, because of her responsibility for the deaths of innocent persons. Schiller portrays her as guilty of having broken a vow of spiritual virginity. Brecht makes her blameworthy, because her idealism and pacifism forestall a riot by striking laborers. Shaw justifies as socially necessary the historic verdict against her because of her avant-garde nonconformity to the status quo. Tournier depicts her as being indirectly responsible for the horrific crimes committed by Gilles de Rais.

This attribution of guilt to Joan of Arc belies the evidence of her innocence in the historical records and demonstrates, in Girardian terms, the constant tendency of myth to represent the victim as guilty, in order to conceal the injustice of the community, whose very existence as a civilization depends on the repeated "founding murder" of a scapegoat. What is particularly striking in the Jehannine fictions surveyed here is the employment of classical patterns and mythic allusions in the rendition of a medieval Christian martyr's life and death as a tragedy. The incidence of explicit mythical allusion increases, moreover, in those fictions that represent Joan of Arc as guilty. Tournier, for example, draws on the myths of the two-faced Janus and of warring twins. Brecht refashions Joan of Arc as an Oedipus. Schiller's *Maid of Orléans* is virtually saturated with Greco-Roman, mythic allusions.

Not every author depicts Joan of Arc as guilty, however; for many, especially those strongly influenced by the Judeo-Christian biblical tradition, Joan of Arc is and remains an innocent victim of persecution and thus a representative of countless other victims. Sometimes, as in the writings of Twain and Bernanos, Joan's spotless innocence stands in such stark contrast to the evil embodied by her foes that the scapegoat mechanism stays firmly in place, ready to be directed vengefully against her killers. More often, however, the authorial concern for victims, grounded in the biblical commandments that forbid killing and require charity, inspires a range of antisacrificial, narrative, and dramatic strategies.

Six chapters follow this introductory chapter. The first of these focuses attention on the Joan of the Jacobins, as depicted in the epic poem of Southey, the poetry of Coleridge, and an essay by De Quincey. Inspired by the French Revolution, the Jehannine poems by Southey and Coleridge demonstrate most obviously the linkage between the modern author and the medieval saint. I argue that the successive revisions of Southey's *Joan of Arc* illustrate in sequence the various kinds of sacrifices entailed in authorship: the killing of the king, the excision of the literary precursor, the removal of the brother-rival, and the scapegoating of Joan of Arc herself. To these sacrifices of art and ideology, De Quincey responds with a powerful, antisacrificial critique.

Chapter 2 reverses this sequence. It shows Schiller making a sacrificial response in his *Maid of Orléans* to Goethe's antisacrificial drama, *Iphigenia in Tauris*. In Schiller's writings on aesthetics and in his self-consciously mythic departure from the facts of history in his Jehannine tragedy, I find a fully articulated, theoretical understanding of the necessity of sacrifice vis-à-vis the evolution of civilization and a profound, systematic unfolding of the structures of identity uniting the figures of the artist and Johanna.

Chapter 3 is devoted to Twain's *Personal Recollections of Joan of Arc*. Written during a period of financial bankruptcy and artistic crisis, Twain's historical romance is riddled with symptoms of authorial and fatherly guilt over the sacrifice of a beloved, idolized child and the conversion of the purity of love and art into lucre. It dramatizes the rivalry between the inventors of literary fictions and of machines in an age when technological advances were influencing artistic production in unprecedented ways. The pictures reproduced in this volume (figures 1–8) are chosen from among Frank Du Mond's illustrations of the original, 1896 edition of Twain's *Joan;* they illustrate the aura with which Twain sought to imbue his artistry in the face of its decay.

Chapter 4, on the Marxist Joan, continues the exploration of economic themes begun in chapter 3. It offers a survey of the depictions of Joan of Arc by three Marxist authors—George Bernard Shaw, Bertolt Brecht, and Lillian Hellman. I argue that sacrificial structures within Marxism itself support the retelling of Joan's story as myth and tragedy. Like the revolutionary Joan of the Jacobins, the Marxist Joan is a heroine of the people. She defends one set of victims, however, at the expense of creating others. Shaw's Joan could, therefore, be used by the Nazis against the British and against the Jews.

In Chapter 5 I discuss four twentieth-century authors—Shaw, Sackville-West, Woolf, and Tournier—whose representations of Joan of Arc foreground issues relating to gender. For Shaw, Joan is a manly woman, with a heterosexual potential. For Sackville-West, she is a cross-dresser, with a homosexual potential. Woolf sees in her the gifted madwoman who is the victim of a patriarchal past. Tournier emphasizes Joan's boyishness and links it perversely to the pedophilia of her comrade-in-arms, Gilles de Rais. For all four writers, the manner of Joan's attire is a key to her identity, but it remains an outward sign of indeterminacy that makes a meditation on the figure of Joan of Arc analogous to the contemplation of a work of art and of the artist.

I have called chapter 6 a "contrapuntal conclusion," because its focus on Catholic and Jewish portrayals of Joan of Arc enables a discussion of the antisacrificial strategies that belong to sacrificial authorship, to the extent to which it is aware of its own costly practice of sacrifice and is prophetically opposed to it. Drawing inspiration from the biblical Word and from God himself as author, these writers are relatively free from the Bloomian anxiety of influence. Charles Péguy, the earliest and most original author of the twentieth-century French Catholic renaissance, found a mystic connection between the unique vocation of Joan of Arc and the new type of holiness to which she was called, on the one hand, and his own calling to defend Alfred Dreyfus, the innocent Jewish victim of the notorious Dreyfus Affair, on the other. In the century of the Holocaust, he was the first of several to discover a Jewish Joan of Arc and to articulate an antisacrificial stance.

Roger B. Salomon summarizes it well when he writes: "The story of Joan of Arc—at once strong in outline, vague in many of its details, dramatic in its historical consequences, and romantic with its young heroine—calls forth endless interpreters, each of whom reveals as much about himself as about Joan."[40] For the interpreter who is also an author, whose "book" brings Joan back to an earthly life and death, the decisions about whether and what and whom to sacrifice are entailed in the very act of writing and sentencing. In this authorial context the exhortation of Rabbi Jesus assumes renewed force: "Judge not, that you be not judged. For with the judgment you pronounce you will be judged" (Matthew 7:1–2).

Last evening lone in thought I wandered forth.
—ROBERT SOUTHEY

Maid beloved of Heaven!
—SAMUEL TAYLOR COLERIDGE

It is singular, indeed, to find a long poem on an ancient subject,
adapting itself hieroglyphically to a modern purpose.
—THOMAS DE QUINCEY

CHAPTER ONE

THE JOAN
OF THE JACOBINS

Southey, Coleridge, and De Quincey

From the viewpoint of English literary history, Robert Southey's earliest epic poem, *Joan of Arc* (1796), is of unquestionable importance. Coauthored in part by Samuel Coleridge, it antedates William Wordsworth's preface to the second edition of *Lyrical Ballads* (1800), and it furnished, as Coleridge himself later suggested, the "original occasion to this fiction of a new school of poetry."[1] Published fifty-five years before Wordsworth's *Prelude, Joan of Arc* directly aligns the aesthetic concerns of Romanticism with the politics of the French Revolution and thus lays an early basis for William Hazlitt's famous assertion that "the Lake school of poetry . . . had its origin in the French revolution, or rather in those sentiments and opinions which produced that

17

revolution."[2] Southey's epic is, moreover, the first poem in the English language to represent the visionary French battle leader, Joan of Arc, England's late-medieval foe, as a heroine. It antedates Friedrich Schiller's *Die Jungfrau von Orleans* (1801) and may be said to have paved the way for all subsequent portrayals of Joan as a literary heroine.

Southey's *Joan of Arc* also demonstrates with a certain crudeness all that is entailed in the notion of "sacrificial authorship" and thus provides a rudimentary blueprint for the works discussed in subsequent chapters. From its earliest drafts in 1793 to its subsequent revisions in six editions published between 1796 and 1837,[3] *Joan of Arc* displays a series of sacrificial moves by its author. First, there is the self-sacrificing move of the idealistic, young, republican poet, who symbolically kills a long-dead English king, Henry V (d. 1422), on behalf of the oppressed masses of his own time and thus puts at rhetorical risk the finding of a wide English audience for his work. In so doing, Southey identifies himself not only with Joan of Arc and the contemporary French revolutionaries but also with the great patriotic English poets of the past: John Milton (1608–1674), who approved the regicide of King Charles I in 1649; and Edmund Spenser (1552–1599), who had honored Queen Elizabeth I by exposing (albeit under an allegorical veil) English error. Southey's conscious goal in writing a Jehannine epic is his own literary canonization, to be achieved through a deliberate king killing and a self-chosen martyrdom. Blending politics and poetry, Southey kills the king imaginatively in order to take the king's place as a laureated poet.[4]

At the second stage in the sacrificial process, marked by the second edition of *Joan of Arc* in 1798, Southey goes further; he symbolically puts to death the literary models who have been most important to him by excising the two "Visions" that appear in the original edition of 1796. He removes the 255 lines in Book II that were written by his pantisocratic "brother" and rival, Samuel Taylor Coleridge (1772–1834), and he replaces the whole of Book IX, where his indebtedness to Spenser's *Faerie Queene* was most obvious.

The guilty betrayals that make scapegoats of kings, fathers, and brothers are ultimately grounded for Southey in the very subject matter of his poem. In the self-divided guiltiness of Joan of Arc as Southey portrays her, he confronts the sacred violence of the French Revolution. Attributing the glory and the guilt of the modern revolution to Joan of Arc requires a mythic expulsion of the Joan of medieval history and a swerving away from the facts of her persecutory trial. Retrieving these facts, as the work of historians made them accessible to him, and confronting the Napoleonic outcome of the Revolution, Southey came to recognize his own mythmaking. In the end, Joan of Arc returns to haunt him as the Spenserian Duessa from whose ghost he had fled.

Arising to defend the saint of history, Thomas De Quincey (1785–1859) answers both to the French historian Jules Michelet and to Southey, his older contemporary and fellow Englishman. De Quincey praises Southey for his praise of Joan but sharply criticizes him for his sacrifice of her on the altar of Jacobin ideology, pointing to the way her place at the stake has been cruelly occupied by the victims of the guillotine. Joan herself, De Quincey insists, would have opposed all such sacrifices.

Joan of Arc, Self-Sacrificing Southey, and Spenser's Redcrosse Knight

As James Darmesteter emphasizes, "In 1796, it was an audacious idea to choose the Maid of Orléans for the central figure of an epic."[5] An unsigned article in the June 1796 issue of the *Critical Review* pointedly raises the issue: "How can he expect to interest the English nation in the fortunes of a heroine who was an active champion against his own countrymen, or be hardy enough to felicitate those successes that involved the English in disgrace? Many of his readers will undoubtedly ask these questions—and, at a time when the course of public opinion is more than ordinarily influenced by recent occurrences, will not be over forward to compliment his patriotism."[6]

In his preface to the first edition, Southey anticipates such objections and comments directly on his choice of Joan: "It has long been established as a necessary rule for the Epic, that the subject be national. To this rule I have acted in direct opposition and chosen for the subject of my poem the defeat of my country" ("Preface," p. 4). In a rhetorical gesture that recalls Milton's stated preference for readers "fit . . . , though few," for his *Paradise Lost*,[7] Southey declares, "If among my readers there be one who can wish success to injustice, because his countrymen supported it, I desire not that man's approbation" ("Preface," p. 4).

The sacrificial stance taken by Southey in choosing deliberately to alienate a politically conservative audience through criticism of his own country did not go unnoticed by his first readers. In a poem entitled "After Reading Southey's *Joan of Arc*," published in 1797 in the *European Magazine*, Anna Seward praised Southey's poetic gifts but blamed his lack of patriotism, calling Southey an "unnat'ral Boy" and a "beardless Paricide," because of his condemnation of King Henry V, his branding of the "hallow'd lustre of . . . ENGLAND," and his besmirching of England's "name / With slavish Meanness, with rapacious Avarice, / And the Wolf's rage."[8]

Whereas Seward uses the language of parricide, Southey's (chiefly Jacobin) reviewers use the imagery of a noble self-denial and self-sacrifice. In the *Critical Review* we read: "A regard to truth produces the true sublime; and to sacrifice, on the altar of justice, a national prejudice that engenders many follies and leads to the perpetration of many crimes, takes nothing from the dignity of the epic, but adds to it considerably; though it is contrary to the method pursued by Homer and Virgil" (*CH*, p. 44). Similarly, the anonymous review in the *Analytical Review* (1796) declares, "The moral lesson which the story teaches is of universal importance, that unjust ambition and tyranny must expect punishment: and it is no objection that this lesson is taught at the expense of the author's native country; for he who wishes success to injustice, because his countrymen support it, is a traitor to humankind" (*CH*, p. 48).

Although his Jacobin sympathies and his choice of a French heroine exposed Southey to the superficial charge of a lack of patriotism, he himself clearly understood his epic to be profoundly patriotic. In a letter to Grosvenor Bedford, dated July 20, 1794, he wrote, "Grosvenor, I shall inscribe Joan of Arc to you, unless you are afraid to have your name prefixed to a work that breathes some sentiments not perfectly in unison with court principles. Corrections shall take up some time, for the poem shall go into the world handsomely: *it will be my legacy to this country, and may, perhaps, preserve my memory in it*."[9]

The unspoken, underlying connection between a poem at odds with "court principles," on the one hand, and the "preservation of [his] memory" as a poet-patriot, on the other, is striking. It juxtaposes two crowns—the gold crown of the king and the laurel wreath of the poet—and suggests the ability of the republican poet to take the king's place as both sovereign and victim. René Girard, pointing to the importance of sacral kingship in primitive societies, has argued that the development of kingship as a modern institution depends on the elaboration of multiple substitutes for the victim-king, to prolong the originally brief "interval between the selection of the victim and the sacrifice."[10] "The relation between sacrifice and monarchy is too intimate to be dissolved all at once," he writes, "but it does change. Since sacrifice is always a question of substitution, it is always possible to make a new substitution and henceforth to sacrifice only a substitute of the substitute."[11] Self-sacrifice, according to Girard, is another such substitute, especially if it is willed in the conscious hope of a heavenly or temporal reward that is a reflex of the mythic deification of sacrificial victims—literary or ecclesiastical canonization, for example.[12] In the French Revolution, when king killing was real and not just symbolic, as in Southey's poetic repudiation of Henry V of England, the question of who and how many would take the king's vacated place was pressing enough to prompt even a poet's desire for prominence, as well as his fear of incurring, in turn, a similar expulsion from the throne.

An English poet whose patriotism expressed itself in youthful antiroyalist proclamations against tyranny, Southey looked to Milton as an exemplar, as did his fellow Romantics. Milton, writes Joseph A. Wittreich Jr., "was the quintessence of everything the Romantics most admired. A rebel, a republican, an iconoclast, a mighty poet, a lofty thinker, Milton was an exemplar of noble, though not flawless, character," whose political stances were more constant than their own.[13] Wordsworth liked to imagine himself as being Milton reincarnated, at a time when England had need of Milton's return: "Milton! thou shouldst be living at this hour: / England hath need of thee."[14] Coleridge, too, called Milton his "idol."[15] In Coleridge's view, however, no poet of the Lake school more resembled Milton than did Southey: "That scheme of head, heart, and habitual demeanour, which in his early manhood, and first controversial writings, Milton, claiming the privilege of self-defense, asserts of himself, and challenges his calumniators to disprove; this will his school-mates, his fellow-collegians, and his maturer friends, with a confidence proportioned to the intimacy of their knowledge, bear witness to, as again realized in the life of Robert Southey."[16]

There can be no doubt that Southey consciously followed in Milton's tread, when he wrote the opening lines of *Joan of Arc*, attempting to compose an English epic in blank verse on a French subject "unattempted yet in Prose or Rhyme" (*Paradise Lost* I.16):

> War's varied horrors, and the train of ills
> That follow on Ambition's blood-stain'd path
> And fill the world with woe; of France preserv'd
> By maiden hand, what time her Chiefs subdued,
> Or slept in death, or lingered life in chains,
>   I sing; nor wilt thou *Freedom* scorn the song. (I.1−6)

The verse form and political resonances of *Joan of Arc* are distinctly Miltonic, but, I would argue, the plot and characterization are inspired less by Milton than by Spenser, the poet whom Southey called "the favourite of [his] childhood" ("Preface," p. 4).

As Greg Kucich has amply demonstrated, the Romantics discovered in Spenser a poet of great complexity. Wordsworth's generation saw him "as both a poet of thought and beauty, caught between two poles."[17] They associated "Spenserian poetics with psychological depth and, more specifically, with mental doubling."[18] Even more important, perhaps, "in adapting Spenser's allegorical duality to their own situation, the Romantics also radicalized his politics, both to give him a more palatable social consciousness and to intensify his drama of the mind."[19] Stressing Spenser's "political sufferings rather than his courtly obedience . . . moved some of them to drop the eighteenth-century convention of a patriotic Spenserian art and cultivate instead the more subversive, dissatisfied element of Spenser's political experience, a discontent that of course greatly appealed to the revolutionary sentiments of the young Wordsworth, Coleridge, and many of their contemporaries."[20]

From Spenser and Milton alike, Southey learned that a patriotic poet could also be a suffering dissident. In Spenser's *Faerie Queene,* in particular, Southey recognized the possibility for chivalric romance to represent, and to comment on, contemporary, political situations. Spenser's contemporaries and later readers knew full well that, as Spenser declares in his prefatory letter to Sir Walter Raleigh, *The Faerie Queene* presents a veiled and not altogether complimentary portrait of Queen Elizabeth I and her reign.[21] Similarly, when *Joan of Arc* first appeared, John Aikin was not alone in recognizing in Southey's epic "a strong allusion to later characters and events": "We know not where the ingenuity of a crown lawyer would stop, were he employed to make out a list of innuendoes. In particular, War and the lust of conquest, are everywhere painted in the strongest colours of abhorrence" (*CH*, p. 42).

The early reviewers of Southey's poem were reminded of Milton and Spenser. Aikin declares: "The glow of feeling and genius animates the whole. The language is, for the most part, modelled on that of Milton" (*CH*, p. 42). Another reviewer praises the poem's heroic inspiration but complains about Southey's use of "quaint and antiquated expressions . . . in the manner of Spenser" and Milton (*CH*, pp. 44–45). In a letter to Coleridge, dated June 10, 1796, Charles Lamb enthused, "I expect Southey one day to rival Milton" (*CH*, p. 46). Coleridge shared Lamb's sentiments, declaring in a letter of November 19, 1796, to John Thelwall, "Homer is the Poet for the Warrior—Milton for the Religionist—Tasso for Women—Robert Southey for the Patriot."[22]

Whereas the reviewers noted immediately the Latinate diction and Miltonic syntax of Southey's poetry, Southey himself in his preface invited a comparison of his epic and Milton's on another, more fundamental basis. Noting his own Romantic departures from epic conventions, Southey refers to the "lawless magic of Ariosto, and the singular theme as well as the singular excellence of Milton," which "render all rules of epic poetry inapplicable . . . ; so likewise with Spenser, the favourite of my childhood, from whose frequent perusal I have always found increased delight" ("Preface," p. 4).

"The general fault of Epic Poems," Southey maintains, "is that we feel little interest in the Heroes they celebrate. . . . There must be more of human feelings than is generally to be found in the characters of Warriors" ("Preface," p. 3). He endeavors to avoid this "common fault" in his own epic by rendering "the Maid of Orleans interesting": "With this intent I have given her, not the passion of love, but the remembrance of subdued affection, a lingering of human feelings not inconsistent with the enthusiasm and holiness of her character."[23]

Southey's Joan is gently in love with Theodore, the companion of her childhood, who disguises himself in order to fight at her side and protect her on the battlefield. She is also the sympathetic counselor of Conrade, a valiant soldier and the bitterly disappointed lover of Charles VII's mistress, Agnes Sorel. At Orléans, Joan cares for the happiness of another pair of young lovers, Francis and Isabel. In retelling Joan's story thus, Southey follows his master Edmund Spenser in combining pastoral and martial subject matters in order to sing of "fierce warres and faithfull loues."[24] At the same time, Southey explores in the person of a historic medieval warrior, saint, and virgin-martyr the possibility, rejected earlier by Milton, of a chivalric romance that celebrates the "better fortitude" (*Paradise Lost* IX.31) of a saint.[25]

Despite the strong evocation of Milton and Spenser in Southey's epic, there are few direct verbal echoes of either *Paradise Lost* or *The Faerie Queene*. The important exception to this rule is Book IX of the original edition of *Joan of Arc*. There the "Delegated Maiden" wanders in her dream through a desolate, cloud-covered heath, illuminated by an occasional ray of light that makes "the moving darkness, visible" (IX.2, 16).[26] Her nocturnal journey recalls not only the opening book of *Paradise Lost* but also Dante's *Inferno*. More important, however, as Arnold Ray Beath notes, "Joan's confrontation with Despair [in lines 68–349] is very similar to the episode of the Redcrosse Knight and Despair (*FQ* I.ix) in its situation, its argument, and several particulars, such as the owl, the dagger, and Joan's blushes."[27]

Book IX offers internal evidence that Southey was consciously modeling himself on Spenser and Milton and confirms what we know from external sources, not only Southey's own preface to *Joan of Arc*, but also his letters. Greg Kucich remarks: "Southey liked to think of himself as the reincarnated 'Spirit of Spenser,' and he claimed to have read *The Fairie Queene* thirty times."[28] Writing from Balliol College in 1792, the year before he first drafted *Joan of Arc*, Southey describes himself as taking delight in his "constant study, Spenser."[29]

By consciously evoking Milton and Spenser, two of England's canonical poets, in the language and form of *Joan of Arc*, Southey could refashion his French heroine, making her simultaneously English and French. At the same time, he could invent himself as a patriotic poet in the republican tradition of Milton and Spenser. Finally, he could use a Spenserian plot in order to assign a new part to an English audience, a part that would allow them to be the penitential celebrators of a rehabilitated Joan of Arc.

Casting Joan in the Spenserian part of Redcrosse allows Southey to reinvent his historical French heroine as English in multiple ways. First, and most obviously, Southey thereby identifies her with Saint George, the patron saint of England, through direct allusion to the patriotic epic of a canonical English poet, Spenser. That literary identification is, however, only the tip of a deeper, intertextual relationship between *The Faerie Queene* and Southey's *Joan*—a relationship that provides a key to Southey's rhetorical success in presenting Joan of Arc as a heroine to an English audience.

As Southey intuitively understood, Redcrosse's sin against Una is a version of England's crime against Joan of Arc. Under the influence of an evil spell, wrought by Archimago, Redcrosse sees the chaste Una in Cantos I and II not as she really is but as a whore, and he therefore abandons her and embraces her double, Duessa. Similarly, the English leaders and soldiers of the fifteenth century falsely condemned Joan, an Una-like saint, as a Duessa-like heretic, whore, and rebel. Seeing and accepting Joan as the heroine she is thus allows Southey's English audience an opportunity also to play the part of a Redcrosse, who realizes his error, accepts forgiveness, and is reunited with his pure Lady. What is at stake for Southey in 1796 is not merely a national atonement for a historical injustice of the late Middle Ages but also the winning of English sympathy for the contemporary Jacobin cause his Joan implicitly supports.

Joan of Arc in the Cave of Despair

The full extent of Southey's debt to Spenser as a political allegorist becomes apparent in Book IX, the book that Southey called the "Original Sin" of the 1796 edition of *Joan of Arc* ("Preface," p. 6). There, in a retelling of Spenser's Cave of Despair episode, Southey casts his republican French heroine in the same literary role Spenser had assigned to the Redcrosse knight, "Saint George of mery England, the signe of victoree" (I.x.61). The identification of the two figures is bold. As Southey must have known from Shakespeare's *I Henry VI*, if not from the historical record, English soldiers during the Hundred Years' War invoked Saint George, England's warrior patron saint, against the French, who were invoking the name of Joan the Maid as that of a living saint, sent by God himself to bring them victory.[30] Identifying George and Joan through Spenserian allusion, Southey imaginatively overcomes that impossible, historical warring of saints and provides a means for his English audience to accept a rehabilitated Joan as their own heroine.

The superficial grounds for such an identification are evident. Both Joan and George are humble figures who are transplanted by divine decree from peaceful, pastoral surroundings into a world of violent warfare, where they fight heroically for the causes of justice. Saint

George's name, as Spenser notes, recalls the *Georgics* of Virgil and bespeaks his rural origins: "thee a Ploughman all vnweeting fond, / As he his toylesome teme that way did guyde, / And brought thee vp in ploughmans state to byde, / Whereof *Georgos* he thee gaue to name" (I.x.66). Similarly, Southey's Joan spends her childhood in Bizardo's hermitage, her youth as a shepherdess in Domremy: "Here past my unruffled days. Sometimes at morn / With pleasing toil to drive the woolly flock / To verdant mead or stream, sometimes to ease / The lowing cattle of their milky load, / My grateful task" (I.327–331).

Entrusted with martial destinies, both Joan and George are warrior saints from a legendary, medieval past: George, a knight and slayer of dragons; Joan, an armored virgin, commissioned to do battle by Saint Michael the Archangel, another warrior saint. In Spenser's *Faerie Queene*, the Redcrosse knight wears on his shield and "on his brest a bloudie Crosse . . . / The deare remembrance of his dying Lord" (II.1.ii). He is clad "in mightie armes and siluer shielde / Wherein old dints of deepe wounds did remaine, / The cruell markes of many a bloudy fielde" (I.1.i). This ancient armor is mysterious, for it is not his own: "Yet armes till that time did he neuer wield" (I.1.i). The prefatory letter addressed to Raleigh explains that Redcrosse must wear this armor, which is "the armour of a Christian man specified by Saint Paul" (p. 17) in Ephesians 6:10–17, if he is to succeed in the chivalric quest assigned to him. The poem, however, only indicates that the young, untried knight is wearing armor in which others have done battle before him. He takes up, as it were, the role of a romance hero, occupying and continuing a literary tradition of knightly, errant adventure, which Spenser employs as an allegory of personal growth in holiness.

In combining a moral allegory with a historical fiction, Spenser sees himself as following Homer, Virgil, and Ariosto, who "comprised . . . in his Orlando" both "a good gouernour and a vertuous man."[31] In *Joan of Arc,* Southey follows Spenser back to Ariosto's Orlando. In a remarkable, overt departure from history, Southey clothes Joan in the battle gear of Orlando (Roland), whose ivory horn, Olivant, miraculously sounds at the approach of the Maid to the warrior's sepulcher in the Church of Saint Catherine: "the lifted trump / pour'd forth a blast whose sound miraculous / Burst the rude tomb. Within, the arms appear'd: / The crested helm, the massy bauldrick's strength, / The oval shield, the magic-tempered blade" (IV.128–132). After this

spectacular event and a second sounding of Orlando's horn have pub-
licly confirmed the Maid's mission to "wield / The sword of vengeance"
(IV.142–143) against the oppressors of the innocent, the court of King
Charles feasts and celebrates, while a minstrel sings of Rinaldo and
Orlando:

> . . . Meanwhile the minstrel struck
> His harp: the Palladins of France he sung;
> The Warrior who from Arden's fated fount
> Drank of the bitter waters of aversion,
> And, loathing beauty, spurn'd the lovely Maid,
> Suppliant for Love; soon doomed to rue the charm
> Revers'd: and that invulnerable Chief
> Orlando, he who from the magic horn
> Breath'd such heart-withering sounds, that every foe
> Fled from the fearful blast, and all-appall'd,
> Spell-stricken Valour hid his recreant head.
>
> (IV.165–175)

This passage incorporates Ariosto's song of Orlando into Southey's song
of Joan, clothes his French heroine in Orlando's armor, and prompts a
citation of Spenser. As Southey wrote to his friend Grosvenor Bedford
in 1796, he was going to gloss (but never actually did) the allusion to
Orlando's magic horn with a "very quaint" footnote, displaying "great
erudition in quotations from Boyardo, Ariosto, Archbishop Turpin,
and Spencer [sic]."[32]

In the revised edition of *Joan of Arc* that appears in Southey's collected works, the passage calling for a Spenserian footnote has disap-
peared. The trumpet of Orlando does not sound. The tomb does not
open miraculously at its blast. The armor in the tomb "where some
warrior slept" (IV.125) is not, by any suggestion, the armor of Orlando.
There is no mention of magic. When the tomb is opened by ordinary
means, and Joan dons "the crested helm, / The bauldrick, and the
shield, and sacred sword" (IV.134–135), a feast ensues, but the minstrel
sings not of the palladins of France but rather "Of Lancelot du Lake"
(IV.176) and other Arthurian heroes, whose adventures have little in
common with Joan's. Indeed, the troubador's song in the revised *Joan
of Arc* symbolizes the court's extravagance and escapist disregard for
the historical plight of the people beseiged at Orléans.

The use of Orlando's trumpet in Book IV of the first edition may be regarded as a venial, Spenserian sin, stemming from the "original sin" manifested in Southey's original Book IX. That book, later removed from *Joan of Arc* and published separately as "The Vision of the Maid of Orleans," is the first of several imaginative reworkings by Romantic poets of Spenser's Cave of Despair episode, which gradually became (in the words of Greg Kucich) "a focal point of Romantic commentary on *The Faerie Queene*." Southey—like Keats, Shelley, and Blake after him—interprets that episode as "a sustained psychodrama of the mind's quest for transcendent ideals coming into conflict with its apprehension of bitter reality."[33] In particular, he uses it to depict, and thus to clarify, what Edward Meachen describes as "Southey's growing disillusionment with the Revolution and its increasingly violent means of reordering society."[34]

In Canto IX of the first book of Spenser's *Faerie Queene*, the Redcrosse knight, who has recently been released from his imprisonment by Orgoglio and Duessa, meets a pale, mirrorlike image of himself in Sir Trevisan, a fugitive from Despair. Trevisan reluctantly leads him back into a "darke, dolefull, drearie" landscape, strewn with corpses and haunted by "wand'ring ghosts" (I.ix.33–34). There Redcrosse encounters Despair, another double of himself, who confronts him with his guilt in having abandoned Una, to whose service he had pledged himself but sold himself instead "to serue Duesse vilde" (I.ix.46), defiling himself in the process. Offered various means of self-destruction—"swords, ropes, poison, fire" (I.ix.50)—Redcrosse accepts a dagger, which Una snatches out of his hand. She then leads him away from Despair's dwelling to the House of Holiness and finally to the Mount of Contemplation, in which wholesome places he repents, converts, and gains the strength he needs to fulfill his dragon-slaying mission.

In Book IX of *Joan of Arc* (and the numerical parallel between Southey's book and Spenser's canto cannot be accidental), Southey's "Delegated Maiden" follows in the footsteps of Redcrosse. She has just delivered Orléans and put the English forces to flight. Joan has done so, however, at the cost of many warriors' lives, including that of her beloved Theodore, who died, disguised, protecting her. At his funeral in an eerie cloister, Joan foresees her own martyrdom, "her pale lips trembling, and her cheek / As wan as tho' untenanted by life" (VIII.803–804).

That night, in a visionary dream, Joan makes her soul journey to Despair "Along a heath, / Barren, and wide, and drear, and desolate" (IX.10–11). Guided by a witchlike female pilot across a "fenny lake," she encounters an old man in a shroud, who welcomes her to the "regions of Despair" (IX.17, 69). He shows her many corpses, among them Theodore's: "This murdered man: murdered by thee! for thou / Didst lead him to the battle from his home" (IX.166–167). From the hand of Despair she accepts a dagger for self-destruction. When she rallies to fight temptation, Despair paints for her the picture of her own future death at the stake. Only after she rejects a second offer of a dagger for suicide does Theodore appear to her in the likeness of an angel to offer her hope: "For the grave / Is but the threshold of Eternity" (IX.369–370).

Like Una, who accompanied Redcrosse, Theodore escorts Joan away from Death and Despair into a purgatorial realm: "Here the dungeons are / Where bad men learn repentance: souls diseased / Must have their remedy" (IX.408–410). She sees the avaricious, the voluptuous, the gluttonous, and other groups of sinners, each atoning in an appropriate way (reminiscent of Dantean *contrapasso*) for their sins. Finally, she sees the purgatory of "the *Murderers of Mankind!*" (IX.695), the monarchs, each of them crowned with fire. In their midst, King Henry V of England greets Joan and acknowledges to her his crimes in persecuting the Lollards and invading France out of an ambitious greed for wealth and power: "I sent abroad / *Murder* and *Rape*" (IX.736–737). As punishment, he informs her, he is doomed to remain in purgatory until a new, republican society emerges on earth: "one brotherhood, / One universal Family of Love" (IX.743–744). That prophecy leads to the final, paradisiacal phase of Joan's dream-vision, which affords the Maid a glimpse of a glorious, future age, when people will have learned from the mistakes and sins of the past: "*Oppression* shall be chain'd, and *Poverty* / Die, and with her, her Brood of Miseries" (IX.859–860).

"Original Sin," Authorial Anxiety, and Fraternal Strife

This consoling Vision, indeed the whole of Book IX in the 1796 edition of *Joan of Arc*, is missing in the 1798 edition. Missing, too, is the Vision in Book II, which Samuel Taylor Coleridge had composed, as Southey duly acknowledged: "The 450 lines at the beginning of the second book, were written by S. T. Coleridge. But from this must be excepted the lines 141, 142, 143, and the whole intermediate passage from 148 to 222. The lines from 266 to 272 are likewise mine, and the lines from 286 to 291" ("Preface," pp. 2–3).

These two Visions include personification allegory, and their excision has usually been justified on purely aesthetic grounds as Southey's attempt to bring a greater stylistic unity to the work as a whole. In his preface to the first edition, Southey admitted, "The ninth book is the Original Sin of the poem. That it is a defect, I am myself sensible; but it is not uncommon at the age of twenty-one for the imagination to out-run the judgment" ("Preface," p. 6). In a letter to John Thelwall, dated December 31, 1796, Coleridge declared, "The ninth book is execrable" (*CL*, 1.170, p. 293). Southey, however, at first resisted suggestions to omit the book, because he doubted "that satire is misplaced," and he found "the lines good in themselves."[35] In the end, however, he decided to strike it from the second edition

The strong phrase used by Southey in referring to Book IX as "the Original Sin of the poem" suggests, however, an entire psychohistory that provides an ascetic rather than an aesthetic explanation for the excision. Southey's "Original Sin" in Book IX is to cite Spenser and Milton directly, making extensive use of personification allegory and disrupting the normative temporality of the epic through a visionary poetics that brings Joan in direct contact with the past and future. Book IX points to the very origins of Southey's own vocation and practice as a poet and to the Spenserian inspiration for his peculiar representation of Joan of Arc. "Strong poets," Harold Bloom has argued, wrestle with the "ghostly fathers" who have given them life as poets, in part because their own creative impulse, the desire to be original in their work, is so strong that they cannot bear to be belated or derivative; they suffer "the melancholy of the creative mind's desperate insistence upon priority."[36]

The phrase "Original Sin" evokes an experience of guilt in the very act of imitating Spenser, which is for Southey a Satanic mimesis of a pure model for which he must atone perversely by utterly distancing himself. In excising Book IX, cutting it out of *Joan of Arc,* Southey accomplishes a sacrificial self-purgation that Bloom, in his taxonomy of anxious, "revisionary ratios," calls *askesis,* defined as "a movement of self-purgation which intends the attainment of a state of solitude."

The ascetical poet, according to Bloom, "undergoes a revisionary move-ment . . . of curtailing; he yields up part of his own human and imagi-native endowment, so as to separate himself from others, including the precursor."[37] In jettisoning his Spenserian book, Southey thus reaches out for a direct, unmediated inspiration, such as he imagines Joan of Arc to have received when she "lone in thought . . . wandered forth" (I.483) in the evening and first heard the Voices that summoned her to her mission.

René Girard's theoretical viewpoint, deriving from anthropology rather than Freudian psychology, would concur with a Bloomian analy-sis of Southey's Spenserian excision. All learning and desire, accord-ing to Girard, is mimetic, as Plato and Aristotle recognized. The fledg-ling poet imitates the master poet, whom he admires and from whom he learns. If the two become very closely identified, the younger poet imitates not only the older poet's practice but also his desires. When the two poets want the same thing—poetic fame, for example—the mimesis becomes competitive, and the one who had been a life-giving father becomes a rivalrous brother or twin, with whom the younger poet competes as his double. This mimetic crisis can be so severe that it seeks its resolution in the severing of ties, the expulsion or killing of the once revered model.

This Girardian shift from the "father" to the "brother" seems es-pecially apropos to the present instance, because Southey does not ex-cise the Spenserian Book IX alone but also the Coleridgean Vision in Book II. Like Southey, Coleridge admired Spenser and learned from him as his student and poetic son, a relation of literary influence that in itself established a brotherhood between the first-generation Roman-tic poets.[38] In Book II Coleridge envisions the Vision of Joan of Arc, and he does so in an allegorical fashion that allowed him to enter into the mode of perception that he attributed to the inspired people—prophets and poets alike—of premodern times, including Spenser him-self. In Joan's Vision he thus saw Spenser's as well, albeit belatedly, even as Southey attempted to do in the Vision of Book IX. The two Visions compete with each other for a Spenserian and Jehannine acquisition and in their representation of Joan of Arc as an artist figure with whom they can identify.

Coleridge's poetry gives allegorical expression (via personifica-tion) to Joan's Voices and visionary forms. In Book II of Southey's *Joan of Arc,* Coleridge prefaces his narrative of Joan's inspiration with lines that anticipate his discussion of symbol, allegory, fancy, and imagination in *Literaria Biographia*.[39] He defines true freedom as "the unfetter'd use / Of all the Powers which God for use had given," especially the poetic ability to view the Creator in his creation: "For all that meets the bodily sense I deem / Symbolical, one mighty alphabet / For infants' minds" (II.13–14, 19–21). In the evolutionary development of humankind, "Fancy is the power / That first unsensualizes the dark mind / Giving it new delights; and bids it swell / With wild activity; and peopling air, / By obscure fears of Beings invisible / Emancipates it from the grosser thrall / Of the present impulse" (II.80–86). Fancy draws on images stored in the memory, recombines them, and thus provides the mind with a means gradually to forge a vision of the future and a programmatic basis for action: "Wild phantasies! yet wise, / On the victorious goodness of high God, / Teaching Reliance and medicinal Hope" (II.114–116).

According to Coleridge, such fantasies, perhaps under the direction of a guardian Power—"If there be Beings of higher class than Man" (II.120)—flooded the soul of Joan of Arc and caused her to brood and meditate, until a beneficial "Superstition with unconscious hand / [Sat] Reason on her throne" (II.87–88). Reason's gradual dominance over the images of fancy is represented in the 1796 *Joan of Arc* by the transformation of Joan's "Voices and strange Shapes, illusions apt, / Shadowy of Truth" (II.135–136) into the clear, ideational forms of Spenserian personification allegory: Ambition, Oppression, Cruelty, Revenge, Avarice, Justice, Freedom, and Peace. Personification combines images and concepts. When stripped of its "Shapes," personification allegory, in turn, becomes the philosophical rhetoric of the revolutionary ideology for which Joan is a mouthpiece. Thus, at the end of Coleridge's part of Book II, Joan responds to the visionary edict "Save thy country!" with a hymn of praise to "Nature's vast ever-acting Energy," the "God" that inspires her death-defiant, military action (II.439, 444).

In Southey's epic Joan first receives her call, not in a daytime apparition of Saint Michael, but rather in a troubled dream, following a conversation with Conrade, a patriotic warrior, who has taken shelter at the hearth of Theodore's mother. As she listens, trembling, she is stirred by his passionate account of England's crimes against her poor countrymen: "Then in mine heart tumultuous thoughts arose / Of high atchievements [*sic*], indistinct, and wild / And vast, yet such they were that I did pant / As tho' by some divinity possess'd" (I.376–179).

During the night, she sleeps restlessly, beholding "strange forms, sent as I do believe / From the Most High" (I.443–444). When she awakes from that dream, Joan is altered in mood and appearance: "From that night I could feel my burthen'd soul / Heaving beneath incumbent Deity" (I.460–461). She hears "strange voices in the evening wind" and beholds "strange forms / . . . in the twilight air" (I.465–466). She becomes a melancholy wanderer, who frequents the forest shade and sits, brooding, by the brook.

Such a Joan is a prototype of the inspired Romantic poet, as Coleridge recognized.[40] In a handwritten note beside Book II, lines 223–264, in his copy of *Joan*, Coleridge explicitly identifies his poetic inspiration with Joan's Voices. In the poem the "tutelary Power" addresses her: "Maid beloved of Heaven!" (II.223). Those same words came to Coleridge, he attests, in a possession by the Muse, who inspired him to speak words whose meaning was unknown to him: "These are very fine lines, tho' I say it that should not: but hang me if I know or ever did know the meaning of them, tho' my own composition."[41]

Elsewhere, in a letter to Joseph Cottle, dating from early April 1797, Coleridge expresses regret at the publication of Southey's *Poems* and applies lines 460–461 from *Joan of Arc*, Book I, to his friend, ironically contrasting Joan's fulsome inspiration to his meager one:

> Notwithstanding the Reviews, I, who in the sincerity of my heart am *jealous* for Robert Southey's fame, regret the publication of that volume. Wordsworth complains, with justice, that Southey writes *too much at his ease*—that he seldom "feels his burthened breast / Heaving beneath th'incumbent Deity." He certainly will make literature more *profitable* to him from the fluency with which he writes, and the facility with which he pleases himself. But I fear, that to posterity his wreath will look unseemly. (*CL* I.184, p. 320)

As Lynda Pratt observes, Coleridge's letter quotes Wordsworth quoting Southey's own "description of divine inspiration in order to reveal how rarely in their shared opinion (or so Coleridge would have it) his poetry was able to attain a comparable level of intensity."[42]

Coleridge goes on to comment critically on the speed (six weeks) with which Southey boasts of having composed his Joan of Arc epic in twelve books. (See "Preface," p. 2.) Taking Milton as his model, Coleridge compares himself with Southey and declares that were he to write an epic, he would devote a full twenty years to preparatory research, writing, and correction: "So I would write haply not unhearing of that divine and rightly whispering Voice which speaks to mighty minds of predestined Garlands, starry and unwithering" (*CL* I.184, p. 321). The letter to Cottle, written during a time of painful estrangement (1795–1799), shows Coleridge—eager for Southey's success but also "jealous" of his positive reception by reviewers—in competition with his brother poet, imaginatively standing in his place, listening to Jehannine Voices of poetic inspiration, stripping Southey of the poet's laurel wreath, and doing so in league with others, Wordworth and (potentially) Cottle.

The *Joan of Arc* that began as a collaborative work between Southey and Coleridge fractured into multiple, competitive Joan poems. As we have seen, the *Joan of Arc* of 1796 appeared in a much revised second edition in 1798. Southey published Book IX as a separate poem, entitled "The Vision of the Maid of Orleans," in the first volume of his collected works. On January 1, 1797, he wrote to Grosvenor Bedford to say that he had "sketched out a tragedy on the martyrdom of Joan of Arc, which is capable of making a good closet drama."[43] In 1796 Coleridge wrote an unpublished Joan poem, variously entitled *The Progress of Liberty* or *The Vision of the Maid of Orleans* or *Visions of the Maid of Orleans* or *Visions of the Maid of Arc* or *The Vision of the Patriot Maid*.[44] About this work, later published with the additional lines that had been withdrawn from Book II of Southey's *Joan* as *The Destiny of Nations*, Charles Lamb wrote enthusiastically to Coleridge on February 13, 1797:

> [Y]our personal account of the Maid far surpasses anything of the sort in Southey. . . . After all this cometh Joan, a *publican's* daughter, sitting on an alehouse *bench*, and marking the *swingings* of the *sideboard*, finding a poor man, his wife, and six children, starved to death with cold, and thence roused into a state of mind proper to receive visions, emblematic of equality; which, what the devil Joan had to do with, I don't know, or, indeed, with the French and American Revolutions, though that needs no pardon, it is executed so nobly![45]

The tension in Lamb's compliment to Coleridge derives from several sources. Lamb mentions the Jacobin ideal of equality in the same breath that he praises Coleridge's surpassing of Southey. He names Joan of Arc as he exclaims to the devil. He honors Coleridge's poetic "execution" in the same sentence that he mentions bloody political "revolutions." And he divorces the Joan of history from the Joan of Coleridge's Jacobin imagination.

A similar, monstrous combination of things emerges in Coleridge's famous long letter of November 13, 1795, written on the eve of the publication of *Joan of Arc,* in which he denounces Southey for his defection from the ideals of pantisocracy, his clinging to personal possessions, and the egoism evident in his literary dealings with his would-be collaborator and "brother," Coleridge. Students together in Oxford in 1794, Coleridge and Southey had quickly formed an intense bond, grounded in their common love of poetry; their literary ambitions; their kindred, republican politics; and their mutual friends. Their desires were so mimetic that they were later to marry sisters—Southey taking Edith Fricker to be his own and Coleridge claiming Edith's sister, Sara, as his bride. Together with their fellow planners—Robert Lovell (a poet who married a third sister in the Fricker family), George Burnett, Robert Allen, and Edmund Seward—they had at first decided to form an egalitarian society in the New World, on the banks of the Susquehanna River, and then tentatively decided on a settlement in Wales. Southey's *Joan of Arc* was to be a vehicle for this pantisocracy in more ways than one, as his letter of July 20, 1794, to Grosvenor Bedford makes clear: "Yesterday I took my proposals for publishing Joan of Arc to the printer; should the publication be any ways successful, it will carry me over [to America], and get me some few acres, a spade, and a plow. My brother Thomas will gladly go with us."[46] By the end of 1795 all their plans were in disarray, Edmund Seward had died, and the personal tensions between Coleridge and Southey had grown to such a point that Coleridge was ready to break off their friendship.

The *Joan of Arc* that had symbolized their common republication ideals became a particular subject of complaint for Coleridge. He was appalled that the life of a saint should be told by a man like Southey, who was, he believed, "lost to Virtue," because selfish, dishonest, and egotistical (*CL* I.93, p. 163). He felt, moreover, that Southey had not recognized the full extent of his contribution: "I wrote with vast exertion of all my Intellect the parts in the Joan of Arc, and I corrected that and other Poems with greater interest, than I should have felt for my own" (*CL* I.93, p. 172). Alison Hickey rightly discovers in Coleridge's self-sacrificing description here and elsewhere of his working relationship with Southey an "obsession with wholes and parts" and an anxiety about himself as an "author of fragments—and thus a fragmentary author."[47] Coleridge complains that he has contributed most of the labor of thinking, whereas Southey has done the easy work of automatic writing, supplying words for Coleridge's critical reading and editorial correction. Elsewhere, in a letter to John Thelwall, dated December 31, 1796, Coleridge muses: "I think that an admirable Poet might be made by *amalgamating him & me*. I *think* too much for a *Poet;* he too little for a *great* Poet"(*CL* I.170, p. 294). The incompletion of each one as a separate identity, the refusal to share all things in common, and the inability to complement each other without exacerbating each other's limitations had worked to produce not a harmonious whole, as they had dreamed, but rather a monstrous, disjointed combination of things.

At this crisis a scapegoat must be found; something monstrous and guilty must be sacrificed as a substitute for the troubled communal relationships that have become so contaminated by mimesis as to have become (in the words of Girard) "*interdividual . . .* , rather than *interindividual,*" causing the "mixing and interference effects that determine the composite nature of ritual *masks* as well as the monstrosity of mythological creatures."[48] Such a monster is the Duessa of Spenser's imagination, and the Jacobin Joan of the Visions of Southey and Coleridge, excised from the second edition of *Joan of Arc.*

Joan of Arc as Duessa: The Monster and the Mythic Lie

Southey's preface to the edition of 1796 calls attention to the monstrosity of the historical image of Joan of Arc, whether one considers the medieval and Renaissance view of her held by the English or a combination of the opposing, English and French views. Referring to Thomas Fuller's 1642 *The Holy State and the Profane State,* Southey notes that "Fuller, of quaint memory," draws on Early Modern English chronicles, such as Edward Hall's *The Union of the Two Noble and Illustre Famelies of Lancastre and Yorke* (1548) and Holinshed's *Chronicles* (1587), in his portrayal of Joan, even as Shakespeare did in *I Henry VI.*[49] Fuller characterizes Joan as a "'handsome, witty, and bold Maid,'" who cut her hair and wore man's clothes in contradiction of nature and "'against God's express word'"; and he flatly "classes her among witches" ("Preface," pp. 5–6). Against this English account of Joan, Southey quotes from Aubin-Louis Millin's 1790 *National Antiquities of France,* which tells of "'outrages'" the Maid suffered at the hands of the English and the Burgundians during her flagrantly unjust trial and cruel imprisonment. "To satisfy [the English], it was necessary to destroy the unhappy Joan," and so "'Joan the Heretic—the Sorceress—the Lascivious'" was burned at the stake ("Preface," p. 7).

Through the juxtaposition of these two contrasting accounts, Southey points to nationalistic bias in the construction of Joan's history— a bias that has led the English chroniclers to demonize Joan and the French historians to sanctify her. What fascinates Southey is the apparent impossibility of knowing Joan's historical "truth" and thus the heightened potential of her story for imaginative retelling. "The History of JOAN of ARC," he writes, "is one of those problems that render investigation fruitless" ("Preface," p. 6).

At the time when Southey first published *Joan of Arc,* the work of modern historians of Joan of Arc was only beginning, but Southey placed his confidence in Joan's irreducible mystery, a mystery that the facts, such as they were, would only serve to confirm: "M. Laverdy is now occupied in collecting whatever has been written concerning the Maid of Orleans. The result of his enquiries I anxiously expect" ("Preface," p. 7).[50]

Southey's anxiety as he awaited the published work of historians stemmed from several sources. Knowing little, he hoped and expected that little more would ever be known, leaving him free to imagine much. Unlike Schiller, writing soon after him, Southey was reluctant to contradict the historical record directly but perfectly content to shape its contradictory materials through abridgment and imaginative amplification. Regarding the known history of Joan of Arc as largely mythic—a product of national prejudices—he felt free to substitute one myth for another, replacing the French myth of her holiness and angelic vocation with an analogous, Jacobin, ideological myth of noble revolt, ending in "liberty, equality, and fraternity." For the myth of English prejudice, he substituted the lie of a guilty, self-divided Joan, conscience-stricken and tempted to suicidal despair on account of the innocent victims caught in the tide of a necessary violence. Joan's guilt and the necessity of her death, alongside the putative necessity of other murders, remain in place in Southey's modern, mythic retelling of her medieval, English legend. Southey's Joan is thus no less monstrous in the end than Shakespeare's, albeit in a different way. Southey would have her be a Spenserian Una, but she remains irreducibly a Duessa, standing in the midst of corpses and in the shadow of the guillotine.

In choosing Joan of Arc, an armed French shepherdess, as his heroine, Southey could immediately evoke in the minds of his readers the militant, downtrodden French rebels of his own time. As Thomas De Quincey was later to remark, "What he needed in his central character was a heart with a capacity for the wrath of the Hebrew prophets applied to ancient abuses, and for evangelic pity applied to the sufferings of nations. . . . A French heart it must be, or how should it follow with its sympathies a French movement? There lay Southey's reason for adopting the Maid of Orleans as the depository of hopes and aspirations on behalf of France as fervid as his own."[51]

Perhaps out of an awareness of his own mythmaking in using the Joan of Arc story to serve an obvious, ideological end, Southey presents himself as demythologizing her history. Southey's revision of the 1796 preface, published in the 1837 edition, emphasizes the mysterious source of Joan's inspiration and enthusiasm: "The history of Joan of Arc is as mysterious as it is remarkable. . . . This mysteriousness renders the story of Joan of Arc peculiarly fit for poetry."[52] By "mystery" Southey does not mean, however, the supernatural instrumentality that the historical Joan claimed for herself; rather, he asserts a natural cause for her actions: "The aid of angels and devils is not necessary to raise her above mankind; she has no gods to lackey her, and inspire her with courage, and heal her wounds: the Maid of Orleans acts wholly from the workings of her own mind, from the deep feeling of inspiration."[53]

Against both the conventions of epic, which demand divine involvement, and the evidence of the medieval chronicles, which declare Joan's miracles and depict her either as a saint or a witch, Southey avoids in his poem "the palpable agency of superior powers," whose intervention would, he feels, "destroy the obscurity of [Joan's] character, and sink her to the mere heroine of a fairy tale."[54] At the same time, he claims to adhere closely to the historical record: "The alterations which I have made in the history are few and trifling. . . . Whatever appears miraculous is asserted in history, and my authorities will be found in the notes."[55]

Southey minimizes the extent of his departures from the historical record, in keeping with the critical principle, cited by one of his reviewers, that "an epic poem should be founded in true history, though it admits the additional embellishments of fiction" (*CH*, p. 44). Although Southey's later editions of *Joan of Arc* are in some respects factually more accurate than the first edition, none of them remedies the basic incongruities to which the original reviewers called attention. Writing in the *Monthly Review* (1796), John Aikin observed, "The sentiments . . . are less adapted to the age in which the events took place, than to that of the writer. . . . In many parts, a strong allusion to later characters and events is manifest" (*CH*, p. 42). The anonymous critic writing for the *Analytical Review* similarly noted that "a manifest incongruity runs through the piece, in ascribing to characters of the fifteenth century the politics and metaphysics of an enlightened philosopher of the eighteenth" (*CH*, p. 48). Southey's "allegorical personages, dreams, and visions" not only "ill supply the place of that grand machinery, which produced so powerful an effect in the epics of Homer and Virgil" (*CH*, p. 48), but they also stand as inferior substitutes for the historical Joan's Voices and saintly visions.

The too obvious discrepancies between his heroine and the Maid of history, and his own changing political views, prompted the poet to keep revising the work over and over again. In Southey's words, "The second edition differed almost as much from the first, as that from the copy which was originally intended for publication. Less extensive alterations were made in two subsequent editions; the fifth was only a reprint of the fourth. . . . My intention then was to take no further pains in correcting a work of which the inherent defects were incorrigible."[56] Southey changed his mind, however, and revised the poem one more time, in preparation for its inclusion in his collected works. In his preface to the 1837 edition, he writes: "And for those [faults] which expressed the political prejudices of a young man who had too little knowledge to suspect his own ignorance, they have either been expunged, or altered, or such substitutions have been made for them as harmonize with the prevailing spirit of the poem."[57]

The language of metamorphosis is striking. Southey's obsessive revision of *Joan of Arc* thus curiously confirms the allegory he originally encoded in it—that of a Redcrosse, wandering in a mutable world of revolutionary change, whose limited, historical perspective leads him again and again to err (however pardonably) in the way he sees persons and things. Southey's 1829 *Sir Thomas More: Or, Colloquies on the Progress and Prospects of Society* suggests that Southey himself may have recognized this parallel. In this dialogue, Southey's alter ego, Montesinos, converses not with Joan of Arc but with the ghost of another martyred political saint, Thomas More. Alluding to his *Utopia,* More comforts his interlocutor by pointing to what they have in common: "We have both speculated in the joy and freedom of our youth upon the possible improvement of society; and both in like manner have lived to dread with reason the effects of that restless spirit, which, *like the Titaness Mutability described by your immortal master,* insults Heaven and disturbs the earth."[58] More models for Montesinos the attitude that constantly seeks revision: "By comparing the great operating causes in the age of the Reformation, and in this age of revolutions, going back to the former age; looking at things as I then beheld them, perceiving wherein I judged rightly, and wherein I erred."[59] With regard to the French Revolution in particular, More describes a truly Spenserian transformation of a Jacobin Una into a Duessa:

> The French had persuaded themselves this was the most enlightened age of the world, and they the most enlightened people in it, . . . the politest, the most amiable, the most humane of nations, . . . and that a new era of philosophy, philanthropy, and peace was about to commence under their auspices, . . . when they were on the eve of a revolution which, for all its complicated monstrosities, absurdities, and horrors, is more disgraceful to human nature than any other series of events in history.[60]

When in 1829 Southey alludes to Spenser in order to fashion himself into another Redcrosse, confronted with the terrible duality of the French Revolution, he restores the Spenserian intertext that he had earlier excised from *Joan of Arc.* Una again becomes a Duessa. From the perspective of this essay, the most notable revision of that poem was Southey's deletion of Book IX, the "Original Sin" of the epic, and of the lines written by Coleridge at the beginning of Book II—revisions he accomplished already in the second edition. These passages laid bare Southey's conceptual debt to Spenser, especially in the use of personification allegory. Both were "sins" against Southey's fiction, because

they revealed rather than concealed his art. They offered overt remind-
ers to Southey and his audience that he was allegorizing a historical
subject—that is, fictionalizing it as other than it really was and using
its images to convey a predetermined, political message.

Such an ideological allegorization, unavoidable as it was in practice, had to be hidden rhetorically and (at least temporarily) forgotten,
in the interest of a truly Romantic art and a republican politics. The
role played by allegory had to be elided, and its literal space in the
narrative emptied, to allow for a symbolic identification between a
medieval saint and modern revolutionaries. In the absence of personification allegory, however, the already wide gap in Southey's *Joan of Arc*
between the two histories, past and present, became too wide for an
effective symbolism. Southey failed, but his attempt was grand and appealing enough to inspire subsequent British writers—from Thomas De
Quincey to Vita Sackville-West—to try to discover the truth of Joan's
story and to retell it as their own.

After the Revolution: Rehabilitating Joan

Southey's reading of Spenser showed him an imaginative, literary way
to triumph over a historical narrative in which England had played a
villainous part. By making that ignoble past a part of a larger romance
plot of error, maturation, and enlightened reform, Southey enabled
English writers after him to celebrate Joan of Arc without any stain to
their patriotism and to participate in their own Rehabilitation of her.
Indeed, as Thomas De Quincey (1785–1859) was quick to understand,
Southey's epic actually made it a patriotic act to honor her and thus
to redeem England's historical failing and atone for Shakespeare's inaccurate portrayal of her in *I Henry VI*.

In 1847, when the French historian Jules Michelet, citing Shakespeare's play, accused the English of being incapable of praising Joan,
due to pride and nationalistic prejudice,[61] De Quincey deplored "the
bitter and unfair spirit in which M. Michelet writes against England."[62]
He pointed to Southey's correction of the bard: "Fifty years before
M. Michelet was writing this flagrant injustice, another Englishman
(viz., Southey) had, in an epic poem, reversed this misjudgment and
invested the shepherd girl with a glory nowhere else accorded to her,
not even by Schiller."[63]

In his "Joan of Arc," De Quincey himself follows Southey in singing her praises and enters into a veritable contest with Michelet "to convince him that an Englishman is capable of thinking more highly of *La Pucelle* than even her admiring countrymen" (p. 30). As De Quincey recognizes, Michelet's history of France is interpretive, imaginative, and literary; it can fittingly, therefore, be answered by historical fiction and subsumed by literary history.[64] In this context Southey's epic and De Quincey's essay constitute a continuation of Joan's trial in which the English outdo the French in their rehabilitation of her: "Here is France calumniating *La Pucelle:* here is England defending her" (p. 31).[65] Indeed, De Quincey predicts that generations of English writers will serve their country's honor by telling Joan's true story: "La Pucelle d'Orleans, the victorious enemy of England, has been destined to receive her deepest commemoration from the magnanimous justice of Englishmen" (p. 6).

De Quincey credits Southey for his positive depiction of Joan of Arc, but he also criticizes Southey for misrepresenting her, to make her serve his own political and ideological agenda. In so doing, De Quincey suggests, Southey continues the allegorical erring of Redcrosse, for he sees and portrays Joan as "other" than she was and thus as a Duessa, who is subject to an endless series of doublings.

According to De Quincey's analysis, Southey's depiction of Joan is false on several major counts. First of all, in making her a mouthpiece for Jacobin sentiments, Southey represents Joan as less concerned with the expulsion of the English invaders and the safeguarding of the Dauphin's succession to the throne of France than with protecting the civil liberties of the lower classes. Joan's sympathies "never coincided with that of the revolutionary period,"[66] and therefore the speeches Southey places on her lips and those of her companions never ring true.

For Southey's Joan, the enemies are the "mighty ones" (V.94, 160) of every nation, who abuse their power over the poor. She is "To England friendly . . . / Foe only to the great blood-guilty ones, / The masters and murderers of mankind" (VIII.642–644). She shows mercy to the English captives, not out of a charitable love for one's enemy, but because they, like the French peasantry, are "the victims of the mighty" (VIII.526). France is, as Conrade exclaims, "King-cursed" (IV.158) and oppressed as much by its own nobility as by England's. Charles rules by popular choice (V.369–370: "France will only own as King / Him whom the people chuse") but only as long as he protects the lowly, feeds the hungry, and protects widows and orphans. On the very day when Southey's Joan—not the archbishop of Rheims!—anoints and crowns Charles king of France, she threatens him with deposition: "Believe me, King! that hireling guards, / Tho' flesh'd in slaughter, would be weak to save / A tyrant on the blood-cemented Throne / That totters underneath him" (X.743–746).

Second, Southey attributes to Joan his own youthful anti-Catholic prejudices and reinvents her as a proof of Rousseau's educational theory. Orphaned at a young age, Southey's Joan of 1796 is raised by the hermit Bizardo in a forest, far from the corrupting influences of city, Church, and state. Summoned before the theologians at Poitiers to give evidence that she has truly been commissioned by God to save France, Joan tells them that she has never participated in Holy Mass, never received the Eucharist, and never gone to Confession. "Ignorant of sin," she claims to have worshiped God instinctively: "Twas Nature taught my early youth / Religion—Nature bade me see the God / Confest in all that lives, and moves, and is" (III.384, 389–391). As De Quincey notes, "All this deistical confession of Joanna's, besides being suicidal for the interest of her cause, is opposed to the depositions" in the records of both her trial and her rehabilitation, which affirm the Maid's intense participation in the sacramental life of the Church: "Joan was a girl of natural piety, that saw God in forests, and hills, and fountains, but did not the less see him in chapels and oratories" (p. 19).

Throughout the epic, Joan has recurring visions of her future death at the stake: "Her snow-white Limbs by iron fetters bruis'd, / Her breast expos'd" (II.291–292). De Quincey ignores this effort on Southey's part to tell the whole of Joan's story. He charges him with having pursued only Joan's "brief career of *action*," which ends (as the epic does) in triumph at Rheims, while omitting "the saintly passion of her imprisonment, trial, and execution" (p. 20).[67] Referring to "the law of epic unity," De Quincey asserts that "Joanna's history bisects into two opposite hemispheres, and both could not have been presented in one poem, unless by sacrificing all unity of theme, or else by involving the earlier half, as a narrative episode, in the latter" (p. 20).

De Quincey's either-or does not allow for the possibility of involving the latter half of Joan's story as prophetic vision in the earlier half. Why? Perhaps because his standard is classical, not Romantic, and such a prophetic technique is little used by Homer and Virgil, who clearly favor beginning "in medias res," the artificial ordering of material, and retrospective narrative. At a deeper level, however, De Quincey may be suggesting that the macabre, Gothic visions of Southey's Joan are so spectral that they fail to represent the historical truth of Joan's Christian heroism and faith-filled martyrdom. Thus in the visions of death, as well as in the conclusion of the epic, "the grander half of the story was . . . sacrificed, as being irrelevant to Southey's political object."[68] Southey does not merely alter the facts of Joan's life; he substitutes Joan's dreams and daydreams of her death for her actual trial, torture, and execution.[69]

In 1796 Southey had reasons not to depict Joan's burning at the stake. To do so would invite comparison of the fate of his republican heroine and that of Marie Antoinette (1755–1793)—the one a victim of royalists; the other, of revolutionaries. Southey had completed a first draft of *Joan of Arc* in 1793, the year of the queen's execution. In a letter dated October 29, he replies testily to Charles Collins: "To suppose that I felt otherwise than grieved and indignant at the fate of the unfortunate Queen of France was supposing me a brute, and to request an avowal of what I felt seemed a suspicion that I did not feel. You seemed glad, when arguments against the system of republicanism had failed, to grasp at the crimes of wretches who call themselves Republicans and stir up my feelings against my judgment."[70] By November 11 news of other atrocities had reached him, and he wrote gloomily to Grosvenor Bedford, "The murder of Brissot has completely harrowed up my faculties. . . . I look round the world and everywhere find the same mournful spectacle—the strong tyrannizing over the weak, man and beast. . . . Oppression is triumphant everywhere, and the only difference is that it acts in Turkey through the anger of a grand seignior, in France of a revolutionary tribunal, and in England of a prime minister."[71]

Joan of Arc veils the spectacle that Southey sees, in an attempt to protect the ideals if not the practice of the Jacobin party. De Quincey, however, brings graphically to the fore what Southey keeps hidden, and he does so as a pointed rejoinder to him. In the conclusion of his "Joan of Arc," De Quincey brings before the view of the imaginary inhabitants of "far telescopic worlds" the "spectacles" of three women on the scaffold. Marie Antoinette, "the widowed queen," steps forward, "her head turned gray by sorrow," and kneels "humbly to kiss the guillotine, as one that worships death" (p. 28). After her comes the youthful Charlotte Corday (1768–1793), guillotined for her assassination of the Jacobin leader Jean-Paul Marat, whom she killed in a vain attempt to put an end to the republican bloodbath. Last of all, Joan of Arc appears, "conducted before mid-day, guarded by eight hundred spearmen, to a platform of prodigious height" (p. 29).

De Quincey's association of Joan with two women executed by the Jacobins gives a startling answer to Southey's depiction of her. Whereas Southey deconstructs nationalistic prejudice in order to reinvent the French Joan of Arc as an English heroine, De Quincey works to deconstruct the two simple oppositions of oppressor and oppressed, master and slave, guilty and innocent, to which the young Southey adheres. De Quincey recognizes in Marie Antoinette's execution the operation of the Girardian scapegoat mechanism.[72] Whereas Southey in his first epic, *Joan of Arc,* as well as in his last epic, *Roderick,* maintains a belief in the virtuous use of violence and what Edward Meachen calls "the cleansing power of war,"[73] De Quincey argues from Joan's example for nothing less than the love of one's enemies, the acceptance of one's own guilt, and the refusal to sacrifice another person as a scapegoat.

In De Quincey's imagination yet another scaffold arises before the eyes of the assembled peoples of France and England. The two nations, once warring twins engaged in fraternal strife, have each rehabilitated the Maid, whom the French had abandoned and the English executed. United in their newfound love for Joan, they place the whole blame for her death on the shoulders of a scapegoat, the bishop of Beauvais, who tried her and condemned her as a heretic. In De Quincey's essay, the guilt-ridden bishop mounts the scaffold to stand in Joan's place, alone and without counsel, as a prisoner at the bar. Before him "the tumult is wondrous, the crowd stretches away into infinity" (p. 35). In a dramatic, antisacrificial conclusion, De Quincey imagines no better advocate for the bishop than Joan of Arc herself, whose charity impels her to come back from the dead to plead for her mortal enemy.

Did not Diana, far from being angry,
At loss of ancient bloody sacrifice,
Give ample hearing to your gentle prayer?
—JOHANN WOLFGANG VON GOETHE

To many of your countrymen I'll still bring death,
And many widows shall I make, but finally I,
Myself, shall perish and shall thus fulfill my fate.
—FRIEDRICH SCHILLER

For from an innocent creature, man became a guilty one,
from a perfect child of nature an imperfect moral being,
from a contented instrument a discontented artist.
—FRIEDRICH SCHILLER

CHAPTER TWO

SCHILLER'S JOHANNA

Civilization, Art, and the Scapegoat

In the book that was the "original sin" of his 1796 epic, Robert Southey depicted a conscience-stricken Joan of Arc, tempted to despair in the belief that she had committed murder. Southey removed the book and with it the too strong implication of Jehannine and Jacobin guilt, in order to maintain the innocence of his revolutionary heroine and the guilt of tyrannical kings. In 1801, on the eve of the Napoleonic invasion of Germany, Friedrich Schiller (1759–1805) boldly presented Joan of Arc on the stage as a guilty sinner-saint, a scapegoat, whose expulsion and death united fifteenth-century France in the face of the English invader. The first of his "fatherland dramas," *Die Jungfrau von Orleans* (*The Maid of Orléans*) served a similarly uniting function in early-nineteenth-century Germany, where performance after performance—in Leipzig, Berlin, Hamburg, and Weimar—roused the public. As banner after banner fell in tribute over the body of the slain virgin on the stage in the final scene of the play, the divided principalities of Germany were being welded together into what Benjamin W. Wells has termed "a moral feeling of racial unity."[1]

Disputing the claim that *Die Jungfrau von Orleans* is "a product of Schiller's patriotism, a nationalist manifesto to the Germans in the era of the revolutionary wars," E. L. Stahl makes the commonsensical observation: "If it had been [Schiller's] intention to rouse [the Germans] against the French invaders, he would surely have chosen another subject.... He planned his tragedy as a sublime, not a patriotic spectacle, for by that means he hoped to meet what he considered to be the need of the age."[2] Stahl is surely right to maintain that Schiller's goals extended beyond immediate political propaganda, but he errs in setting the "sublime" against the "patriotic" and in opposing the immediate to the underlying "need of the age" addressed by the play. Schiller himself emphatically joined the two. There can be no doubt that Schiller sought to unify Germany through his play—not for Germany's immediate political salvation alone, however, but for the sake of Germany's role as a modern, united nation in the larger work of human civilization. As he writes, "It is a poor and little aim to write for one nation.... The most powerful nation is but a fragment; and thinking minds cannot grow warm on its account, except in so far as this nation or its fortunes have been influential on the progress of the species."[3]

Schiller's *Uber die Ästhetische Erziehung des Menschen* (*Letters on the Aesthetic Education of Man*) first appeared as a complete and revised text in 1801, the same year in which Schiller completed *The Maid of Orléans*. In those letters Schiller portrays humanity as being insufficiently prepared for modern democracy—a truth evidenced by the barbaric course of the French Revolution. Schiller saw the Revolution (in the words of Walter Hinderer and Daniel O. Dahlstrom) as "a brutal attempt to turn a people's natural instincts into moral virtue overnight, the fate of a people 'not yet ripe for civil liberty' because of what it lacked in 'human liberty.'"[4] There is, Schiller writes, at long last the "*physical* possibility of setting law upon the throne, of honoring man at last as an end in himself, and making true freedom the basis of political associations," but "the *moral* possibility is lacking." In the "drama of the present time" humanity portrays itself in extreme images of "human depravity": "On the one hand, a return to the savage state; on the other, to complete lethargy."[5] These extremes result from the fragmentation of the separate faculties of feeling, thinking, and willing within the individual—a fragmentation fostered by the specialized, societal divisions of knowledge and labor. We must therefore "continue to regard every attempt at political reform as untimely, and every hope based upon it as chimerical, as long as the split within man is not healed."[6] Seeing the desired unity within the individual and among people to be an essential property of beauty, Schiller urges the political importance of aesthetic education: "If man is ever to solve that problem of politics in practice he will have to approach it through the problem of the aesthetic, because it is only through beauty that man makes his way to freedom."[7]

In *The Maid of Orléans* Schiller faces the "problem of the aesthetic" and models aesthetic freedom by departing as widely as possible from the facts of history. Rather than tell the truth about Joan of Arc, he refashions her story as myth and tragedy, portraying her in classical rather than Christian terms as a scapegoat. He substitutes for the persecution text of the medieval trial that condemned her and for the hagiographic text of her rehabilitation a mythic text that first demonizes and then deifies her. Internally divided, Schiller's Johanna is guilty, not innocent. As such, she makes a fitting, surrogate victim for a divided kingdom, which is restored (albeit temporarily) to unity through its sacrifice and expulsion of her and through her sacrifice of herself. Johanna's story thus becomes a vehicle for exploring the relationship between nature and art, art and civilization, guilt and human progress, beauty and death.

Schiller gave *The Maid of Orléans* the subtitle *A Romantic Tragedy* (*Eine romantische Tragödie*)—a generic designation that has long puzzled critics of the play.[8] As early as 1825, however, Thomas Carlyle called attention to *Die Jungfrau* as a scapegoat play and thus a tragedy in the classical sense of a sacrificial goat song. In his biography of Schiller, Carlyle relates that Schiller, then a professor of history at Jena, originally sought to tell the truth, "to represent Johanna and the times she lived in, as they actually were." Relinquishing that task as "too difficult"—in part because of the "rude horror" that "defaced and encumbered the reality" of Joan's martyrdom—Schiller chose instead to retell her tale according to the primeval, mythic pattern of a sacrificial victim. As a "sacrifice doomed to perish for her country," Johanna resembled, in Schiller's view, "the Iphigenia of the Greeks."[9] Carlyle's allusion to the legendary daughter of Agamemnon, who was offered in sacrifice by her own father as a purchase price for favorable winds, is a telling one. Schiller had read the *Iphigenia in Tauris* of his friend, Johann Wolfgang von Goethe (1749–1832), in 1780, only a few months before he began writing *The Maid of Orléans,* and Goethe's play no doubt inspired Schiller's conception of Joan of Arc.[10]

Indeed, *The Maid of Orléans,* written as his relationship with Goethe was cooling, may best be understood as Schiller's sacrificial response to Goethe's attempt to imagine an antisacrificial development of human civilization. In *Iphigenia in Tauris* Goethe presents a noble heroine, who has been rescued by the goddess Diana from Agamemnon's altar of sacrifice. As Diana's priestess on the island of Tauris, Iphigenia discontinues the local custom of offering as human sacrifices those persons who reach the shores after shipwreck. Tauris is blessed with prosperity, and King Thoas seeks to marry Iphigenia. The arrival at Tauris of her own brother, Orestes, prompts a crisis, when the king wants to force Iphigenia to revive the ancient sacrificial practice. In Goethe's play, Iphigenia manages to obtain in the end the king's permission for both Orestes and her to return to their homeland, and she secures the royal promise that there will be no more human sacrifices offered on the island. Schiller's Johanna, like Goethe's Iphigenia, saves her people, but she does so through sacrificing and being sacrificed. In Schiller's view, civilization is necessarily founded on the tragic sacrifice of those outstanding persons who lead its advance. "Goethe may try to avoid tragedy," as Frank G. Ryder observes,[11] but that attempt only prompts Schiller's passionate reaffirmation of it as inevitable.

The decision to transform Joan's history into myth in competition with his literary father, Goethe, seems also to have clarified Schiller's notion of the mimetic relationship between the historian and the poet. As twins engaged in an acquisitive competition over shared subject matter, the writers of history and poetry quarrel with each other in a perennial manner that can only be held in check, Schiller believes, through repeated sacrifice. Not only does Schiller's heroine enact the onstage role of a mythic victim, but Schiller himself acts behind the scenes to sacrifice the truth of Joan's history in favor of its mythic representation.[12]

As Schiller asserts in "On the Art of Tragedy," "Tragedy has the power, indeed, the obligation of *subordinating* the historical truth to the laws of literary art and of reworking the given material as the art requires.... [P]oetic truth often suffers when historical truth is strictly observed and ... poetic truth stands to gain when *historical truth is rudely violated*."[13] Writing to Goethe on December 24, 1800, about *Die Jungfrau von Orleans*, Schiller exults that he has "overcome" the historical facts in an entirely "poetic" and "naïve" way: "Das historische ist *überwunden*, und ... die Motive sind alle poetisch und grösstentheils von der naiven Gattung."[14] Elsewhere, in *Aesthetic Education*, Schiller affirms, "In a truly successful work of art, the contents should effect nothing, the form everything.... Subject matter, ... however sublime and all-embracing it may be, always has a limiting effect upon the spirit, and it is only from form that true aesthetic freedom can be looked for. Herein, then, resides the real secret of the master in any art: *that he can make his form consume his material*."[15]

Civilization began, in Schiller's view, with humanity's ability to distinguish between form and substance and to exercise mimesis, the imitative "art of semblance" that derives from this fundamental distinction: "Inasmuch as need of reality and attachment to the actual are merely consequences of some deficiency, then indifference to reality and interest in semblance may be regarded as a genuine enlargement of humanity and a decisive step toward culture."[16] Emerging from "the slavery of the animal condition," which responds blindly to instinctual needs and desires, human beings are marked by "delight in *semblance*, and a propensity to *ornamentation* and *play*."[17] As civilization advances, they increasingly claim "the sovereign human right" to exercise the "art of semblance," to separate "form from substance," and to give "autonomy ... to the former."[18]

A practical consequence of this freedom to separate form from substance is the poet's ability to depart from historical reality, to transform its matter in the process of imitating it, and thus to give the world itself new, mythic models and ideals. Schiller looked to the history plays of William Shakespeare as examples of such departures and transformations. In particular, Shakespeare's *King Henry VI, Part I* showed Schiller the possibility of seeing Joan of Arc from a dual perspective, as a French saint and an English witch, and of creating fictive doubles for her through an anachronistic sequence of events and pairing of characters. In its imitation of history, Shakespeare's play reveals history itself to be mimetic in its rivalries, tragic divisions, and cycles of revenge.[19]

In Schiller's treatment of Joan of Arc, the aesthetic "form" of tragedy as a dramatic, quasi-ritualistic representation of the scapegoat myth completely "consume[s]" the historical matter of Joan's life and death by fire at the stake, so much so that, as George Bernard Shaw was later to complain, Schiller's "play . . . is not about Joan at all."[20] The full significance of Schiller's depiction and aesthetic use of Joan of Arc as a scapegoat has eluded critics of the play, in part because Schiller's own extensive writings on tragedy, on the sublime and the pathetic, and on aesthetics give no explicit treatment of the topic of the scape-goat (*Sündenbock*); in part because Schiller's work antedates the great psychological and anthropological studies of victimage by Sigmund Freud, Claude Lévi-Strauss, and (most important) René Girard. Inter-preted in conjunction with the anthropology of his aesthetic essays, however, Schiller's sacrificial, onstage use of a virginal scapegoat may be said to anticipate and to confirm many of the insights of these later writers with an uncanny exactitude. Indeed, as a commentary on his aesthetics, *Die Jungfrau von Orleans* highlights a dark undercurrent in Schiller's theoretical view that too often goes unnoticed, masked as it is by his Enlightenment narrative of cultural progress.

Freud, Schiller, and the Origins of Civilization

In certain respects Freud's debt to Schiller is well known. Linking his theory of libidinal instincts to Schiller, Freud himself confesses in "Civilization and Its Discontents" (1929): "In my utter perplexity at the beginning, I took as my starting point the poet-philosopher Schiller's aphorism, that hunger and love make the world go round."[21] Eliza-beth M. Wilkinson points out that it was Schiller who, in anticipa-tion of Freud's view of dreams and of artistic images, first "formulated the poet's task as 'making the unconscious conscious'" in a letter to Goethe (March 27, 1801): "Die Poesie, däucht mir, besteht eben darinn, jenes Bewußtlose aussprechen und mittheilen zu können."[22] Freud's as-sertion in *Totem and Taboo* (1913) and later in "Civilization and Its Discontents" that civilization itself originated in a guilty, primordial sacrifice—the murder of the primal father by the united horde of his sons—may similarly be seen as the development of a scapegoat theory latent in Schiller's aesthetics and symbolically expressed in *Die Jung-frau von Orleans.*

Drawing an "analogy between the process of cultural evolution and of individual development," Freud argues that the place of the murdered father within a society is filled by the communal superego, whereby the father is resurrected to live on in the form of high ethical ideals "based on the impression left behind them by great leading personalities, men of outstanding force of mind, or men in whom some one human tendency has developed in unusual strength and purity, often for that reason very disproportionately." During their lives, Freud observes, very often "such persons are ridiculed by others, ill-used, or even cruelly done to death, just as happened with the primal father, who also rose again to become a deity long after his death by violence."[23]

Freud famously gives Jesus Christ as an example of such a communal scapegoat, but he may well have had Schiller's heroine also in mind. Anticipating Freud, Schiller put forward a theory of cultural evolution based on the disproportionate or one-sided development of a single human faculty within a leading individual:

> One-sidedness in the exercise of his powers must, it is true, inevitably lead the individual into error; but the species as a whole to truth. Only by concentrating the whole energy of our mind into a single focal point, contracting our whole being into a single power, do we, as it were, lend wings to this individual power and lead it, by artificial means, far beyond the limits that nature seems to have assigned it.[24]

In this remarkable passage, Schiller adumbrates the fate of the scapegoat, who, as an individual, must "err," must wander as an outcast and exile, but who is also destined for deification through the taking of "wings." Isolated as a result of a one-sided development of their potential, individual persons of genius may have benefited little "from this fragmentation of their being," Schiller writes, "but there was no other way in which the species as a whole could have progressed."[25]

Except in a few significant passages to which I return later, Schiller does not dwell in *Aesthetic Education* on the sacrificial fate of the outstanding individual, whom he describes as suffering "under the curse of this cosmic purpose" of cultural development;[26] instead he speaks of the violent sacrifice of natural wholeness that the one-sidedness of the individual arts as competing specialties necessarily entails and on which the process of civilization depends. The "antagonism of faculties and functions is the great instrument of civilization," in Schiller's view, but civilization as such remains unachieved as long as "the cultivation of individual powers involves the sacrifice of wholeness. . . . [H]owever much the law of nature tends in that direction, it must be open to us to restore by means of a higher art the totality of our nature that the arts themselves have destroyed."[27] Civilization itself, which is characterized by "the increase of empirical knowledge" and the "increasingly complex machinery of state," has "inflicted this wound [of division] upon modern man," severing "the inner unity of human nature," as well as the harmony of the community, which is subject to an ever more "rigorous separation of ranks and occupations."[28]

In *Aesthetic Education* Schiller metaphorically likens the divisive sins of the modern world to the murder of the father, even as he compares the poet to an avenging Orestes, raised to maturity "under a distant Grecian sky" ("unter fernem griechischen Himmel"): "Let [the artist] return, a stranger to his own century; not, however, to gladden it by his appearance, but rather, terrible like Agamemnon's son, to cleanse and purify it."[29] That artistic cleansing or catharsis, Schiller suggests, requires a substitutive victim, a goat-sacrifice who takes the place of the murdered father in a tragic ritual play. Division itself, both within the individual psyche and in the state, must be cast out through the sacrifice of the one for the all.

The divisive one-sidedness of Johanna is represented visually in *Die Jungfrau von Orleans* by the helmet she wears. When Bertrand first bears the helmet, a gypsy's offering, with him to Domremy from Vaucouleurs, Thibault calls it an "evil token" of war: "Das böse Zeichen."[30] Johanna eagerly snatches it from Bernard's hand, declaring, "The helmet's mine, and it belongs to me" (Prologue.iii.193): "Gebt mir den Helm!" No sooner has she placed it on her head than, like one possessed by a spirit, she begins to speak in prophecy about the defeat of the English invaders "through a tender virgin" chosen by God (Prologue.iii.326): "Durch eine zarte Jungfrau." Astonished at her speech, Raimond attributes her tranformation to the helmet: "It is / The helmet, that inspires her martial soul" (Prologue.iii.328–329): "Es ist / Der Helm, der sie so kriegerisch beseelt." Later, in soliloquy, Johanna contradicts her father, calling the helmet not an "evil token" but the "token Heaven . . . has foreordained" for her (Prologue.iv.425): "Ein Zeichen hat der Himmel mir verheißen."

When Johanna first appears to the French forces, she steps forth from the forest like a divine apparition: "a virgin, helmet on her head, / Like to a martial goddess, fair at once / And fearsome to behold" (I.ix. 955–957): "eine Jungfrau, mit behelmtem Haupt / Wie eine Kriegesgöttin, schön zugleich / Und schrecklich anzusehn." Talbot, too, likens her to a goddess of war, calling her a "terror-goddess" (II.v.1543): "Die Schreckensgöttin." Later, Agnes Sorel begs her to take off her helmet and breastplate, saying that she is frightened by Johanna's coldness of heart and martial appearance: "Thou art like the rigid Pallas" (IV.ii. 2639): "du der strengen Pallas gleichst." Driven from the city, Johanna continues to wear the helmet, even though Raimond pleads with her to discard it: "Lay the helmet and armor off. / They mark you out and offer no protection" (V.ii.3102–3103): "Legt den Helm ab und die Rüstung, / Sie macht Euch kenntlich und beschützt Euch nicht." In the last act, when the French come to Johanna's rescue, Dunois exhorts the troops to courage with an allusion to Pallas Athene: "Now arm yourself! Your honor is suspended! / The crown and *palladium* expended. / Set all your blood and all your life at stake! / Free must she be before the day is ended! (V.viii.3320–3323; emphasis added): "Bewaffne sich! Die Ehre ist verpfändet, / Die Krone, das Palladium entwendet, / Setzt alles Blut! Setzt euer Leben ein! / Frei muß sie sein, noch eh der Tag sich endet!"

A virgin warrior, Johanna mirrors the Queen of Heaven whom she serves. In a vision, the Holy One gives Johanna a banner and a sword, commanding her to go to war on behalf of her people. "Enraged and scolding" ("scheltend"), the Sainted One exhorts a reluctant Johanna to the "obedience . . . / And stern forbearance" (I.x.1101–1103) that is a woman's lot: "Gehorsam ist des Weibes Pflicht auf Erden, / Das harte Dulden ist ihr schweres Los." Victory will be hers, she promises, as long as Johanna remains untouched in her heart by "love of men" (Prologue.iv.411): "Männerliebe." On the battlefield, Johanna kills against her own will, obligated by what she calls an "awful, binding contract" ("der furchtbar bindende Vertrag") to slaughter anyone who crosses her path and to offer them as victims to the Holy Virgin. Johanna tells Montgomery, who seeks her mercy: "[D]eadly is encounter with the virgin" (III.vii.1600, 1598): "Doch tödlich ists, der Jungfrau zu begegnen."

When Johanna finally breaks her vow to abstain from love, she imagines the War Queen's anger: "See how she glares and how she knits her
brow" (IV.iii.2736): "Seht, wie sie herblickt und die Stirne faltet." As
Lesley Sharpe remarks, "the de-Christianizing of the Christian context
of the play" is so complete that the "Virgin becomes representative of
some cruel female goddess, a sort of Amazonian Queen, who demands
absolute obedience to an inhuman pattern of behaviour."[31] Through
the vengeful Queen of Heaven, Johanna's own violence and that of others toward her becomes inextricably associated with what René Girard
calls "the sacred."[32]

The sustained pattern of imagery suggests that the comparison of
Johanna to Pallas Athena is not mere, allusive coloring but rather a
controlling idea in Schiller's tragedy. Indeed, a letter to Unger, his publisher, dated November 28, 1800, indicates that Schiller wished the head
of Athena ("eine Minerva") to appear as an illustration on the title
page of the drama.[33] In *Aesthetic Education* it is Athena to whom Schiller
points as an emblem for the dawn of civilization: "Not for nothing
does the ancient myth make the goddess of wisdom merge fully armed
from the head of Jupiter. For her very first action is a warlike one. Even
at birth she has to fight a hard battle with the senses, which are loath
to be snatched from their sweet repose."[34] Saying no to the urge of the
natural instincts, Athena represents the power of thinking humanity
to choose among alternatives and to develop one-sidedly. In its mythic
structure, then, the emergence of the goddess from Jupiter's head, like
the stepping forth of a helmeted Johanna from the forest, is, as John D.
Simons suggests, "a veiled retelling of man's first step out of nature"
and out of Eden, from wholeness into division.[35]

Johanna and the Naive Poet

Johanna is, in many ways, a child of nature par excellence. Her anguished abstraction from nature renders her both pathetic and sublime, even as her final reintegration with nature makes her ideal. Schiller
uses her story as a mythic art object to narrate, and thus to promote
and effect, the ongoing work of civilization. The "assembly of contradictions" within Johanna makes her "the supreme poetic figure" in
the play, as E. J. Engel and W. F. Mainland remark.[36] Johanna does not

merely stand as a personification of poetry, however. In her Schiller creates a portrait of the artist—indeed a self-portrait.

Schiller provides a definite key to his aesthetic interpretation of Joan of Arc in *Die Jungfrau von Orleans* (1801) in a short lyric, three stanzas in length, entitled "Das Mädchen von Orleans" (1802).[37] (For a complete translation, see Appendix 1.) The first two stanzas contrast the ways in which a personified War and Mockery, on the one hand, and Poetry, on the other, have treated Joan, whom the poet addresses in the intimate second person as "du":

> Das edle Bild der Menscheit zu vehöhnen,
> Im tiefsten Staube wälzte dich der Spott,
> Krieg führt der Witz auf ewig mit dem Schönen,
> Er glaubt nicht an den Engel und den Gott,
> Dem Herzen will er seine Schätze rauben,
> Den Wahn bekriegt er und verletzt den Glauben.
>
> Doch, wie du selbst, aus kindlichem Geschlechte,
> Selbst eine fromme Schäferin wie du,
> Reicht dir die Dichtkunst ihre Götterrechte,
> Schwingt sich mit dir den ew'gen Sternen zu,
> Mit einer Glorie hat sie dich umgeben,
> Dich schuf das Herz, du wirst unsterblich leben.

War has rolled Joan in the dust in order to deride and dishonor in her the noble image of humanity ("das edle Bild der Menschheit") and the beauty that she represents. Poetry, however, has surrounded her with a halolike glory or aura ("Mit einer Glorie") and exalted her to the skies, mounting with her to the eternal stars: "Schwingt sich mit dir den ew'gen Sternen zu" (line 10). War seeks to rob the heart of its treasures ("Dem Herzen will er seine Schätze rauben"), whereas Poetry encloses Joan as a favorite creation within its heart: "Dich schuf das Herz" (line 12). War does not believe in angels, or in God ("Er glaubt nicht an den Engel und den Gott"), but Poetry possesses and offers divine rights and powers ("Götterrechte"), even as Joan does ("wie du").

The close association—indeed, the identity—between Joan and poetry emerges from a series of wordplays. Addressing Joan as a devout shepherdness ("selbst eine fromme Schäferin"), Schiller puns on the word *Schafferin*, meaning "a creative female artist, shaper, or maker" (from the verb *schaffen*). Schiller signals the pun through his use of "schuf" in line twelve: "Dich schuf das Herz" (literally, "The heart has created you"). Poetry ("die Dichtkunst") acts as Joan does ("wie du selbst, . . . wie du"), with Joan ("mit dir"), and on Joan's behalf: "Mit einer Glorie hat sie *dich* umgeben" (line 11). Seven second-person pronouns in the space of six lines have the effect of making the art of poetry itself you-oriented toward Joan as its ultimate subject and objective correlative: "*Dich*tkunst." Shining in the everlasting stars ("ewigen *Ster*nen") with and through poetry, Joan attains immortality: "du wirst un*ster*blich leben" (line 12), even as poetry becomes immortal through its association with her: "Schwingt sich mit dir den ew'gen Sternen zu" (line 10).

   In the third stanza of "Das Mädchen," the speaker turns from Joan herself to address the auditor, who identifies with her and her sufferings: "Do not be afraid!" ("Doch fürchte nicht!")

> Es liebt die Welt das Strahlende zu schwärzen,
> Und das Erhabne in den Staub zu ziehn,
> Doch fürchte nicht! Es gibt noch schöne Herzen,
> Die für das Hohe, Herrliche entglühn,
> Den lauten Markt mag Momus unterhalten,
> Ein edler Sinn liebt edlere Gestalten.

Even as War has mistreated Joan, the World loves to blacken the radiant one and to drag what is sublime into the dust: "Es liebt die Welt, das Strahlende zu schwärzen / Und das Erhabne in den Staub zu ziehn." But, Schiller reassures himself and us, there are still "beautiful hearts" ("schöne Herzen") that nobly glow for high ideals: "Die für das Hohe, Herrliche erglühn." A nobler sensibility ("Ein edler Sinn") than that which panders to the raucous marketplace ("Den lauten Markt") takes delight, he says, in nobler figures. The closing words of the poem, "edlere Gestalten," recall the opening words, "Das edle Bild," while making the singular plural. The "noble image" of Joan of Arc has been extended to other figures and images of nobility, including that of the poet, who spurns the popular values of the marketplace and endures the "blackening" of inappreciative critics. Joan of Arc was, of course, burned to death in the marketplace at Rouen, and Schiller's repetition of the word *Staub* ("Im tiefsten Staube . . . in den Staub") in the second lines of the first and third stanzas links the image of the dust, into which the world's mockery drags the sublime, to the ashes of the saint. At the same time, it draws a connection between the marketplace of the popular press and the marketplace of Joan's martyrdom. Similarly, the repetition of the word *Schön* ("mit dem Schönen . . . schöne Herzen") in the first and third stanzas directly associates the beauty of saints like Joan with the aesthetic appreciation for her beauty in the hearts of true artists and their audiences.

Each of the three stanzas of "Das Mädchen von Orleans" contains the word *Herz* (heart) and thus continues a theme that Schiller developed in *Die Jungfrau von Orleans.* In an often-quoted letter from Schiller to his publisher Göschen, dated February 10, 1802, the playwright states: "Dieses Stück floß *aus dem Herzen* und *zu dem Herzen* sollte es auch sprechen. Aber dazu gehört, daß man auch ein Herz habe und das ist leider nicht überall der Fall."[38] According to H. B. Garland, the word *Herz* occurs seventy-eight times in the play and the expression "Mir sagts das Herz" three times. It was, Garland writes, "probably no coincidence that [that same clause] is already found in Goethe's *Iphigenie,* where Orest speaks the words (1.1358)."[39]

It is difficult to know exactly what Schiller means when he speaks of *Die Jungfrau von Orleans* as a play flowing "from the heart" and speaking "to the heart." Schiller's use of the word *Herz* in the play and his thrice-repeated quotation of Orestes' line may be, as Garland suggests, "a mere unimportant act of self-indulgence" by an emotive poet.[40] A passage in "On Naïve and Sentimental Poetry" suggests a weightier significance, however, for the word *heart:*

> The poet of the world in its youth, naïve and inspired, just like the sort of person who comes closest to him in ages of artificial culture, is austere and shy. Distrustful, like the virgin Diana in her forest, *he flees the heart that seeks him,* the need that would embrace him. The arid truthfulness with which he treats his subject matters often appears as insensitivity. The subject matter takes complete possession of him; *his heart does not lie like some cheap metal right beneath the surface, but rather wants to be sought, like gold, in the depths.* Like the divinity behind the structure of the world, he stands behind his work.[41]

The passage merits close inspection. It gives a descriptive definition of the naive poet—a topic of relevance to *Die Jungfrau von Orleans*. As we have seen, in a letter to Goethe Schiller explicitly characterizes the play as being a composition "of the naïve sort" ("von der naiven Gattung").[42] Schiller distinguishes the naive poet, typical in antiquity, from the sentimental poet, who predominates during modern times. According to Schiller, a naive poet, such as "Homer among the ancients and Shakespeare among the moderns,"[43] depicts the world of the play's action without intruding in his own voice (as the sentimental poet does) to comment explicitly on the difference between his own world and the play's. The poet thus hides his personal view of present conditions while allowing the work of art to function as a veiled commentary on them. In the act of hiding his "heart," the naive poet resembles the virginal huntress, Diana.

The comparison to Diana inevitably invites a comparison of the naive poet also to the "austere and shy" warrior maiden, Johanna, the heroine of Schiller's play. As we shall see, in the play Johanna speaks as a sentimental poet, apostrophizing the past, commenting on her distance from the idyllic, pastoral world she has forever left behind, and agonizing over her own self-division. She thus serves as an artistic double for the hidden, naive poet, who is the writer of her play. The poet's "heart," like that of his virginal heroine, is buried, even as the play's hidden significance as an allegory of art is encoded.

In his representation of Johanna's story as a portrait of the artist, Schiller gives dramatic expression to a general principle of correspondence, which he articulates in "On Naïve and Sentimental Poetry." There he writes that the "road taken by the modern poets is . . . the same road human beings in general must travel, both as individuals and as a whole. Nature makes a human being one with himself, art separates and divides him; by means of the ideal he returns to unity."[44] As an outstanding individual, Johanna follows a course of psychological development that makes her life something beautiful, an artistic work that is accomplished through her own striving and that furthers the larger work of civilization in which it participates.

Telling Johanna's story allows Schiller to reify its status as an art object and at the same time identify himself with her as agent and artist. The life of Johanna, as Schiller imagines it, bears remarkable correspondences to his own. Johanna looks back on her sheltered childhood in Domremy as paradisiacal, and Schiller, too, remembered his

own boyhood, as Viola Geyersbach observes, "immer als eine glück-
liche und harmonische Zeit . . . 'mit dem Paradies und dem Goldenen
Zeitalter, mit einer ursprünglichen menschlichen Gleichheit und Freiheit verbunden.'"[45] Like Johanna, whose inspired calling met with her
father's doubt and disapproval, Schiller also experienced a painful, pa-
rental testing. His desire to study the humanities and to become a poet
evoked the stern opposition of his pious father, who had desired him
to become a Protestant clergyman, and of Duke Karl Eugene, in whose
military academy at Solitude Castle the young Schiller studied from
1773 to 1780.

Like Johanna, a guilty Schiller suffered expulsion for the sake of
his art. Destined by the despotic duke for a medical career in the army,
for which he himself had no inclination, Schiller began the clandestine
composition of poetry and plays, correspondence with publishers, and
secret journeys to Mannheim and Stuttgart. When Schiller's authorship of the acclaimed republican play, *The Robbers*, became known, he
was arrested for neglect of his duties as an army surgeon, commanded
to devote himself wholly to the ducal military service, and forbidden
"all further literary work" by official mandate.[46] Finally the sense of his
own vocation as a poet became so great and of his imprisonment so
unbearable that Schiller left Solitude Castle at night on September 17,
1782, as a fugitive. In a letter to the duke, Schiller made a final plea for
the blessing of the "Anointed One" on his literary pursuits, acknowl-
edging that "otherwise he would be the most wretched of men, driven,
banished from kindred and home; he must needs wander forth into
the world, an outcast!"[47] Schiller was, in fact, to spend eleven years in
exile from Würtemberg.

Having suffered much, Schiller was well aware of the vulnerability
of artists as social critics and outsiders. In "On Naïve and Sentimental
Poetry" he describes the fate of the naive poet in terms that strikingly
recall his own experience and comment on Johanna's fictive expulsion:
"In an artificial age poets of this naïve sort are rather out of place. In
such an epoch . . . they are possible only by *running wild* in their age
and being protected from its mutilating influence by some benign fortune. They can never emerge from society itself, but outside it such
poets still occasionally appear, though more as strange individuals
whom people stare at."[48] Crossing into a divided, fragmented society
from the realm of "uncultivated nature," such poets "offend" their contemporaries through the manifestation of natural wholeness, to which

they bear a prophetic witness. For this they pay a price of division within themselves and of mutilation and expulsion by others, because "the critics, the real border patrol of taste, detest these naïve poets for *disrupting the boundaries* and would rather see them suppressed."[49]

Johanna and the Sentimental Poet

A liminal creature, Johanna clearly figures the naive poet's closeness to nature but also the sentimental poet's separation from it. From the opening scenes of the play, Johanna's relationship to nature appears problematic. Thibault, on the one hand, faults her unnatural coldness to Raimond, her suitor in Domremy, and her slowness in flowering as a woman, wife, and mother. He interprets her attraction to the wilderness and her haunting of the oak tree as a brooding intercourse with paganism and evil spirits. Raimond, on the other hand, sees Johanna's love as a "noble, tender fruit of Heaven" that, precisely because it is precious, "ripens still and slowly" (Prologue.ii.67–68): "Die Liebe meiner trefflichen Johanna / Ist eine edle zarte Himmelsfrucht, / Und still allmählich reift das Köstliche!" Observing Johanna the shepherdess "on lofty lea," where she "Amid her herd . . . stands alone, erect" (Prologue.ii.74–75), Raimond finds in her a symbol of eternal things: "She then portends to me a higher something, / And oft me thinks she stems from other ages" (Prologue.ii.78–79): "Da scheint sie mir was Höhres zu bedeuten, / Und dünkt mirs oft, sie stamm aus andern Zeiten." Answering to Thibault's charge of pride and sterility, Raimond describes Johanna as pious, humble, and serving. The virginal Johanna is, he says, especially attuned to nature and thus an indirect source of its fecundity: "Your herds and likewise too your crops are thriving" (Prologue.ii.140): "Gedeihen Euch die Herden und die Saaten."

Raimond's description of the shepherdess Johanna in harmony with nature recalls Schiller's discussion of natural objects of beauty in "On Naïve and Sentimental Poetry." Natural objects affect us "with a certain melancholy" ("mit einer gewissen Wehmut"), he writes, because they "*are* what we *were*; they are what we *should become* once more. We were nature like them, and our culture should lead us along the path of reason and freedom back to nature. Thus they depict at once our lost childhood . . . [and] at the same time they portray our supreme perfection in an ideal sense."[50] Because nature and childhood represent being itself in an organic wholeness, they are "holy."[51]

Johanna's poignant soliloquy, in which she bids adieu to the beloved mountains, meadows, and vales of her youth, draws a sharp contrast between the bloody battlefields to which she is being summoned and the bedewed, grassy fields of the sheep's pasture. At the same time, however, the speech offers hope for a final, higher integration of the two, because Johanna uses natural metaphors for her work as a battle leader and civil servant: "There's another herd that I must treasure / On danger's fields, that will be wet with gore" (Prologue.iv.397–398): "eine andre Herde muß ich weiden, / Dort auf dem blut'gen Felde der Gefahr." She compares her calling, moreover, to that of two biblical shepherds, Moses and David, whose closeness to nature enabled them to be wise leaders of the people.

Leaving the fields behind her, Johanna enacts an aesthetic withdrawal from the world of nature, a stepping back that places it at a contemplative distance. Thus, in Schiller's words, nature itself becomes for Johanna, as for the sentimental poet, "something naïve," because it "contrast[s] with art and put[s] it to shame."[52] Seeing nature outside of herself, Johanna becomes increasingly differentiated from it; at the same time, a whole world "becomes manifest to [her] because [she] has ceased to be one with it."[53] Distanced from nature, Johanna also becomes internally divided, even as she hopes by means of the ideal to return to the unity symbolized by nature.

Johanna's very costume points to the tension within her, for she generally appears onstage "with her banner, wearing helmet and breastplate; otherwise attired as a woman" (stage directions to Act II, scene iv): "mit der Fahne, im Helm und Brustharnisch, sonst aber weiblich gekleidet."[54] Only in Act III, scene iv, does she appear "in armor but without helmet, . . . wearing a wreath in her hair" ("im Harnisch, aber ohne Helm, und trägt einen Kranz in den Haaren"). Charles notes her change of dress, saying, "Thou comest as a priestess decked" (III.iv.2026): "Du kommst als Priesterin geschmückt, Johanna." Burgundy, too, observes the contrasts signaled by Johanna's outward appearance: "How dreadful was the Maiden in the fight, / And how, in peace, so radiant with charm!" (III.iv.2028–2029): "Wie schrecklich war die Jungfrau in der Schlacht, / Und wie umstrahlt mit Anmut sie der Friede!"

Schiller highlights the duality within Johanna by pairing her with unlike female doubles of herself: the gentle mistress of the Dauphin,

Agnes Sorel, and the heartless queen mother, Isabeau. Like Sorel, Johanna is beautiful and inspires the worship of chivalrous lovers. Sorel shares Johanna's strong allegiance to Charles VII. She freely sacrifices her jewels in order to replenish his coffers, she urges him to the defense of Orléans, and she offers to risk her life with Charles on the battlefield: "Come! Come! We'll share alike both want and danger!" (I.iv.643): "Komm! Komm! Wir teilen Mangel und Gefahr!" To Sorel Charles first applies the prophecy traditionally applied to Joan of Arc: "A woman, so the nun declared, would make / Me victorious over all my enemies" (I.iv.654–655): "Ein Weib, verhieß die Nonne, würde mich / Zum Sieger machen über alle Feinde." On the day of Charles's coronation, Johanna herself calls Sorel "holy" and "pure" ("selig"), because Sorel's heart, unlike Johanna's, has found in the king a proper object for her affection: "Thou lovest where all love!" (IV.ii.2686): "Du liebst, wo alles liebt!" Sorel, loving and beloved, represents exteriorly the natural power that Johanna must suppress and redirect within herself for the sake of her calling.

The ruthless Isabeau stands at a greater distance from Johanna, but she too serves as an obvious double for her. Isabeau, Johanna's antagonist, first discredits her son Charles through her adultery and then physically places the English boy-king, Henry VI, on the throne in the place of Charles, whom Johanna seeks to restore to his rights. Banished by Charles, as Johanna later will be, she, like Johanna among the French troops, goes "Full clad in steel . . . riding through the camp" (Prologue.iii.241: "In Stahl gekleidet durch das Lager reiten"), rousing the English forces and their allies. Indeed, she offers herself to the English explicitly as an altera Johanna, "a substitute for prophetess and virgin" (II.ii.1378): "Statt einer Jungfrau und Prophetin." She proclaims aloud and seeks to satisfy the lust that Johanna feels, hides, and resists. "Give me this man" (II.ii.1453: "Gebt mir diesen da"), she brazenly demands, pointing to Lionel, the English lord with whom Johanna later falls in love.

The conflict within Johanna between the demands of her calling and the desires of her womanly nature is powerfully dramatized in the scene when Montgomery falls at her feet to plead for mercy: "O, by the gentleness of thy mild, tender sex / I beg of thee! Have mercy on me still a youth" (III.vii.1606–1607): "O bei der Milde deines zärtlichen Geschlechts / Fleh ich dich an. Erbarme meiner Jugend dich!" Johanna replies by denying her womanhood and her capacity for pity: "Don't call me woman! . . . [T]his, my armor, covers up no heart" (III.vii.1608, 1611): "Nenne mich nicht Weib. . . . [D]ieser Panzer deckt kein Herz." Contrasting the cruel sword in her hand to the "innocent and pious shepherd staff" (III.vii.1657: "den unschuldig frommen Hirtenstab"), Johanna describes herself as having been violently "torn away from [the] fields" of her pastoral home against her own desires ("weggerissen von der heimatlichen Flur"), forced by the "divine voice" ("die Götterstimme") that impels her to kill and ultimately to be killed, a "victim" ("Opfer") like her victims (III.vii.1658–1663).

Johanna's anguished, merciless slaughter of Montgomery and her prophecy of her own death on the battlefield recall the "violent condition" that Schiller associates with the one-sided development of human powers: "any separation and *isolation* of these powers is a violent condition, and the ideal of recreation is the rejuvenation of our nature as a whole in the wake of one-sided tensions."[55] Nature itself inspires the quest for this ideal, renewed unity of mind and heart. In Johanna's case, nature asserts itself when she suddenly falls in love with Lionel and, against her own principle of unconditional slaughter, spares the life of the man whom she was about to kill, as she had earlier slain Montgomery. The spontaneous awakening of Johanna's natural power to love endows her, as nature endows the sentimental poet, "with a vital urge to restore, from out of [her]self, the unity that abstraction had destroyed within [her]."[56]

Schiller's anthropological aesthetics identifies the self-division caused by abstraction with sin and guilt but also with cultural progress, so that civilization itself is seen as resting on a series of necessary sins. Johanna speaks in precisely these terms about the guiltiness of her calling away from nature. In her soliloquy at the beginning of Act IV, Johanna regrets having ever exchanged her "pious staff" for a "battle-sword" (IV.i.2582–2583): "Frommer Stab! O hätte ich nimmer / Mit dem Schwerte dich vertauscht!" Burdened by a "formidable vocation" ("Diesen furchtbaren Beruf"), she laments her failure in relation both to the pure nature she has abandoned and denied and to her high calling as her "fatherland's deliveress" (IV.i.2595, 2546): "Ich meines Landes Retterin." Addressing the Queen of Heaven, Johanna complains: "Guiltless once I drove my lambkins / On the quiet mountain heights. / Thou hast thrust me into living / In the haughty princes' hall, / Thus to guilt my being giving" (IV.i.2608–2612): "Schuldlos trieb ich meine Lämmer / Auf des stillen Berges Höh. / Doch du rissest mich ins Leben, / In den stolzen Fürstensaal, / Mich der Schuld dahin zu geben." Later, hearing the familiar sounds of her sisters' voices, Johanna remembers their "paternal home" ("väterliche Flur") as an Eden from which she has been exiled: "There, where I drove the herds upon our highlands, / There was I happy as in Paradise— / Can I not once again be or become so?" (IV.ix.2898–2990): "Da ich die Herde trieb auf unsern Höhen, / Da war ich glücklich wie im Paradies— / Kann ichs nicht wieder sein, nicht wieder werden!"

Johanna as Scapegoat

Johanna's achievement of a final, ideal unity that reconciles nature and art, sensuality and reason, depends on personal acts of atonement (at-one-ment) and self-sacrifice. Similarly, the community, which is divided on her account, is restored to peace through the sacrifice of Johanna. It is Schiller's genius to have discovered in the classical myth of the scapegoat and its dramatic representation in tragedy a means of joining the plots of psychological growth, artistic process, and cultural development, as he understood them.

As the myth of Oedipus and a vast array of anthropological evidence suggest, the original scapegoat was a king, a father, and thus a fitting, sacrificial representative for the community as a whole.[57] In *The Maid of Orléans*, Schiller traces the institution of kingship back to its sacrificial origins through an initial focus on the French king. At the start of the play, Charles VII has been driven back into a corner of his kingdom—his rightful place on the throne usurped by the English king, Henry VI; his legitimacy denied by his own mother; his cities besieged; his coffers empty; his troops demoralized; his followers deserting him. Adjudging the house of Valois to be guilty of "heinous deeds," accursed, and pursued by "the furies' wrath" (I.v.779–780), Charles determines to accept his own expulsion by withdrawing voluntarily across "the Stygian waters of the Loire" (I.v.816): "Das stygsche Wasser der Loire." As Johanna reveals, Charles has begged God to pour out his wrath upon him alone, taking his life as a sin offering for his people, if "any . . . grievous guilt, still yet / Left unatoned e'en from [his] father's time, / Had called this tear-filled conflict into being" (I.x.1026–1028): "Wenn eine andre schwere Schuld, noch nicht / Gebüßt, von deiner Väter Zeiten her, / Diesen tränenvollen

Krieg herbeigerufen, / Dich zum Opfer anzunehmen für dein Volk." By a king's paternal sacrifice of himself, Charles hopes to unify the realm once more. Indeed, Schiller depicts Charles as a new King Solomon, ready to renounce his claim to the throne in order to save the lives of his people: "Shall I, like that unnatural mother, / Let my own child be quartered with the sword?" (I.v.822–823): "Soll ich gleich jener unnatürlichen Mutter / Mein Kind zerteilen lassen mit dem Schwert?"

Having established Charles's position as a sacrificial scapegoat, ready to suffer expulsion, Schiller then removes him from that role, leaving it open in order that another victim, Johanna, might occupy it in his stead. Dunois vehemently opposes Charles's decision to withdraw, insisting that no king has the right to sacrifice himself and "give a crown away"; instead "the folk must sacrifice itself unto its king. / That is the fate and law of all the world" (I.v.844–845): "Für seinem König muß das Volk sich opfern, / Das ist das Schicksal und Gesetz der Welt."

As a representative of "the folk" and a substitute for the victim-king, Schiller's Johanna possesses all the classical features of a scapegoat. From the very beginning of the play, she stands out from the crowd as different. Even among her family members and fellow villagers in Domremy, she is an outsider.[58] Her father, Thibault, complains, "She flees the joyous company of her sisters, / Seeks out the desert mountains" (Prologue.ii.81–82): "Sie flieht der Schwestern fröhliche Gemeinschaft, / Die öden Berge sucht sie auf." Her reluctance to marry suggests to him "some grave perversion in the ways of nature" (Prologue.ii.62): "eine schwere Irrung der Natur." She remains silent in the opening two scenes, while her father and Raimond speak in her praise and blame. As Lesley Sharpe notes, "Her silence . . . emphasizes her remoteness."[59] Later, in the army (as a woman among warriors) and in the court (as a lowborn shepherdess among genteel courtiers), she remains marked by her difference, an outsider, whose lack of personal membership in the community enables her to be its focal point at a time of crisis and the means of its reunification. As Girard phrases it, "The community belongs to the victim, but the victim does not belong to the community."[60]

Before Johanna's expulsion at Rheims, she works with preternatural effectiveness as a peacemaker. Even before she arrives at court, her announced military victory over the English reconciles Dunois with the king: "Lords, embrace! / Let all your grudge and discord vanish now /

Since Heaven itself proclaims that it's for us" (I.ix.933–935): "Umarmt euch, Prinzen! / Laßt allen Groll und Hader jetzo schwinden, / Da sich der Himmel selbst für uns erklärt." On the battlefield, her "sweet eloquence" (II.x.1742: "süßer Rede") convinces the duke of Burgundy to switch his allegiance back from the English to the French and to be reconciled with Charles. Johanna points to her peacemaking as a proof of her divine mission: "Is making peace, / Dispelling hate, the work of hell?" (II.x.1778–1779): "Ist Frieden stiften, Haß / Versöhnen ein Geschäft der Hölle?" Her climactic mediation occurs when Burgundy, breaking his "awful oath of vengeance" (III.iv.2071: "schrecklich Rachgelübde"), embraces and pardons even Du Chatel, the murderer of his father.

Johanna's peacemaking powers do not, however, merely restore and re-create the community whose existence is endangered through strife; they also threaten to undo the community from within and from without. As the one beloved by all her countrymen, she sparks new division by inspiring love's rivalry and jealousy. Anticipating an ultimate French victory, Dunois and La Hire, who have been "cordial friends and war-time brothers" (III.i.1811: "Herzenfreunde, Waffenbrüder"), begin to quarrel over Johanna. Dunois pleads with La Hire, "Let not the love of woman rend this [fraternal] bond" (III.i.1814): "Laßt Weiberliebe nicht das Band zertrennen." Similarly, Charles gently chides Johanna, "Two distinguished wooers, / Alike in martial fame and hero's virtues! / —Wilt thou, who reconciled my foes to me, / My realm united, part my dearest friends?" (III.iv.2174–2177): "Zwei treffliche Bewerber / An Heldentugend gleich und Kriegsruhm! / — Willst du, die meine Feinde mir versöhnt, / Mein Reich vereinigt, mir die liebsten Freunde / Entzwein?"

Shortly after the scene in which Charles speaks these words to the Maid, the circle of Johanna's lovers widens to include Lionel, the English prince whose life Johanna spares on the battlefield after falling in love with him at first sight. Schiller's amatory twist of plot has often been ridiculed as historically inaccurate and dramatically contrived. Nonetheless, considered from a mythic point of view, Johanna must be contaminated by the love of the enemy, since it is the mission and fate of the scapegoat to reconcile opposing factions. The more she unites the French among themselves, the closer she comes to reconciling them as a group with their common foe, the English. This, indeed, is the ideal conclusion that must be drawn from Johanna's speech to

Burgundy: "A gracious master throws his portals wide / For all his guests, and no one is excluded; / Free, as the firmament surrounds the world, / So must his grace embrace both friend and foe" (III.iv.2054–2057): "Ein gütger Herr tut seine Pforten auf / Für alle Gäste, keinen schließt er aus; / Frei wie das Firmament die Welt umspannt, / So muß die Gnade Freund und Feind umschließen." Such inclusiveness, however, threatens the existence of the community from without by extending its boundaries beyond the limits that have defined it.

Johanna inspires love, but she is unable to be the spouse of any man without failing in her vow of virginity and dividing the community anew. Thus Johanna's life, in her own eyes and in those of others, becomes a threat to its oneness and her death a seal for its unity. As Schiller's tragedy unfolds, it conforms to the mythic pattern whereby the sacrifice of a virgin daughter, such as Iphigenia, at the hand of a father figure secures the unity of a people—a unity threatened at its origins, as Girard avers, by acquisitive mimesis over "objects which the community is incapable of dividing peacefully: women, food, weapons, the best dwelling-sites, etc."[61]

Johanna's own father, Thibault, brings the charge of guilt against her on the public occasion of the king's coronation feast at Rheims. Stepping out from the crowd, Thibault confronts Johanna in the presence of the king and his court and announces to all present that Johanna's victories have been wrought "through the devil's wiles" ("durch des Teufels Kunst") and by means of sorcery, as a result of a pact with Satan: "Here unto the enemy / Of man she bartered her immortal soul, / That he with brief and earthly fame extol her" (IV.xi.2975, 2992–2994): "Hier verkaufte sie / Dem Feind der Menschen ihr unsterblich Teil, / Daß er mit kurzem Weltruhm sie verherrliche." In placing such a demonizing accusation on the lips of Johanna's father, Schiller accomplishes a dramatic, mythic transfer of the persecutory material from the trial records at Rouen, where the historical Joan was charged with witchcraft and condemned as a heretic.[62]

Johanna also attributes to herself the polluting guilt that is the scapegoat's burden. Recoiling from Agnes Sorel's sisterly embrace, the conscience-stricken Johanna cries out, "Forsake me! Turn from me! Do not pollute / Thyself with my pestiferous encounter! / Be happy! Go! Let me in deepest night / Conceal my horror, my disgrace, and my / Misfortune"(IV.ii.2702–2706): "Verlaß mich. Wende dich von mir! Beflecke / Dich nicht mit meiner pesterfüllten Nähe! / Sei glücklich, geh,

mich laß in tiefster Nacht / Mein Unglück, meine Schande, mein Entsetzen / Verbergen." Later, when Johanna shrinks from carrying the
banner of the Queen of Heaven, she addresses the Virgin within the
hearing of Dunois, La Hire, and Du Chatel to welcome her destruction
at the Virgin's hand: "Destroy and punish me, take e'en thy lightning /
And let it fall upon my guilty head! / My bond I've broken, and I have
profaned / And desecrated thy most holy name!" (IV.iii.2743–2746):
"Verderbe, strafe mich, nimm deine Blitze, / Und laß sie fallen auf
mein schuldig Haupt. / Gebrochen hab ich meinen Bund, entweiht, /
Gelästert hab ich deinen heilgen Namen!" As if in answer to her prayer
for punishing lightning bolts, violent claps of thunder sound repeatedly during Thibault's denunciation of Johanna. Heaven itself seems
to speak in witness against her.

Johanna herself remains silent and motionless during the scenes
that represent her trial and condemnation. As Girard emphasizes, the
victim of ritual sacrifice is always silent and silenced—often by being
gagged or drugged—in order to confirm the myth of its guilt and thus
the community's innocence of murder.[63] Unlike the historical Joan,
who defended herself heroically under repeated inquisition, the mythic
Joan/Johanna refuses to contradict her father's witness against her.
Sorel begs Johanna to break her "unpropitious silence" (IV.xi.3001:
"dies unglückselge Schweigen") in answer to "this horrid accusation"
(IV.xi.3005: "die gräßliche Beschuldigung"); La Hire begs her to declare
her innocence: "The guiltless has a tongue" (IV.xi.3010–3011): "Die
Unschuld / Hat eine Sprache"; and Thibault challenges her to speak:
"Say thou art innocent! Deny the foe / Is in thy heart and brand me as
a liar!" (IV.xi.3022–3023): "Sprich, du seist schuldlos. Leugn es, daß der
Feind / In deinem Herzen ist." Mute, she refuses to give even tokens of
her innocence by clasping the crucifix or taking the friendly hand of
Dunois, which he extends to her.

One by one, Johanna's supporters believe in her guilt, turn away
from her, abandon her, and concur in her expulsion from the city into
the wilderness—an expulsion that necessarily exposes her to capture
and death at the hands of the English. The stage directions in scenes xi,
xii, and xiii of Act IV powerfully enforce the "all-against-one structure" that, according to Girard, is definitive of narratives of victimage.[64] "All draw back in astonishment" ("Alle treten mit Entsetzen
zurück") when Thibault points his accusing finger at his daughter to
name her a witch. Then all eyes are fixed on her, as she stands motion-

less and silent: "Allgemeine Stille, alle Blicke sind auf sie gespannt, sie steht unbeweglich." Agnes Sorel pleads with her, then "walks away from her in dismay": "Agnes Sorel tritt mit Entsetzen von ihr hinweg." La Hire at first draws near, then "retreats affrighted" from Johanna: "La Hire tritt entsetzt zurück." At the crashes of thunder, "the populace flees": "Das Volk entflieht zu allen Seiten." Then the king and his courtiers depart, leaving only Dunois onstage with the Maid, who "turns away from him with convulsive emotion": "Sie wendet sich mit einer zuckenden Bewegung von ihm hinweg." Du Chatel returns briefly to summon Dunois ("You have no honor / To linger here") and to command the expulsion of Johanna D'Arc: "You may leave the city unmolested. / For you the gates stand open" (IV.xiii.3042–3044): "Der König will erlauben, / Daß Ihr die Stadt verlasset ungekränkt. / Die Tore stehn Euch offen."

Driven out into the wilderness during the storm, Johanna counsels her faithful friend Raimond to leave her: "Thou seest, a curse pursues me and all else flees me; / Care for yourself and leave me to my fate" (V.iv.3110–3111): "Du siehst, mir folgt der Fluch, und alles flieht mich, / Sorg für dich selber und verlaß mich auch." She learns to her dismay that even Raimond regards her as someone "guilty of grave sin" ("der schweren Sünde schuldig"), as "an outcast spurning God" ("die Verworfne, / Die ihrem Gott entsagt"), on the basis of "silence," her "confession": "Euer schweigendes Geständnis" (V.iv.3133–3134, 3139). To Raimond she confides her innocence of sorcery, telling him that she kept silent in the face of a monstrous charge out of a double piety, submitting to her God-given fate as a divine "visitation" ("eine Schickung") and accepting Thibault's action as a fatherly "proving" (V.iv.3156, 3151): "Und väterlich wird auch die Prüfung sein."

Even in this intimate exchange, however, Johanna does not declare herself to be (or to have been) innocent of all guilt. The stormy expulsion, which she identifies with the cleansing work of God in nature, has, she says, "healed" and "purified" her being, ending the confusion and "strife within [her] heart" (V.iv.3175, 3177, 3172). Writing about this "strife" ("der Streit"), E. L. Stahl observes: "Schiller invented the inward conflicts of both Maria [Stuart] and Johanna, for they are not attested by history or legend."[65] Schiller, in short, chose to make his Johanna impure, anguished, and guilty in a way the historical Saint Joan was not, in order to refashion her into a tragic heroine in the root meaning of that word: that is, as a scapegoat. According to myth, as Girard insists, the scapegoat must always be guilty. The "mythical lie" is that "of the guilty victim who deserves to die."[66]

Critics of Schiller's *Maid of Orléans* usually declare Johanna innocent of the "false" charges brought against her by her father and interpret her silence as an act of expiation for a "real" and "different" sin, known only to Johanna herself. Edna Purdie phrases it thus: "By suffering silently a false charge, she . . . atones for a different fault."[67] From a mythic point of view, however, the charge that Johanna's father brings against her is literally true and cannot be contradicted without perjury. When Thibault finally adjures her in the name of "the God who o'er us thunders" to "deny the foe / Is in thy heart" (IV.xi.3022–3023: "Antworte bei dem Gott, der droben donnert! . . . Leugn es, daß der Feind / In deinem Herzen ist"), she cannot do so.

Schiller's word choice is deliberate and striking. The word *foe* refers, on the one hand, to the devil, the eternal Adversary and Diabolos; on the other hand, to Lionel, the English prince for whom Johanna has conceived a passion. What Schiller as an interpreter of myth and culture has recognized is that the scapegoat always has "the foe" in his or her heart, because the victim is sacrificed as a means of reconciling forces within the community, forces whose violent antagonism—at first acquisitive, then mimetic, and finally contagious—threatens the very existence of the community. Because the victim becomes a generalized surrogate for the "foe," it is and must be demonized, because the Satan is, by definition, the "stumbling block," the "one who opposes."[68] Part of the horror of the victim is that it absorbs into itself the differences that have separated the one from the other, that have atomized the community and defined everyone as a "foe" of everyone else. At a time of crisis, everyone has come to oppose everyone else; now all turn suddenly against the one whom they choose to embody (and thus to exteriorize) their strife. Expelling the victim provides a means of putting division itself to a temporary end.

The Guilt of All and the Guiltiness of Art

Like Freud and Girard after him, however, Schiller clearly recognized that such an expulsion does not cleanse the community of guilt. Unlike Sophocles' *Oedipus the King*, *The Maid of Orléans* does not end with Johanna being driven from the city into the wilderness. It follows her there, but it also represents the happenings in the French camp after her condemnation. As the storm clears, one and all regret their hastiness in banishing France's savior: "But now cool-headedness returns to us. / We see her as a wanderer in our midst, / And find in her not any fault at all. / We are confused—we fear we have committed / A grave injustice—E'en the King repents" (V.vii.3267–3271): "Jetzt kehrt uns die Besonnenheit zurück, / Wir sehn sie, wie sie unter uns gewandelt, / Und keinen Tadel finden wir an ihr. Wir sind verwirrt—wir fürchten schweres Unrecht / Getan zu haben.—Reue fühlt der König." Dunois publicly maintains Johanna's innocence, and the archbishop declares the guiltiness of the community: "One of two faults we have been guilty of: / We have defended us with magic arms / Of hell, or else a saint of God we've banned!" (V.vii.3284–3286): "Eins von den beiden haben wir verschuldet! / Wir haben uns mit höllschen Zauberwaffen / Verteidigt oder eine Heilige verbannt!"

The response of the community is to try to atone for its actions by rescuing Johanna from her English captors. Dunois issues the call to arms: "Oh rescue her, as she once rescued you, / From a most fear-provoking death!" (V.viii.3316–3317): "O rettet sie, die euch gerettet hat, / Von einem grausenvolle Tode!" Johanna, chained and in prison, also offers atonement for her own heart's infidelity by refusing to accept the proffered love and assistance of Lionel, who begs her to disown her French loyalties as a fitting act of revenge, since she herself has been disowned by the French.

Both in its sin and in its atonement, however, the community is relatively passive in comparison to Johanna, who exerts a powerful agency throughout. The community is confused by Thibault's accusation and Johanna's determined silence, so that its violent expulsion of her as victim appears rather to be Johanna's self-chosen departure from their midst. When the French forces rally to her rescue, Johanna at first hopes that they will triumph over the English without her direct assistance. They begin to experience a devastating defeat, however. Dunois is wounded and seized, Charles arrested, the soldiers killed or put to flight. Their weakness and need inspires miraculous strength in Johanna, who as a new Samson breaks her chains, appears suddenly as an omnipresent warrior on the battlefield, rescues the king, and reverses the tide of battle.

Victory belongs in the end to France but only, as King Charles admits, at the price of Johanna's death. She dies, but no one murders her.

The play does not even show her receiving a mortal wound from any single combatant. Her murder as murder is hidden, in keeping with the myth of victimage, which attributes all blame not to the community but to the demonized scapegoat and all glory and power to the victim, whom the community deifies. In the words of Girard, "The community thinks of itself as entirely passive *vis-à-vis* its own victim. . . . The victim is held responsible for the renewed calm in the community and for the disorder that preceded this return. It is even believed to have brought about its own death."[69]

The closing scenes of divinization carefully invert the scenes of Johanna's condemnation. Reluctant to bear her banner at the time of Charles's coronation, because of her sense of her own unworthiness, the dying Johanna eagerly takes it into her hands as the sign of the accomplishment of her life's mission: "Without my banner I dare not arrive. / It was entrusted to me by my Master, / And I must lay it down before his throne" (V.xiv.3531–3533): "Nicht ohne meine Fahne darf ich kommen, / Von meinem Meister ward sie mir vertraut, / Vor seinem Thron muß ich sie niederlegen." Whereas she had been surrounded by thunderbolts at the time of her condemnation, Johanna is now granted a vision of a rainbow as a token of Heaven's restored favor. Her spirit mounts "upward—upward," while "Earth doth backward fly" ("Hinauf—hinauf—Die Erde flieht zurück"), and she sinks down to her death. "No more rejected and despised" ("nicht mehr verachtet und verstoßen") by her own people, Johanna is acclaimed by them as "an angel passing" (V.xiv.3526, 3508): "Seht einen Engel scheiden!" As banner after banner covers her body in tribute, Johanna dies a beautiful death—her corpse literally screened from view—and her passing in glory, like her expulsion in shame, seals the unity of her people.

Johanna dies on a battlefield, adoringly surrounded by her worshipful countrymen, whereas Joan of Arc was burned to death at the stake, abandoned by the French, wrongly condemned by Church authorities, and tortured and cruelly executed by the English. Schiller presented to his audiences not the historic scandal of Joan's martyrdom but the myth of Johanna in the classic form of tragedy. Spectacular as the ending of *Die Jungfrau von Orleans* undoubtedly is, its disturbing difference from the ending of Joan's real life continues to disquiet audiences, to provoke unease, and to raise the question, Why?

To reply, as Stahl does, that Schiller's "reasons for violating a truth of this kind . . . were artistic, not moral, reasons" is to beg the question, which is and remains an ethical one.[70] The problem is compounded, moreover, because Schiller himself did not isolate moral, political, and aesthetic concerns but rather saw them as closely intertwined.

In his consideration of the historical matter of Joan of Arc, Schiller clearly understood its form, its higher truth, to be mythic. Schiller contemplated Joan of Arc and discovered in her a scapegoat. Retelling her life as a tragedy thus enabled him and us to see powerful mechanisms at work in her history—mechanisms of rivalry, of communal self-preservation and victimage, of condemnation and rehabilitation, of expulsion and reclamation, of violence and the sacred, and of institutional formation—that would otherwise remain obscure. Such an endeavor necessarily demands the recognition of similarities and results in an aesthetic doubling of Joan as Johanna, but it also requires one to ignore or deny the profound differences that exist between a classical tragedy and a medieval saint's life. As we have seen, Schiller had to de-Christianize Joan of Arc; to invent her self-division, guilt, and silence; and to deny her execution.

It may be that Schiller, at odds with the faith of his father and of his upbringing, understood Christianity, as Freud did, to be a profoundly sacrificial religion, not unlike the cults of antiquity, aimed at the purging of communal and personal guilt and at the prevention or containment of violence through prohibition, memorial, and ritual. W. White observes: "The basic concepts of Christian belief—redemption through sacrifice, sin and atonement, a paradise lost and a paradise to be regained—all these loom large in Schiller's writing, not in their orthodox Christian sense, but as forms of thought and imagery in which his mind habitually moves."[71]

And yet the striking absence of overt Christian references in the play suggests that Schiller must have been aware of unbridgeable differences between the pagan contexts in which tragedy thrives and the antimythic, antisacrificial ethos of Christianity. Christian references are, in fact, almost entirely lacking in *Die Jungfrau von Orleans*. There are some significant biblical allusions, alongside many classical ones, but they are almost all from the Old Testament.[72] The major biblical figures to whom Johanna is explicitly compared, Moses and Samson, are carefully selected as sinner saints, whose expulsion from the community results in part from their own wrongdoing, even as it contributes to the unfolding of a beneficent, providential plan.[73] Even in suffering, Johanna is not a Christ figure. Innocent of sorcery, she is guilty—inescapably, pathetically, sublimely guilty—of other things.

Christianity, which Schiller once called "the only aesthetic religion," has, in short, been expelled, along with history, from the story of Joan of Arc, and art has taken its place.[74] In *Die Jungfrau von Orleans* Schiller concerns himself less with Joan of Arc than with Johanna as a figure of the artist, but that substitution veils a hidden murder—not only Joan's, but also Christianity's. In a world where religion has been cast out, art serves as a substitute means for the fostering of spirituality, the purging of guilt, and the ending of division. Tragedy as a cathartic play form remains behind, long after actual goat sacrifices are no longer offered in ritual observance. "Since sacrifice is always a question of substitution," Girard writes, "it is always possible to make a new substitution"—in this case, not only of Johanna for Joan, and of pagan cult for Christianity, but also of art for religion.[75]

But art, too, in an increasingly materialistic age, is and remains in danger of being cast out as something useless and guilty, because beautiful. As Schiller recognized, beauty offends a fragmented society, because of the untouched wholeness it represents and prophesies. For beauty, therefore, there awaits a prophet's fate. To forestall that tragic outcome, Schiller composed his "romantische Tragödie" as a ritual performance, designed to avert the real crisis that the sacred violence of the French Revolution presaged for the modern world, where victims multiply uncontrollably. In a prophetic speech, Johanna tells Charles that her place, as a peasant supporter of the throne, will one day be taken by poor rebels who overthrow their king—a violent action setting in motion a series of sacrificial substitutions (see III.iv.2098–2101). As a tragedy about tragedies—a play about the tragic fate of artists and art forms—*Die Jungfrau von Orleans* thus celebrates not just the beautiful death of its heroine but the death of beauty itself. Onstage, beauty holds its position, albeit in death, even as it evokes fear about what shall come in the place of Johanna, of the artist, and of art itself.

We know that for the present the force which could remove
mountains is pretty much gone out of the world.
Faith has ceased to be, but we have some lively hopes
of electricity. We now employ it to exanimate people;
perhaps we shall yet find it valuable to reanimate them.
Or will faith come back, and will the future ages be
some of them religious?
—WILLIAM DEAN HOWELLS

CHAPTER THREE

THE AURA OF
SANCTITY AND ART

Mark Twain's *Personal Recollections of Joan of Arc*

Mark Twain's strong aversion to the nostalgic medievalism of his contemporaries—a contagion he called the "Walter Scott disease"—is well known.[1] Three of his novels—*The Prince and the Pauper* (1882), *A Connecticut Yankee in King Arthur's Court* (1889), and *Personal Recollections of Joan of Arc* (1896)—do indeed deal with medieval subjects but with the ostensible purpose of contrasting the barbarity of the Middle Ages with modern civilization, and thus of combating the medievalist revival.[2] Yet, as Kim Moreland and others have shown, Twain's attitude toward the Middle Ages is deeply conflicted, and his novels reveal an almost obsessive attraction to the past he repudiates.[3] The ambivalence of Twain's medievalism shows itself particularly in his *Joan of Arc*, which he named his favorite work and the "best of all [his] books."[4]

Written abroad in two spurts of concentrated activity in 1892–1893 and 1894–1895, the actual composition of *Joan of Arc* coincides with the bankruptcy of Twain's publisher, Charles L. Webster and Company, in April 1894, and the ultimate failure in 1895 of the Paige typesetter, a revolutionary machine in which Twain had invested much of his fortune over a period of fifteen years. This coincidence of technological failure with intense hagiographic writing suggests that Twain was seeking almost desperately to imbue his artistic work not only with the personal aura of the saint whose story he told[5] but also with the aura that belonged to art in an age before mechanical reproduction.

In a famous essay dealing with aesthetics, Walter Benjamin (1892–1940) asserts that "that which withers in the age of mechanical reproduction is the aura of the work of art. . . . The technique of reproduction detaches the reproduced object from the domain of tradition. By making many reproductions it substitutes a plurality of copies for a unique existence."[6] The art of the Middle Ages possessed "aura," Benjamin explains, because it, like an object of natural beauty, was "unique," had a definite "presence in time and space," was "embedded in the fabric of tradition," possessed a quality of "distance" from the beholder, and found its special use in cult and ritual.[7] This kind of "aura," which is indispensable to any "authentic" artwork,[8] was gradually lost to art through the process of mechanical reproduction, which substitutes simulacra for a unique original; aims at bringing art close to its viewers rather than keeping it distant from them; detaches a work from the tradition in which it came to be; and emphasizes its "exhibition value" before a mass audience rather than a "cult value" before a company of initiates.

Benjamin's older contemporary, Mark Twain (1835–1910), enthusiastically supported and promoted the new technologies that enabled the mechanical reproduction of art. Fascinated by the inventions of his age and greedy for the wealth they promised, Twain entered into a series of business speculations. Beginning in the 1880s, he made significant financial investments in the technology of publishing.[9] In February 1880 he purchased 80 percent of the stock in a printing process known as Kaolatype. In 1881 he made his initial investment in the typesetter that was being developed by James W. Paige. The Paige typesetter became an obsession for Twain. In Moreland's words, for fifteen years Twain "alternated between euphoric optimism and despairing pessimism about the future of the machine—an enormously complex apparatus of over 18,000 separate parts, which he refused to market until it was absolutely perfect."[10] Twain invested much of his fortune—a total of $300,000 — in the development of the typesetter, which had a voracious appetite for improvements, refinements, and repairs.[11] Twain was bankrupt and nearly $100,000 in debt when the typesetter finally collapsed in 1894–1895.

The disastrous failure of the typesetter, which had been for Twain the symbol of nineteenth-century progress, brought with it a severe financial and psychological challenge to his own powers of artistic invention. Twain had identified with Paige as an artist and inventor, calling him in 1890 "a most great and genuine poet, whose sublime creations are written in steel." Paige was, in Twain's estimation, "the Shakespeare of mechanical invention."[12] In Twain's imaginary competition with Thomas Edison, the archinventor of the nineteenth century, Paige had been Twain's alter ego and protagonist. With the failure of Paige, Twain was thrown back into reliance on his now dwindling personal resources as an artist.

The Machine and the Manuscript

Confronted with mechanical failure and financial disaster, Twain seems to have faced, more frankly than he had in the past, the loss of aura in his own literary production — an aura that he associated (reportedly from childhood on) with the subject of Joan of Arc. He endeavored to counter, forestall, and overcome that loss by writing a romance in vital contact with unique historical documents and artifacts, extant from the distant world of fifteenth-century Europe. As Twain, using the persona of the supposed translator, Jean François Alden, states in an opening note, "The Peculiarity of Joan of Arc's History," her biography is "unique" in that "it is the only story of a human life which comes to us under oath." This uniqueness gives it aura, as does the specific location in time and space of the medieval transcripts of Joan's trials: "The official records of the Great Trial of 1431, and of the Process of Rehabilitation of a quarter of a century later, are still preserved in the National Archives of France." The title page refers in parallel fashion to the "Original Unpublished Manuscript" of the *Recollections* itself, which is housed "in the National Archives of France" and which has been "Freely Translated out of the Ancient French into Modern English." At one remove from the rehabilitation records, wherein the actual testimony of the historical Louis de Conte appears, the fictive manuscript yet participates in their aura, because, we are told, "the Sieur Louis de Conte is faithful to [Joan's] official history in his personal recollections."[13]

Significantly, the "recollections" are "personal"—a quality that distinguishes them from the reproductions of a machine. That the word choice in the novel's title was important to Twain becomes apparent if one refers to "What Is Man?" (1906), an essay written in Twain's old age. There an Old Man engages in a dialogue with a Young Man, perhaps Twain's own younger self, and argues that evolution has brought about "Man the machine—man the impersonal machine," who is incapable of "personal recollection": "*Personally* you cannot claim even the slender merit of *putting the borrowed materials together*. That was done *automatically*—by your mental machinery, in strict accordance with the law of that machinery's construction."[14]

As Hamlin Hill has suggested, the definition of man as a machine echoes—albeit with a bitter, parodic difference—Twain's earlier, exultant description of the operation of the Paige typesetter.[15] Writing to his brother Orion on January 5, 1889, Clemens enthused:

> At 12.20 this afternoon a line of moveable type was spaced and justified by machinery for the first time in the history of the world! And I was there to see. It was done *automatically*—instantly—perfectly. . . . All the other wonderful inventions of the human brain sink pretty nearly into common-place contrasted with this awful mechanical miracle. Telephones, telegraphs, locomotives, cotton gins, sewing machines, Baggage calculators, Jacquard looms, perfecting presses, Arkwright's frames—all of them are mere toys, simplicities! The Paige Compositor marches alone and far in the lead of human inventions.[16]

If the Old Man in "What Is Man?" asserts the factual existence of "Man the machine" in an age of mechanical reproduction, Louis de Conte, the eighty-two-year-old narrator of *Personal Recollections of Joan of Arc,* speaks in 1492 for the existence of another, more authentic kind of humanity in an age when the spoken word was laboriously recorded by scribes on manuscripts. Given Twain's heavy investment in the Paige typesetter, it can be no accident that the opening lines of Twain's novel refer to Joan's "page" and to "the late invented art of printing": "In all the tales and songs and histories of Joan of Arc which you and the rest of the world read and sing and study in the books wrought in the late invented art of printing, mention is made of me, the Sieur Louis de Conte—I was her page and secretary" (p. 27).[17]

As many have noted, Twain's narrator, whose initials conveniently match those of Samuel L. Clemens, is a close double for Twain himself. He writes his tale for his "great-great-grand nephews and nieces" (p. 27), even as the sixty-year-old Twain read aloud in the evenings to his wife and daughters the manuscript of *Personal Recollections,* on which he had worked during the daytime. De Conte's high esteem for Joan of Arc, "the most noble life that was ever born into this world" (p. 28), matches that of Alden the translator, who calls her "the most innocent, the most lovely, the most adorable [child] the ages have produced" (p. 21), and that of Twain himself, who speaks in his own voice in the essay "Joan of Arc" (1904) to name her "the Wonder of the Ages" and "the most extraordinary person the human race has ever produced" (pp. 448, 452).

De Conte begins the story of his life much as Twain himself would begin his own in a late reminiscence, "The Turning Point" (1910). De Conte pictures himself as a frightened child in a world filled with war, famine, plague, and contagion: "Epidemics swept away the people like flies, and the burials were conducted . . . at night" (p. 31). At the age of five he was orphaned in a Burgundian raid and left "all alone, except for the company of the dead and the wounded" (p. 32). Similarly, Twain describes himself at the age of twelve, the year of his father's death, in a season of pestilence: "The summer came, and brought with it an epidemic of measles. For a time a child died almost every day. The village was paralyzed with fright, distress, despair."[18]

In "The Turning Point," Twain links his near-fatal, suicidal childhood bout with measles to his subsequent apprenticeship to a newspaperman and thus to the beginning of his literary career.[19] Similarly, de Conte shows, as Susan Harris observes, "how events conspired to make him the chronicler of [Joan's] life."[20] Orphaned, he was entrusted to the care of the priest in Domremy, Joan's childhood home: "The priest in the course of time taught me to read and write, and he and I were the only persons in the village who possessed this learning" (p. 32). Because of his literacy, Joan asked him to accompany her on her mission: "I may need you in Vaucouleurs; for if the governor will not receive me I will dictate a letter to him, and must have some one by me who knows the art of how to write and spell the words" (p. 79). Later,

Figure 1.　Frank Du Mond, "Joan Dictating to Her Parents."

as her appointed page and secretary, he took down her dictated letters to the English and French commanders and to her parents. (See figure 1.) In the end, his ability as a scribe placed him in the "strange position" of being "clerk to the [chief] recorder" (p. 317) during Joan's trial at Rouen and a witness to her martyrdom.

De Conte's fictional *Recollections* thus purports to provide a commentary on the authentic documents of the trial and rehabilitation of Joan of Arc, which possess (in Benjamin's terms) an indisputable aura because of their uniqueness, their definite placement in time and space, and their distance. As much as possible, Twain sought to familiarize himself with these and other documents, devoting at least twelve years (by his own, probably somewhat exaggerated testimony) to careful research and translation, in preparation for his writing of Joan's story (*MTB* 3:1034). Joseph C. Jurick asserts that already during their 1879 residency in Paris, the members of the Clemens family "studied French, read French history, and Twain renewed his interest in Joan of Arc."[21] According to Albert Bigelow Paine, "there is a bibliographi-

cal list of various works on the subject [of Joan of Arc], probably com-
piled for him not much later than 1880, for the latest published work of
the list bears that date" (*MTB* 3:958). The research of Alan Gribben,
Ruth Mary Bradley, and Lionel Carl Nadeau into Twain's sources for
Joan of Arc confirm an early date for the start of the project and extensive reading on Twain's part.[22]

The sheer amount of time Twain devoted to this work suggests a
conscious determination to set its duration, and the possibility for meditation it offered, in opposition to the quick rate of mechanical reproduction. As Twain was to admit later, "*Joan of Arc*... furnished me seven
times the pleasure afforded me by any of the others: 12 years of preparation & 2 of writing. The others needed no preparation, & got none"
(*MTB* 3:1034). Even if Twain exaggerated the amount of time he actually invested in *Personal Recollections* and minimized that which he
spent in research for his other writings (as he indeed did), he clearly
associated temporal duration with the aura of his *Joan*, with regard to
both its medieval subject matter and his authorial *modus agendi*.

As Twain recognized, the historical documents related to Joan's
trial and rehabilitation possess an incontestable authenticity that participates (in a way that Twain himself did not) in an unbroken tradition of religious belief and cultic practice, leading up to (and beyond)
Joan's canonization as a saint on May 16, 1920. Sensing the inter-
dependence of aura and tradition to which Benjamin was later to
point, Twain faced the challenge of preserving Joan's place within a
tradition from which he himself, an avowed anti-Catholic, stood apart.[23]
Twain scholars often point to his disparaging remarks about Catholicism, Mariolatry, sacramental Confession, the clergy, and saintly ap-
paritions and find in them a possible basis for the artistic failure of
Personal Recollections, which celebrates a medieval Catholic saint.[24]
Yet, as Nadeau has demonstrated, Twain carefully compensates for his
own lack as a skeptical non-Catholic by using a medieval Catholic
narrator, Signeur Louis de Conte, as one of his personae in the novel.
Whatever Twain may have said and written outside the context of *Personal Recollections*, in the novel itself he speaks with the voice of de
Conte, whose personal viewpoint becomes increasingly embittered
and like that of Clemens but who remains faithful to history in his depiction of Joan's devotional practices.[25] Twain represents Joan's achievement, according to William Searle, "as due in large part to her direct

involvement in medieval tradition. In this respect she forms a particularly instructive contrast to the Yankee, whose relation to that tradition remains always that of an outsider."[26]

At the same time, however, there is in *Personal Recollections* a strong
impulse to see Joan as someone outside of her century and ahead of her
time, as an exceptional personality (in the words of Roger B. Salomon)
"who is clearly outside the logical processes of history."[27] Seeing de
Conte as a mask for Twain, Harris has argued that de Conte's perspective on things subtly changes as the novel progresses, so that by its end
"De Conte . . . has lost not only the companions of his youth, but the
ability to share his contemporaries' values as well."[28] The "narrative
patterning" of the novel, Harris writes, charts "the evolution of his estrangement from the society that condemned [Joan]" and thus "provides resolutions for the tensions created by Mark Twain's use of a
Catholic narrator to communicate an essentially anti-Catholic theme."[29]

De Conte's impassioned denunciation of the faction of the Church
that condemned Joan, of the king who abandoned her, and of the English who killed her certainly gives voice to Twain's own sense that the
fifteenth century was "the brutalest, the wickedest, and the rottenest
in history since the dark ages" (p. 19). Moreland may also be correct
when she writes that the "almost hysterical rhetoric" of de Conte's
outcry against Bishop Cauchon "reveals Twain's visceral disgust with
the medieval Catholic Church."[30] But the problem remains: de Conte
and Twain cannot place themselves rhetorically outside of the Middle
Ages and against the Church without distancing themselves also from
Joan of Arc, whose aura depends on her participation in the life of the
Church, who loved her contemporaries, who served her king, and who
died forgiving her enemies.

The Saint and Susy

Eager to preserve the aura of his heroine but unable to give his portrayal of her a religious "cult value" (to use Benjamin's term) comparable to that given her by Catholic biographers, Twain instinctively
compensated by substituting a corresponding, cultic attachment to the
beloved family members—his wife, Olivia ("Livy"), and his daughter
Susy—who mediated between him and his heroine and provided real-
life models for his Joan. Here, too, Twain's practice anticipates Ben-

jamin's theoretical observation that "cult value does not give way without resistance. It retires into an ultimate retrenchment: the human countenance. . . . The cult of remembrance of loved ones, absent or dead, offers a last refuge for the cult value of the picture."[31]

On the anniversary of their wedding, Twain dedicated *Personal Recollections of Joan of Arc* to Livy "in grateful recognition of her twenty-five years of valued service as [his] literary advisor and editor" (*MTB* 3:1033). After making six false starts in writing Joan's story— each meeting with the "deadly criticism" of Mrs. Clemens's "silence"— Twain at last found confirmation for the present form of the work in Livy's response: "When . . . I found the right form I recognized at once that it was the right one and I knew what she would say. She said it, without doubt or hesitation."[32] Twain's letters indicate the extent to which Livy provided Twain with emotional support throughout the time of the novel's composition. In a letter to his close friend and adviser, Henry Huddleston Rogers, dated August 25, 1894, for instance, an impoverished Twain writes: "Mrs. Clemens . . . requires me to drop the lecture platform out of my mind and go straight ahead with Joan until the book is finished."[33] Working steadfastly, day after day, at their residence in Viviani, Twain read to Livy and the others nightly what he had written (*MTB* 3:960).

Moreland points out that Twain "apostrophized Olivia as sister and saint" throughout their courtship, and his extant love letters to her parallel, and participate in, Twain's worshipful attitude toward Joan of Arc.[34] To Livy he wrote: "You seemed to my bewildered vision, a visiting *Spirit* from the upper air—a something to *worship*, reverently & at a distance—& *not* a creature of common human clay, to be profaned by the *love* of such as I."[35] Similarly, Twain's principal narrator de Conte describes Joan of Arc "clothed all in white armor, dreamy, beautiful, and in her face a deep, deep joy, a joy not of earth, oh, she was not flesh, she was a spirit!" (p. 265). Twain's second narrator, the comic figure Paladin, seeks to marry Joan, even as Clemens married Olivia, but (as de Conte asserts) "there was no fit mate in that village for Joan of Arc" (p. 67). (See figure 2.)

The Joan of *Personal Recollections* is, as Peter Stoneley remarks, "Twain's ideal of womanhood."[36] As such, she also represents Twain's careful modification of Livy's own feminist ideal. In her magisterial work, Laura E. Skandera-Trombley has underscored Livy's admiration for the suffragette lecturer Anna Dickinson, who was popularly known

Figure 2.   Frank Du Mond, "In the Forest."

as the "juvenile Joan of Arc"[37] because of her public lectures in Joan's praise.[38] Worried that his fiancée would be "unsettled by Anna Dickinson's fiery words," Twain wrote to Livy on January 22, 1869, "You cannot do Anna Dickinson's work, & . . . she cannot do yours. Livy you might as well reproach yourself for not being able to win bloody victories in battle, like Joan of Arc. In your sphere you are as great, & as noble, & as efficient as any Joan of Arc that ever lived. Be content with the strength that God has given you, & and the station He has given into your charge."[39] In dedicating *Personal Recollections of Joan of Arc* to Livy, Twain offered to her the image of a feminine Joan with whom she could identify herself—indeed, a Joan whom he had fashioned in Livy's own likeness.

Twain's more immediate model for Joan, however, was not his wife Olivia but their daughter Susy. In January 1902 Twain admitted, "Susy at 17—Joan of Arc at 17. Secretly, I drew Joan's physical portrait from the Susy of that age, when I came to write that book." Twain goes on to indicate that Susy's spiritual qualities—"vivacity, enthusiasm, precocious wisdom, wit, eloquence, penetration, nobility of character"—also helped him to comprehend and depict Joan's character.[40] According to Susy's own testimony, listening to her father's novel-in-progress in 1892–1893 also affected her, increasing her piety: "My old religious feeling has suddenly come back to me and I find going to church and reading the Bible the greatest comfort."[41] She was moved by Twain's *Personal Recollections*, which, she said, "promises to be his loveliest book. . . . The character of Joan is pure and perfect to a miraculous degree. Hearing the M.S. read aloud is an uplifting and revealing hour to us all."[42]

In summer 1894 Susy accompanied Clemens to Rouen to visit the site of Joan of Arc's imprisonment, trial, and death at the stake. There, exposed to the damp of the dungeon, Susy fell ill—a circumstance that delayed their departure from the city and reinforced the association in Clemens's mind of the two young women (*MTB* 3:989). In August 1896 Susy, afflicted with spinal meningitis, died suddenly at the age of twenty-four, only months after the publication of *Personal Recollections*. Two years later, in 1898, Twain recalled with special poignancy the evening of April 28, 1895, when he had read aloud to a weeping Susy the chapter recounting Joan of Arc's martyrdom: "The last ms. of mine that ever I read to her was four-fifths of the last chapter of Joan— and the last words of that which I read were 'How rich was the world etc.' And to me these words have a personal meaning now."[43] Twain refers to the lament of de Conte and uses it to eulogize his own daughter: "Yes, she was gone from us: JOAN OF ARC! What little words they are, to tell of a rich world made empty and poor!" (p. 434). As William Searle notes, the notebook reference suggests that "the pain of Joan's loss" had "merged in Twain's mind with that of Susy's."[44]

Twain's main source for the chapters dealing with Joan's trial and martyrdom (as well as other episodes in Joan's life) was an 1873 French edition of the *Jeanne d'Arc* of the historian Jules Michelet (d. 1874). Nadeau rightly suggests that Twain found a kindred spirit in the French poet-historian, whose sentimental romanticism and anticlerical bias matched his own.[45] What has not been observed is an uncanny parallel in the biographies of these writers, both of whom projected onto the religious cult of Joan of Arc the memorial cult of a beloved and deceased woman.

In 1841 Michelet wrote in passionate, idealistic, even romantic terms about the life and death of Joan of Arc at the conclusion of the fourth volume of his monumental *History of France*. In 1840 his young wife, Pauline, had died. He was thus literally visiting the site of Joan's execution at the same time that he was visiting Pauline's grave and writing about the end of the Middle Ages. At Rouen, where Joan was burned at the stake, he stayed at the home of a married woman, the mother of one of his students. She was dying of cancer, and Michelet's brief, paradoxically healing love affair with her marked the transition between two periods in his personal life and two volumes of his *History of France*. Entries in his journal suggest that his portrayal of Joan of Arc creatively combines the images of two beloved women, his dead wife Pauline and his dying mistress, Madame Dumesnil, and that his historical narrative of Joan is inescapably autobiographical.[46]

A similar aura surrounds Mark Twain's Jehannine romance—so much so that Paine's sentimental response to *Personal Recollections of Joan of Arc* in his biography of Twain effectively merges the cult of the martyred saint with Twain's mourning for Susy: "We find ourselves all the time as in an atmosphere of consecration, and feel that somehow we are helping him to weave a garland to lay on Joan's tomb" (*MTB* 3:1030). Even as Twain had resorted to an idolatrous, familial worship in order to compensate for a personal lack of Catholic devotion to the saints, his biographer Paine now substitutes a funereal wreath for the saint's halo.

Twain was, however, also seeking in *Joan of Arc* to weave for himself another sort of garland, the writer's laurel crown, by identifying his own imagination as an artist with the visions and prophecies of Joan of Arc. Twain's letters and recorded statements make it clear that he associated *Joan of Arc* with his serious literary ambitions and set that work against the contrary impulse, so strong in him, for popular acclaim and financial remuneration. In a letter to Mrs. Clemens, he imagines himself bidding "Farewell—a long farewell—to *business!*" and embracing instead a life of letters: "I will live in literature, I will wallow in it, revel in it; I will swim in ink! *Joan of Arc!*" (*MTB* 3:978). To H. H. Rogers he wrote on January 29, 1895, "Possibly the book may not sell, but that is nothing—it was written for love."[47] To Mrs. Fairbanks he wrote in similar terms, describing *Joan of Arc* as "private & not for print, . . . written for love & not for lucre."[48] He determined to publish the book anonymously because, as he told Mrs. Clemens and Susy, "I shall never be accepted seriously over my own signature. People always want to laugh over what I write and are disappointed if they don't find a joke in it. This is to be a serious book. It means more to me than anything I have ever undertaken" (*MTB* 3:959).

Twain's Turning Points

The opposition that is expressed in these declarations—of love to lucre, of literature to business, of serious art to public pandering—figures in two radically different accounts of the conversion of Samuel Clemens into Mark Twain, the writer. The first is by Twain himself; the second, by his friend, biographer, and close confidant during his last four years, Albert Bigelow Paine (1861–1937). Each is entitled "The Turning Point," and each makes striking mention of Joan of Arc. Twain's account orients his life forward into the modern era of capitalism, investment, and mechanical reproduction. Paine's biography, by contrast, depicts Twain's artistic progress as a visionary medievalism, grounded in antiquities and aimed at capturing from the present a saintly aura from the past. In the pages of Twain's profoundly ambivalent romance, *Personal Recollections of Joan of Arc,* these two contradictory orientations may be said to meet and merge.

In "The Turning Point of My Life," an essay written for *Harper's Bazaar* shortly before his death in 1910, Twain describes his life as a series of linked chains that, through a process of historical determinism, have made him a writer: "I know how I came to be literary, and I will tell the steps that led up to it and brought it about."[49] Characterizing his life's course as the inevitable result of a combination of circumstance with temperament, Twain tells how he made the transition in 1856 from the life of a printer to that of a riverboat pilot. Reading a traveler's book about the Amazon River, the twenty-year-old Clemens had become obsessed with a get-rich-quick scheme "to ascend the Amazon," harvest "*coca*, a vegetable product of miraculous powers," and establish "a trade in coca with all the world" (p. 459). At that juncture, Twain relates, "Circumstance came to my aid. Circumstance, to help or hurt another man, made him lose a fifty-dollar bill in the street; and to help or hurt me, made me find it. I advertised the find, and left for the Amazon the same day. . . . Circumstance furnished the capital, and my temperament told me what to do with it" (pp. 459–460).

Commenting on this incident, Searle observes that "the sum involved was equivalent, in current purchasing power, to some four hundred dollars. People do not 'find' that kind of money. Nor do they leave it lying about for the wind to take."[50] Whether or not Searle is right in his surmise that Twain's belated tale of a lucky find covers a crime of theft that burdened Twain's conscience the rest of his life, it is certain that Twain's story of finding a banknote "in the wind" (as Searle puts it) just at a time when his desire for cash was keen makes an odd beginning for his portrait of himself as an artist.[51] In Twain's "Turning Point," the fifty-dollar bill, sent to him by Circumstance with a capital *C*, functions as a kind of angelic sign, which tells and enables him to move on. Looking back on the episode, Twain remarks, "By temperament I was the kind of person that *does* things. Does them and reflects afterwards. . . . I still do the thing commanded by circumstance and temperament, and reflect afterward. Always violently" (pp. 460–461).

Paine's four-volume, 1912 biography of Twain has a chapter entitled "The Turning Point" that gives a very different genesis for Twain's literary career. Paine looks back to Twain's childhood in Hannibal, when he was an apprentice to the newspaper publisher, Joseph Amant. Like Twain's account of a turning point, Paine's involves a discovery of a paper, blown in the wind down the street: "There came into his life just at this point one of those seemingly trivial incidents which, viewed in retrospect, assume pivotal proportions. He was on his way from the office to his home one afternoon when he saw flying along the pavement a square of paper, a leaf from a book. . . . He caught the flying scrap and examined it. It was a leaf from some history of Joan of Arc" (*MTB* 1:81).

Paine uses this incident as a controlling narrative for the whole of his biography of Mark Twain. From that fateful day onward, Paine writes, Twain's interest in Joan of Arc "would grow steadily for more than half a lifetime and culminate in that crowning work, the *Recollections [of Joan of Arc]*, the loveliest story ever told of the martyred girl" (*MTB* 1:81). Paine images Twain's entire literary output to grow, as it were, from this single page, which awakened Twain's interest in history and foreign languages—German, French, and Latin—and which "crystallized suddenly within him sympathy with the oppressed, rebellion against tyranny and treachery, scorn for the divine rights of kings" (*MTB* 1:82). For Paine, the wind that blew the "stray leaf from another life" into Twain's own life was symbolic of the *pneuma*, the breath of prophecy, and the inspiring muse of authorship that shaped Twain's "career as one of the world's mentally elect" (*MTB* 1:82).

Paine was (in Hamlin Hill's words) "the victim of a fastidious Victorian sense of propriety."[52] It was his ambition as Clemens's literary executor to fashion the life and complete works of Mark Twain into what Robert Paul Lamb terms "a monument of Victorian respectability"— a goal with which Twain himself did not easily cooperate.[53] Puzzled that Twain himself "for some reason did not mention this incident" in his essay "The Turning Point," Paine insists that "if there *was* a turning point in [Twain's] life, he reached it that bleak afternoon on the streets of Hannibal," when he first learned about Joan of Arc. Paine thus endeavors to correct Twain's account, to fill a gap in Twain's memory of himself, by substituting a new "turning point" for Twain's own, setting biography against autobiography.[54]

But Paine is wrong to imply that Joan of Arc goes unmentioned in Twain's "Turning Point" essay. There, Twain explores the linked chain of causation back to "the scene of the real turning point of my life (and of yours) . . . the Garden of Eden" (p. 463). "It was there," Twain writes, "that the first link was forged of the chain that was ultimately to lead to the emptying of me into the literary guild" (pp. 463–464). That first link was God's creation of an Adam whose weak temperament made his disobedience inevitable. Before God commanded Adam "to let the fruit alone," He first issued an earlier, contradictory command, one that "Adam would *never* be able to disobey," namely, "'Be weak, be water, be characterless, be cheaply persuadable'" (p. 464). Made of "butter" by their very temperaments, Adam and Eve naturally were "melted" when they came into "contact with fire" (p. 464).

The image of fire (an important image throughout Twain's writings) moves Twain to imagine an alternative "first link" in the chain of causation: Joan of Arc at the stake.[55] "What I cannot help wishing is, that Adam and Eve had been postponed, and Martin Luther and Joan of Arc put in their place—that splendid pair equipped with temperaments not made of butter, but of asbestos. By neither sugary persuasions nor by hell fire could Satan have beguiled *them* to eat the apple" (p. 464).[56] Had an unfallen Joan of Arc been at the beginning, Twain muses, things would have been different: "There would be no *you;* there would be no *me.* And the old, old creation-dawn scheme of ultimately launching me into the literary guild would have been defeated" (p. 464).

In substituting a page from a history of Joan of Arc for a fifty-dollar bill, then, Paine gives to Twain's literary career a lofty, paradisiacal beginning that Twain himself imagines, longs for, but emphatically denies in his autobiographical "Turning Point" essay. In his *Personal Recollections of Joan of Arc,* however, Twain suggests that his literary career stems not from one but from two mutually opposed impulses—one idealistic, one opportunistic—which turn to meet and converge, if only for a time, before separating again. He adumbrates that writerly calling of his in another "turning point": the angelic vocation of Joan of Arc.

Mark and Saint Michael

De Conte, nicknamed "The Scholar" by his childhood companions because of his literacy, notices that a change has taken place in Joan of Arc. She, who was a "light-hearted creature" by nature, has become "mainly grave; not melancholy, but given to thought, abstraction, dreams" (p. 69). Suspecting that she has a "secret," he detects a prophetic tone in her utterances. Passing through the oak forest on the fateful day of May 15, 1428, he chances on a solitary Joan, who is sitting there on the gnarled roots of "the haunted beech-tree" of the fairies, whose branches the children annually adorned with flower garlands

(p. 73). He hides himself, with the intention of surprising her, only to become an "eye-witness" of her historical visitation by Saint Michael the Archangel: "I saw a *white* shadow come slowly gliding along the grass toward the Tree. It was of grand proportions—a robed form, with wings" (p. 73). Uncovering his head "in the presence of something not of this world," de Conte is possessed by "terror and awe," and his breath grows "faint and difficult" (p. 73). His sight of Joan's vision allows the reader to see what he saw, in anticipation of the beatific vision in heaven (figure 3):

> The shadow approached Joan slowly; the extremity of it reached her, flowed over her, clothed her in its awful splendor. In that immortal light her face, only humanly beautiful before, became divine; flooded with that transforming glory her mean peasant habit was become like to the raiment of the sun-clothed children of God as we see them thronging the terraces of the Throne in our dreams and imaginings. (P. 74)

The shift from "I saw" to "we see" in this remarkable passage absorbs the onlooker's gaze through a series of mediations—through Twain's imaginative vision as author, into de Conte's as witness and narrator, and finally through his reported vision into Joan's vision of the angel and "our" common vision of the saints in heaven.

Behind the believing Sieur Louis de Conte (S. L. C.) stands a more skeptical Mark Twain. The narrative renders even him present through an extraordinary device of authorial inscription. In fear and in doubt whether he wakes or dreams, de Conte flees "deeper into the wood," stopping there to carve "a *mark* in the bark of a tree" (emphasis mine). He tells himself: "It may be that I am dreaming and have not seen this vision at all. I will come again, when I know that I am awake and not dreaming, and see *if this mark is still here;* then I shall know" (p. 74; emphasis mine). Later Joan herself tells him, in a voice of prophetic authority, "It was not a dream. . . . And you were not dreaming when you cut the *mark* in the tree" (p. 75; emphasis mine).

The mark/Mark stands as a mute witness to the truth of de Conte's and Joan's vision and thus participates in its aura. But it is not an unambiguous witness, for it also participates obliquely in de Conte's guilt as a lurking spectator and eavesdropper. Joan's vision of God, and God's of her, has (in Benjamin's terms) a pure cult value, whereas

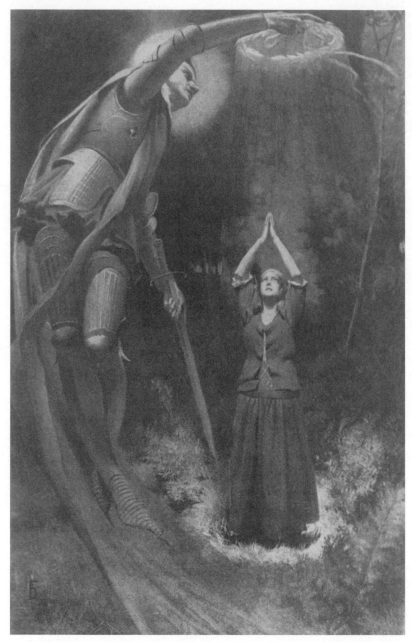

Figure 3.   Frank Du Mond, "Joan's Vision."

de Conte's reported vision of her encounter with the angel exploits the exhibition value of the same scene. In a profound rendering of the original sin of the artist, Twain describes de Conte's shame and confusion: "Then I came to myself. I reflected that I had been intruding upon a mystery of God—and what might my punishment be? I was afraid, and went deeper into the forest. Then I carved a mark in the bark of a tree" (p. 74). To cover his guilt, de Conte hides himself in the foliage, even as the biblical Adam and Eve hid from God and attempted to cover their nakedness with fig leaves. Behind him, however, stands an even guiltier party, the author "Mark," who hides himself behind the persona of de Conte.

To underscore the theme of guilt, Twain establishes a parallel between de Conte's lurking sight of the visionary Joan and an incident in the novel that occurs shortly before—namely, Dame Aubrey's unseen witness of the fairy dance:

> But late one night a great misfortune befell. Edmond Aubrey's mother passed by the Tree, and the fairies were stealing a dance, not thinking anybody was by; and they were so busy, and so intoxicated with the wild happiness of it, . . . that they noticed nothing; so Dame Aubrey stood there astonished and admiring, and saw the little fantastic atoms holding hands, . . . tearing around in a great ring. (P. 39)

"Heartless," "foolish," and "thoughtless," the woman, who could not contain herself, "went straight home and told the neighbors all about it" (p. 39). As a result of her report and the talk of the villagers, the priest finds himself with no choice but to perform an exorcism: "Père Fronte held the function under the tree and banished the fairies" (p. 40). (See figure 4.) The plain result of her onlooking and her gossip was, according to de Conte, a palpable loss of the aura surrounding the tree: "The great tree—l'Arbre Fée de Bourlemont was its beautiful name— was never afterward quite as much to us as it had been before. . . . No, the place was not quite the same afterwards" (p. 40).

The contrast between two kinds of vision—one worshipful, reverently distant, and suffused with religious aura; the other up close, intrusive, guilty, and instrumental in the loss of aura—helps to explain the several traditions about the "Vision of the Tree" to which de Conte refers.[57] Children of the Tree are said to have a "mystic privilege"

Figure 4. Frank Du Mond, "The Fairy Tree."

of seeing the fairy tree before their deaths (p. 36). To the "sinless dying forlorn in distant lands" it comes as a consolation, reminding them of their childhood home in Domremy and promising them an eternal home-going to Paradise (p. 36). To sinners it comes once or twice— once, in its "desolate winter aspect," as a fearsome warning to repent; twice, if repentance has occurred, "this time summerclad and beautiful" (p. 36).

In the *Personal Recollections,* Joan of Arc sees the vision of the Tree three times as an omen and a consolation before her martyrdom (p. 425): "The death-warning had nothing dismal about it for her; no, it was a remission of exile, it was leave to come home" (p. 241). Like Joan, de Conte is granted the comforting vision of the Tree: "I myself, old and broken, wait with serenity; for I have seen the vision of the Tree; I have seen it, and am content" (p. 37). De Conte can therefore speak with authority about the vision given to the Tree's pure children. Others—notably Jacques d'Arc, Joan of Arc's own father (another of Twain's several personae in the novel)—claim to know for certain that "the vision appear[s] twice—to a sinner" (p. 37).

The notion of a vision granted to a sinner—a vision of the same Tree beheld by saints but in a radically different, desolate form—hints at Twain's authorial uneasiness about imaginatively seeing Joan and penetrating into her visionary experience, for the sake of depicting her and exhibiting her life in novelistic form to a mass audience of readers. It may be, as Searle suggests, that a Faustian Twain at the age of sixty experienced the loss of his fortune as a punishment by God for his greed and the prostitution of his artistic talents; that he accepted it as a call to repent; and that he felt compelled to write *Personal Recollections of Joan of Arc* "for love & not for lucre" as an act of atonement.[58] Twain may well have sought to purify and renew his artistry through a vital contact with the cultic aura of a saint and the anonymous publication of her story. But Twain surely must also have sensed the desperate irony whereby an act of atonement can turn into temptation and sin, for to publish the novel meant for him to sell *Joan* and to profit from the beauty of the saint's life and death, even as her enemies had done. It was one thing to hold the manuscript in his hand and to read it aloud to his own family; quite another thing to have it reproduced mechanically.

Skandera-Trombley suggests a complex relationship between the private, familial audience and the public, popular one. According to her,

Twain's Joan is not just a heroine designed to please and edify Livy and Susy by embodying their personal, womanly ideals; she is also someone with whom a large readership of politically engaged women might be expected to identify. (See figures 5, 6.) "Well aware of Joan of Arc's popularity among female reformers and suffragists," Twain set out to write a novel "incorporating WCTU [Women's Christian Temperance Union] interests," hoping in this way "to attract a large audience and perhaps have the WCTU embrace his work."[59] As Skandera-Trombley observes, "Clemens's Joan of Arc espouses all the 'pet' causes of the WCTU: she is an adamant defender of children's rights, animal rights, dress reform, and temperance. Joan stops the troops from engaging in whoring, drinking, and swearing; at no time, even in the midst of battle, does Joan ever lose her feminine characteristics."[60]

Side by side with Twain's declarations of high intent and selfless motives in writing *Joan* we do indeed find early indications that he hoped to gain financially through its publication. A letter to Fred J. Hall, dated February 3, 1893, describes *Personal Recollections of Joan of Arc* as a "companion piece" to *The Prince and the Pauper*: "And I have had the idea that if it were gotten up in handsome style, with many illustrations and put at a high enough price, maybe the L. A. L. canvassers would take it and run with that book. . . . It could be priced anywhere from $4 up to $10, according to how it was gotten up, I suppose."[61] One year later, on December 22, 1894, a desperate Twain is ready to travel immediately to the United States in a last-ditch attempt to save the Paige typesetter. He writes to H. H. Rogers from Paris: "I can write Joan on board ship and lose no time. Also I could discuss my plan with the publisher for a *de luxe* Joan, time being an object, for some of the pictures could be made over here cheaply and quickly, but would cost much more time and money in America."[62] Although Twain did not at first want *Joan* to be published in a magazine,[63] *Harper's* published it serially, beginning in April 1895. Reversing his earlier resolve to maintain his anonymity, Twain wrote to J. Henry Harper, expressing the wish that his name be printed as the author of *Joan,* although (as he subsequently admitted) his wife was "a little troubled by [his] wanting [his] *nom de plume* put to the *Joan of Arc* so soon" (*MTB* 3:1006).

In 1895 Twain, with Livy and their daughter Clara, left Susy, their eldest daughter, and Jean, their youngest, behind in Hartford to go on a worldwide lecture tour, in an effort to pay their debts and restore their

Figure 5.   Frank Du Mond, "Joan Puzzles the Scholars."

Figure 6.   Frank Du Mond, "Joan before the Governor."

finances.[64] From Paris on April 29, 1895, Twain wrote to H. H. Rogers in New York City, declaring his intention to read aloud from *Joan of Arc:* "In these Joan proofs which I have been reading for the September Harper I find a couple of tip-top platform readings—and I mean to read them on our trip. If the authorship is known by then; and if it isn't, I will reveal it. The fact is, there is more good platform stuff in Joan than in any previous book of mine, by a long sight."[65]

Already in the fictive world of *Personal Recollections,* Twain foresees himself in the comic person of the Paladin, who mounts the speaker's platform to tell the story of Joan of Arc: "Then the Paladin began to walk up and down his platform with a great deal of dignity and quite at his ease; and as he walked he talked, and every little while stopped and stood facing his house and so standing continued his talk" (p. 130). (See figure 7.) Like Twain himself, the Paladin responds to calls from his audience for a rendition of particular episodes from Joan's story: "The people sat down and began to hammer on the table with their flagons and call for 'the King's Audience!—the King's Audience!—the

Figure 7. Frank Du Mond, "The Paladin Tells How He Won Patay."

King's Audience!'" (p. 130). Forgiven by one and all for his exaggerations of truth, the Paladin is chosen by Joan to be her standard-bearer. "Of old you were a fantastic talker, but there is a man in you, and I will bring it out," she tells him (p. 147).

Having written *Personal Recollections,* on tour Twain returns to the platform once more as a "fantastic talker." He must have felt it an ambiguous way of carrying the banner of Joan of Arc, for it is well known that he had a conflicted attitude toward the lecture circuit, sometimes reveling in his popular performances, sometimes finding them degrading and incompatible with the life of a genuine artist. According to Paine, "He abominated the platform and often vowed he would never appear before an audience again."[66] A letter to William Dean Howells from London, dated October 19, 1899, joins the subjects of Joan of Arc and platforming. He tells Howells that while in Sweden he has written "an introduction to a nobler book—the English translation of the Official Record (*unabridged*) of the Trials and Rehabilitation of Joan of Arc," and that he has "declined 45 lectures" in England and Scotland: "Nothing is so loathsome as gadding around platforming. . . . I wanted the money, but not the torture."[67]

The mention of torture suggests, paradoxically, that Twain may also have justified and sought to redeem his popular lecture appearances by likening himself on the speaker's platform to Joan, a public spectacle staked on the platform of execution (figure 8). There can be no doubt, at any rate, that Twain associated his artistic labors with Joan's saintly ordeal. To H. H. Rogers he wrote on January 29, 1895: "At 6 minutes past 7, yesterday evening, Joan of Arc was burned at the stake. With the long strain gone, I am in a sort of physical collapse today, but it will be gone to-morrow. I judged that this end of the book would be hard work, and it turned out so. I have never done any work before that cost so much thinking and weighing and measuring and planning and cramming, or so much cautious and painstaking execution."[68]

Twain's "physical collapse" associates him with the saint who has been burned, but his artistic "execution" of her story puts him in the position of those who plotted and brought about her death for their own gain. When twenty-four-year-old Susy, Twain's model for Joan, died of meningitis in Hartford in August 1896—suddenly and unexpectedly, while Twain was in England, at the end of a world tour of "platforming"—Twain's intense feelings of guilt, coupled with his

Figure 8. Frank Du Mond, "The Martyrdom of the Maid of Orleans."

understanding of her death as a cruel, divine punishment for sin, strongly suggest an underlying, authorial anxiety about his artistic use of Joan, his selling of her story, and his imaginative identification of Susy with the saint.

Writing to Livy from Guildford on August 19, 1896, the day after Susy's death, Twain confesses, "I have spent the day alone . . . [r]eproaching myself for laying the foundation of all our troubles and this final disaster."[69] Tracing a linked chain of events back to his support of Annie Moffett's marriage to Charles L. Webster, Twain blames himself in that letter for the creation of the Webster publishing company, its subsequent bankruptcy in 1894, and the global lecturing tour that their penury necessitated. It would be easy to place the writing of *Personal Recollections of Joan of Arc* as a link in that same chain. "My crimes," he laments, made Susy "a pauper & an exile."[70]

Whereas *Personal Recollections* had held Twain's optimism and pessimism about human nature in a precarious balance, by juxtaposing a perfect, all-forgiving Joan against the evil of her enemies, Susy's death prompted only despair, as Twain projected his own guilt on to the whole human race. His misanthropy was so bitter and severe that Livy wrote to him in distress: "Do darling change your mental attitude, try to change it. . . . Where is the mind that wrote . . . Jeanne d'Arc. . . . Bring it back! . . . the side [of you] I know, the sweet dear, tender side— that I love so. . . . Why always dwell upon the evil until those who live beside you are crushed to the earth & you seem almost like a monomaniac."[71]

Livy did not realize the extent to which "the mind that wrote Jeanne d'Arc" tormented Twain's conscience. Through a complex chain of mediation and culpability, Twain's novel, which reproduces the authentic documents of Joan's condemnation, participates in their original crime: "What a strange document that was, and what an exhibition and exposure of the heart of man, the one creature authorized to boast that he is made in the image of God" (p. 377).

For Sale: A De Luxe "Joan"

Only months before Susy's death, *Personal Recollections of Joan of Arc* had been published as a book in the *de luxe* format Twain had envisioned. The first edition had a striking red cover, decorated with golden fleurs-de-lis, on which the book's title appeared within the frame of a gold and red shield, intersected by a silver sword. Mark Twain's name stood in gold letters beneath the shield, as well as on the book's spine. The title page aimed at capturing the aura of antiquity and left Twain himself unnamed as author:

Personal Recollections of
Joan of Arc
by
The Sieur Louis de Conte
(Her Page and Secretary)

Freely Translated out of the Ancient French into Modern
English from the Original Unpublished Manuscript in the
National Archives of France
by
Jean François Alden

Copiously illustrated by Frank V. Du Mond, a young American artist who was studying in Paris at the time of the Clemens family's residency there in 1893–1894,[72] the 1896 edition of *Personal Recollections* employed a pattern of illustration that duplicates the narrative strategy of a mediated distance from authentic Jehannine matter. As the title page and captions indicate, interspersed among Du Mond's thirty original drawings for Twain's text (in some of which Joan wondrously resembles a young, nineteenth-century lady) are photographic reproductions of "old paintings and statues."

The edition visibly strove to bring Joan of Arc close to a late-nineteenth-century reading audience, to popularize her story, to make it accessible, and to place her life literally into the hands of a mass readership. In studying Joan's history, Twain had reached out for a share in its aura; in publishing it in novelistic form, however, he actually contributed to what Benjamin terms "the contemporary decay of the aura." That decay, Benjamin explains, results from two circumstances "related to the increasing significance of the masses in contemporary life. Namely, the desire of the . . . masses to bring things 'closer' spatially and humanly, which is just as ardent as their bent toward overcoming the uniqueness of every reality by accepting its reproduction."[73]

The cultic "distance" of a saint is, however, resistant to such a bringing closer; his or her uniqueness repels reproduction. Paine acknowledges that the early sales of *Personal Recollections* were "disappoint-
ing" and that reviewers voiced the "general verdict that, in attempting
Joan of Arc, Mark Twain had gone out of his proper sphere" (*MTB*
3:1029).[74] Paine himself praises the work lavishly, however, and he
does so precisely because of the "closeness" it effects: "But that is just
the very wonder of Mark Twain's Joan. She is a saint; she is rare; she
is exquisite; she is all that is lovely, *and she is a human being besides*"
(*MTB* 3:1029; emphasis added). Reading Twain's book sympatheti-
cally, Paine insists, "[the reader] will love her as the author loved her"
(*MTB* 3:1030).[75]

But how did he love her? In "What Is Man?" Twain's Old Man
replies that the author of *Personal Recollections,* like all authors, necessarily loved his heroine egotistically, for his own selfish gain: "In *all*
transactions, the Interior Master looks to it that *you get the first profit.*"[76] He also loved his Joan "impersonally," as an inventor loves the
mechanical invention of his own mind. The process by which
Shakespeare wrote his plays and invented his characters, the Old Man
claims, is the same process whereby Thomas Edison made his
mechanical inventions: "The process is the same. . . . The rat's mind
and the man's mind are the same machine, but of unequal capaci-
ties—like yours and Edison's; like the African pygmy's and Homer's;
like the Bushman's and Bismarck's."[77]

In the philosophy of Twain's Old Man, Edison's way of thinking
is paradigmatic for all forms of human thought: "Man's thought-
machine works just like the other animals', but it is a better one and
more Edisonian."[78] In supporting the invention and perfection of the
Paige typesetter, Twain had entered into a kind of competition with
his great American contemporary: "The Paige Compositor marches
alone and far in the lead of human inventions."[79] When the typesetter
failed, Twain devoted his energies to an invention of a different sort,
Joan of Arc.[80] William Dean Howells, Twain's close friend, hints at the
hidden contest between Twain, the author of *Joan,* and Edison, the
electrical inventor, in his 1896 review of *Personal Recollections* in
Harper's Weekly. There he contrasts Joan's religious faith with his contemporaries' belief in technological progress: "We know that for the
present the force which could remove mountains is pretty much gone

out of the world. Faith has ceased to be, but we have some lively hopes of electricity. We now employ it to exanimate people; perhaps we shall yet find it valuable to reanimate them."[81]

Howells's remark about animation may be taken as an unintended prophecy of the motion picture. It is one of the great ironies of history that in 1895, the same year that saw the serial publication of Twain's novel, Thomas Edison filmed a historical reenactment of the execution of Joan of Arc.[82] In the competition between Twain and Edison as inventors, the illustrated novel about Joan of Arc had to vie with a movie showing her burning at the stake. Walter Benjamin traces the evolution of the mechanical reproduction of art from the woodcut to the lithograph to the photograph to the motion picture. Benjamin makes no mention of Edison's experiment in filmmaking, which may have been unknown to him, but he uses as an example of the contemporary loss of aura another film about Joan of Arc: Carl-Theodore Dreyer's 1928 classic silent movie, *The Passion of Joan of Arc*. A pioneering film in its extensive use of close-ups, *The Passion* brought its viewing audience face-to-face with the saint in her agony.[83] As Benjamin observes in a note, the Danish director departed "from stage practices," selecting actors as if they were hard-to-find "stage properties" and using them, without makeup, as props.[84] At the same time, Dreyer allowed actual stage props—a spinning instrument of torture, a crown of straw, the bars of a light-filled window, a flying dove—to move on the screen and thus to function metaphorically as actors.

Perhaps Dreyer would have agreed with Twain that man is a machine, and that the martyrdom of a saint like Joan of Arc—in history and in fiction—only proves the point. What tormented Twain was the awareness that the reproduction of Joan's story—which mechanically brought Joan to life again, albeit as a shadow of herself, only to execute her anew—was the guiltier of the two killings. Why? Not simply because it involved a profit motive, but because it cast doubt on Joan's truth, stealing from her unique aura in the act of appropriating it for oneself. Twain sensed what Benjamin was later to declare: "The authenticity of a thing is the essence of all that is transmissible from its beginning. . . . Since the historical testimony rests on the authenticity, the former, too, is jeopardized by reproduction. . . . And what is really jeopardized when the historical testimony is affected is the authority of the object."[85] The author's invention of de Conte's "manuscript," in short, diminishes the aura of the actual manuscripts related to Joan's trial and rehabilitation, weakens the power of their testimony, and withers Joan's own prophetic authority in the process of duplicating it: "Yes, she was gone from us: JOAN OF ARC! What little words they are, to tell of a rich world made empty and poor!" (p. 434).

Nothing is easier than to give Christian asceticism a Socialist tinge.
— THE COMMUNIST MANIFESTO

A real public-bar angel, a gutter seraph!
In any case now we know where those
'Voices" come from.
— BERTOLT BRECHT

CHAPTER FOUR

THE MARXIST
JOAN OF ARC

Shaw, Brecht, and Hellman

Given the inimical stance of Karl Marx (1818–1883) and Friedrich
Engels (1820–1895) toward religion, one might at first be surprised
that Marxist playwrights—principal among them, George Bernard
Shaw (1856–1950), Bertolt Brecht (1898–1956), and Lillian Hellman
(1905–1984)—have repeatedly chosen Saint Joan as a dramatic subject. Sacrificial structures within Marxism itself, however, find a ready
ideological vehicle in the story of Joan when it is retold as myth and
tragedy. For Shaw, Joan is a Galtonic visualizer, whose farsightedness
signals and contributes to the rise of the urban bourgeoisie and thus
the historic supercession of medieval, Catholic feudalism by modern
nationalism, Protestantism, and capitalism. For Brecht, Joan is an Oedipal figure, both blind and sighted, in *Die heilige Johanna der Schlachthöfe* (1929, *Saint Joan of the Stockyards*) and a childlike, alienated visionary in *Die Gesichte der Simone Machard* (1942, *The Visions of Simone*

109

Machard). For Hellman, Joan is a radical heroine of the people, doomed by her own courage. For all three playwrights, Joan is a figure of the socially committed artist whose aesthetic production is inseparable from politics and therefore impure, infectious, and subject to expulsion. Whereas the historic Joan falls and fails, however, precisely through her failure, the Marxist playwright hopes to bring about a fictional triumph over the illusions of religion and capitalism, on the one hand, and of their literary precursors, on the other.

The Theater of Ideology and Ideological Theater

Noting that "Marx was a great devotee of classical drama—especially that of Aeschylus and Shakespeare," John McMurtry has argued that "Marx employs an implicit dramaturgical model throughout his work in his description of ideological phenomena."[1] Every historical conflict between social classes takes place for Marx not only at a given stage in time but also on a public, theatrical stage, where the superstructural realm reveals itself to be illusion and pretense. Marx himself develops this dramaturgical model at length in "The Eighteenth Brumaire of Louis Bonaparte" (1852). Commenting on Hegel's remark that "all facts and personages of great importance in world history occur, as it were, twice," Marx writes: "He forgot to add: the first time as tragedy, the second as farce."[2] Revolutionary activity that aims at the creation of something new always, he insists, "conjure[s] up the spirits of the past and . . . borrow[s] from them names, battle cries and costumes in order to present the new scene of history in this time-honored disguise" (p. 120). Thus "Luther donned the mask of the Apostle Paul," and "the masses of the old French Revolution performed the task of their time in Roman costume and with Roman phrase" (pp. 120–121). As we shall see, among the many masks of the Marxist revolutionaries and playwrights is that of Joan of Arc.

Marx would like to distinguish sharply, however, between the theatrical pretenses of the dominant, capitalist ideology and those of the Communists. Whereas ideological deception systematically supports the interests of the ruling class and clothes them in an attractive guise, Marxist theater aims at disclosing that same ideological superstructure as deceptive through a process of defamiliarization that Bertolt Brecht famously names the "a-effect" (alienation effect). In place of ideological deception, Marxism offers an equally dramatic morality play in which (as Robert Tucker observes) the "*dramatis personae* are My Lord Capital and the Collective Worker."[3] Like the myths of old, Marxist theory imagines an eschatological conflict between the proletariat and the bourgeoisie as forces of light and darkness, a conflict leading to the end of all class divisions. Pointing to the mythic origins of philosophy, Tucker links Marxist mythology to Hegelian philosophy, declaring, "[Marx] had gone beyond philosophy into that out of which philosophy, ages ago, originated—myth."[4]

When Marxist myth is enacted, it becomes first "tragedy" and then "farce," mirroring the sequence of plays in ancient Greek performance and the antique rituals of sacrifice associated with them. Even as the Athenian democracy had confirmed its political identity through tragedies depicting the deaths of Homeric kings, so too the Marxist revolution aimed at a latter-day reenactment of their slaughter in that of the contemporary ruling classes. In an inflammatory speech delivered on April 14, 1856, Marx directly compares the work of the Communist Party to that of the medieval *Vehmgericht*:

> To revenge the misdeeds of the ruling class, there existed in the middle ages, in Germany, a secret tribunal, called the "*Vehmgericht.*" If a red cross was seen marked on a house, people knew that its owner was doomed by the "*Vehm.*" All the houses of Europe are now marked with the mysterious red cross. History is the judge— its executioner, the proletarian.[5]

This passage follows the ideological moves described in the "Eighteenth Brumaire," clothing contemporary rebels in medieval costumes, reviving an older vocabulary ("Vehm"), and employing an established iconography (the red cross). It points to the "misdeeds" of the rich and powerful as a tragic flaw, warranting their slaughter. At the same time that it alludes to the Christian Middle Ages, however, it also evokes the biblical narrative of the Exodus, wherein the doorposts of the Israelites were marked with the blood of the Passover lamb (Exodus 12:7). A Jewish convert (of sorts) to (a nominal) Christianity, Marx subtly inverts the Judeo-Christian imagery of salvation and protection, making it a mark of death. At the same time, he identifies the Jews in an archetypal fashion with the doomed capitalists.

The Marxist insistence on the need to eliminate the Jews rests on a double basis: Marx's identification of the Jews with a profiteering praxis and his view of religion as the most comprehensive and threatening form of ideology, given its ability to compete with Marxist theory. Looking back to Hegel's Frankfurt writings on Judaism and tragedy and forward to Hitler's war against the Jews,[6] Marx's 1843 essay "On the Jewish Question" offers a horrific "final solution": "In the final analysis, the *emancipation* of the Jews is the emancipation of mankind from *Judaism.*"[7] Looking for "the secret of the Jew" not in his religion but in the "real Jew" and his monetary practice, Marx identifies the "profane basis of Judaism" as "*self-interest*"; the Jew's "worldly cult" as "*Huckstering*"; his "worldly god" as "*Money*" (p. 48). For Marx, the Jew "only manifests in a distinctive way the Judaism of civil society" and the essential Judaism of Christianity: "Christianity is the sublime thought of Judaism; Judaism is the vulgar, practical application of Christianity" (p. 52). The elimination of Christianity is thus entailed for Marx in the destruction of Judaism and "real Jew[s]."

Appropriating the medieval, persecutory charge of idol (Mammon) worship and child murder, Marx repeatedly describes the capitalists as devouring the flesh and blood of the children who work in their factories. In a memorable passage in *Capital* (1867), Marx places upon the lips of a personified Capital the words of Shakespeare's Shylock, whose "Shylock-clinging to the letter of the law of 1844" enables him to abuse "children of 8."[8] In an accompanying footnote, Marx refers to the "Shylock-law of the Ten Fables" and speculates in all seriousness about the historicity of Jewish demands for payment in the flesh, as well as early Christian, Eucharistic cannibalism.[9] Citing this text and many other anti-Semitic passages in his writings, Amy Newman observes that Marx "portrayed contemporary commercial practice as the abstract continuation of the religious practice of human sacrifice," putting forth "the notion that modern-day capitalism had transformed the distinctively 'Jewish' practice of ritual murder from a religious into a commercial practice."[10]

Representing all capitalists as Jews and reviving the anti-Semitic mythology of Judaism as a sacrificial religion, Marx would justify the violent overthrow of the upper classes by the communist leaders of the oppressed workers. The question arises: Is the Jewish mask he puts on the face of Capital an incidental coloring, or does it indicate that the real target of his attack is, first and foremost, the Judeo-Christian tradition that prohibits hatred and killing? Much in Marx's writings suggests that he perceives religion, not capitalism, as the greatest opponent of communism, the rivalrous twin with which Marxist thought must engage in a fraternal strife.

Marxism generally ignores whatever similarities may exist between itself and religion, in order to represent religion as Other. As early as 1906, Sergei Bulgakov pointed to the theologian Ludwig Feuerbach as "Marx's untold secret."[11] Similarly, Robert Tucker maintains that Marxism is a "religion of revolution," whose "religious essence . . . is superficially obscured by Marx's rejection of the traditional [Western] religions."[12] In his "Theses on Feuerbach" (1845), Marx explicitly identifies himself as someone who continues the theological work that Feuerbach had begun by moving beyond a recognition of the "religious self-alienation" on earth that projects itself into Heaven toward an insight into the fundamental societal divisions, the secular "self-cleavage and self-contradictoriness," that produce self-alienation.[13] In this way, as Tucker explains, Marx actually "projected upon the real conflicts of [nineteenth-century, industrial] society a conflict out of the inner life of man," extending Feuerbach's projective self-alienation in the opposite direction, not toward the spiritual realms of Heaven and Hell, but toward the material domain of secular society.[14]

Because Marx sees "society as a whole . . . splitting up into two great hostile camps," he blames "the social principles of Christianity" for preaching "the necessity of a ruling and oppressed class," for sacralizing the rulers, and for exhorting the workers to bear their hard lot patiently, either as "the just punishment of original sin and other sins or [as] trials that the Lord in his infinite wisdom imposes on those redeemed."[15] According to Marx, the sweet promise of heavenly reward makes religion "the *opium* of the people," rendering them passive.[16] Because Marxism also offers happiness to the people as the goal and fruit of revolution, it must supplant religious ideology with its own: "The abolition of religion as the *illusory* happiness of the people is required for their *real* happiness. The demand to give up the illusions about its condition is the *demand to give up a condition that needs illusions. The criticism of religion is therefore in embryo the criticism of the vale of woe,* the *halo* of which is religion."[17]

In competition with religion, Marxism first reduces religion to myth, depicting the Judeo-Christian continuum as a sacrificial system, and then it incorporates religion into its own mythological, sacrificial structure as a necessary victim. At the same time it denies its own mythic status, declaring itself to be truth. "One of the characteristics of true mythic thinking," Tucker notes, "is that the thinker is not aware of it as mythical. For him it is a revelation of what empirically *is*."[18]

In presenting Marxism's "truth," however, the theoretical writings of Marx continually reproduce the mythic patterns and images of ancient Greek tragedy, casting him in the role of Prometheus, the giver of light; of Tiresias, the Seer; or of Oedipus, the solver of riddles. In his *Economic and Philosophic Manuscripts of 1844,* for example, Marx describes the factory worker as returning "to a cave dwelling, which is now, however, contaminated with the pestilential breath of civilization, and which he continues to occupy only *precariously,*" because he must pay even for "this mortuary," from which he can be evicted.[19] The worker, Marx laments, is denied "a dwelling in the *light,* which Prometheus in Aeschylus designated as one of the greatest boons, by means of which he made the savage into a human being."[20] The allusion to Prometheus makes the "dwelling in the light" not just a literal reference to better housing but also a metaphor for the enlightenment offered by Marxist theory in competition with Judeo-Christian revelation and its heavenly imagery. Presenting himself as one endowed with light and sight, Marx refers again and again to the class conflict that is taking place "under our very eyes." Tucker notes: "The frequency with which this expression appears in his writings after 1844 is remarkable."[21] As the one with hard-won insight, Marx is a latter-day Oedipus who can declare: "Communism is the riddle of history solved, and knows itself to be this solution."[22]

No one has grasped the mythic, quasi-religious quality of Marxism more firmly than Georges Sorel, whose radical essays, collected in his *Reflections on Violence* (1908), openly celebrate the "contemporary myths" that "lead men to prepare themselves for a combat which will destroy the existing state of things."[23] Belief in "such myths" as the "syndicalist 'general strike' and Marx's catastrophic revolution" (p. 42) renders genuine revolutionaries "secure from all refutation" (p. 52) and ready to act with apocalyptic fervor in the present moment, regardless of the cost to themselves. Comparing the modern socialists of his generation to the fated heroes of Greek epic and tragedy, to the early Christian martyrs, and to the most fervent of the Protestant reformers, Sorel applauds their strict discipline, their sectarian aloofness from the society around them, their fear of contamination by it, and their

readiness to tear it down for the sake of a new order, the historical triumph of which they hold to be inevitable. From a motivational point
of view, myth is indispensable, because it forms a whole way of life. "A
myth," declares Sorel, is what "gives to socialism such high moral value
and such great sincerity" (p. 46).

Opposing the "prejudices against violence," Sorel argues that "in
the new [economic] state of things, political crime is an act of simple
revolt which cannot carry with it disgrace of any kind" (p. 111). The
memory of past revolutions, including "the adventures . . . of Joan of
Arc," assumes "epical" force for incipient radicals if, and only if, they
can view those historical actions as "reproducible in a near future"
(p. 102).[24] A viable "myth," according to Sorel, "must be judged as a
means of acting on the present" (p. 126).

Joan of Arc as Oedipus

Sorel's "epical" ethics has its aesthetic counterpart in the "epic theatre"
of Bertolt Brecht, even as Marx's Oedipal myth finds a Jehannine expression there. Representing Joan of Arc as Oedipus allows Brecht
both to identify himself with her as a seeker for truth and an agent of
revolution and to sacrifice her as guilty for crimes committed unwit-
tingly, as a result of her complicity in the status quo. In the Marxist
plays about Joan, she is always in some sense guilty; her death, always
necessary. This assertion holds true even in those plays that allow her
a posthumous victory.

Bertolt Brecht's *Saint Joan of the Stockyards* (*Die heilige Johanna
der Schlachthöfe*) clearly demonstrates the direct link between the Oedipus of Greek mythology and the Marxist Joan. Composed between
1929 and 1931, the play may best be understood as Brecht's response
to a performance in Berlin in January 1929 of Sophocles' *Oedipus Rex*,
in which Helene Weigel, whom Brecht was soon to marry, played the
part of Jocasta's maidservant. In an article of February 1, 1929, written for the *Berliner Börsen-Courier*, an exultant Brecht celebrates the
experimental directions in German theater that are leading it into a
philosophical future. This movement, Brecht declares, "does not run
straight. Sometimes . . . it is so swift that it goes through several stages
in a single year. The last of these seems to be *Oedipus*."[25] Countering the
traditional, Aristotelian presupposition of the spectator's emotional

identification with Oedipus and Jocasta, the performance strove instead to alienate the audience from the protagonists and to forestall empathy for them, so that, as Brecht notes, the dramatic " 'experience,' if it comes from anywhere, comes from the philosophical realm."[26]

At the same time that Brecht praises the *Oedipus* of 1929, he calls attention to its shortcomings. The audience, disposed toward an older, emotionally cathartic mode of reception, generally refused to distance itself coolly from the tragic hero and thus "failed to take part in the moral decisions of which the plot is made up."[27] The performance, in fact, was innovative in inviting and urging the audience to see the tragedy as far from inevitable:

> The theatre as we know it shows the structure of society (represented on the stage) as incapable of being influenced by society (in the auditorium). Oedipus, who offended against certain principles underlying the society of his time, is executed: the gods see to that; they are beyond criticism. . . . Human sacrifices all around! Barbaric delights! We know that the barbarians have their art. Let us create another.[28]

Brecht aimed at creating a new sort of theater wherein the audience would consider in a detached way the fate of the hero and see it not as a matter of "inexorable fate" but of "human contriving" and thus capable of reversal.[29] If "in a performance of *Oedipus* one has for all practical purposes an audience full of little Oedipuses,"[30] the work of the producer is to avoid presenting Oedipus's fate as necessarily their own. If they are alienated from Oedipus, they can witness his blinding and expulsion, knowing that the story could and should end differently. Thus, "the theatre becomes a place for philosophers, and for such philosophers as not only wish to explain the world but . . . to change it."[31] Brecht imagines as his ideal audience Karl Marx himself: "This man Marx was the only spectator for my plays."[32]

To counter the tendency of the audience to identify emotionally with the hero, Brecht experimented with various alienating strategies in order to create an a-effect. In *Saint Joan of the Stockyards*, Brecht's answer to *Oedipus*, he retells the story of the medieval saint in the contemporary setting of the meatpacking plants in Chicago, where an idealistic girl named Joan Dark, a leader in the Salvation Army (here identified as the Black Straw Hats) works among the poor laborers. The various groups onstage sometimes speak in chorus, to emulate one of the "forms of alienation" that Brecht had discovered in Greek dramaturgy.[33] The capitalists typically speak in metered verse, reminiscent of Schiller's plays, whereas the workers speak in the freer rhythms of street talk. The novel subject matter itself contributes to the a-effect, for in *Saint Joan of the Stockyards* Brecht endeavors to present "money in the form of iambics," letting his plot be structured by cyclical changes in the stock market.[34]

Brecht's Joan Dark is a modern Oedipus. Her surname does not merely pun on the French appellation "D'arc," it also personifies her spiritual condition. Like Oedipus, Joan at first thinks that she sees reality as it is, only to discover in the end that she has been blind: "I was in the dark too long" (p. 75): "ich hab's zu lang nicht gewußt" (p. 60).[35] Confronted by the misery of the thousands of workers who have been laid off by the sudden closing of the factories, Joan seeks to know the real cause of this catastrophe: "Whose fault is all this? That's what I want to know" (p. 36): "Dann will ich aber wissen, wer an all dem schuld ist" (p. 20). When the Black Straw Hats try to stop her, discrediting the testimony of the poor as the lies of "gluttonous slackers," she repeats: "No, I want to know" (p. 36): "Nein, Ich will's wissen" (p. 20). At this point the Black Straw Hats speak a prophetic warning: "Then, Joan, your coming fate looks grim to us. / Keep out of earthly fights! / The meddler in a fight becomes a victim. / His purity swiftly perishes" (p. 37): "Dann sehen wir schwarz für dein weiteres Schicksal, Johanna. / Nicht misch dich in irdischen Zank. / Dem Zank verfällt, wer sich hineinmischt! / Seine Reinheit vergeht schnell" (p. 20). When Joan repeats for the third time "I want to know," she begins a quest like Oedipus's for the murderer who is the cause of the city's pestilence.

Asked whether she wishes to witness the conditions of the poor, she replies, "I want to see it" (p. 45): "Ich will ihn sehen" (p. 29). Later she temporarily loses sight of the poverty-stricken masses, whose utter misery is symbolically screened by the falling snow: "The very snow that kills them withdraws them / from every human eye. / How easily / I forgot what everyone gladly forgets" (p. 74): "Und dieser selbe Schnee, der sie umbringt, entzieht / Sie jedem menschlichen Aug. Daß ich so leicht / Vergessen hab, was jeder gern vergißt" (p. 58). Even as the rich are blind to the poor, the poor have been kept at a distance from the wealthy: "We never saw people like that before" (p. 61): "Solche Leute sahen wir nie sonst" (p. 46). Brecht's play brings these unseen realities into Joan's view and that of the audience.

Joan's Oedipal investigation into the secret, economic causes of things leads her to discover the manipulations of the capitalists and the collaborative role of organized religion, as represented in the Salvation Army, but in the end she finds the most blameworthy person to be herself. Paulus Snyder accuses her of pride—the tragic flaw of hubris—in her willful quest and expels her from the ranks of the Salvation Army: "Without any humility / You followed your first impulse!" (p. 75): "Ohne alle Demut bist du / Dem nächsten Trieb gefolgt!" (p. 61). Driven out by the Black Straw Hats because of her activism on behalf of the poor, Joan enters the no-man's-land of the peacemaker and probable scapegoat: "Go, thou celestial one / out in the rain and abide in righteousness in the blizzard!" (p. 76): "Jetzt geh, du Überirdische / Hinaus in den Regen und bleib rechthaberisch im Schneetreiben!" (p. 61).

Joan gradually learns the truth of Snyder's warning that the would-be mediator between opposed forces is destined to become a victim, useless to either side. First, she proves useless to the capitalist "meat king," Pierpont Mauler, who recognizes her genuine holiness and seeks from her a blessing on his greed and cruelty: "So you must work with us, and even if you make no sacrifices, which / we wouldn't ask of you anyhow, still approve the sacrifices" (pp. 81–82): "Darum müßt ihr / Mitmachen und wenn ihr schon nicht opfert, was / Wir auch nicht von euch wollen, so doch gutheißen die Opfer" (p. 67). Joan refuses to give the sacrificial approval Mauler seeks, even when he offers to donate money to the Salvation Army: "If the Black Straw Hats / accept your money, they are welcome to it, / but I will take my stand among the people / waiting in the yards" (p. 82): "Und wenn die S. S. Ihr Geld annehmen, so sollen sie's nur / Tun, aber ich geh von Ihnen weg hinaus zu diesen / Und will mich setzen zu den Wartenden auf die Schlachthöfe" (p. 67).

Then she proves useless to the workers when, in the midst of a riot, she fails to deliver a crucial message to Communist leaders. Rejecting the use of force (p. 98: "What's done by force cannot be good"), she becomes the weak link in the chain, the cause of the workers' defeat. When, hearing the reproachful voices of conscience, she recants her abjuration (p. 103: "I must turn back!"), it is too late. Joan can only die of pneumonia, confessing her guilt: "Speeches I made in every market-place / and dreams were past counting but / I did injury to the injured, / was useless to the injurers" (p. 119): "Aber geredet habe ich auf allen Märkten / Und der Träume waren unzählige, aber / Den Geschädigten war ich ein Schaden / Nützlich war ich den Schädigern" (pp. 103–104). The Leninist lesson she learned too late is the one Brecht wishes to teach his audience: "Only force helps where force rules, and only men help where men are" (p. 122): "Es hilft nur Gewalt, wo Gewalt herrscht und / Es helfen nur Menschen, wo Menschen sind" (p. 106).

When Joan dies at the age of twenty-five, Snyder eulogizes her as a saint "in the service of God, a fighter, and a sacrifice" (p. 122): "im Dienste Gottes, Streiterin und Opfer!" (p. 106). A brilliant parody of Schiller's *Maid of Orléans,* Brecht's closing scene shows Joan's lifeless body covered in tribute with the flags of the Salvation Army. Mauler and Snyder, the respective spokesmen for capitalism and religion, honor her departing spirit, naming Joan the holy victim of Faustian self-division and class conflict. Sharing in death the saint whom they both rejected in life as a criminal, capitalism and religion forge a deeper bond through the very one who sought to expose their culpability. She dies as a sacrificial substitute for themselves.

René Girard has argued that the persecutory texts of the Middle Ages—the records of trials, such as Saint Joan's, for heresy and witchcraft—enable us to read ancient myth as a canonical cover-up for the historical sacrifice of arbitrary victims, innocent persons, whom myth represents as guilty.[36] According to Girard, Oedipus the King stands as an archetype for all the victims sacrificed as scapegoats for the restoration of health and unity to disturbed communities. In refiguring the medieval, Christlike Joan as a mythic Oedipus, the Marxist artist works against this demythologizing trend to reverse it and to reassert the actual guilt of the saintly victim.

The sacrificial themes and images in *Saint Joan of the Stockyards* are powerful and overt in their linkage of myth, ritual, and tragedy to Marxist theory. Envisioning the world as a slaughterhouse, Brecht transforms the medieval Dauphin and his nobles into the "meat kings" of modern Chicago. At the top of the sacrificial system, "King" Mauler senses that the animals being killed are in some sense a substitute for himself: "Remember, Cridle, the steer, fair-haired and big / and dully gazing heavenward as he took / the blow I felt that it was meant for me" (p. 27): "Erinnere, Cridle, dich an jeden Ochsen / Der blond und groß und stumpf zum Himmel blickend / Den Streich empfing, mir war's, als gelt er mir" (p. 11). Haunted by the bellowing of the steers, Mauler, "the well-known meat king and philanthropist" (p. 29) ("dem bekannten Fleischkönig und Philanthropen" [p. 14]), withdraws from the glutted meat market in order to protect himself both morally and financially. (The convenience of a moralistic ideology, on the one hand, and of practical profiteering, on the other, is anything but subtle here.)

When the steers cease to be sacrificial substitutes for himself, Mauler elects a series of other victims in order to avert his downfall through theirs. "Cut-throat prices" (p. 28) become a sacrificial means, as do reductions in wages, layoffs, and the closing of factories. When seventy thousand workers lose their jobs, they lament, "Bloody Mauler grips / our exploiter by the throat and / we are the ones who croak!" (p. 30): "Der blutige Mauler hält / Unsere Ausbeuter am Hals und / Uns geht die Luft aus!" (p. 14). For his part, Mauler justifies the chain of victimage by ascribing guilt to the victims: "On oxen I take pity, man is wicked" (p. 44): "Mit Ochsen hab ich Mitleid, der Mensch ist schlecht" (p. 28).

When an outspoken Joan protests Mauler's actions, she echoes Deuteronomy 25:4, likening herself to an unmuzzled ox: "You / even muzzle the ox that's yoked to the thresher! / And so I speak" (p. 61): "Du sollst / Nicht einmal dem Ochsen, der da drischet, das Maul verbinden / Aber ich red doch" (p. 46). Later she warns the rich traders who exploit the poor: "Some day you may not be looked upon as human beings either, but as wild beasts that have to be slaughtered in the interest of public order and security!" (p. 75): "Da könnt es passieren, daß man euch auch nicht mehr als Menschen ansieht, sondern als wilde Tiere, die man einfach erschlagen muß im Interesse der öffentlichen Ordnung und Sicherheit!" (p. 60). Because she insists that "men shouldn't be treated as steers" (p. 75)—neither the workers nor the capitalists—she attempts to stand outside the sacrificial systems of capitalism and communism alike: "mit Menschen soll man nicht umgehen wie mit Ochsen" (p. 60).

In her mythic analysis of the sacrificial structures in capitalism, Joan identifies the original sin of Adam as a doe slaying. She imagines God intruding on Adam at the very moment when his arms are wet to the elbows with the blood of the beast he has slain: "Adam's standing behind a bush again, with his arms in a doe again" (p. 79): "Adam steht gerad wieder hinter einem Gesträuch und hat die Hände sozusagen wieder bis über die Ellenbogen in einer Hirschkuh" (p. 64). So, too, the godlike Joan seeks out the meat king, Mauler, who blushes on her unexpected arrival. As a latter-day Adam, Mauler has committed the original sin of killing a doe—a sin he repeats in the destruction of Joan herself, when she resists his seductions and refuses to "approve the sacrifices" (p. 82) he offers in order to preserve his kingship.

Perversely, not only Mauler the capitalist king but also Brecht the playwright doom Joan Dark. Her idealism results only in her own victimage and the immediate failure of the workers' revolt. She—not Mauler and not the workers—dies onstage as the solitary, real sacrifice of the play, the primary target of attack, the guiltiest of the guilty. Joan's crime is her idealism, her pacifism, her refusal to sacrifice the lives of other people. Only if all the Joans die on stage and in the audience can the final, forceful revolution come. The decision Brecht seeks from his auditors is the decision to kill the Joan in themselves, to refuse to be her—or rather, to avoid her fatal flaw not of pride but of nonviolence.

Offering a trenchant commentary on Brecht's *Saint Joan of the Stockyards*, a play that he calls "the central work of [Brecht's] dialectical theater," Theodor Adorno reiterates his often-quoted statement that "it is barbaric to write poetry after Auschwitz."[37] The barbarity of Brecht's art shows itself, according to Adorno, in turning "victims . . . into works of art, tossed out to be gobbled up by the world that did them in" (p. 88). Committed to a violent, Leninist revolution rather than a Socialist evolution, "the young Brecht . . . betrays the false courage of the intellectual who, out of despair about violence, shortsightedly goes over to a violent praxis of which he has every reason to be afraid" (p. 86). Brecht's "political flaws become artistic flaws," when an improbable plot too obviously serves his Marxist tenets and when "the process of aesthetic reduction . . . works against political truth" by oversimplifying it (pp. 86, 83, 82). By mythologizing Joan, Brecht "the anti-ideological writer paves the way for the degradation of his own doctrine to ideology" (p. 83). When Adorno complains that "the demeanor of [Brecht's] didactic drama recalls the American expression 'preaching to the saved'" (p. 84), Brecht's naive declaration that Marx was "the only spectator for [his] plays" assumes an ironic ring.[38]

Influence, Anxiety, and Sacrifice

Brecht aimed at the instruction of his audience, a goal he consciously shared with his great dramatic precursor, Friedrich Schiller (1759–1805). "According to Schiller," Brecht observes, "the theatre is supposed to be a moral institution. . . . The epic theater was likewise often objected to as moralizing too much."[39] Even as Schiller's dramaturgy was revolutionary in its own day in its bourgeois challenge to the feudal dukes, so too Brecht's Marxist theater opposed the sentimental dramaturgy of the twentieth century and its ideological reinforcement of capitalism. Brecht's parody of Schiller's *Die Jungfrau von Orleans* in *Saint Joan of the Stockyards* is usually taken either as his rude dismissal of Schiller and of German classical theater[40] or (more subtly and accurately) as his critique of the current, capitalist, ideological appropriation of Schiller's art.[41] Following Harold Bloom, I would argue that Brecht's simultaneous sacrifice of Joan Dark and of Schiller's *Jungfrau* is a swerving away from the literary father figure with whom Brecht both identified himself closely and vigorously competed. As Siegfried Puknat notes, "The intended irony of the photograph taken of Brecht posing as a 'new Schiller' in one of the poets' niches in the Augsburg Memorial Theatre . . . is softened" by the many scholarly observations, supported by Brecht's own words, of similarities between the two men as playwrights and aesthetic theorists.[42]

Brecht had, according to Peter Thomson, a "lifelong habit of allowing himself to be provoked into writing by the urge to counter another author's work."[43] He boasts, in fact, of his experience as a "copyist": "As a playwright I have copied the Japanese, Greek, and Elizabethan drama, . . . yet I have never felt my freedom restricted."[44] Brecht's twofold antidote for the Bloomian "anxiety of influence" would seem to have been a conscious cultivation of copying, of making "use of what has already been achieved, without of course stopping there," on the one hand; a predilection for authorial collaboration, on the other.[45] Embracing "a collective method drawing upon all possible experiences,"[46] Brecht rejected the role of the solitary author, choosing to work with such artists as Elisabeth Hauptmann (1897–1973), Margarete Steffin (1908–1941), and Ruth Berlau (1906–1974), among many others.

Brecht's collaboration may, however, have provoked rather than lessened his anxiety, for he seldom credited his coauthors duly. John

Fuegi has demonstrated that Elisabeth Hauptmann, in love with Brecht, was largely responsible for *Saint Joan of the Stockyards* and for other "Brecht" masterpieces written between 1925 and 1932 and again between 1945 and 1956. "Despite the fact that her work was vital to reshaping the modern stage," Fuegi laments, "there is no entry under her own name in the main reference works on the German or on world drama."[47] Hauptmann attempted suicide twice during Brecht's lifetime, the first time in April 1929, after he had casually announced his marriage to Helene Weigel.[48] In the death of Joan Dark, Brecht found an apt artistic expression for his own sacrifice of Hauptmann, his lover and closest collaborator, to whom he owed a tremendous debt, the extent of which he never acknowledged publicly. At the same time Hauptmann figured herself in the dying saint. Whose anxiety of influence, one wonders, was the greatest? That of Hauptmann, who devoted herself foolishly and helplessly to Brecht? Or that of Brecht, who callously stole from her?

In making Joan Dark a member of the Salvation Army, Hauptmann and Brecht were influenced by George Bernard Shaw's *Major Barbara* (1905) and, to a lesser extent, by his *Saint Joan* (1923). Shaw had read Marx's *Capital* (*Das Kapital*) enthusiastically in 1882–1883. A great fan of Shaw's, Brecht first saw a performance of *Saint Joan* in Berlin on October 14, 1924, two years before he began his own reading of Marx's *Capital*. On July 25, 1926, Brecht dimly recognized in Shaw a fellow Marxist (albeit of the Fabian sort): "I get the impression that a lot revolves for him round a particular theory of evolution."[49] In that same essay, in which Brecht gives "three heartfelt cheers for Shaw," he praises him for his "terrorist" humor, his conceitedness, and his rationality: "The reason why Shaw's own dramatic works dwarf those of his contemporaries is that they so unhesitatingly appeal to the reason."[50] Brecht, in short, saw in Shaw a fellow traveler and a kindred spirit.

Like Brecht, Shaw evinces through denial a considerable anxiety of influence over his treatment of Joan of Arc, the play for which he was awarded the Nobel Prize in literature in 1925. To Sydny C. Cockerell he wrote on February 27, 1924, about *Saint Joan:* "I am not inordinately proud of it. You see, it was very easy to write: the materials were there, and even the historical manufacture had been worked over by so many hands that I am only the author in the sense that Michael Angelo was the architect of St. Peter's."[51] To John Middleton Murry, Shaw writes in a radically different vein on May 1, 1924, to deny the influence of artistic predecessors and of Anatole France in particular:

> But all this about A. F. is nonsense. My Plutarch was the report of the trial and the rehabilitation: contemporary and largely verbatim. I took particular care not to read a word of anything else until the play was finished. Then I amused myself by looking through Anatole, Lang, and Mark Twain. . . . I owe absolutely nothing to anyone except Joan herself (to whom be the glory) and my own knack of dramatic reporting.[52]

In the first account given above, Shaw describes himself as a mere arranger of preexistent materials, building on the work of "many hands." In the second, he claims to have drawn only from the historical record, while he admits a certain anxiety and deliberate avoidance: "I took care not to read anything else." The suggestion that Joan herself inspired him was later developed by Shaw into a mythology of direct, divine inspiration: "'As I wrote,' he told Theatre Guild director Lawrence Langnor, 'she guided my hand, and the words came tumbling out at such a speed that my pen rushed across the paper, and I could barely write fast enough to put them down.'"[53]

Shaw admits to having read only Anatole France, Andrew Lang, and Mark Twain, but in his 1924 preface to *Saint Joan*, he mentions in addition the representations of Joan of Arc by Shakespeare, Schiller, and Voltaire and discusses the differences between their portrayals and his. His remarks on Schiller's play are particularly interesting, because of the emphatic denial of any influence: "We find Die Jungfrau von Orleans drowned in a witch's caldron of raging romance. Schiller's Joan has not a single point of contact with the real Joan, nor indeed with any mortal woman that ever walked the earth. There is really nothing to be said of his play but that it is not about Joan at all."[54] Similarly, he writes to René Viviani on March 13, 1924, that he has written his play as an act of justice and piety to defend Joan against the previous, outrageous treatments of her by Shakespeare, Schiller, Voltaire, and Anatole France.[55]

The discrepancies between and among these statements point to a real anxiety on Shaw's part about the roles, conscious and unconscious, played by others in the writing of *Saint Joan*. Not only the ghost of Joan herself weighs on him, but also the spirits of a burdensome list of departed precursors. Among these, I wish to call attention to the ghost of Schiller. Like Brecht, Shaw seems to have felt a special affinity to that great German playwright. On April 12, 1916, he wrote to Thomas Demetrius O'Bolger about a period of illness: "I was not alarmed; but I had always, from my boyhood, had an impression that 38 to 40 was a dangerous age for a man of genius, and that I should possibly die like Mozart, Schiller, and Mendelssohn at that crisis."[56] Writing to the same correspondent on June 28, 1922, he declared: "My health broke down very much as Goethe's and Schiller's did in midlife; and Schiller, you may remember, died."[57]

Shaw emphatically and defensively denies any possible likeness between his *Saint Joan* and Schiller's *Jungfrau*, which he erroneously describes as a "romance" rather than a "romantic tragedy." Perhaps Shaw honestly reports that he did not read (or reread?) Schiller's classic; perhaps he only knew of it in a secondhand fashion, from plot summaries. If so, it is amazing (1) that in Shaw's play, as in Schiller's, Joan appears as a genius, an agent of historical change within civilization; (2) that in both plays a guilty Joan is already justly condemned at the time of the coronation; and (3) that for both Schiller and Shaw Joan's judges are not villains but well-intentioned people, an extension of the play's own audience. Perhaps Shaw feared, and therefore denied, the ghost of Schiller, sensing what Benjamin Bennett has called the "chain of influences" connecting them.[58]

Viewed from this perspective, the controversial epilogue to Shaw's *Saint Joan* gains another level of meaning. The ghost of Joan returns and receives a fitting tribute on bent knee from Charles, Dunois, Warwick, Cauchon, and others, after a clerical gentleman reads the proclamation of Saint Joan's canonization, dated May 16, 1920. One by one, the same individuals who pay her reverence as a saint steal away, unable to answer "yes" to her question: "Shall I rise from the dead and come back to you a living woman?" (p. 158). From their point of view, the only good saint is a dead one. When Joan's own voice mingles with the ringing bells, it sounds in the ears of the audience, even as the voices of Saints Catherine, Margaret, and Michael had sounded in Joan's, to ask the troubling question with which the play ends: "O God that madest this beautiful earth, when will it be ready to receive Thy saints? How long, O Lord, how long?" (p. 159).

The saint can only return as a ghost to haunt the living; she cannot be resurrected. As Shaw understands it, canonization—both

ecclesiastical and literary—allows the precursors to haunt their followers but prevents them from threatening one's peaceful, here-and-
now existence. Those who disrupt the status quo must first be killed;
only after their death can they become a bond of cultural unity. Schiller,
Shakespeare, Lang, France, Twain, and Voltaire cannot come back, except as ghostly influences to be denied; Saint Joan cannot return, except as a direct inspiration for the genius of Shaw, who alone among
all authors on earth can claim to have told her story rightly.

Shaw's Saint Joan: *Judging Joan and Her Judges*

Shaw's *Saint Joan* is set in fifteenth-century France. In approaching his
subject matter, Shaw draws on Marxist discussions of the Middle Ages,
which characterize it as the age when the bourgeoisie, nascent in the
urban guilds, first arose to challenge the then-dominant feudal aristocracy. According to Friedrich Engels, the Church and the aristocracy
were so interdependent as institutions that "all the generally voiced
attacks against feudalism were above all attacks against the Church,
and all the social and political, revolutionary doctrines were necessarily at the same time and mainly theological heresies."[59] Because "the
existing social conditions had to be stripped of their halo of sanctity
before they could be attacked," revolutionary opposition to feudalism
"took the shape of mysticism, open heresy, or armed insurrection,
all depending on the conditions of the time."[60] In the case of Joan of
Arc, celebrated as a mystic, acknowledged as a battle leader, and condemned as a heretic, all three forms of opposition to feudalism may be
said to have coincided.

    Not surprisingly, therefore, the "real Joan" is for Shaw quintessen-
tially the foe of feudalism,[61] because her allegiance to the king, to the
people, and to France as a nation does not take the smaller dukedoms
into account. Already in the first scene of the play, Robert de Beaudricourt denies Joan's peasant, rural origins (as Shaw does in the preface), declaring: "She's a bourgeoise. . . . I know her class exactly" (I.i,
p. 55). Although Beaudricourt helps Joan at the start of her career, his
words portend the eventual conflict between the classes they represent
and, more immediately, Joan's betrayal by the lords—French, Burgundian, and English alike. He replies ominously to the steward's tale
of a spell on the hens, who have ceased to lay eggs: "That story's not

good enough for me. Robert de Beaudricourt burns witches" (I.i, p. 50). Frightened by Joan's use of the unusual, nationalistic terms "Englishmen" and "Frenchmen," a nobleman declares: "If this cant of serving their country once takes hold of them, goodbye to the authority of their feudal lords, and goodbye to the authority of the Church" (I.iv, p. 87).

Chief among the feudal aristocrats, Charles the Dauphin seeks at first to possess Joan as an ideological warrant for kingship: "My grandfather had a saint. . . . My poor father had two saints. . . . I will have my saint too" (I.ii, p. 67). Later he is eager to be rid of her, because she would subjugate even his authority to that of the God for whom she speaks. As Joan tells Beaudricourt: "It is the will of God that you do what He has put into my mind" (I.i, p. 53). Positing an economic basis for Joan's "two ideas," Warwick admits the fundamental identity of her nationalism and Protestantism. Her protest against feudalism manifests itself, he says, in the "protest of the individual soul against the interference of priest or peer between the private man and his God" (I.iv, pp. 98–99). For Shaw, Joan is "one of the first Protestant martyrs" ("Preface," p. 7), because she cannot have opposed feudalism without having departed from the Church's teaching through her insistence on an unmediated access to God's voice.

As a Marxist heroine, Shaw's Joan is problematic precisely because of this marked individualism of hers, which sets her apart from the aristocrats, on the one hand, and the poor masses, on the other.[62] As long as the people follow her enthusiastically, the French aristocrats favor her and the English fear her. Joan reminds Bluebeard and Dunois: "You locked the gates to keep me in; and it was the townsfolk and the common people that followed me, and forced the gate, and showed you the way to fight in earnest" (I.v, p. 108). Dunois correctly predicts, however, that she will act without a popular following, separating herself from the collective: "Up to now she has had the numbers on her side; and she has won. But I know Joan; and I see that some day she will go ahead when she has only ten men to do the work of a hundred. And then she will find that God is on the side of the big battalions" (I.v, p. 109). Lacking the support of the aristocrats, the blessing of the Church, and finally also the enthusiasm of the masses, Joan stands alone, sharing the loneliness of God. "I am alone on earth," she declares. "I have always been alone" (I.v, p. 112).

The aristocrats and Church leaders condemn Joan for her pride and predict her downfall precisely at the time of her triumph in Charles's coronation: "The old Greek tragedy is rising among us. It is the chastisement of hubris" (I.v, p. 106). Like Schiller's *Jungfrau,* which depicts Joan as a scapegoat, accused of pride and exiled from the city by the king, Shaw's *Saint Joan* describes her leaving the court of the newly crowned king as a lonely outcast, already marked for death: "I believed that you who now cast me out would be like strong towers to keep harm from me. But I am wiser now" (I.v, p. 112). Joan goes out to the common people to accept their cheers, but she knows that she will find a lasting place in their hearts only after her death: "If I go through the fire, I shall go through it to their hearts for ever and ever" (I.v, p. 112). Using the image of fire, as Schiller had used that of rain, as an image of purification, Shaw admits Joan's guiltiness as an untimely agent for societal change, even as he approves her enduring value as an icon for the modern world that has come into being through her victimage.

Shaw invokes Greek tragedy at the heart of his *Saint Joan.* In his preface to the play, he compares Joan to Socrates (p. 8), even as Schiller had likened her to Athena. Shaw probably also had Oedipus in mind in his characterization of Joan, because he strongly associates her with the sense of sight and the ability to solve the riddles of history. "She was," he writes, "what Francis Galton and other modern investigators of human faculty call a visualizer" ("Preface," p. 18). Shaw describes her as a genius possessing "an appetite for knowledge and power, . . . an appetite for evolution" ("Preface," p. 15). For Shaw, a saint is a special kind of genius, that is, someone who, "seeing farther and probing deeper than other people, has a different set of ethical valuations from theirs" ("Preface," p. 10). Joan of Arc was "a religious person" who "conceive[d] . . . herself to be the instrument of some [high] purpose in the universe" and of "the native power of evolution—that is, of a continual ascent in organization and power and life."[63]

Like Schiller before him, Shaw believed that the martyrdom of geniuses, heroes, and saints occurs because "their fellows hate mental giants" ("Preface," p. 9). As Dunois exclaims to Joan, "Do you expect stupid people to love you for shewing them up?" (I.v, p. 102). In their sight she is guilty, "blinded by a terrible pride and self-sufficiency" (I.vi, p. 132) and deceived by the voices that come "from [her] imagination" (I.i, p. 59).

Set apart from her contemporaries by her natural genius, marked as different from them, Joan is destined to be a scapegoat. Rejecting the "melodramatic legend of the wicked bishop and the entrapped maiden" ("Preface," p. 39), Shaw (like Henrik Ibsen, whom he greatly admires) seeks to tear away the ideological masks that "hide the unbearable face of the truth."[64] Joan was not judged and killed, according to Shaw, by wicked men. Rather, Joan was "burnt by normally innocent people in the energy of their righteousness" ("Preface," p. 43). Social tolerance for the remarkable and the handicapped alike weakens, Shaw asserts, depending "on the strain under which society is maintaining its cohesion" ("Preface," p. 36). At best, the legal system only slows down and partially regulates the victimage mechanism endemic to human society, whose very existence depends on intolerance. As the Inquisitor insists:

> Remember also that no court of law can be so cruel as the common people are to those whom they suspect of heresy. . . . Before the Holy Inquisition existed, . . . the unfortunate wretch suspected of heresy, perhaps quite ignorantly and unjustly, is stoned, torn in pieces, drowned, burned in his house with all his innocent children, without a trial, unshriven, unburied save as a dog is buried. (I.vi, p. 123)

In an intolerant society, the fate of outspoken, socially committed artists like Henrik Ibsen (1828–1906) and Shaw himself is likely to parallel that of Joan of Arc. Alluding to Ibsen's persecution by the public, Shaw writes: "Terrified . . . at the rending of the beautiful veil they and their poets have woven to hide the unbearable face of the truth," they "crucify him, burn him, . . . ostracize him, brand him as immoral, profligate, filthy, and appeal against him to the despised Philistines, specially idealized for the occasion as SOCIETY."[65]

In *Saint Joan* Shaw's mythological view of things places the "all" (feudal, Catholic) against the "one" (bourgeois, Protestant) in a conscious if unsuccessful attempt to expose and thus perhaps retard the victimage mechanism at work in all societies, including twentieth-century England. Haunted by the military trials during World War I of political dissidents such as Edith Cavell and Roger Casement, Shaw declares: "If Joan had to be dealt with by us in London she would be treated with no more toleration than Miss Sylvia Pankhurst, or the Peculiar People, or the parents who keep their children from the elementary school, or any of the others who cross the line we have to draw, rightly or wrongly, between the tolerable and the intolerable" ("Preface," p. 27). Feeling powerless to oppose the drawing of the lines that "we *have* to draw" (emphasis added), Shaw recognizes the victim as such but defensively makes the victimizers relatively innocent (as the maintainers of social order); the victim, relatively guilty (as a disturber of it). Echoing the biblical word of the High Priest in John 11:49–50, the Chaplain declares: "Let her perish. Let her burn. Let her not infect the whole flock. It is expedient that one woman die for the people" (I.iv, p. 100).

To a certain, unavoidable extent, Shaw argues, every society maintains itself in existence through sacrificing its avant-garde, its sages and saints, along with its lunatics and criminals. This guilt, he insists, should be owned and not displaced. In one of his religious speeches, Shaw declares: "I want to destroy the hope in every human soul that we could possibly shift our responsibility for guilt on any sacrifice whatever."[66] Therefore Shaw (in the words of Benjamin Bennett) "casts us as Joan's murderers," and he does so "for the same ultimate poetic reason Schiller casts us [as Joanna's and Maria Stuart's], to awaken us to the possibility of infusing even this terribly imperfect world with our own creative energy," our ability to shape a better one.[67]

But does Shaw succeed? Alick West complains that Shaw's social philosophy leads him to overemphasize the guiltiness of (the innocent) Joan, the (supposed) inevitability of her victimage, and the innocence of her (guilty) judges. When Shaw declares, "There are no villains in the piece" ("Preface," p. 43), he actually "ennobles the enemies of the people with that impartiality and justice with which bourgeois idealism always endows the State."[68] Shaw's artistic unmasking of the victimage mechanism then only renders it more operative than ever, licensing the multiplication of victims in societies under stress. Looking back to World War I, Shaw's *Saint Joan* of 1923 ominously prophesies the annihilation of millions of Jews and thousands of physically and mentally handicapped people, as well as religious and political opponents of Fascism. With the ovens of Auschwitz in mind, Shaw's paranomastic epigram assumes a horrible resonance: "The question raised by Joan's burning is a burning question still" ("Preface," p. 34).

A man of many contradictions, Shaw had a mixed reception in Hitler's Germany. Because of his Marxist and Stalinist leanings, his writings came under close scrutiny by the Nazis. Because of his intimate connections to the German Jewish intelligentsia of the Weimar Republic and his published protests against Nazi anti-Semitism and eugenics, he was denounced as an Irish Jew ("der irische Jude Shaw"). And yet, as Glenn R. Cuomo has thoroughly shown, "contrary to what would have been expected, Shaw's works fared exceptionally well in one of the most volatile cultural environments that ever existed."[69] Shaw enjoyed the "high-placed protection" of the Führer himself, who issued "no less than two edicts . . . on Shaw's behalf," and of Propaganda Minister Joseph Goebbels (p. 437). After September 1939 Shaw and Shakespeare were "the only two 'British' authors whose dramas were still tolerated in the Third Reich" (p. 445). In fact, more than merely tolerated, Shaw was actually celebrated as a canonical writer of the Reich. His plays were among those most frequently performed on German stages. According to Cuomo, "As late as 28 September 1943, the Propaganda Ministry still stressed the extreme importance the performance of Shaw's works had for the regime's cultural politics" (p. 450).

How is this to be explained? In part, as Cuomo demonstrates, the Nazis capitalized on Shaw's anti-British satires in their own propaganda against the English. They also made use of Shaw's occasional praise of Hitler as a strong leader and of his policies, especially the Hitler-Stalin pact. "A great deal of Shaw's writings," Cuomo notes, "were in fact quite compatible with the aims of the National Socialist regime" (p. 437), and his criticisms of it could be (and effectively were) ignored or suppressed.

Among Shaw's plays, *Saint Joan* (*Heilige Johanna*) was especially popular among the Nazis. In 1941 the Chemnitz Theater actually chose "to commemorate the eighth anniversary of Hitler's 30 January assumption of office" with its performance (p. 450). Cuomo suggests that what appealed to Goebbels and Hitler in *Heilige Johanna* was the focus on Joan as a heroine of the people ("Volk-martyr"); her willingness to do and to suffer everything for the victory of her "Führer," Charles; her criticism of the English and of Church leaders; and her outspoken nationalism.[70] I would add that Shaw's ambivalent exoneration of Joan's judges ("There are no villains in the piece") and his defense of her death at the stake as a sacrifice necessary for the good of fifteenth-century society offered indirect support to the Reich's own systematic victimage of Jews and dissidents and to its characteristic "banality of evil."[71]

Brecht's Visions of Simone Machard: *Reading "the Book" Wrong*

Brecht realized, much more clearly than Shaw, the ideological potential in the history of Joan of Arc. His *Visions of Simone Machard* (*Gesichte der Simone Machard*), written in collaboration with Lion Feuchtwanger in 1941–1942, answers to Shaw's depiction of Joan as a nationalist by showing the dangers and inadequacy of traditional patriotism in the face of global capitalism. Set in France in June 1940, *Visions* tells the story of a young girl, Simone Machard, who reads a book about Joan of Arc. She then has a series of visions of an angel, who directs her to beat the drum of resistance to the invading Nazis and their French collaborators. Never performed during Brecht's lifetime and oddly dismissed by Thomson as "the most conventional of Brecht's approaches to the Joan of Arc theme,"[72] it stands among the least known and most surreal of Brecht's works.

The book that Simone reads is meant to make her "the victim of a patriotic education" (to quote a phrase from Brecht's journal, dated May 28, 1943).[73] Never named by title or author, the book stands as an ideological tool of the wealthy innkeepers for whom Simone works. Scolding Simone for reading during her work hours, the Patron complains: "That's not what I gave you the book for" (p. 7): "Dazu habe ich das Buch nicht gegeben" (p. 1847).[74] He defends the educational value of the history, observing, "Our young people don't know what France means any longer" (p. 7): "Diese Jugend weiß ja nicht mehr, was Frankreich ist" (p. 1848). Obviously hoping that Simone will aspire to a Jehannine part, he remarks to Père Gustave: "God knows we could do with another Maid. . . . It could be her" (p. 7): "Weiß Gott, wir könnten eine Jungfrau von Orléans brauchen. . . . Sie könnte es sein" (p. 1848). Behind the Patron's back, Père Gustave mocks his hypocrisy: "How about that, Georges? Now even the scullery maid is to be re-educated to become the Maid of Orléans, just in her spare time of course" (p. 8): "Ist das zu schlagen, Georges? Jetzt soll noch das Abwaschmädchen zur Jungfrau von Orleans erzogen werden, natürlich nur in ihrer freien Zeit" (p. 1848).

The Patron apparently wants Simone to be patriotic by helping to defend his personal property from loss and destruction during the war. In the book Simone reads the often-repeated sentence: "France is the most beautiful country in the whole world" (p. 6): "Frankreich [ist] das schönste Land in der ganzen Welt" (p. 1846). To be patriotic, in the view of the Patron, is to protect the aesthetic beauty of France, even at the cost of passively welcoming the invaders and collaborating with them. When, therefore, Simone courageously commits sabotage, setting afire the Patron's store of hidden petrol lest it be given to the Germans, the Patron perversely sees her act of patriotism as a crime against France: "Oh, I see, it was my brickworks, but the crime was against the Germans. . . . You people are worse than the Germans" (pp. 46–47): "Ach so, es ist zwar meine Ziegelei, aber die Brandstiftung wandte sich gegen die Deutschen. . . . Ihr seid schlimmer als die Deutschen" (pp. 1891–1892).

At issue in Simone's act of sabotage and in her distribution of food from the inn's pantry to refugees is the right to private property in the face of a national threat. The patriots—Simone, her coworkers, the Mayor, and the masses of refugees—put the needs of the people first, whereas the wealthy continue to place private interests ahead of the nation's. The Mayor tells the innkeeper: "In times like these whatever we have belongs to France. My sons are at the front, so is [Simone's] brother. Not even our sons belong to us anymore" (p. 25): "In einer Zeit wie dieser ist unser aller Habe die Habe Frankreichs. Meine Söhne sind an der Front, und so ist ihr Bruder. Das heißt, daß nicht einmal unsere Söhne uns gehören!" (p. 1867). To which the outraged Patron exclaims: "So there's no more law and order? So private property has ceased to exist, has it?" (p. 25): "Also es gibt keine Ordnung mehr! Besitz hat aufgehört zu existieren, wie?" (p. 1867).

Brecht's imagination connects Joan of Arc's historical burning at the stake to Simone's act of arson and to the controversial "scorched earth" policy used by patriots against invaders. He notes in his journal on December 19, 1941: "our social circumstances are such that in wartime not only the ruled but also the rulers of the two hostile countries have common interests. the [sic] owners and the robbers stand shoulder to shoulder against those who do not recognize property—the patriots. this [sic] illuminates among other things the difficulty which a *scorched earth* policy must face in certain countries."[75] The wealthy French oppose what the patriots advocate.

In a scene depicting one of Simone's visions, Brecht links the historical division among medieval French dukedoms to the contemporary division between Frenchmen of different social classes. Just as the Maid in Simone's book is "sentenced by French judges and rightly so since she is French" (p. 51), Simone's greatest enemies turn out to be wealthy French collaborators with the Nazis. From the viewpoint of the Patron, the child "didn't read her book right" (p. 49), because she associates "France" with the common people of that country rather than its wealthy citizens: "Sie hat ihr Buch nicht gut gelesen" (p. 1894). Madame Soupeau, the Patron's mother, exclaims in exasperation: "Are you in the least aware who *is* France?" (p. 55): "Weißt du denn überhaupt, wer Frankreich ist?" (p. 1901). Later she grabs hold of Simone and shakes her: "Are you teaching us how to be patriotic? The Soupeaus have owned this hostelry for two hundred years. . . . *We* are France, do you get that?" (p. 61): "Willst du uns lehren, wie man patriotisch ist? Die Soupeaus haben diese Hostellerie seit 200 Jahren. . . . Wir sind Frankreich, verstanden?" (p. 1909).

When Simone is finally expelled, Madame Soupeau confiscates the book from her suitcase, declaring, "This is the hostelry's property" (p. 62): "Es gehört der Hostellerie" (p. 1910). When the Patron objects, saying, "I gave it to her," his mother observes sarcastically: "It didn't do her much good" (p. 62): "Es hat bei ihr nichts genützt" (p. 1910). Simone learns from the book to burn rather than to be burned.[76]

Simone's ability to read the book wrong, against its intended purpose, mirrors Brecht's own practice of copying the literary classics of the past while swerving away from them in the form of a contemporary retelling. Simone's ability to defamiliarize and alienate the history of Joan of Arc, to interpret it against the grain of the dominant ideology, depends on her childlike, wondering, and wonderful naïveté. Brecht consciously accompanied her childlikeness with an a-effect "by showing how the thirteen-year-old is sent out to work before her time and forced to do a grown-up's job, forced likewise to speak, think, and behave like an adult."[77] Her "painful inadequacies" in the face of the responsibilities placed on her; her wearing of clothes too big for her; her witnessing of inexplicable behavior, both in the historical reality and in her visions—all provoke and enable the involvement of the villagers (and the audience) in assisting her in what she cannot accomplish alone.[78]

Several entries in Brecht's journal indicate that he struggled with the problem of Simone's characterization. Unable to "motivate simone's [*sic*] patriotism," Brecht decided to make her a child.[79] But what child could fulfill the ideological function that Brecht's argument in the play required? Unwilling to let Simone's speech be dictated by her psychology, Brecht found himself unable "to formulate a single sentence for simone," to whom he wanted to ascribe a voice with "literary tones, . . . latinate tones, highly developed language treated sensuously."[80] When he sat down to write the first scene of the play, he found himself "with no picture of the principal part, simone."[81] Newly arrived in the United States, Brecht could not tailor the part for a specific actress of his acquaintance, as was his usual practice, and was left, according to James Lyon, "without a known model in mind."[82]

Reading Brecht's play about Simone Machard and her brother André, however, one cannot avoid the thought that Brecht indeed had in mind a "known model"—namely, the "Red Virgin," Simone Weil (1909–1943) and her older brother, André.[83] A Marxist and a Jew, Simone Weil went to Germany in 1932 "to try to understand on what the strength of Nazism rested."[84] There she attended meetings of the Communist Party, and she may also have attended plays.[85] Brecht may have met her in Berlin. In Paris in 1935 for the International Writers' Congress, Brecht also may have met Weil there. Like Weil, who involved herself in the Spanish Civil War in 1936–1937, Brecht called in 1937 "for solidarity with the Spanish people and armed intervention."[86] In 1937 Weil had the first of the profound mystical experiences that drew her to Christianity and that catalyzed within her a unique synthesis of Christian, Platonic, and Marxist thought. Even if Brecht did not know Weil personally, he almost certainly knew her writings, which appeared regularly in French leftist journals, such as *Libres Propos, La Révolution Prolétarienne,* and *L'Ecole Émancipée.* Weil and Brecht, moreover, moved in overlapping circles of friends and acquaintances. Weil had, for example, a famous quarrel with Georges Bataille (1897–1962),[87] who knew and assisted Brecht's Jewish friend, Walter Benjamin, during his tragic exile. A brilliant philosopher and a clumsy, pacifist fighter on the side of the downtrodden, Simone Weil possessed a saintly, patriotic spirit not unlike that of Brecht's selfless young heroine, Simone Machard.[88]

In Brecht's play, Simone sets fire to the store of gasoline by herself, but in the last scene, as she is being driven to her confinement in a mental hospital, she witnesses the burning of the town hall, which has been set afire by the villagers in protest of the Germans' occupation and in imitation of her own patriotism. Georges declares, "Simone will see the fire from the car" (p. 63) ("Da kann Simone vom Wagen aus das Feuer sehen" [p. 1911]), and the remark teaches the audience to see the blaze with her eyes and to spread it, in keeping with the angel's command to her to scorch the earth before the enemy's advance: "Whatever can't be burned has to be hidden. . . . / Go forth now and ravage!" (p. 37): "Was ihr nicht brennen könnt, sollt ihr verstecken. . . . Geh hin und zerstöre!" (pp. 1880–1881).

The reason that the people follow Simone is that she herself is guided by the voice of the people, in keeping with the proverb quoted by Brecht in his journal: "la voix de dieu est la voix du peuple."[89] From the point of view of the capitalists, French and German alike, "the people are the enemy" (p. 9) ("Das Volk ist der Feind" [p. 1850]), as Père Gustave attests. When Simone admits that the angel who appears to her resembles her soldier-brother André, whom she loves and for whose safety she fears, Madame Soupeau reviles him: "A real public-bar angel, a gutter seraph! In any case now we know where those 'Voices' come from. From the taverns and sewage farms" (p. 54): "Ein richtiger Weinschwemmenengel und Gossengabriel! Jedenfalls wissen wir jetzt, was es mit diesen 'Stimmen' auf sich hat. Sie kommen aus den Weinhäusern und hinter den Jauchegruben vor" (pp. 1900–1901).

In her dream-visions, Simone encounters not only the patriotic angel but also people from her own town, whose speech is sometimes French, sometimes an unknown dream-language (p. 21: "Okkal grisht burlap"), sometimes a combination of familiar and unfamiliar words and sounds: "Workers of unfurled, ignite!" (p. 18): "Arbeiter kaller Fender, befeinigt kei" (p. 1859). Composing a fictional French in actual German, Brecht plays with the layering and combining of languages to show the international dimension of the workers' movement. The prophetic status of the "vox populi" makes it sound at first like a Babel, then as a speaking in tongues that requires a commensurate gift of interpretation. (See 1 Corinthians 14:6–13.) Overhearing Simone's voices, the audience becomes involved in listening attentively to them too, in the hope of understanding them. The strange sanity of the charismatic voice of the people is confirmed in the political action it directs, even as the authoritative voice of the capitalists and the Church is aligned with madness when Simone is condemned for her good deeds to imprisonment in an insane asylum run by cruel nuns.

The dream-language Brecht employs in *The Visions of Simone Machard* may also serve as a metaphor for the linguistic and cultural frustration he felt during his exile in the United States. Brecht's decision to use dream sequences for four of the nine scenes of the play was an attempt on his part to achieve an alienation effect while appealing to a commonsensical American audience. A journal entry reads: "In a dream [a non-naturalistic style] at least has a naturalistic basis."[90] The play, however, went without a buyer either on Broadway or in Hollywood. Samuel Goldwyn read Brecht's play and admitted that he did not understand it. Feuchtwanger turned it into a less alienating and artistic novel, Goldwyn bought the film rights to it in early 1944, and Feuchtwanger gave Brecht two-fifths of the $50,000 that had been contracted.[91]

Hollywood, HUAC, and Hellman: The Un-American Joan

As it turns out, Goldwyn never made a movie based on Feutchwanger's novel, perhaps because French resistance to Nazi invaders was no longer topical. The theme of a modern, Marxist Joan of Arc retained its appeal for Hollywood, however. In 1948 Republic Pictures released Irving Pichel's *The Miracle of the Bells*, the screenplay that was based on Russell Janney's 1946 novel by the same title. Like Brecht's *Visions of Simone Machard* and Feuchtwanger's novel, *The Miracle of the Bells* features a youthful, contemporary heroine who becomes a latter-day Joan of Arc for poor workers oppressed by wealthy capitalists. Olga Treskovna (played by Alida Valli) is a girl from poverty-stricken Coaltown, Pennsylvania. She leaves her hometown with the dream of becoming a Hollywood star and thus a sign of hope to her people. When a famous European actress walks off in a huff, abandoning her starring role in a motion picture about Joan of Arc, Olga wins the part, which she performs brilliantly. Afflicted with the black lung disease common to coal miners, the beautiful Olga dies, immediately after filming the final scene of Joan's execution. *The Miracle of the Bells* begins after her death when press agent William Dunnigan (played by Fred MacMurray) accompanies her body back to Coaltown for burial in Saint Michael's Church, a poor parish where Father Paul (Frank Sinatra) serves as pastor.

Pichel's *Miracle of the Bells* follows Janney's novel closely. The major plot difference is that Janney's 1946 heroine does not play the Hollywood part of Joan of Arc but rather stars in a movie entitled *The Garden of the Soul*, about a girl who becomes a nun.[92] The overlong novel focuses on Dunnigan as a modern-day Saint Michael the Archangel, coming to the rescue of Olga and the townspeople, whereas the movie devotes equal or more attention to Olga as Saint Joan. Indeed, Janney's novel contains only two explicit mentions of Joan of Arc. When Father Paul inspects the supports in the basement of the church, in order to discover a natural explanation for the seemingly miraculous turning of the statues, he is interrupted not by the voice of Saint Michael but by the voice of Dunnigan: "It might have been some other saint sent by Heaven, as the Voices were sent to Joan of Arc! It was neither of these. It was a Broadway press agent."[93] Later, when Bishop O'Conner arrives on the scene in Coaltown, he invokes the example of Joan of Arc in order to encourage the young pastor to foster the people's faith in miracles instead of undermining it: "What blunders have sometimes been made of such things. The Maid of Orleans. . . . We burnt her, but the heart of the people knew even then. The voice of the people, Villon in his gutter, knew more surely than all our Hierarchies."[94]

Pichel's film expands on these passing references to Joan of Arc. In 1948 Pichel was certainly responding to and capitalizing on the popular cult of the Swedish actress Ingrid Bergman (1915–1982), who played the Maid of Lorraine in Victor Fleming's *Joan of Arc* (1948), after having starred in Maxwell Anderson's Broadway play, *Joan of Lorraine* (1946). As Hollywood recognized, a film about a historical heroine like Joan of Arc is never simply about her; it is also about the actress who plays her, becomes her. In 1948 Bergman was Joan; so was Olga Treskovna; so was Alida Valli playing Olga playing Ingrid playing Joan.[95]

Between 1946 and 1948, however, another event occurred to suggest the Hollywood part of Joan for Olga—namely, the summons of nineteen Hollywood leftists to appear before the House Committee on Un-American Activities (HUAC) in Washington, D.C. In September 1947 Bertolt Brecht was subpoenaed, along with eighteen others—screenwriters, producers, directors, actors—from Hollywood. The "unfriendly nineteen" included Irving Pichel, director of *The Miracle of the Bells*.[96] Brecht was the only alien resident among them and the only one to use a strategy of seeming cooperation with HUAC.

As James K. Lyon has shown, Brecht rehearsed his answers ahead of time and chose a cigar as a theatrical prop.[97] Employing a strategy he may have learned from the dream sequences of *The Visions of Simone Machard*, Brecht in his answers to the committee highlighted the related problems of translating from one language to another and of literary interpretation, in order to emphasize the possibility of reading a book wrong. Appearing before HUAC on October 30, Brecht directly denied membership in the Communist Party. When asked about revolutionary passages in his writings, Brecht skillfully misled his questioners while seeming to cooperate with them. Again and again he corrected the translations of his work or disavowed their accuracy: "No, I wrote a German poem, but that is very different from this."[98] At the end of an hour, Brecht was free to leave Washington, D.C. The following day he flew home to a postwar Europe, while a very different fate befell the "unfriendly" Hollywood witnesses who testified before Brecht, read prepared statements of protest, were cited for contempt of Congress, and served prison terms.

Janney's 1946 novel and Pichel's 1948 movie directly answer to HUAC's persecution of Hollywood by sacralizing its self-sacrificing actress-heroine, by associating real miracles with publicity stunts (e.g., the hired ringing of the church bells nonstop for four days), and by giving a savior's role to Hollywood (represented especially in the producer played by Lee J. Cobb). Whereas Marx couples the arts and religion as ideological superstructures useful in the maintenance of the dominant class, Janney and Pichel emphasize the transformative potential of the two. Although one Catholic pastor in Coaltown (Father Spinsky) accepts donations, such as a new organ, from the wealthy in return for preaching sermons to the miners "about working hard and being happy with your lot," the other priest (Father Paul) genuinely cares about improving the physical, economic, and spiritual conditions of the poor.[99] The debt-ridden parish under Father Paul's care becomes the place of socially transformative miracles, even as the pastor becomes the friend of actors and their agents. As the bishop in Janney's novel tells Father Paul, "The real Theater is like the Church—or should be—a source of guidance and wisdom and inspiration. I believe in the Theater. . . . I believe our America is morally sound and healthy and that most of the plays that last are good" (p. 301).

The Miracle of the Bells effects a strange synthesis of Marxist and American ("rags to riches") ideology: "Cinderella stuff always went, as Dunnigan well knew. It gave every girl in America a new hope" (p. 74). Its plot puts Hollywood on the side of the poor, immigrant coal miners; aligns its artists and entertainers with the masses of common laborers; and sets them against the wealthy mine owners, only to bring about finally a miraculous, rather than violent, change in Coaltown's living and working conditions. At the beginning of Janney's novel, the Breaker at the mines is a monstrous symbol of capitalism: "This Breaker, and the mines that fed it, devoured men also—men and children who were early put to work in them—took greedy toll of their strength each day while planting a dark, sinister imprint of life-bondage inside each human lung" (p. 4). The rich mine owners are quick to vilify "foreigners and Catholics" and to complain that "the working classes are getting entirely out of hand! . . . Socialism! Communism! Open anarchy next!" (pp. 412–413). By the end of the novel, however, the wealth has been voluntarily redistributed by the owners, who have had a change of heart. The sight of a thousand miners loudly singing a hymn and marching to Saint Michael's Church symbolizes their newfound hope, improved conditions, and human solidarity: "The fervor of fellowship—of man shoulder to shoulder with his fellow man. . . . The charity toward one's fellows. . . . The pulsing breath of comradeship that is more potent for good than a million solitary converts each locked in a selfish cell of righteousness" (p. 489). Such miracles are possible, Janney insists, "for this, thank God, is America" (p. 497).

It is hard to imagine two more different renditions of the latter-day, Marxist Joan of Arc than Brecht's *Visions of Simone Machard* and *The Miracle of the Bells*. Written within five years of each other in the atmosphere of America's Hollywood, the former is alien, surreal, German, and artistic; the latter, unabashedly American, sentimental, and naturalistic. Brecht's young visionary reads the story of Joan of Arc and learns from it to defend her country from Nazi invaders and French capitalists alike. The poor Coaltown orphan of Janney's novel and Pichel's film literally memorizes Joan's script and wins her stardom both in Hollywood and in Heaven, giving hope to all those who would rise to fame and prosperity. Whereas the "unfriendly eighteen" maintained that it was not necessarily "un-American" to be communist, given the constitutional freedoms of speech, Brecht could avoid the issue altogether, since no "non-American" can be "un-American."

Even as the capitalists and patriots in *The Visions of Simone Machard* were contesting the definitions of "France" and "Frenchmen," the congressmen of HUAC and the leftist artists of Hollywood and Broadway struggled during the Red scare of the McCarthy era over the ideological meaning of "America" and "American." Called before HUAC in 1952, the playwright Lillian Hellman invoked American values to justify her "un-American" refusal to answer questions concerning other people whom she regarded as innocent of wrongdoing: "I was raised in an old-fashioned American tradition, and there were certain homely things that were taught to me: to try to tell the truth, not to bear false witness, not to harm my neighbor, to be loyal to my country, and so on. . . . It is my belief that you will agree with these simple rules of human decency and will not expect me to violate the good American tradition from which they spring."[100] Forced to invoke the Fifth Amendment in order to avoid incriminating not herself but others, Hellman chose silence as a form of conscientious objection—a successful tactic that contributed to the eventual silencing of HUAC and the end of its questions.

Unlike her lover, Dashiell Hammett, who went to jail in 1951 for refusing to name contributors to the bail bond fund of the Civil Rights Congress, Hellman survived the HUAC investigation. According to Hellman, Hammett and she had different notions about the fate of prophets in society. Hammett understood scapegoating to be inevitable: "If you differ from society, no matter how many pieties they talk, they will punish you for disturbing them" (p. 49). Hellman, by contrast, naively believed "there could be no punishment for doing what [she] had been taught to do by teachers, books, American history"—namely, "to speak or act against what [she] thought was wrong or dangerous" (p. 49). Like Simone Machard, who read the book of French history and the story of Joan of Arc wrong, interpreting it against the interests of the ruling class, Hellman found a basis for her radical opposition to the congressional witch-hunt in her patriotic education.

Already at the time of her testimony before HUAC on May 21, 1952, Hellman seems to have had Joan of Arc in mind as a model for herself. Her reminiscences of that episode in *Scoundrel Time* (1976) highlight, at any rate, implicit parallels between herself and Joan. Lawyer Abe Fortas had had the "hunch," she recalls, "that the time had come, the perfect time, for somebody to take a moral position before these disgraceful congressional committees" (pp. 53–54). In her famous letter of May 19, 1952, to Rep. John S. Wood, chair of HUAC, she took that high moral ground of obedience to the inner voice of conscience, declaring: "I cannot and will not cut my conscience to fit this year's fashions" (p. 93). On the morning of her appearance before HUAC, her attorney Joseph Rauh had had second thoughts about that letter, telling Hellman:

"Thurman Arnold called me. He says that I am sending you straight to jail with the lettter we wrote. . . . His exact words were, 'You and Fortas are making a martyr of this woman'" (pp. 101–102).

Despite her fears, Hellman was prepared to take a martyr's part in the proceedings. *Scoundrel Time* records her psychosomatic trauma, her physical illness, her mental suffering, and her financial troubles during the time of the HUAC investigation and in the years immediately following. Like Joan of Arc, she endured a form of torture. Like Joan, too, she complains about the inaccuracy of the official court record of the proceedings: "I am convinced that . . . either the court stenographer missed some of what was said and filled it in later, or the documents were, in part, edited. Having read many examples of the work of court stenographers, I have never once seen a completely accurate report" (p. 107).[101] Unlike Joan, however, she had the assistance of shrewd legal counsel. Whereas Joan sometimes replied in a cheeky way to her judges and prosecutors, Hellman heeded Rauh's advice. "Almost everybody," he observed, "when they feel insulted by the Committee, makes a joke or acts smart-aleck. It's a kind of embarrassment. Don't do it" (p. 103).

In a striking passage in *Scoundrel Time*, Hellman recalls a quasi-miraculous intervention by an unknown voice:

> But in the middle of one of the questions about my past, something so remarkable happened that I am to this day convinced that the unknown gentleman who spoke had a great deal to do with the rest of my life. A voice from the press gallery had been for at least three or four minutes louder than the other voices. . . . The loud voice had been answered by a less loud voice, but no words could be distinguished. Suddenly a clear voice said, "Thank God somebody finally had the guts to do it."
>
> It is never wise to say that something is the best minute of your life, . . . but I still think that unknown voice made the words that helped to save me. (P. 109)

The repetition of the words "voice" and "voices," which appear six times in the passage; the reference to God; the salvific, transformative impact of the mysterious utterance—all work together to make Hellman's "voice" parallel to the heavenly Voices of Joan of Arc that instructed her to "answer bravely."[102]

The theatricality of her appearance before HUAC was evident to Hellman. In her memoirs she calls attention to the excited presence of the newspaper reporters, who formed an audience, and she observes that the congressmen "were to sit on a raised platform, the government having learned from the stage, or maybe the other way around" (p. 104).

In 1955, only three years after her hearing before HUAC, Hellman translated and adapted Jean Anouilh's *L'Alouette* to create *The Lark*. A Broadway hit with a run of 229 performances, *The Lark* featured Julie Harris as Joan of Arc, Christopher Plummer as Warwick, and music by Leonard Bernstein. It opened on November 17, 1955, to the enthusiastic praise of New York reviewers. William Wright notes: "The theme of a woman being coerced by the State to testify to things she was unwilling to say had a rather direct connection with Hellman's own experience at that time," but none of the reviewers mentioned that parallel, perhaps to spare the flamboyant, alcoholic Hellman, "who was no saint," from "charges of grandiosity."[103]

Carl Rollyson has listed some of the obvious biographical similarities between the Joan of *The Lark* and Hellman. They are both, he indicates, "down-to-earth" women.[104] Joan, like the playwright who adapts her, is "a patriot sharply critical of her own country, but profoundly loyal" (p. 355). A "vulnerable" heroine, Joan, like Hellman before HUAC, is afraid, but she acts bravely nonetheless (p. 356). Joan's judges and prosecutors display "the crazed, almost prurient interests" of investigative committees like HUAC (p. 356). The English "intelligence service," to which the earl of Warwick refers,[105] stands as a medieval "precursor of the national security state put into business by Truman at the end of the war" (p. 356).

Finally, and most important, Joan's loyalty to herself, her ideals, and convictions stands as a model for Hellman's own moral integrity. To HUAC Hellman had written, "I am most willing to answer all questions about myself. I have nothing to hide from your Committee and there is nothing in my life of which I am ashamed."[106] Similarly, Hellman's Joan twice repeats: "But what I am, I will not denounce. What I have done, I will not deny" (*The Lark*, pp. 590–591). Answering to the questions of the congressmen, Hellman had heard an "unknown voice" declaring: "Thank God somebody had the guts to do it."[107] In the play Warwick hears Joan herself singing as a lark: "The unknown, the unguessed—God, if that's the way you believe. The girl was a lark in the skies of France, high over the heads of her soldiers, singing a joyous, crazy song of courage" (*The Lark*, p. 580). Doomed by her own courage, Hellman's Joan momentarily commits the "great sin" of being untrue to herself: "I still believe in all that I did, and yet I swore against it" (*The Lark*, p. 599). Of this sin, she repents. Unlike the Joan of history, who died crying out the name of Jesus, Hellman's Joan dies silent at the stake with her head held high—silent like Hellman, who invoked the Fifth Amendment: "I must not answer."[108]

Hellman's *Lark* ends, however, not with Joan's execution, but with a reenactment of "her happiest day" (*The Lark*, p. 601), the day on which she witnessed the solemn coronation of Charles VII in the cathedral at Rheims. To conclude with her death at the stake would be to falsify her life, because, as Ladvenu insists, "The true story of Joan is not the hideous agony of a girl tied to a burning stake. She will stand forever for the glory that can be" (*The Lark*, p. 601). Whereas Brecht's *Saint Joan of the Stockyards* and Shaw's *Saint Joan* end with satiric representations of Joan's posthumous canonization, Hellman's *Lark* moves backward in time to remember the royal crowning of Charles as a metaphor for Joan's own crowning glory as a saint. The substitution of a political crown for an ecclesiastical one underscores Joan's patriotism and this-worldly involvement. The curtain falls as the chorus sings the "Gloria" of the Mass in grateful celebration of Joan's victory for France. "I wanted [Charles] crowned because I wanted my country back," Joan explains. "And God gave it to us on this Coronation Day. Let's end with it, please, if nobody would mind" (*The Lark*, p. 602).

The various endings of the Marxist stories of Joan of Arc are significant in their ideological statements. *Saint Joan of the Stockyards* and *Saint Joan* are consciously anti-ideological plays that try to rob Joan of any halos that capitalism and the institutional Church would give to her to secure their own societal dominance. In so doing, the arguments of the plays imitate, continue, and fulfill in modern times the revolutionary work that Joan left unfinished, validating in the process the historical charges of pride, disobedience, subversion, and heresy that were leveled against her long ago. The anti-ideological, Marxist ideology of Brecht and Shaw incorporates the story of Joan of Arc into its own sacrificial mythology as the tragedy of an idealistic outsider, whose vision exceeded that of her contemporaries but who grew wise—that is, became a conscious proto-Marxist—too late to save herself but not too late to galvanize others.

Brecht's *Visions of Simone Machard* illustrates the double ideological potential of Joan of Arc—the capitalists using the book of Joan's history to teach a patriotism of property rights, the true patriots learning from it the necessity of sacrificing private ownership for the good of the nation. Simone Machard becomes another Joan, sacrificed by the Nazis and their French collaborators, but she succeeds in the end in inspiring others to spread the fire that she set when she, as a solitary resister, ignited the hidden store of gasoline. That final blaze at the hands of the refugees is her glory and her hope.

The most hopeful endings of the Joan of Arc story are those related by Janney and Pichel in *The Miracle of the Bells* and by Hellman in *The Lark*. Placed on the defensive by HUAC, their patriotism called into question, these three artists—a novelist, a producer, and a playwright—resisted sacrifice (their own and that of others) by answering ideology with ideology and celebrating a peculiarly American brand of Marxism. For them, Joan of Arc stands as a symbol of common decency, democracy, hard work, equal opportunity, freedom of expression, human dignity, and love of country. Marxist ideology found a mask for itself in Joan of Arc, as did Nazism, but only in America, the home of Hollywood and Broadway, could Joan be both a rags-to-riches capitalist and a would-be communist at the same time. In the United States that ideological miracle can occur, and for that reason the last sentence of Janney's *Miracle of the Bells* declares: "This, thank God, is America."[109]

*She must be thought of as a girl. Our understanding of her must always
be enclosed in the envelope of her age and gender.*
——MARY GORDON

She was the sort of woman that wants to lead a man's life.
——GEORGE BERNARD SHAW

She was not even a man. . . . She was a girl dressed up.
——VITA SACKVILLE-WEST

If Jeanne is neither a girl nor a boy, then she must be an angel.
——MICHEL TOURNIER

CHAPTER FIVE

THE JOAN OF GENDER

Shaw, Sackville-West, Woolf, and Tournier

For the nineteenth-century writers about Joan of Arc—Robert Southey, Friedrich Schiller, Jules Michelet, and Mark Twain—Joan's wearing of man's armor had been a matter of relatively little interest, for they saw her as a definitively feminine heroine, whose beauty and virginity were protectively and temporarily sheathed in steel. For twentieth-century authors, by contrast, Joan's transvestism is a key issue, even as it was for her judges at Rouen in 1431.

Given the scriptural mandate against cross-dressing in Deuteronomy 22:5 and Saint Paul's opposition to the cutting of women's hair (1 Corinthians 11:6), the judges questioned Joan repeatedly about her motive for wearing masculine attire, wondering at whose command or suggestion and for what reasons she did so. As Susan Crane, Valerie R. Hotchkiss, and Susan Schibanoff have noted, Joan's practice did not match that of the woman saints who had disguised themselves so completely that they passed as men.[1] Instead, the cross-dressing that Hotchkiss terms "Jeanne's trademark" distanced Joan "from her sex without concealing it": "The male clothing set her apart from other women, whereas her transparent femininity distinguished her from the men with whom she fought."[2] To be sure, Joan's male clothes helped to protect her and to enable her soldierly work on the battlefield, but those benefits alone do not explain her practice, for Joan also wore them elsewhere—at court, for example. When questioned, Joan sometimes offered practical, self-protective, and instrumental explanations for her transvestism, but she also pleaded the necessity of obeying her Voices.

For Joan's medieval and modern judges alike, her dressing as a man had one of two possible functions. Her jurors at Poitiers in 1429, on the one hand, accepted it provisionally as a sacramental sign of her special, virginal vocation from God as a warrior maiden and thus (as Hotchkiss phrases it) of Joan's "transcendence and uniqueness."[3] Her judges at Rouen in 1431, on the other hand, rejected it as a blasphemous offense against God, the Creator of two different sexes, male and female, because it fashioned an androgynous self-identity for Joan with a hetero- and homosexual potential. For both juries, Joan's chosen garb was problematic and required interpretation. Taking their bearings from psychology and sociology rather than theology, Joan's modern critics tend to side with the medieval judges at Rouen, concluding, as Crane does, that "Joan's transvestism refers to her sexuality as well as to her campaign to save France."[4] It has something, rather than nothing, to do with her very identity as a gendered person. Depending on where the accent falls in these discussions, the outward sign of Joan's cross-dressing corresponds to the inward reality of grace, of gender, or of sexuality.

As a false man and an unwomanly woman, Joan was guilty, in the eyes of the medieval judges who condemned her, of idolatry, because of the misdirected worship she inspired from others and rendered to her saints and Voices. Schibanoff observes: "With what would soon become a fatal symmetry, Joan's visible idolatry, her attire, had been synchronized with her invisible idolatry, her visions."[5] As a mix of the two genders, masculine and feminine, Joan similarly became, in the opinion of the moderns, the quintessential androgyne and creative author of fictions.

Both Joan's historical condemners and her modernist admirers thus mythologize her. At Rouen she was condemned for heresy and idolatry, charges that link her to pagan belief, cultic practice, and mythology. In the twentieth century that same mythologized Joan is not condemned but rather praised as a new Narcissus, a mythic model for feminist warriors, same-sex lovers, androgynous artists, and heroic suicides. For the medievals and the moderns alike, the definition of Joan's gender provides a basis for determining her historical genre as a sinner or a saint and for choosing the literary genres most suited to the telling of her story.

Shaw's Engendering of Joan

In the published text of his *Saint Joan,* George Bernard Shaw (1856–1950) represents Joan's gendered double identity by employing two different genres: the "Preface" of 1924 and the chronicle play of 1923, for which the "Preface" prepares the reader. The "Preface" highlights the contemporary relevance of the story of Joan of Arc. According to Shaw, the historical Joan had two abnormalities: first, she heard Voices and saw visions; second, she dressed as a man and did manly things. Shaw does not relate these two qualities directly to each other; rather he connects them both to Joan's genius as an artistic agent of social and cultural change. In so doing, he made a significant contribution to the ongoing, modern conversation about gender and genius, a conversation in which Virginia Woolf (1882–1941), Vita Sackville-West (1892–1962), and Michel Tournier (b. 1924), among many others, were soon to make their voices heard.

Shaw discusses aspects of the gender of Joan of Arc under three different headings in his "Preface": "Joan the Original and Presumptuous," "Joan's Good Looks," and "Joan's Manliness and Militarism." Already in the first paragraph he calls attention to her masculine attire: "She was the pioneer of rational dressing for women, and, like Queen Christina of Sweden two centuries later, to say nothing of Catalina de Erauso and innumerable obscure heroines who have disguised themselves as men to serve as soldiers and sailors, she refused to accept the specific woman's lot, and dressed and fought and lived as men did."[6]

This first passage both raises and suppresses questions. If Joan was "the pioneer of rational dressing for women," then her transvestism would seem merely instrumental and practical, a "rational" anticipation of the wearing of slacks and trousers by modern women, including feminine and heterosexual women, in their professional work. In support of an instrumental interpretation, Shaw then compares Joan to both famous and obscure "heroines who have disguised themselves as men to serve as soldiers and sailors," without admitting that Joan's so-called disguise was not a disguise at all but rather a uniform or habit. It did not allow her to pass as a man and was never intended to do so. Joan was known to be a virginal woman, who called herself and was celebrated as "the Maid." Finally, Shaw emphasizes that Joan acted as she did by her own choice, willfully and rebelliously "refus[ing] to accept the specific woman's lot." Shaw represents Joan as an early feminist and overlooks entirely Joan's statements that she had excelled at womanly household tasks, such as weaving, and that she had dressed as a man not only for practical reasons but also out of obedience to God's command.

Later Shaw explicitly rejects as sufficient a purely self-protective motive for Joan's transvestism, noting that she "presented herself in her man's dress" even during times of peace, when she was at court and could have worn "feminine attire with perfect safety and obviously with greater propriety" ("Preface," p. 19). Unwilling to accept an orthodox, sacramental understanding of Joan's male clothing as a quasi-religious habit appropriate to her special vocation, Shaw sees it as Joan's personal expression of her gender as a manly, managerial woman. "Why did she . . . in every action repudiate the conventional character of a woman?" he asks. "The simple answer . . . is that she was the sort of woman that wants to lead a man's life" ("Preface," p. 20). The external and internal identities of the Shavian Joan are thus, as J. Ellen Gainor puts it, "of a piece: [her] physical appearance coincides with the essential gender orientation [she] feel[s]."[7]

Shaw's understanding of feminism minimizes the differences between the sexes while engendering the societal roles traditionally fulfilled by men and women as masculine and feminine. For him, woman is simply "the female of the human species, and not . . . a different kind of animal with specific charms and specific imbecilities" ("Preface," p. 11). Depending on her temperament and physical condition, a woman, in Shaw's view, could and should do masculine things, surpassing men in the process. Since Joan of Arc was "like most women of her hardy managing type" ("Preface," p. 11), she could and did lead men, inspiring their fear of her, reducing her sexual appeal to them, and thereby neutralizing her own sexuality. Men feared Joan, according to Shaw, not because of her numinosity as a saint or witch, but because of her bossiness. Joan "seemed neutral in the conflict of sex," Shaw writes, "because men were too much afraid of her to fall in love with her" ("Preface," p. 11).

Shaw clearly equates this sexual neutrality with a kind of androgyny well suited to the life of genius. Joan had a woman's body "in the bloom of youth, and was neither ugly, awkward, deformed, nor unpleasant in her person" ("Preface," p. 11). She combined this quite ordinary female body with a temperamental "craze for soldiering and the masculine life" ("Preface," p. 19). As a result, "she herself was not sexless," and "she never excluded the possibility of marriage for herself"; rather, she set marriage aside for the time being, vowing to remain a virgin as long as "she had something else to do" ("Preface," p. 11)— namely, saving France.

Whereas Shaw discovers a potential heterosexuality behind the veil of Joan's adolescent androgyny, Vita Sackville-West perceives a potential homosexuality or bisexuality. She does so, moreover, in answer to Shaw, whose "romantic" depiction of Joan she explicitly criticizes.[8] Although Sackville-West mentions Shaw by name only once in *Saint Joan of Arc* (1936), describing him as a "brilliant and trustworthy artist" (p. 12), her own interpretation of the fifteenth-century battle leader is clearly indebted to him. Following a prompt in Shaw's "Preface," she levels strong, sustained criticism against Anatole France as a biographer of Joan (pp. 12, 65, 90–91, 107, 110).[9] Like Shaw, Sackville-West compares Joan of Arc to Socrates (p. 331) and finds a possible, modern explanation for Joan's visions and Voices in Sir Francis Galton's theory of visualization (pp. 332–333). Most important, Sackville-West follows Shaw's lead in focusing attention on Joan's transvestism as a clue to her personality, gender, and (latent) sexuality.

Vita's (Auto)Biography of Saint Joan

When Vita Sackville-West picked up her pen in 1935 to begin writing a full-length, formal biography of Joan of Arc, she became the first notable woman writer after Christine de Pizan (ca. 1364–ca. 1431) to take Joan as her subject. Her *Saint Joan of Arc* is generally regarded (in the words of Nadia Margolis) as "the best English-language biography"[10] of the medieval heroine. As Karyn Z. Sproles has demonstrated, Sackville-West's biography of Joan is also in many respects an autobiography, for she foregrounds the intrusive "I" of the biographer, mediates between her modern audience and her historical subject, and suggests a host of connections between her own experience and Joan's.[11] In doing so, I argue, Sackville-West fashioned her (auto)biography of Joan of Arc as a conscious response to Virginia Woolf's *Orlando: A Biography* (1928), the classic picaresque that fictionalized Vita's life story, via a series of metamorphoses, across four centuries of English literary history.[12] Generally neglected by Woolf scholars, Sackville-West's *Saint Joan of Arc* has an important place in the ongoing, amorous, and literary dialogue between Vita and Virginia, looking back, on the one hand, to Sackville-West's *Aphra Behn* (1927) and Woolf's *Orlando* and forward, on the other, to Sackville-West's *Pepita* (1937) and Woolf's *Roger Fry: A Biography* (1940), a book that was published not long before Virginia's suicide on March 28, 1941.[13]

As is well known, Woolf wrote *Orlando* when her friendship with Sackville-West was still passionate, in order both to console her aristocratic lover for the loss of Knole, the ancestral estate that she had failed to inherit, and to chide her jealously for her recent affair with Mary Campbell. Woolf's second and greater purpose was to attempt a new, novelistic form of (auto)biography and literary history, in response not only to Sackville-West's biography of Aphra Behn and her family history, *Knole and the Sackvilles* (1922), but also to the interconnected biographies of Tennyson and Byron in Harold Nicolson's *Some People* (1927).

As Thomas S. W. Lewis has argued, "While the subject of *Orlando* had its genesis in Woolf's relationship with Vita Sackville-West, the method of *Orlando* had its genesis" in her reading of the book by Vita's husband, Harold Nicolson.[14] Commenting on Nicolson's *Some People* in a 1927 essay entitled "The New Biography," Woolf praises it for its attempt to combine "truth of fact and truth of fiction."[15] Since the sheer abundance and complexity of the facts encourages the modern biographer to select and arrange them in an artistic way, the biographer's art—to the extent that it is art and not mere craft—tends in the directions of the novelistic and the autobiographical. Aiming at the revelation of personality rather than the enumeration of notable deeds, "the biographer's imagination is always being stimulated to use the novelist's art of arrangement, suggestion, [and] dramatic effect to expound the private life."[16] At the same time, biographers shape the lives of their subjects to make them mirrors of their own. Thus, Nicolson "is as much the subject of his own irony and observation as [Tennyson and Byron] are. . . . Indeed, by the end of the book we realize that the figure which has been most completely and most subtly displayed is that of the author."[17]

In *Orlando*, Woolf pushed the conventions of the biographical genre as far as possible in the direction of the novelistic. Subtitled *A Biography*, *Orlando* is nevertheless frequently designated a "novel" in critical discussions, and the confusion of terms is a telling one. In its most obvious features, *Orlando* is fantastic, romantic, and novelistic. At another level, Woolf's dedication of the book to Vita Sackville-West and her use of illustrative photographs reveals a factual, historical, and truly biographical reference while concealing autobiographical allusions to herself. What Woolf says of Nicolson's subjects applies to her portrayal of Sackville-West in *Orlando*: "Each of the supposed subjects holds up in his or her bright diminishing mirror a different reflection" of the author.[18] *Orlando*'s hero/heroine is Vita and Virginia combined, and thus its perilous mirror becomes a vehicle for narcissism, her own and Vita's.

Sackville-West's immediate response to *Orlando* is recorded in her letters to Woolf. On October 11, 1927, Vita wrote to accept Virginia's proposed portrayal of her: "My God, Virginia, if ever I was thrilled and terrified it is at the prospect of being projected into the shape of Orlando. . . . You have my full permission. Only I think that having drawn and quartered me, unwound and retwisted me, or whatever it is that you intend to do, you ought to dedicate it to your victim."[19] Vita actively cooperated in the production of *Orlando*, supplying Virginia with historical and biographical information, family portraits, and photographs of herself. On October 11, 1928, exactly one year after she had given her "full permission" to Virginia, Vita responded enthusiastically to the finished work: "It seems to me the loveliest, wisest, *richest* book that I have ever read. . . . Also, you have invented a new form of Narcissism—I confess—I am in love with Orlando—this is a complication I had not foreseen."[20]

Sackville-West's delayed response to Woolf's book came eight years later, after their friendship had cooled, in *Saint Joan of Arc*, the first of her biographies to appear after the publication of *Orlando: A Biography*. Whereas Woolf had dedicated *Orlando* to her lover and collaborator, Sackville-West, Sackville-West dedicated *Saint Joan of Arc* to Philippa, the daughter of her Catholic sister-in-law, Gwen St. Aubyn. If Vita's first response to *Orlando* had been a mixture of thrill and terror, with the accent on the thrill, her later reply focused attention on a medieval martyr who had been burned at the stake, rather than "drawn and quartered," but who was nonetheless a mirror of her own victimization. Sackville-West had been complimented by Woolf, yes, but also used by her. Canonized as a novelistic character by Woolf's literary masterpiece, Sackville-West turned to celebrate a recently canonized saint, Joan of Arc. In *Orlando* Woolf's narrator declares that "her ancestors"—that is, Orlando's and Vita's—"had none of them been saints or heroes, or great benefactors of the human race."[21] In *Saint Joan of Arc* Sackville-West imaginatively challenges that assertion to claim her own spiritual descent from the Maid of Orléans.

In *Orlando* Woolf describes at length the physical appearance of her hero, noting the shapely legs, the forehead and eyes, and accompanies these descriptions with reproductions of paintings and photographs. The biographer's task consists, the narrator declares, in describing the outward signs of the hero's looks and deeds: "From deed to deed, from glory to glory, from office to office he must go, his scribe following after" (*O*, p. 15). Debarred from the knowledge of the hero's inmost thoughts, Woolf's parodic biographer focuses on the external evidence of facts, clothing, and facial expression.

Whereas Woolf uses irony to address the limitations of the biographer indirectly, Sackville-West faces the problem directly. Again and again she emphasizes that outward appearances give us at best a very limited insight into the inward mystery of a personality, be it Charles VII, Joan of Arc, or anyone else: "Who really knows himself? Who can really know another? So, logically, if we fail to know ourselves or our contemporaries, how can we hope to know a person who lived five hundred years ago, and whose character we can reconstruct only from very inadequate . . . contemporary records?" (*SJA*, p.122). In direct contrast to Woolf's physical descriptions of Orlando, Sackville-West reports: "No contemporary portrait of Jeanne d'Arc is known to exist. . . . There is nothing to tell us what Jeanne d'Arc looked like" (*SJA*, p. 2). Nor do the posthumous portraits of Joan by artists and historians agree in their representation of her. Instead, a false, simplistic "double image" clearly emerges: "the image of Jeanne pensive and pastoral, or the image of Jeanne embattled and heroic" (*SJA*, p. 2).

Sackville-West aims to deconstruct this simple division of Jeanne's personality into separate spheres, arguing that Jeanne possessed "as queer a mixture of feminine and masculine attributes as ever relentlessly assaulted the enemy and then must cry on seeing him hurt" (*SJA*, p. 11). Among her feminine attributes, Sackville-West cites Jeanne's "richly decorative taste," her "womanly voice, and her ready tears" (*SJA*, pp. 10–11). Among the masculine ones, she numbers Jeanne's "severity" and "single-mindedness" (p. 10).

Emblematic of Jeanne's androgyny, as Sackville-West understands it, is her wearing of man's clothes. Throughout *Saint Joan of Arc,* Sackville-West calls attention to Jeanne's cross-dressing as a way of establishing a point of identification between herself and Jeanne. Sproles explains: "Joan represents what Sackville-West sees herself as— not as a woman passing as a man, as the outside world might occasionally see her, but as a woman in a man's clothes, masculine and feminine at once. . . . What Sackville-West sees when she looks at Joan is the ambiguity of her gender."[22]

The autobiographical account in *Portrait of a Marriage* reveals that Sackville-West frequently dressed (and passed) as a man named "Julian" during her lesbian affair with Violet Trefusis.[23] Sackville-West indirectly alludes to her own experience when she comments on the problem of measuring Jeanne's physical height: "The truth probably is that, although sufficiently tall for a woman, she probably looked much shorter when dressed as a man, a contention which may be personally endorsed by anyone who has ever seen *a tall woman in men's clothes*" (*SJA*, p. 5; emphasis added).

What causes continual wonderment for Sackville-West is that Jeanne's cross-dressing does not seem to have altered her fundamental identity to the same extent that her own wearing of a man's or a woman's clothes did. Joan of Arc remains fundamentally true to herself, no matter what she wears, whereas Sackville-West, who longs for a stable self, finds in her own life history the multiple selves represented in Woolf's Orlando, who had "a great variety of selves to call upon" (*O*, p. 309). In *Orlando* sex and gender changes abound, in correspondence with changes in clothing, but it remains unclear which of these metamorphoses cause the others. On the one hand, the clothes we wear "change our view of the world and the world's view of us" (*O*, p. 187);

on the other hand, "clothes are but a symbol of something hid deep beneath," of an inward disposition that dictates one's "choice of a woman's [or man's] dress and of a woman's [or man's] sex" (*O*, p. 188).

Part of the challenge Woolf had put to herself in *Orlando* was the problem of the biographical subject as both constantly changing and yet recognizably the same. When Orlando experiences the first of his sex and gender changes, Woolf's narrator observes: "Orlando had become a woman—there is no denying it. But in every other respect, Orlando remained precisely as he had been" (*O*, p. 138). At the end of *Orlando*, the hero/heroine, who has now become a twentieth-century woman, seeks to discover something unchanged in herself: "Yet, through all these changes, she had remained, she reflected, fundamentally the same" in temperament and interests (*O*, p. 237). Answering to this view of herself in Woolf's *Orlando*, Vita Sackville-West sought to portray herself not as a man who had become a woman but as a woman whose wearing of man's clothes highlighted masculine features in herself that were always already there, always a part of her self. Whereas *Orlando*'s picaresque narrative places the emphasis on what constantly changes, while admitting a minimal consistency in character, *Saint Joan of Arc* stresses what remains constant—namely, Jeanne's androgynous identity.[24]

If Jeanne's male attire stresses the masculine in her self, her dressing in a woman's clothes bears witness to her femininity. Sackville-West refers again and again to Jeanne's red dress, the traditional garb of peasant women in the Lorraine.[25] Before Jeanne left Baudricourt to ride with Jean de Metz and Bertrand de Poulengy to Chinon, she accepted the male clothes offered to her by de Metz. Sackville-West writes: "It is noteworthy, I think, that Jean de Metz should so quickly have turned to tackle the problem of her outward appearance, whether it should remain feminine or become masculine" (*SJA*, p. 86). In a footnote Sackville-West explains that his "apparent, instant preoccupation with her dress" may be less "noteworthy" when considered in the context of the accusations brought against Joan at Rouen (*SJA*, p. 87). The annotation, however, signals a self-consciousness on the part of Sackville-West, who finds Jeanne's change of clothes "noteworthy" for other reasons—her own practice of transvestism. Sackville-West's fascination with the redness of Jeanne's dress may well reflect another red dress that she vividly recalls in *Portrait of a Marriage*. There she writes of her first sexual attraction to Violet Trefusis: "She appealed to my unawakened senses; she wore, I recall, a dress of red velvet that was exactly the colour of a red rose."[26]

Like George Bernard Shaw, Sackville-West enumerates reasons why Jeanne's cross-dressing was a wise, practical choice, enabling her to perform her military duties and protecting her virginity. Unlike Shaw, however, Sackville-West does not see Jeanne as thereby rejecting the feminine in her self. Rather, her feminine character remains intact, even when she does a man's work. Sackville-West explicitly denies that Jeanne d'Arc was a "tomboy" and describes her instead as "a serious and aloof little girl" (SJA, p. 25). Sackville-West acknowledges that Jeanne's visionary spirit became "restive" and that she eventually came to find "the feminine occupation of spinning . . . scarcely adequate as a pastime" (SJA, p. 92). Even then, however, Jeanne used a maternal metaphor for her manly work: "She was, it must be remembered, impatient as a woman great with child" (SJA, p. 92). Noticing this metaphor of Jeanne's, Sackville-West—herself the mother of two sons—emphasizes that Saint Margaret, one of Jeanne's Voices, was the traditional patroness of pregnant mothers in labor (SJA, pp. 69, 82, 90–92).

Attempting a psychological explanation for Jeanne's androgyny, Sackville-West departs from the vast majority of Jehannine interpreters, who tend to stress the estrangement between Jeanne and her father, Jacques. Sackville-West argues instead for a unique closeness between father and daughter. "Poor Jacques d'Arc," Sackville-West exclaims. "He seems to have been endowed with his share of his daughter's gift of divinization" (SJA, p. 29). Commenting on her father's prophetic dream, Sackville-West suggests that "some curious sympathetic bond existed between Jeanne and her father, which . . . can only be explained by some sort of telepathic communication between them" (SJA, pp. 59–60). "Dreaming her unrevealed thoughts" (SJA, p. 60), the father is the daughter's second self, even as the daughter is the father's extended self. It was by listening attentively to her father, Sackville-West suggests, that Jeanne gained the knowledge that enabled her to recognize Baudricourt later on (SJA, p. 64).

Closely identified with her father, Jeanne possessed an adolescent androgyny that had, Sackville-West suggests, a homosexual as well as a heterosexual potential. Unlike other biographers of Jeanne d'Arc, Sackville-West calls emphatic attention to Jeanne's relationships with other women. Although Sackville-West is careful to deny any suspicion of immorality, she nevertheless finds it important to mention that

Hauviette, Jeanne's "most intimate friend from childhood," uses "the rather curious expression *jacuit amorose*" with reference to Jeanne, with whom she "slept . . . in her father's house," according to what was "a common custom, especially between girls who had made their first communion together" (*SJA*, p. 81). After Jeanne left Domremy to embark on her great mission to save France, she was regularly entrusted to the guardianship of women during those times when she was not at the front. At Bourges, for example, she slept "according to custom" with her hostess, Marguerite La Touroulde, with whom she also "went to church and to the public baths" (*SJA*, p. 227). During the months "between September 1429 and April 1430," Sackville-West notes, "a number of women pass across Jeanne's stage" (*SJA*, p. 232), among them, Marguerite La Touroulde, Catherine de la Rochelle, Héliote Poulnoir, La Pierronne, Saint Colette de Corbie, and (of course) Jeanne's attendant guides, Saints Catherine and Margaret.[27] Shortly after her capture at Compiègne, moreover, Jeanne "was put under the care of three women for whom she evidently conceived a great devotion"— namely, Jeanne de Luxembourg, Jeanne de Béthune, and Jeanne de Bar (*SJA*, p. 253).

Joan of Arc and Sackville-West both bedded with other women. Both dressed in men's clothes. These superficial commonalities, noted with so much interest by Jeanne's biographer, mark Sackville-West's persistent effort to find her own image in the mirror of the medieval martyr. Ever conscious of the spiritual and religious differences between the two, however, Sackville-West also uses the personae of the harlot and the biographer in a rhetorical attempt to narrow the gap separating herself from the saint.

Eschewing the frequent historical fallacy that makes Agnes Sorel a doublet of Joan of Arc,[28] Sackville-West turns instead to the figure of Alison Dumay, the ill-fated mistress of Joan's contemporary, Charles of Lorraine, in order to bridge the distance between "the harlot and the saint, the material and the spiritual" (*SJA*, p. 95). Sackville-West, Jeanne's aristocratic biographer, downplays Jeanne's sharp rebuke of Charles's marital infidelity. Instead, she expresses empathy for Alison, who suffered misfortune and disgrace when Charles died, likening her attachment to her wealth to Jeanne's love for France and God:

> Poor Alison Dumay. . . . Harlot though she was, our sympathy goes out as we imagine her losing her house, her furniture, her gold

and silver plate, her security, at one sweep. These things must have
meant so much to her—quite as much, in her own limited way, as
the salvation of France meant to Jeanne. . . . Judging each according to the capacity of each, there is very little difference in values.
(*SJA*, p. 95)

The anguish of the dispossessed Alison is for Sackville-West, herself dispossessed of her ancestral inheritance at Knole, analogous to the martyrdom of Jeanne d'Arc.

This angle of identification between Vita and Jeanne found a surprising sequel in *Pepita* (1937), Sackville-West's biography of her gypsy
Spanish grandmother. Ten days after the publication of *Saint Joan of
Arc,* Sackville-West discovered among the belongings of her deceased
mother the depositions of the Spanish witnesses taken before the Knole
succession case of 1910. According to Victoria Glendinning, she was
"'absolutely thrilled'" by these testimonies and declared, "They are exactly like the Jeanne d'Arc witnesses: all labourers and suchlike people,
living in a little village in Spain. . . . They are all people who knew
Pepita and her mother."[29] Linking the biographies of Pepita and Jeanne,
Sackville-West thus made of them a complex response to Woolf's *Orlando,* which narrates Sackville-West's life and family history under a
fictive veil. In Woolf's book, Orlando as a man had secretly married
"Rosina Pepita, a dancer, father unknown, but reputed a gypsy" (*O*,
p. 132). Whereas in Woolf's fiction Orlando as a woman triumphs in
court and retains her estate, in the biographies of Jeanne and Pepita
Sackville-West gives veiled expression to the injustice she had personally suffered.

The persona of the biographer, however, provides Sackville-West
with what is perhaps the most effective way to join her story to Jeanne's.
As Sackville-West understood, the work of the biographer, who follows imaginatively in the footsteps of her subject, naturally forges a
structure of sympathy and identification between the two. Sackville-
West made it a point to visit the important sites in the history of Jeanne
d'Arc in 1935, and her description of them places herself rhetorically
in Jeanne's position. "If Jeanne were to return to Domremy today,"
Sackville-West opines, "she would notice but little change in the features of the landscape" (*SJA*, p. 35). Alone in the nearby hermitage of
Our Lady of Bermont, where Jeanne d'Arc often prayed, Sackville-
West enters into that spiritual atmosphere: "Poor simple, deserted and

utterly countrified, it is a strangely moving place. . . . It is perhaps at Bermont, on a still afternoon, with no other company than the rabbits nibbling beside the gorse, that one comes closest to the spirit of Jeanne d'Arc and of the influences that made her" (*SJA*, pp. 48–49).

Musing about whether and to whom Jeanne may have revealed anything about her visions and Voices while still in Domremy, Sackville-West concludes that the girl must have confided in her confessor, "for, after all, he was a neighbour as well as a priest: they were all friends together" (*SJA*, p. 77). This fact, in turn, provides another point of convergence of her own life story and Jeanne's. Sackville-West interrupts her reporting to exclaim: "How queerly life turns out! How impossible that Jeanne, in spite of all her prescience, could have foreseen that I, trying in 1935 to interpret the facts of her existence from 1412 to 1428, should receive a visiting card from the Curé-Doyen de Domremy-la-Pucelle, Chanoine honoraire de Saint Dié et de Orléans, Chapelaine d'honneur de Jeanne d'Arc, téléphone Greux 7" (*SJA*, p. 77).

Later, when Sackville-West discusses Jeanne's rash attempt to escape from the tower at Beaurevoir, where she had been imprisoned, the biographer again occupies Jeanne's position, albeit with great discomfort: "Let anyone stand on a tower the height of Beaurevoir, and ask himself if he would care to throw himself over with any reasonable hope of not being smashed at the bottom" (*SJA*, p. 257). From the perilous height of Beaurevoir, Sackville-West contemplates the possible motives behind Jeanne's apparently self-destructive actions—not only her leap from the tower, but also her ultimate refusal at Rouen to renounce her male clothes and to deny the divine origin of her Voices. (Sackville-West's imagination is misleading here. The historical Joan did not in fact leap from the tower but rather used a rope of bedsheets to lower herself; the shortness of that rope required her to let go and to fall the rest of the way—a considerable distance—to the ground.)

Unable to penetrate the world of Jeanne's religious devotion and supernatural experience, Sackville-West reserves for herself the role of a respectful observer of Jeanne's words and actions. What she cannot do is either hear Jeanne's Voices with her or believe in the Maid's madness. With less conviction than Shaw's, she presents the available psychological explanations while implying their inadequacy. In the end, as Sproles asserts, "Sackville-West's identification with Joan of Arc . . . is disrupted by God."[30]

Better than any biographer, perhaps, the author of a saint's biography confronts and realizes the limitations of the genre, the inability of the biographer to penetrate the innermost, mystical experience of his or her subject. Woolf writes parodically in *Orlando*, using the third-person pronoun to speak in her chosen persona as "the biographer." Sackville-West, by contrast, writes in the first person to interject her serious, personal commentary on events in the life of Joan of Arc. Commenting on what Woolf had learned from Sackville-West's earlier biography, *Aphra Behn*, Sproles observes: "Both women were grappling with the problem of biographical representations of identity and sexuality," and both employed the rhetorical device of "an intrusive narrator who intervenes between the audience and the subject of the biography to triangulate a relationship that is otherwise susceptible to uncritical idealization."[31] Woolf learned about "the biographer" from Sackville-West's *Aphra Behn*, but Sackville-West in *Saint Joan of Arc* resisted Woolf's novelistic approach to biography, as manifested in *Orlando*, choosing instead to counter the (deceptive) objectivity of biography as a genre with the overt subjectivity of autobiography. She writes in *Saint Joan* about Joan of Arc but also about herself in the act of biographical investigation, reflection, and identification.

Whereas Woolf's novelistic biography begins with Orlando's boyhood during Elizabethan times, Sackville-West's formal biography begins with Joan's birth in the Middle Ages. Vita thus competes with Virginia to claim a different, older origin for her self, taking the first place that comes earlier in time. She also claims for herself a mastery of the factual material that is foundational to fiction. In so doing, she competes with Woolf for first place, if not as a novelist, then as a biographer—a challenge to which Woolf responds in turn in *Roger Fry*, the only formal biography in her oeuvre. Woolf began writing *Roger Fry* in 1935, when Sackville-West was writing *Saint Joan*.

Sproles faults Sackville-West for failing to learn from Woolf's artistic technique in *Orlando*, complaining that "in *Joan of Arc* Sackville-West does not demonstrate the flexible irony that gave her distance from her material."[32] Sproles thus joins Woolf herself in expressing dissatisfaction with Sackville-West's biography of the saint. Woolf wrote to Ethel Smyth on October 26, 1937, calling Sackville-West's *Saint Joan of Arc* "a schoolboys [*sic*] essay."[33] In a letter to Julian Bell, dated June 28, 1936, Woolf mingled halfhearted praise with criticism:

"Vita has produced a life of Joan of Arc; a solid, wordy, worthy work, in every way the opposite of Lytton [Strachey], of whom my opinion rises the more I read other peoples [*sic*] lives and essays."[34]

Vita's friends in the Bloomsbury circle objected to her *Saint Joan* on related artistic and personal grounds. An anxious letter of March 28, 1935, from Vita to Virginia shows that Ethel Smyth, for one, was upset by Vita's amorous relationship with Gwen St. Aubyn. Ethel had written to both Vita and Gwen, "saying that we were leading 'a rotten life'; and were not fit to write the life of Joan of Arc."[35] Vita's narrative strategy of sympathetic identification with Joan only served to heighten this objection, which demanded a moral, ethical, and religious likeness between the biographer and the saint. Victoria Glendinning explains: "What Vita's friends were really deploring was her absorption in topics for which they felt she was ill-suited and had only tackled because of the religious preoccupations of her sister-in-law," Gwen St. Aubyn.[36]

Virginia raised the issue of the appropriateness of Vita's chosen subject in a more complex way in a letter to her, dated June 29, 1936. There she jealously counters Vita's praise of Joan's virtues with her own praise of Vita's: "[H]ow angelically you behave to the Hogarth Press! Generous, humane, honourable. In Jeanne's time none of those qualities existed. . . . My perception or your perception is far finer than any 2 womens [*sic*] in 1456."[37] She opposes Vita's stammering confession of belief in God with the assertion of her own idolatry and that of others: "[T]he living belief is now in human beings."[38] Commenting implicitly on Vita's tendency to place herself imaginatively in Joan's position, Virginia contrasts Joan's love of bells with her own repulsion by them: "[T]he Rodmell church bells rouse in me nothing but antipathy to the Xtian religion—more especially as they set Miss Emery's dogs barking."[39]

"Was She Mad?": Virginia and the Maid

Virginia Woolf's attitude toward Joan of Arc is markedly ambivalent. Like Sackville-West, who traveled in 1935 with Gwen St. Aubyn through France to see Domremy, Orléans, and the other places most associated with the Maid,[40] Virginia twice visited Jehannine sites. Indeed, her pilgrimages preceded Vita's. In 1905, when Virginia was not yet fully recovered from the suicidal depression that had overwhelmed her after her father's death on February 22, 1904, she journeyed to Rouen. There the statue of Joan at the place of her martyrdom moved her to reflect (as James King reports) that "the brave woman had not found a sculptor worthy of her achievements."[41] Later, on April 27, 1931, Virginia and her husband, Leonard, visited the Château du Milieu at Chinon, where "Jeanne stood before the King."[42] Virginia's diary records that she visited "a stone crypt in which Joan lived" and "sat on the steps to hear two struck by the clock which has rung since the thirteenth century: what Joan heard. Rusty toned." The entry continues: "What did she think? Was she mad? A visionary coinciding with the right moment."[43]

The references to madness, visions, and voices are significant, given Woolf's own recurrent struggles with bipolar mental illness, in the throes of which she sometimes heard voices commanding her suicide.[44] "Madness" was a word Woolf applied to her condition, as did her friends. The question "Was she mad?" suggests a possible bond between Virginia and the Maid, a ground for their identification. In *A Room of One's Own* (1929), Woolf laments: "[N]othing is known about women before the eighteenth century. I have no model in my mind to turn this way or that."[45] She imagines that "any woman born with a great gift in the sixteenth century would certainly have gone crazed, shot herself, or ended her days in some lonely cottage outside the village, half witch, half wizard, feared and mocked at."[46] Had Woolf extended her historical vision to include the Middle Ages, she would surely have likened Joan of Arc to "Shakespeare's sister" and discovered in the outward sign of her masculine clothes a proof of her thesis that "a great mind is androgynous."[47]

Even as Woolf's portrayal of Sackville-West in *Orlando* is in part a self-portrait, so too Sackville-West's autobiographical biography of Joan of Arc veils a view of two different beloved, visionary women: Gwen St. Aubyn, whose religious piety laid claim to a personal mysticism, and Virginia Woolf, the literary artist. In *The Dark Island* (1934), a novel dedicated to St. Aubyn, Sackville-West depicts Gwen as Christina and imagines in the relationship between Christina and her friend Shirin what Suzanne Raitt describes as a blending of "lesbian feelings and mystic experiences."[48] In February 1935 Sackville-West accompanied her sister-in-law to the church where she was received as a Roman Catholic. That spiritual journey and the pilgrimage they made together to Jehannine sites in France found literary expression in Sackville-West's *Saint Joan of Arc* and in St. Aubyn's

Towards a Pattern (1940), an epistolary memoir in which St. Aubyn relates a mysterious vision of light that she had while sitting in the company of Sackville-West.[49]

Jealous of St. Aubyn, Woolf competed against her, seeking a different sort of identification with the Joan of Arc who so fascinated Sackville-West. Raitt has argued convincingly that *Saint Joan of Arc* inspired Woolf's autobiographical account of her own quasi-mystical experience. In an unpublished paper entitled "A Sketch of the Past," which Woolf delivered to the Memoir Club, a group of her close Bloomsbury friends, in 1939–1940, she relates her "highly sensual," childhood memory of a paradisiacal spot at St. Ives:

> The gardens gave off a murmur of bees; the apples were red and gold; there were also pink flowers; and grey and silver leaves. The buzz, the croon, the smell, all seemed to press voluptuously against some membrane; not to burst it; but to hum round one such rapture of pleasure that I stopped, smelt, looked. But again I cannot describe that rapture. It was rapture rather than ecstasy.[50]

This recollection of paradise and virginity ("all seemed to press voluptuously against some membrane") is immediately followed in her account by two disturbing memories that Woolf associates with a sense of shameful guilt. The first is suggestive of narcissism: "By standing on tiptoe I could see my face in the glass. When I was six or seven perhaps, I got into the habit of looking at my face in the glass. But I only did this when I was sure that I was alone. I was ashamed of it. A strong feeling of guilt seemed naturally attached to it."[51] Woolf explains this guilt in terms of her being a tomboy. Boyish, she was attracted by her own girlish beauty and yet ashamed to acknowledge it.

The second tells the story of her sexual abuse when she was "very small" by her older half brother, Gerald Duckworth, who molested her: "His hand explored my private parts too."[52] Gerald's attraction to her, which doubled her own fascination with the girl's beautiful face in the looking glass, produced a nightmarish disturbance: "I dreamt that I was looking in a glass when a horrible face—the face of an animal—suddenly showed over my shoulder."[53] After that dream, she could hardly bear to look at herself in a mirror and became increasingly disassociated from her own body: "This looking-glass shame has lasted all my life."[54]

According to Raitt, "Woolf's story, perhaps consciously (she had by this time read Sackville-West's biography), recalls Joan's rejection of the sexual, her repeated vaginal examinations, her first vision in the fields—or, in one account quoted by Sackville-West, in the garden—near her home."[55] Woolf offers indirect support to this idea of an identification between her and Joan when she declares that her experience of mystical beauty and instinctive shame "proves that Virginia Stephen was not born on the 25th January 1882, but was born many thousands of years ago."[56] Who indeed is "Virginia" if not "the Maid," born once again?

By Woolf's own admission, *Saint Joan of Arc* provoked her to thought: "Whats [sic] interesting [about *Saint Joan of Arc*] is the whole, however, not the parts. I keep speculating—which is what I enjoy most in all books: not themselves: what they make me think."[57] This remark echoes Sackville-West's comment about Joan: "She makes us think, and she makes us question" (*SJA*, p. 326).

At the end of *Saint Joan of Arc*, Sackville-West declares her personal creed, confessing her belief in "a mysterious central originating force" that one might name "God," and in a supernatural reality that is "one comprehensive, stupendous unity of which we comprehend but the smallest segment" (*SJA*, p. 327). This declaration seems to have prompted Woolf's articulation of her own mystic philosophy in "A Sketch of the Past." Subject to "sudden shocks" of insight, Woolf gains "a revelation of some order; it is a token of some real thing behind appearances; and I make it real by putting it into words. It is only by putting it into words that I make it whole. . . . It is the rapture I get when in writing I seem to be discovering what belongs to what."[58] What Sackville-West describes as a transcendent "unity," Woolf calls an artistic "pattern": "The whole world is a work of art. . . . But there is no Shakespeare, there is no Beethoven; certainly and emphatically there is no God; we are the words; we are the music; we are the thing itself."[59]

In the last years of her life, Woolf felt that she was losing this visionary insight into the whole, even as Joan of Arc had been deprived of the consolation of her visions and Voices in the months of defeat and captivity following the triumphant coronation of Charles VII at Rheims. On April 27, 1935, she wrote in her diary: "All desire to practice the art of a writer has completely left me. I . . . cannot curve my mind to the line of the book: no, nor of an article. Its [sic] not the writing but the architecting that strains."[60]

Woolf's friend Roger Fry had died on September 9, 1934, and she was working on his biography at the same time that Sackville-West was writing *Saint Joan of Arc*. Whereas Sackville-West completed her work in a year, Woolf spent five on *Roger Fry*.[61] As James King emphasizes, "*Roger Fry* was a book which tested its author severely."[62] Pressured to write a formal biography, Woolf found herself confined by the conventions of a genre that she personally disliked and overburdened by the many facts (some of them too troubling to be told) of Fry's life. As a biographer, moreover, she felt herself inferior to the workmanlike Sackville-West, whose affectionate, motherly regard she needed and by whom she felt abandoned. "The writing 'I' has vanished," Woolf admitted in June 1940 while correcting the proofs for *Roger Fry*. "No audience. No echo. Thats [*sic*] part of one's death."[63]

If *Saint Joan of Arc* is Sackville-West's answer to Woolf's *Orlando*, *Roger Fry* is Woolf's reply to Sackville-West's biography of the Maid. The ambivalence of that response becomes apparent when one reads Woolf's essay, "The Art of Biography." There Woolf compares two biographies by Lytton Strachey, *Queen Victoria* and *Elizabeth and Essex*, and confronts the paradox that the one that is a "triumphant success" as a biography is an artistic failure, a work not of art but of *technē*: "In the *Victoria* he treated biography as a craft; he submitted to its limitations."[64] The less successful biography, *Elizabeth and Essex*, by contrast, takes artistic liberties that are improper to the genre. In claiming that "the novelist is free; the biographer is tied,"[65] Woolf argues for the superiority of the genre at which she herself excels, even as she belittles the genre at which she falls short, calling it not art but craft. Building with the facts of life, working with what is by definition "perishable," the successful biographer necessarily creates a work that lacks the "enduring matter" of an artistic production; at the same time, however, the rough fragments of "true facts" are and remain at the very origins of art: "By telling us the true facts, . . . the biographer does more to stimulate the imagination than any poet or novelist, save the very greatest."[66]

Writing a formal biography forced Woolf to reconsider her earlier, novelistic one. Octavia Wilberforce's letter of March 22, 1941, to Elizabeth Robins records a conversation she had had with Woolf only a few days before her death. In it Woolf had asked Octavia whether she had read *Orlando*. Woolf went on to say: "Well that was a fantastic biography and *Roger Fry* is the other one I've attempted and both are failures. . . . I can't write. I've lost the art."[67]

Virginia Woolf drowned herself on March 28, 1941. Commenting on the manner of her death, King observes: "She carefully chose the time and circumstances of her death, very much in the manner of an artist imposing her will upon life."[68] At first sight, Woolf's lonely death by water offers the strongest possible contrast to Joan of Arc's martyrdom at the stake. One must remember, however, that Shaw's *Saint Joan* and Sackville-West's *Saint Joan of Arc* pointedly reopen the questions of madness and suicide that had been posed at Joan's historical trial in Rouen. Woolf must have wondered with Shaw, "Was Joan Suicidal?" ("Preface," p. 29).

Shaw answers "no" and "yes" to that question. For Shaw, Joan's risk taking—first when she rode onto the battlefield and later when she rashly attempted to escape from the prison tower at Beaurevoir Castle by leaping from it—cannot be considered suicidal, since her aim was not to take her own life. She signed the document of abjuration, moreover, out of fear for her life, in an effort to preserve it. But what of her decision to recant and to dress again in male clothes, knowing that her stubbornness would cost her her life? Rejecting a supernatural explanation for her Voices, which he understands to be the imaginative expression of her own genius, and seeking to exonerate Joan's judges, Shaw concludes that Joan willed to die rather than accept a life worse than death: "Her death was deliberately chosen as an alternative to life without liberty" ("Preface," p. 20). Retorting to her judges, Shaw's Joan declares: "You think that life is nothing but not being stone dead" (*Saint Joan*, I.vi, p. 137). After listing the natural sources of her inspiration— "the wind in the trees, the larks in the sunshine, the young lambs crying through the healthy frost, and the blessed blessed church bells" (*Saint Joan*, I.vi, p. 137)—Shaw's Joan insists: "Without these things I cannot live" (*Saint Joan*, I.vi, p. 138).

Reflecting on the question of Joan's possibly suicidal bent, Sackville-West both agrees and disagrees with Shaw. Noting that "the accusation of attempted suicide provid[ed] a point of considerable value in the eyes of the Church, which will not allow any human being, however wretched, the right to dispose of his own life" (*SJA*, p. 256), Sackville-West puzzles over Joan's sixty-foot jump from the tower at Beaurevoir, a leap that left her unconscious but from which she quickly recovered.

Like Shaw, Sackville-West dismisses the charge of a suicidal motive, insisting that Joan "was far too good a Catholic for that. Escape was all she thought of" (*SJA*, p. 256). Unlike Shaw, however, Sackville-West is reluctant to accept a purely natural, consequentialist explanation for Joan's recanting of her abjuration and donning anew of man's clothes. As Sackville-West sees it, Joan was aware that her words and actions carried a mortal penalty, but she spoke and acted as she did, not to choose death for herself, but rather in simple obedience to her Voices, choosing to be true to them and to herself whatever the cost.

Woolf's position on the question of what motives if any might justify suicide seems to have combined the possibilities outlined by Shaw and Sackville-West in their Jehannine meditations. In 1940–1941 England was bracing itself for an anticipated German invasion. According to Woolf's biographer, Herbert Marder, Virginia and Leonard Woolf first discussed a suicide pact on May 15, 1940: "As a Jew and a prominent socialist, Leonard would be singled out for particularly harsh treatment, and they agreed that suicide would be preferable to falling into Nazi hands."[69] June 5 found them discussing the question of suicide anew.[70] Reasoning from probable consequences, they had decided to kill themselves rather than be killed by the Nazis.

When Woolf drowned herself on March 28, she did so at a time when the Nazi invasion seemed imminent and when the world as she had known it was virtually ended. At the outbreak of World War I, a "steadily more feminist" Woolf had decried it, labeling it a "preposterous masculine fiction" and complaining to Margaret Llewelyn Davies that we are "without some vigorous young woman [Joan of Arc] pulling us together and marching through it."[71] The youthful Woolf was ready on January 23, 1916, the date of her letter to Davies, to don Joan's armor. In spring 1941, in the seeming defeat of a second world war, Woolf experienced the death of Joan of Arc within herself—a death she then realized in a lonely suicide by water, setting the self-chosen waves against the flames of execution.

Virginia's suicide notes to Leonard do not refer specifically to the war and the threatened Nazi invasion. In them she alludes instead to her internalization of the distressing atmosphere surrounding them: "Dearest, I feel certain that I am going mad again. . . . I begin to hear voices and cant [*sic*] concentrate. So I am doing what seems the best."[72] Even as Joan of Arc heard her Voices again during the night before she recanted, so too Woolf experienced the return of hers. Earlier Woolf's voices had urged her suicide; now she declares herself ready to obey them. At the same time, however, Woolf speaks of the falling silent of a different sort of voice, the voice of her inspiration as a writer. She complains of her inability to write even a proper suicide note: "I cant [sic] write this even, which shows I am right."[73] She goes on to beg Leonard: "Will you destroy all my papers."[74] For Woolf, the destruction of her papers, the laying down of her pen when she has lost the ability to write, is an ambivalent act, either an abjuration of an improper claim to authorship or a recanting of that abjuration through a refusal to write when, lacking the inspiration that once moved her, she no longer can.

Were the voices that urged Woolf's suicide similar to the Voices heard by Joan of Arc? Catholic orthodoxy shrinks in horror at such a comparison, emphasizing instead the contrast between the two. The much less orthodox Sackville-West also draws back from that abyss, defending Joan of Arc from any taint of mania. Like Shaw, however, Sackville-West cannot adequately explain the Voices that Joan heard. Lacking a religious faith, she draws support for Joan's sanity from the modern psychological research of Frederic Myers and Francis Galton, for whom "genius represents the supreme and ideal sanity, rather than the derangement of a hysterical or over-excitable mind" (SJA, p. 331). Judging by that definition alone, one might conclude that Virginia Woolf, who certainly possessed a writer's genius, chose the sanest of deaths in obedience to voices not unlike the ones that brought Joan of Arc to the stake. Conforming herself to the tragic pattern she perceived in the life of the Maid, Virginia found a way in the end to become the Jeanne about whom Vita wrote and whom she loved.

The Myths of Madness and Literary Influence

In their classic study of the psychohistory of women writers, *The Madwoman in the Attic*, Sandra M. Gilbert and Susan Gubar offer a feminist counterstatement to Harold Bloom's thesis that male authors, troubled by "anxiety of influence," are engaged in an Oedipal struggle with the great literary precursors who are their fathers in the realm of art. They argue that women writers in a patriarchal culture lack notable precursors and are troubled not by an "anxiety of influence" but rather by an "anxiety of authorship" that leads them to seek out female models for themselves rather than to struggle against them. This authorial anxiety forms, in fact, "one of the unique bonds that link women in what we might call the secret sisterhood of their literary subculture."[75]

What Gilbert and Gubar largely ignore is the "anxiety of influence" that exists within this secret sisterhood, in part because the scarcity of female models from the past makes the woman writer inordinately dependent on finding a contemporary female audience and living models—sisterly and maternal—for herself. More than the male author, who can look to the past to find some image of himself, the female artist needs a mirror in the present. If the myth of Oedipus presents a dangerous paradigm for men, the myth of Echo and Narcissus offers an equally threatening, sacrificial pattern for women.

The literal and metaphoric mirror in which Virginia Woolf beheld her own face became the reflecting pool in which the beautiful Narcissus, who was desired by men and women alike, saw and loved his own image. As a child she was guiltily attracted to the sight of herself in the mirror, until her desire found its horrible double in that of the half brother who molested her. After that, she could not bear to look into a mirror, until Vita Sackville-West helped her to see herself anew and differently. Louise DeSalvo notes that one measure of the positive effects of the friendship between the two women is that Virginia, "who so detested mirrors throughout her life, bought herself an antique mirror when she went to France with Vita" in September 1928.[76]

This antique mirror must be understood as symbolic, not only of a certain healing of Virginia's self-image, but also of a new development in her artistry. In 1927–1928, after all, Woolf first formulated her theoretical understanding of the "new biography" as a telling of other people's lives in a way that "mirrored" one's own and dared to compose such a biography in *Orlando*. She had just finished correcting the proofs for *Orlando* when on July 6, 1928, she had a vivid dream-encounter with the deceased novelist Katherine Mansfield, in whose image she best saw herself as a writer: "All last night I dreamt of Katherine Mansfield. . . . [S]he was lying on a sofa in a room high up, & a great many sad faced women were round her. Yet somehow I got the feel of her, & of her as if alive again."[77]

The ghostly apparition of Mansfield, who imparted her living spirit to Woolf, is significant in view of the rivalrous, sisterly relationship between the two writers. Woolf regularly visualized Mansfield after her death wearing a wreath on her head, the equivalent of the crowned poet's laurel.[78] When she first heard the news of Mansfield's death in January 1923, Woolf wrote in her diary:

> At that one feels—what? A shock of relief?—a rival the less? Then confusion at feeling so little—then gradually, blankness and disappointment; then a depression which I could not rouse myself from all that day. When I began to write, it seemed to me there was no point in writing. Katherine wont [sic] read it. Katherine's my rival no more. More generously I felt, But though I can do this better than she could, where is she, who could do what I cant [sic]![79]

With the passing of Mansfield, Woolf grieved the loss of a reader for her work, of an inspiring female model, and of a rival for artistic acclaim. Later, in 1927–1928, Woolf's friendship with another woman writer, Sackville-West, restored to her the sense of a vital contact with Mansfield, whose artistry she admired much more than she did Vita's.

And yet Sackville-West—biographer, novelist, poet—was also a mirror for Woolf, a sister, a friend, a mother, and an artistic rival. The cooling of Sackville-West's friendship brought with it a crippling enervation of Woolf's creative powers and of her will to live. Already on March 11, 1935, Woolf wrote in her diary: "I would here analyze my state of mind these past 4 months & account for the human emptiness by the defection of Vita; Roger's death; & no-one springing up to take their place; & a certain general slackening of letters and fame, owing to my writing nothing."[80]

When in 1935–1936 Sackville-West held up the (auto)biographical mirror of *Saint Joan of Arc*, Woolf saw in it not only Sackville-West's revoking of *Orlando* but also the sacrifice of her own person as a victim and madwoman. In a letter to Vita about *Saint Joan* on June 29, 1936, Woolf writes of discovering in Joan's story the tragic psychohistory of an artist: "I cant [sic] help thinking the general state of mind was so different from ours that voices, saints, came, not through God, but through a common psychology: why was everyone able to write poetry: to carve statues; paint pictures?"[81] Interpreting Joan of Arc as a visionary female artist betrayed by a patriarchal establishment and bereft of womanly companionship, and seeing herself in Jeanne, Virginia Woolf drowned herself, turning a saint's martyrdom into a suicide.

Woolf's psychological interpretation of Joan of Arc must be understood in the larger context of her ongoing reflections on Freudian psychoanalysis. The Hogarth Press had begun publishing the complete works of Sigmund Freud in English translation in 1924, but Woolf did not personally meet "the great Freud" until January 28, 1939, when the Woolfs had tea with him in Maresfield Gardens, Hampstead.[82] On that occasion Freud "ceremoniously presented Virginia with a narcissus,"[83] a gift with mythical connotations that paid tribute to her as an artist and quietly acknowledged her homo- or bisexuality.

Freudian psychology interprets the myth of Narcissus as representing an autoerotic stage in normal human psychological development, during which the sexual impulses find their object in a person's own ego, before they are directed toward an external object. A pathological fixation of this autoerotic condition is possible, so that narcissism in adults appears as the object-oriented, Oedipal love of the mature person. But in Freudian thought narcissism remains primal. As Freud explains in *Totem and Taboo*, "To a certain extent man remains narcistic [*sic*], even after he has found outer objects for his libido, and the objects on which he bestows it represent, as it were, emanations of the libido which remain with his ego and which can be withdrawn into it."[84]

According to René Girard, classical myths, such as the myths of Oedipus and Narcissus, disguise not stages in individual psychological development but real, historical violence, the communal violence that has been directed against sacrificial victims. The community protects itself against destructive self-division by expelling and murdering someone whom it mythologizes (and pathologizes) as the guilty cause of civil unrest and disease. The "mythical lie," asserts Girard, is that "of the guilty victim who deserves to die."[85] The myth of Oedipus renders him guilty of parricide and incest and thus the cause of the plague afflicting Thebes. This mythic attribution of guilt to Oedipus disguises the city's actual, ancient sacrifice of an innocent person, a king or a substitute for the king, whom it has held arbitrarily responsible for general misfortune. Similarly, the myth of Narcissus's pride, self-directed love, and suicide disguises the true history of a murder committed against an outsider, who was the object of desire of competing groups.

According to the myths, Oedipus blinds and exiles himself, even as Narcissus drowns himself. The community thus bears no responsibility for their tragic fates. The myth conceals their actual, all-against-one murder by the group. The unacknowledged burden of communal guilt is then atoned for through memorials of the sacrifice. Since the historic sacrifice of a scapegoat restores peace and unity to the community, the victim, once held to be the cause of division, then becomes a god, the restorer of social order.

Ritual and artistic reenactments of the myth serve to support this process of deification, even as they provide a substitute means of memorial sacrifice to delay or prevent the recurrence of violence. From ancient times the myth of Oedipus has been associated with the fate of the king, the energetic seeker after truth, the seer, the riddle solver, and the savior of the people. The myth of Narcissus belongs, by contrast, to contemplatives, homosexuals, and artists like Pygmalion, who fall in love with their own (created) images. The story of Oedipus is a founding myth of tragedy, even as that of Narcissus/Pygmalion is foundational for other art forms, especially statuary.

The great works of art, according to Girard, answer to myth by opposing it, revealing its fiction to be a rationalization, suggesting the true (or at least relative) innocence of the victim, and curbing the impulse toward spontaneous violence. Propaganda, by contrast, does the ideological work of reifying myth and justifying victimization, often with horrid results.

The artist who accepts the myth as true, taking on him- or herself the moral burden of an Oedipus or a Narcissus, imitates the mythic action, commits suicide, and thus spares the community the guilt entailed in the active destruction of those members it adjudges useless, burdensome, or divisive by their very difference. The self-destruction of the "mad" artist then becomes, in mythic terms, a praiseworthy act; the deed of a politically correct hero or a saint; a self-sacrifice meriting a quasi-religious, literary canonization. Contemporary "performance art" not infrequently verges on the sadistic and suicidal.[86] And how many modern, canonical authors have (however obliquely) secured their position, as Virginia Woolf did, by killing themselves and thus rendering their murder by a Philistine or fascist society unnecessary? Can it be indicative of the extent to which the mythology of the guilty, pathological artist has assumed truth-value?

Desiring Joan of Arc: Mythic Sanctity in Gilles and Jeanne

Michel Tournier's novella, *Gilles and Jeanne* (1983), demonstrates with chilling perversity the interrelated aesthetic and ethical consequences of a mythological reading of Joan of Arc. To a disturbing degree, the narratological perspective and the viewpoint of the principal character, Gilles de Rais, merge in Tournier's decadent, historical fiction about the relationship between Joan of Arc and the infamous French nobleman who fought at her side at Orleáns and who, nine years after her burning at the stake, died in flames at Nantes in 1440. Gilles's mythological interpretation of Jeanne d'Arc leads him to accept the truth of the charges against her, to believe in her guilt, and to imitate the example of depraved sanctity set by her putative heresy, whoredom, and sorcery. Tournier's narrative works to establish as many parallels as possible between the two figures, so that Gilles and Jeanne become doublets, and their initial differences dissolve in the end in a formal, Hegelian synthesis.[87] What is expelled, cast out, and denied in the process are the real differences between the martyr and the criminal. Holiness itself becomes scapegoated, even as Jeanne d'Arc becomes the supposed cause of the crimes of de Rais, the maker of the monster. Drawing an analogy between the fervent religious discipleship that imitates and follows an Other, on the one hand, and artistic mimesis, on the other, Tournier makes his Faustian fiction a Satanic offering to the father of lies.[88]

Tournier represents Gilles's initial devotion to Jeanne as a barely sublimated, pedophilic attraction to a boylike figure whose saintly mystique depends on the indeterminacy of her sex and gender: "If Jeanne is neither a girl nor a boy, then she must be an angel" (p. 10): "Si Jeanne n'est ni une fille, ni un garçon, c'est clair, n'est-ce pas, c'est qu'elle est un ange" (p. 13).[89] To connect Gilles's early worship of Joan of Arc to his subsequent sexual abuse of hundreds of young boys, Tournier depicts Jeanne as so boylike that Charles VII actually "required the opinion of experts as to her sex" (p. 9) ("il attend une expertise de son sexe" [p. 11]) and commanded a physical examination of her, not to prove her womanly virginity, but to decide whether she was female or male. In the opening pages of the novel, the reader first sees Jeanne at Chinon as a boy: "There appeared, with firm step, what looked like a young page boy" (p. 6): "Ils voient survenir à pas décidés un petit page" (p. 8). Tournier plays with this confusion, referring to

Jeanne as "the boy-girl who claimed to be sent from God" (p. 7): "la fille-garçon qui se veut envoyée de Dieu" (p. 9). Placing the emphasis on "boy" as the first noun in the compound, Tournier's English translator dares to use the masculine pronoun for Jeanne: "So there he stood, the young page with the bright eyes" (p. 7): "Le voici donc le petit page au regard de lumière" (p. 9). Later, Alençon explains Jeanne's virginity as something puerile, remarking to de Rais, "I'm not surprised she's a virgin. Unless he liked boys, no man would take it into his head to approach her" (p. 10): "Je ne peux m'étonner qu'elle soit pucelle. A moins d'aimer les garçons, aucun homme n'aurait fantaisie de l'approcher" (p. 12).

After Jeanne has been wounded during the unsuccessful attack on Paris, Gilles, who does like boys, dares to approach her, placing an adoring kiss on her bloody knee: "He bent down and laid his lips for a long time on Jeanne's wound" (p. 24): "Il s'incline et appuie longuement ses lèvres sur la plaie de Jeanne" (p. 28). That kiss of her fetishized wound becomes for Gilles the seal of his communion with her. "I have communicated with your blood," he tells her. "I am bound to you forever. Henceforth I will follow you wherever you go. Whether to heaven or to hell!" (p. 24): "J'ai communié de ton sang. Je suis lié à toi pour toujours. Je te suivrai désormais où que tu ailles. Au ciel comme en enfer!" (p. 28). After Jeanne's execution, Gilles sacramentally renews this first communion with her by offering the blood of his victims in a bowl to the devil and by kissing their severed heads: "When we agreed on which one was the most beautiful, he took it in his hands and put his mouth on its mouth" (p. 116): "Quand on s'était mis d'accord sur la plus belle, il la prenait entre ses mains et appuyait sa bouche sur sa bouche" (p. 132).

The serial killings for which the historical Gilles de Rais was tried and executed date from 1432, the year after Jeanne d'Arc's death. Tournier imagines a causal relationship between the two events. In *Gilles and Jeanne* Gilles secretly makes his way to Rouen in the hope of rescuing the Maid and arrives there just in time to witness the cruelty of her killing. There he hears the sixteen charges for which she has been convicted: "a liar, a pernicious woman, a betrayer of the people, a soothsayer, superstitious blasphemer of God, presumptuous, unbeliever in the faith, boastful, idolatrous, cruel, dissolute, invoker of devils, apostate, schismatic, heretic" (p. 34): "menteuse, pernicieuse, trompeuse du peuple, devineresse, superstitieuse, blasphématrice de Dieu, présomptueuse, mécréante en la foi, fanfaronne, idolâtre, cruelle, dissolue, invocatrice des diables, apostate, schismatique, hérétique" (p. 39). Seeing her final agony, Gilles is so traumatized that he falls in a trance to the ground. When he rises up again, he has been re-created in the image and likeness of that guilty Jeanne; he has "the face of a lying, pernicious, dissolute, blaspheming invoker of devils" (p. 35): "un visage menteur, pernicieux, blasphémateur, dissolu, invocateur des diables" (p. 40).

This metamorphosis, which converts Gilles into "an infernal angel" (p. 35) ("un ange infernal" [p. 40]), depends on his unconditional discipleship and his apparent belief in the truth of the charges leveled against Jeanne. He follows her "to hell" (p. 24), because he believes that that is where she has gone. At the same time, however, he never loses a sense of her sanctity. The either-or binary of "heaven or hell" becomes a monstrous both-and: "Au ciel comme en enfer!" (p. 28). In the end he rests his hope for salvation on Prelati's alchemical principle of inversion, malign and benign, whereby the same path that leads down to hell also becomes a ladder of ascent, leading to a final synthesis through which the sinner is saved, not in spite of his atrocious crimes, but because of them. Gilles comes to understand that if he "wanted to follow Jeanne, he would have to continue the descent into hell" (p. 88) ("s'il voulait suivre Jeanne, il fallait qu'il poursuive la descente aux enfers" [p. 99]), until, reaching the extremity of evil, he touched upon its celestial opposite.

A Girardian analysis shows Gilles's understanding to be mythical in several senses. First of all, Gilles believes in the "mythical lie" of the guilt of the victim, failing to distinguish between Jeanne, an innocent scapegoat, and himself, a convicted, self-confessed murderer. Believing in this lie, he puts Jeanne to death over and over again in the serial killing of innocent children, whose sodomized bodies he burns, renewing the stench he first inhaled at Rouen. He kills Jeanne in them so that he might be killed like her and with her. Believing in the lie of Jeanne's guilt, he utterly debases himself, so that he might be justly sentenced to a death by hanging and fire as cruel (and even more spectacular in its ritual) than hers. At the hour of his death, Gilles calls upon Joan of Arc: "Jeanne! Jeanne! Jeanne!" (p. 124), even as Joan had cried out, "Jesus! Jesus! Jesus!" (p. 34).

Mythological thinking first kills and then deifies its victims. So, too, Gilles dares to hope that he will attain a depraved sanctity through his conformity to the pattern of Jeanne's death. Tournier signals this confusion of pagan deification and Christian canonization through an explicitly mythological reference, when he mentions Gilles's preference for "the combined litanies of the Janus-Jeanne" (p. 38) ("les litanies de Jeanne bifrons" [p. 43]), which first invoke her as a saint and then condemn her under multiple titles. Janus, the Roman god of doorways, the two-faced god of past and future, is, for Gilles, another name for Jeanne.

As Girard explains, the all-against-one victimage mechanism operates in the communal sacrifice of a scapegoat only after sufficient pressure has built up within the community, whose members are divided, all against all, by a mimetic contagion that spreads from some initial, fraternal strife, one against the other. Tournier's fictions repeatedly employ the plot of warring twins, and *Gilles and Jeanne* conforms to that pattern. In Tournier's *récit,* the boyish Jeanne is at once the model and the brotherly-sisterly rival of Gilles. Gilles's competition with Jeanne for an "excessive sanctity" (p. 38) ("des excès de la sainteté" [p. 43]) begins after her death, but already during her lifetime they stand like twins, side by side: "With Jeanne on his right and Gilles on his left, the future king knelt on the altar steps" (p. 20): "Ayant Jeanne à sa droite et Gilles à sa gauche, le futur roi s'agenouille sur les degrés de l'autel" (p. 24). Gilles tells Jeanne, "Jeanne, I never want to leave your side. Jeanne, you are a saint, make a saint of me!" (p. 18): "Jeanne, je ne veux plus te quitter. Jeanne, tu es une sainte, fais de moi un saint!" (p. 22).

The "ineluctable connection" (p. 100) between Gilles's trial and that of Jeanne the Maid depends in the novel on a series of superficial similarities and circumstantial associations between the two figures. Like the parodic hagiography of Jean Genet (1910–1986), Tournier's fictions—especially *Le Roi des aulnes* (1970), *Gaspard, Melchior & Balthazar* (1980), and *Gilles et Jeanne* (1983)—are based "upon a making contiguous of transgressive act and Christian counterpart."[90] Edith Wyschogrod's comment on the "unconcealed doubleness" that characterizes Genet's *Our Lady of the Flowers* (1948) applies equally well to Tournier's *Gilles and Jeanne:* "The allegorical elements . . . endlessly reflect each other in a mirror play of transgressive and salvific acts. . . . '[D]epraved' desire in Genet's [and Tournier's] work carries the weight of its 'sacred' double."[91]

As Gilles becomes more and more Jeanne's double, the mimetic rivalry between them grows contagious. Tournier demonstrates the spreading of this contagion through the introduction of a series of Jehannine look-alikes, who disturb and divide the community. Father Blanchet tells Prelati that after Jeanne's death Gilles was constantly expecting her reappearance, anticipating her reincarnation. Indeed, he sponsored the gala performance of *The Mystery of the Siege of Orléans* on May 8, 1435, as a "sumptuous sacrifice" ("un somptueux sacrifice") in order "to force . . . Jeanne's wandering soul to become re-embodied in the actor appointed to play her role" (pp. 67–68): "pour obliger . . . l'âme errante de Jeanne à venir se réincarner dans le comédien chargé de jouer son rôle" (p. 77). Gilles sees Jeanne not only in her historical impostor and in the actors who audition for her part but also in the hundreds of little boys who become his victims. When Prelati, who becomes Gilles's diabolical mentor, first appears at Tiffauges Castle, Gilles is dumbfounded, because "Prelati resembled [Jeanne] to a strik-ing degree" (p. 76): "Prélat lui ressemblât de façon saisissante" (p. 86).

Perceiving only the similarities between himself and his victims, on the one hand, and Jeanne, on the other, Gilles sees Jeanne's features everywhere. As Prelati remarks to Blanchet, "Gilles . . . was seeking an adored face" (p. 69): "Gilles . . . cherchait un visage adoré" (p. 79). The idolatrous character of that search becomes evident in Gilles's blindness to the actual faces of his individual young victims, all of whom serve as iconic substitutes for the one sacrificial victim, Jeanne d'Arc. Slitting the throats of the children and decapitating them, Gilles commits a particu-larly horrific crime that violates the face-to-face, I-Thou relationship that Emmanuel Levinas describes as one of infinite responsibility for the Other. Like the use of the guillotine in Genet's fiction, Gilles's cutthroat display of heads "violates the source of the prescription against murder, the face."[92] For Gilles, all the faces are alike. The sameness of the face is the object of the depraved, mimetic desire that endlessly copies the Other, whereas (in the words of Wyschogrod) the uniqueness and "oth-erness of the [human] face rather than the chain of signifiers super-imposed on it is the object of disinterested saintly love."[93] Even Gilles's own facial features are transformed into a diabolical, werewolfish copy of Jeanne's: "un masque de loup-garou" (p. 74). "It was," Blanchet muses, "as if the horror of Jeanne's death were imprinted on his face" (p. 64): "On aurait dit que toute l'horreur du supplice de Jeanne s'était im-primée sur son visage" (p. 73).

Tournier rightly figures Gilles's mimesis of Jeanne d'Arc as Satanic. In an early conversation with Jeanne, Gilles contrasts her heavenly Voices to his own devilish ones: "The voices I heard in my childhood and youth were always those of evil and sin" (p. 18). Sitting in Jeanne's tent, Gilles remarks to her, "Good and evil are always so close to one another. Of all creatures, Lucifer was the most like God" (p. 23): "Le bien et le mal sont toujours proches l'un de l'autre. De toutes les créatures, Lucifer était la plus semblable à Dieu" (p. 27). Having witnessed Jeanne's death, Gilles becomes an "infernal angel" (p. 35): "un ange infernal" (p. 40). Practicing the devil's arts and offering devil worship, Gilles the arch-offender "thinks he's Satan" (p. 107), as Malestroit exclaims: "Il se prend pour Satan!" (p. 121).

To believe in the mythic guilt of the innocent Jeanne, in order to justify her murder and that of countless substitute victims, is Satanic, because, as Girard reminds us, "[Satan] is the *accuser*. . . . Satan produces myths and is the principle of systematic accusation that burst forth from the contagious imitation provoked by scandals."[94] Scandalized by the conviction and execution of Jeanne, whom he has taken as his model, Gilles becomes all the more her perverse imitator, entangled in her shadow, projecting her supposed guilt onto the boys who become his sacrificial offerings, and immersing himself in capital offenses.

Because Satan is not only the seducer and accuser but also the scriptural ape of God, Satanic thought produces mythological copies of the divine originals, refusing to see the enormous differences between and among them. Not only does it liken Gilles, the monstrous mass murderer, to Jeanne the Maid, but it also provides a host of biblical typologies for his depravity. Thus Prelati cites in blasphemous defense of Gilles's pedophilic sodomy and murder a series of scriptural proof texts: Abraham's sacrifice of Isaac (Genesis 22:1–19); the Father's sacrifice of Jesus on Calvary; and the words of Jesus, "Let the little children come to me" (Luke 18:16). "Yahweh," Prelati asserts, "loves the fresh, tender flesh of children" (p. 89) ("Yahvé aime la chair fraîche at tendre des infants" [p. 101]), and Gilles is merely imitating God. His mimesis, however, does not honor God but mocks him. Girard rightly observes that "Satan is an imitator in the rivalistic sense of the word. . . . Satan is the ape of God" (p. 45).

Tournier systematically extends the significance of this Satanic aping from the ethical to the aesthetic realm. Each of Gilles's actions is associated with a work of art. As mentioned previously, his desire to see a reincarnated Jeanne impels him to commission a pageant, *The*

Mystery of the Siege of Orléans, in which someone enacts her part onstage. His longing to witness her death over and over moves him to establish a boys' choir, dedicated to the Holy Innocents, whose members he molests and whose singing intensifies his desire. The musical performance of the boys regularly takes place in a hall decorated with a fresco depicting the Slaughter of the Innocents (Matthew 2:13–18). "The artist," we are told, "had spared no detail, and his vision was all the more striking in that, according to the practice of the time, he had costumed his figures like the men, women, and children of his own period, and placed them in a village that was supposed to be Bethlehem, but in which everyone could recognize the houses of Machecoul" (p. 40): "L'artiste n'avait reculé devant aucun détail, et son évocation était d'autant plus saisissante que, selon une tradition consacrée en ce temps, il avait habillé les personnages comme l'étaient les hommes, les soldats, les femmes et les enfants de son temps, et les avait placés dans un village qui était en principe Bethléem, mais où chacun pouvait reconnaître les maisons de la commune de Machecoul" (pp. 46–47). Gilles responds emotionally to the painting in a commingling of pity and pleasure: "It is so moving to see a child suffering! A tiny, blood-stained body in its death throes is such a beautiful sight!" (p. 42): "C'est si émouvant, un enfant qui souffre! C'est si beau un petit corps ensanglanté, soulevé par les soupirs et les râles de l'agonie!" (p. 48). Soon thereafter he reenacts in real life the role of Herod and his soldiers.

The interplay of art and life becomes all the more complicated as Gilles's actual crimes, recounted through the spread of rumors, become bogeyman stories; the "dark, cruel scenes . . . inscribed with all the power of legend in popular imagery" (p. 44): "Des scènes noires et cruelles s'inscrivaient avec force de légende dans l'imagerie populaire" (p. 50). Thus the historical Gilles de Rais comes to be assimilated with the Bluebeard who murdered his seven wives; with the Gothic Erl-King, mounted on horseback, who abducts children by night; and with the eerie fairy tale of Tom Thumb.

This development in the popular art of oral tradition meets and merges, in Tournier's novel, with the latest innovations in the realm of high art. In Florence in 1439, Father Blanchet, Gilles's confessor, meets Francesco Prelati, who introduces him to the new, dissective, anatomical sciences and to their impact on sculpture. Calling particular attention to Donatello's "bronze of David, the boy David" (p. 60) ("David en bronze, le David enfant" [p. 69]), Prelati highlights the pornographic potential of the new, realistic art, which is so lifelike that it allows for the easy substitution of art for life, on the one hand, and for the aesthetic objectification of human bodies, on the other: "Yes, we have abolished the distance that artistic contemplation necessarily requires. So what is left? Love plus anatomy. . . . The skeleton, but also the muscles, the viscera, the entrails, the glands, . . . and the blood!" (p. 62): "Oui, nous avons aboli la distance qu'exige nécessairement la contemplation artistique. Que reste-t-il dès lors? Il reste: amour plus anatomie. . . . Et pas seulement le squelette: les muscles, les viscères, les entrailles, les glandes . . . et le sang!" (pp. 70–71).

Prelati's sinister commentary on Donatello's statue calls attention to the double potential of art. Whereas "distance" and "contemplation" can harmonize the audience and retard its relapse into the sacrificial violence at the origins of ritual and artistic representation, too great a resemblance between art and life can stimulate a violent, repetitive response in the onlooker, an imitation of the mimetic crisis that the artwork memorializes. Even as the mimetic crisis has its beginnings in acquisitive rivalry, the mythic strife of twins, so too art, which is itself a double of life, typically patterns itself in symmetrical pairings, in a ritual dance of doubles. According to Girard, "the model of the most abstract ritual dances is always that of a confrontation of doubles, although it has been entirely 'aestheticized.'"[95]

In *Gilles and Jeanne* such a nocturnal dance occurs on the Feast of Saint Gilles, but it is a pagan, Dionysiac festival that spurs rather than forestalls bloodshed. Rather than harmonize opponents, the ball at Tiffauges is characterized by a frenzied excess. Men dance with men, who shamelessly take the female roles; and humans dress in the skins of animals, leading Prelati to wonder: "Were all these creatures entirely men, or were they all more or less the products of matings with bears, wolves, or some other beasts of the forests of the Vendée?" (p. 79): "Ces êtres étaient-ils tout à fait hommes, ou n'étaient-ils pas tous plus ou moins mâtinés d'ours, de loup ou de toute autre bête de la forêt vendéenne?" (p. 89). Taking the orchestration of Gilles's crimes into his hands, Prelati consciously aims at the conversion into violence of the excessive energy displayed in the bacchanalia, asking himself, "How can I convert all that brute force to my subtle ends?" (p. 80): "Comment convertir à mes fins subtiles toute cette force brute?" (p. 90).

For his part, Tournier seeks to forge an all-encompassing, literary plenum out of the same excess, which blurs all distinctions between pagan and Christian, good and evil, innocence and guilt, male and female, human and beast. Once again, Wyschogrod's words about Genet seem appropriate for Tournier, when she characterizes the former author's decadent hagiography as "a magical plenum in which . . . wholeness without fissure seems to be attainable: ecstasy."[96] "The aspiration" in Tournier's writings, David Gascoigne observes, "is to a series of impossible syntheses."[97] Tournier wants "to deploy an eclectic mythology which can suggest pattern without any specific commitment other than to openness and freedom."[98] Seemingly all-inclusive, this ecstatic, mythological "all" excludes, however, the "one" of real difference. It includes the Gospels only by rendering them mythical; it includes Jeanne d'Arc only as the guilty victim who is the cause of Gilles's crimes, the double of his depravity. Thus Jeanne is at first expelled, only to be reincorporated in Gilles; and Gilles is excommunicated and executed, to return in the company of a sainted Jeanne.

In an extended discussion of Mark 3:23–26, René Girard explicates the saying of Jesus that "Satan expels Satan." "The devil," Girard writes, "does not have a stable foundation; he has no *being* at all. To clothe himself in the semblance of being, he must act as a parasite on God's creatures. He is totally mimetic, which amounts to saying *nonexistent as an individual self*."[99] Satan in his many guises—seducer, ape of God, accuser, father of lies—maintains his control over the kingdoms of this world precisely through the constant shape changing, the metamorphoses, that constitute his identity as an adversarial principle: "The mimetic cycle begins with desire and its rivalries, it continues through the multiplication of scandal and a mimetic crisis, and it is finally resolved in the single victim mechanism, which is the answer to the question asked by Jesus: 'How can Satan expel Satan?'"[100] Tournier represents this final expulsion of Satan by Satan in a prayer addressed by Prelati to the devil, in which he abandons the increasingly wild and reckless Gilles "to the fate that he is forging with his own hands" (p. 95) ("au sort funeste qu'il se forge de ses propres mains" [p. 107])—arrest, trial, and public execution.

Tournier explicitly denies that Gilles's death by fire, like Jeanne's before him, can be considered a scapegoating: "The witches' stake was not a punishment, still less a means of ridding the community of some accursed creature—like the profane death penalty. It was a purificatory trial intended, on the contrary, to save a seriously threatened soul" (p. 87): "Le bûcher des sorcières n'était pas un châtiment et moins encore un expédient pour se débarrasser d'un être maudit—comme la peine de mort profane. C'était une épreuve purificatrice destinée au contraire à sauver une âme gravement menacée" (p. 98). Girard argues to the contrary that "the historians [of the Middle Ages] continue to affirm the actual existence of victims massacred by medieval mobs: lepers, Jews, foreigners, women, those who were disabled, marginal persons of every sort."[101] Girard would have us remember an essential difference between Jeanne and Gilles that Gilles and Tournier are wont to forget: Jeanne, unlike Gilles, was innocent.

In his 1965 edition of the trial records of Gilles de Rais, Georges Bataille sets apart the two figures whom Tournier joins: "Of all the victims offered to the crowd, Joan of Arc and Gilles de Rais, these companions in arms, are opposed to each other in the same way as derided innocence and the crime that exhibits in the same breath the horror and the tears of the criminal."[102] What fascinates Bataille is the compassion of the crowd that witnessed Gilles's death and wept for him after his confession of guilt. Historians record the tears of some witnesses at Rouen in 1431, who wept because of Joan's innocence and their own guilt in burning a saint.[103] At Nantes on October 26, 1440, people wept and prayed for Gilles because, Bataille asserts, "the crowd could discover in their tears that this great lord who was to die, being the most infamous criminal, was like everyone in the crowd," a mortal and a sinner in great need of God's mercy.[104] In these communal tears of compassion for the innocent Joan and the guilty Gilles, there is no doubt a cathartic effect similar to that produced by classical tragedy and the ancient goat sacrifices. What is different in these Christian executions after protracted trials is the acknowledgment of communal guilt rather than its projection onto the single victim and the recognition in Jeanne and in the children slain by Gilles of innocent victims.

Shaw tells the story of a feminist Joan of Arc in two genres, the chronicle play and a prose preface, to suggest the modern timeliness of her medieval life. Sackville-West writes a self-conscious, formal biography of Joan that is at the same time autobiographical, combining a masculine mode of historical objectivity with an intrusive, feminine subjectivity in order to mirror Jeanne's own androgyny. The lesbian potential of Sackville-West's Jeanne becomes, through a strange metamorphosis, the pedophilia of Tournier's Gilles. Tournier writes a macabre novel about Jeanne d'Arc that vaguely resembles Woolf's *Orlando* in the queerly sexualized continuum that links Jeanne to Gilles across the temporal space of a trancelike sleep, in its developmental sense of art history, and in its lush descriptions of costume and scenery. Neither a realistic novella nor a moralistic fable, Tournier's story of Jeanne is, like his other *contes*, a hybrid of the two; it is, in Tournier's own words, a "nouvella haunted by a meaning, like having a ghost in the house; but one never learns what exactly this meaning is."[105] Tournier's self-proclaimed "mystical naturalism" answers to Jeanne's mysticism[106] but only through the depraved sanctity of her bisexual, Satanic double, Gilles de Rais. In a mythological universe, as Girard avers, something must be sacrificed.

*What we need, God, what we finally need is a woman who would also be
a saint . . . and who would succeed.*
—CHARLES PÉGUY

But cannot Joan herself become a glorious flame in the darkness?
—PAUL CLAUDEL

I want to thank you, Joan of Arc.
—LEONARD COHEN

CHAPTER SIX

A CONTRAPUNTAL CONCLUSION

The Catholic and the Jewish Joan

We must distinguish, in the end, between the "catholic" and the "Catholic" Joan. Described with the lowercase adjective, Joan of Arc is truly "catholic," because everyone can identify with her by picking one or the other aspect of her story as a point of identification. What distinguishes her various representations is the eye of the beholder as it contemplates her image, which becomes, in turn, a mirror for those who marvel at her. The need to interpret Joan in order to reach some sort of conclusion about her makes her person—not unlike the dreams, enigmatic visions, and heavenly Voices with which she is associated—akin to a beautiful work of art in its demand for a meditative, discerning, critical response.

In his *Curiosities of Literature* (1791), Isaac D'Israeli (1766–1848) reprints a humorous epitaph that sums up the range of possible opinions about Joan of Arc while reserving a last ruling on the subject for the Final Judgment:

> Here lies Joan of Arc; the which
> Some count saint, and some count witch;
> Some count man, and something more;
> Some count maid, and some a whore.
> Her life's in question, wrong or right;
> Her death's in doubt, by laws or might.
> Oh, innocence! Take heed of it,
> How thou too near to guilt doth sit.
> (Meanwhile, France a wonder saw—
> A woman rule, 'gainst salique law!)
> But, reader, be content to stay
> Thy censure till the judgment day;
> Then shalt thou know, and not before,
> Whether saint, witch, man, maid, or whore.[1]

D'Israeli, echoing Winstanley, calls for an indefinite postponement of the final verdict on Joan's life, but he does so only after the historical Joan has long since been condemned to death and cruelly executed: "Here lies Joan of Arc." This undeniable verdict, already pronounced and enforced, cannot be revoked or postponed, and it provides the common ground for a universal identification with Joan—namely, the ground that is the grave, the ashes that symbolize her mortality and victimhood: "Here lies Joan of Arc." The epitaph points to an absent presence, the body of Joan that was burned and not buried, because, with the exception of her heart, it had been totally consumed by the flames. The place of Joan's body is empty, ready to be taken by a substitute, indeed, by a series of substitutes.

This book has focused on the particular ways in which modern literary artists—poets, essayists, dramatists, biographers, and novelists—have identified with Joan of Arc, seeing her story as an artwork and herself as an artist, inspired with genius, suffering, misunderstood, and scapegoated. Imitating Joan as an artistic model, they typically follow her into the literary marketplace, the place of their martyrdom. In so doing, they identify Joan with all the artists who have gone before them as precursors, as well as with the living writers who are at once their models and rivals. In Joan's death they imagine their own. At the same time, by imaginatively killing her, reenacting her execution, they purify themselves ritually of the influences that limit their own originality, swerving away from them. At once sacrificial victims with Joan and her murderers, they accept as true the myth of her guilt and the necessity of her death as a purchase price for literary canonization. In a modern world, where art has supplanted religion, Joan's authors seek to imbue themselves with the still resplendent aura of the saint.

Catholic writers (and here I employ the uppercase adjective) identify with Joan of Arc no less than their secularist counterparts do, but they necessarily do so in a different way. Their art continues to serve religion rather than displace it. For them, Joan is and remains a saint. They set Joan's *mystique* against her myth. Indeed, they firmly reject the myth of Jehannine guilt and consciously employ antisacrificial strategies in their telling of Joan's story. In so doing, they anticipate René Girard in his insistence that the account of Christ's Passion in the Gospels is antimythic, because it reveals the innocence of the scapegoat and lays bare the single-victim mechanism, whereas myths do precisely the opposite, blaming the victim, claiming the necessity of his death, and concealing the community's responsibility for murder. As Catholic authors see it, the history of Joan's trial and death at the stake, parallel in many respects to the Passion of Christ, is an antimythic, persecution text, because it exposes the lie of the guilty victim.

In sharp contrast to virtually all the authors discussed previously, Catholic and Jewish writers about Joan of Arc—Charles Péguy (1873–1914), Paul Claudel (1868–1955), Georges Bernanos (1888–1948), Franz Werfel (1890–1945), Leonard Cohen (b. 1934), and Erik Ehn (b. 1958)—all focus attention less on Joan's victimhood than on her charity, on her free choice to offer her life to God for her fellow human beings in an act of heroic love and forgiveness. The life of a victim, a scapegoat, is always cruelly taken away from him or her by others, whereas saints give their lives, even in the midst of torture, come what may. What Jesus says of himself is true of the mystic Joan, whose defining trait is an all-consuming charity: "No one takes my life from me, but I lay it down of my own accord. . . . Greater love has no man than this, that a man lay down his life for his friends" (John 10:18; 15:13).

Mystique *and* Politique: *Péguy's Joan of the Jews*

At the fountainhead of modern Catholic writings about Joan of Arc stands Charles Péguy, peasant son of Orléans, socialist, poet, founding editor of *Les Cahiers de la Quinzaine,* prominent Dreyfusard, hero of World War I. Commenting on twentieth-century portrayals of the Maid, the bibliographer Nadia Margolis observes: "The two towering figures of this period in literature are Shaw and Péguy."[2] Whereas Shaw is perhaps the major source for the mythic Joan in her Marxist and feminist manifestations, Péguy opens the way for the mystic Joan of political engagement. Shaw treats the subject of Joan of Arc only once, in his justly famous chronicle play, *Saint Joan* (1923). Péguy, by contrast, was so thoroughly immersed in Joan's spirit that he portrayed her again and again: in *Jeanne d'Arc,* the dramatic trilogy of 1897; in *Le Mystère de la charité de Jeanne d'Arc* (1910); in *Le Tapisserie de la Sainte Geneviève et de Jeanne d'Arc* (1912); and, more allusively, in *Eve* (1913). Shaw emphasizes the external world of Joan's action and witty repartee while Péguy endeavors to capture Joan's innermost being, her attitude toward God and others, her sense of vocation, her anguish of soul, her prayer. Whereas Shaw's *Saint Joan* has been a favorite and frequent stage production, Péguy's plays, combining prose and verse, have never been performed, nor can they be. Their speeches—prolix, repetitive, biblical in their concrete imagery and parallelism, powerfully anaphoric—are written to be read slowly, silently vocalized by a reader who impersonates the parts.

As Shaw's 1924 "Preface" makes clear, *Saint Joan* was inspired in part by his reflections on the military trials of World War I. Concluding that societies in states of crisis are necessarily intolerant, Shaw set out to vindicate Joan's judges by comparison and to render understandable their tragic condemnation of her. Shaw's mythic approach pronounces Joan guilty in the historical present, albeit canonizable in the future, and works to justify society's sacrifice of her. Péguy's Jehannine verse plays were also inspired by a military trial: the courtmartial in January 1895 of Alfred Dreyfus. Péguy's impulse, however, was exactly the opposite of Shaw's. Setting *mystique* against a mythic *politique,* Péguy ardently maintained the innocence of the scapegoat, defending the one against the many.

The link between the Dreyfus Affair and Péguy's writings on Joan of Arc becomes obvious through an examination first of the chronology and then of the texts themselves. On November 2, 1894, Péguy began studies at the École Normal. "Only three days earlier," Marjorie Villiers notes, "*La Libre Parole,* a right-wing and anti-semitic paper, had carried this headline: HIGH TREASON. CAPTAIN DREYFUS, A JEWISH OFFICER, ARRESTED."[3] Convicted on the basis of false evidence, Dreyfus endured a humiliating public ceremony of degradation on January 5, 1895, before a crowd of thousands who shouted, "Death to the Jews, death to traitors, death to Judas."[4] Despite his protestations of innocence and the qualms of conscience of the French president, who resigned his office over the affair, Dreyfus was sentenced to life imprisonment on Devil's Island.

The beginning of the Dreyfus Affair in 1894–1895 coincides exactly with the start of Péguy's research on Joan of Arc at the École Normal Supérieure. Eager to work on *Jeanne d'Arc,* Péguy requested a year of absence from school in 1895–1896, traveled to Domremy and Vaucouleurs, and settled with his mother in his boyhood home at Orléans, where he established a local socialist group, advocated the cause of Dreyfus, and wrote. Retracing Jeanne's steps, Péguy launched into his own campaign to save France, this time from moral ruin through the condemnation of an innocent man.

In spring 1896 Lieutenant Colonel Georges Picquart discovered new evidence to prove that Commandant Walsin-Esterhazy, not Alfred Dreyfus, had been guilty of treason. On his return to Paris in fall 1896, Péguy lent support to his Jewish friend, the journalist Bernard-Lazare, who was working on behalf of Dreyfus. Péguy personally enlisted the help of the socialist leader Jean Jaurès, who had been reluctant to enter the fray. In December 1897, at the height of the Dreyfus Affair, the *Librairie de la Revue Socialiste* published Péguy's *Jeanne d'Arc.* Péguy visited Émile Zola a few weeks later, to encourage him after the publication on January 13, 1898, of his famous letter, "J'accuse," denouncing the army's cover-up of Esterhazy's guilt and Dreyfus's innocence.

Dreyfus was finally exonerated in full on July 12, 1906. In 1908 Péguy, who had styled himself an atheist, confessed himself to be a Catholic. In January 1910 he published *Le Mystère de la charité de Jeanne d'Arc (The Mystery of the Charity of Joan of Arc),* a revision and expansion of part 1 of the earlier *Jeanne d'Arc.* In October 1910 Péguy, responding critically to an essay on the Dreyfus Affair by his socialist friend, Daniel Halévy, published his own memoir in a *Cahier* entitled *Notre Jeunesse.* Taken together, Péguy's famous *Cahier* concerning "cette immortelle affair Dreyfus" and his *The Mystery of the Charity of Joan of Arc* reaffirm (albeit with the greater insight gained through years of work and suffering) the political mysticism of his youth, a mysticism like Joan's own.[5]

René Girard has pointed to the famous Dreyfus case as a modern example of the operation of the scapegoat mechanism, which the anti-Dreyfus party attempted to conceal through the myth of the victim's guilt. Girard mentions Charles Péguy in particular as someone who recognized a parallel between Dreyfus's trial and the Passion of Christ.[6] Girard does not, however, elaborate on Péguy's insight, nor does he comment on the parallel Péguy draws between Jeanne d'Arc and himself, on the one hand, and Jeanne and Dreyfus, on the other.

Péguy's analysis of the Dreyfus Affair, in fact, anticipates with an uncanny exactitude Girard's theoretical model of victimage. Girard insists that the community's choice of a scapegoat is relatively arbitrary but that the one selected is marked by some physical or spiritual difference that makes him or her outstanding and therefore capable of being isolated. Shocked by France's defeat in the Franco-Prussian War, the French were on the lookout for spies who could be held responsible for the nation's loss of Alsace. Jewish and Alsatian, Dreyfus was vulnerable to attack. He was, Péguy writes, "victim in spite of himself, hero in spite of himself, martyr in spite of himself" (p. 135): "Victime malgré lui, héros malgré lui, martyr malgré lui" (p. 134). A flawed and very ordinary man suddenly thrust into a hero's role, Dreyfus lacked the personal virtues that would naturally attract support. "He was as he was," Péguy writes, "but not as we had dreamed him to be" (p. 139): "il était comme il était, et non point comme nous l'avions rêvé" (p. 138). Dreyfus had been unjustly condemned, however, and that fact alone mattered. Péguy remembers the poignant words of his friend, Bernard-Lazare, who defended Dreyfus "with that admirable voluntary blindness of those who really love" (p. 139), declaring simply: "He is innocent, that already means a great deal" (p. 141): "Il est innocent, c'est déjà beaucoup" (p. 140).

The community generates the myth of the victim's guilt, according to Girard, because it believes that its very survival as a community depends on the scapegoat's expulsion. The mythic lie is that the one must die for the good of all. "From this point of view," Péguy writes, "it was evident that Dreyfus should sacrifice himself for France. . . . And if he did not wish to sacrifice himself, of his own free will, if the need

arose, he should be sacrificed" (p. 111): "À ce point de vue il était évi-
dent que Dreyfus devait se dévouer pour la France. . . . Et s'il ne voulait pas se dévouer lui-même, dans le besoin on devait le dévouer"
(p. 110). According to Péguy, the "true position" of the anti-Dreyfusards
was not so much to believe Dreyfus guilty but "to believe and to say
that guilty, or innocent, the life and salvation of a people, the enormous salvation of a people could not be upset, could not be *compro-
mised*, could not be risked, for a single man" (p. 109): "mas de croire et
de dire qu'innocent ou coupable on ne troublait pas, on ne boulever-
sait pas, on ne *compromettait* pas, on ne risquait pas pour un homme,
pour un seul homme, la vie et le salut d'un peuple, l'énorme salut de
tout un peuple" (p. 108).

Distinguishing between the temporal and the eternal salvation of
the people, Péguy characterizes the view of the anti-Dreyfusards as
shortsighted and self-deceiving. Rather than secure the unity, health,
and salvation of the community, the expulsion of a scapegoat has,
Péguy insists, precisely the opposite effect. The unjust condemnation
of a single individual destroys the honor of the nation and contami-
nates the body politic, rendering every one of its members vulnerable.
Péguy voices the antimythic opinion of the Dreyfusards: "We said that
a single injustice . . . is a touch of gangrene that corrupts the entire
body" (p. 111): "Nous disions une seule injustice . . . c'est un point de
gangrène, qui corrompt tout le corps" (pp. 110, 112).

The crucial thing in the Dreyfus case, according to Péguy, was not
so much to decide whether Dreyfus was innocent—after all, many of
the anti-Dreyfusards knew and admitted that—but to decide whether
his innocence mattered enough to come publicly to his defense; to
bring high-ranking people under accusation; to divide the community;
to risk and to suffer the personal loss of friends, reputation, employment; to share, in short, the fate of Dreyfus. In the beginning, Villiers
notes, only a very few were willing to do so: "a few Socialists prepared
to face the wrath of their leaders, a few Catholics ready to be considered pariahs by most of their co-religionists, a few Jews brave enough
to risk a rise in anti-semitism because they had come to the rescue of
a fellow Jew."[7] About this decision to stand with Dreyfus, Péguy writes:
"Our opponents will never know, our enemies could not know all that
we have sacrificed for the sake of this man, and with what a heart we
have sacrificed it. For him we have sacrificed our entire life, since this
case has marked us for life" (p. 105): "Nos adversaires ne sauront jamais,

nos ennemis ne pouvaient pas savoir ce que nous avons sacrifié à cet homme, et de quel cœur nous l'avons sacrifié. Nous lui avons sacrifié notre vie entière, puisque cette affaire nous a marqués pour la vie" (p. 104).

In Péguy's view, the real hero of the Dreyfus case was not Dreyfus but Bernard-Lazare and those other heroes who dared to defend Dreyfus long before it was popular to do so. Bernard-Lazare possessed and supplied all the personal, Christlike virtues that Dreyfus himself lacked. He was, Péguy writes, "one of the greatest among the prophets of Israel" (p. 119): "l'un des plus grands parmi les prophètes d'Israël" (p. 118). A secular Jew who called himself an atheist, Bernard-Lazare "unquestionably . . . possessed elements of holiness, of sanctity" (p. 119): "Il avait, indéniablement, des parties de saint, de sainteté" (p. 118). A poor man, generous beyond his means, Bernard-Lazare willingly took upon his shoulders the burden of the Dreyfus case and the plight of the Rumanian Jews, because he was one of those rare persons who felt themselves truly responsible for others, especially for his fellow Jews: "responsible pour sa race et pour son peuple" (pp. 124, 126). He kept the commandments and in him reverberated, therefore, "the eternal Word" (p. 131): "la parole éternelle" (p. 130). A hero unsung except by Péguy, Bernard-Lazare died in obscure poverty at the age of forty. He was one of those, Péguy writes, who died for Dreyfus and in his stead: "D'autres sont morts pour lui" (p. 134).

The Dreyfus Affair was for Péguy and Bernard-Lazare mystical in its very essence—"une affaire essentiellement mystique" (p. 100)—because it required them to answer a divine call, to place eternal values ahead of temporal ones, and to sacrifice their very selves for the individual stranger on whose fate the eternal salvation of the nation rested. Their action was, consciously or unconsciously, Christian. It found its wellspring, a retrospective Péguy asserts, in charity: "Today we can own that of all the passions which urged us into this ardor and into this effervescence, into this dilatation and into this tumult, one virtue was at the heart of them, and that was the virtue of charity" (p. 103): "Aujourd'hui nous pouvons avouer que de toutes les passions qui nous poussèrent dans cette ardeur et dans ce bouillonnement, dans ce gonflement et dans ce tumulte, une vertu était au cœur, et que c'était la vertu de charité" (p. 102).

The emphatic references to Christian mysticism and to charity in *Notre Jeunesse* (1910) are perhaps the most obvious of the intertextual references linking Péguy's essays on the Dreyfus Affair to his *Mystery of the Charity of Joan of Arc*, which had appeared earlier that same year to great acclaim. The *Mystère*, as noted earlier, is a revision of the Domremy portion of *Jeanne d'Arc*, the trilogy that Péguy had composed during the early years of the Dreyfus case. Although critics like to call *Jeanne d'Arc* the "Socialist Joan" and *The Mystery of the Charity of Joan of Arc* the "Christian Joan," that too neat division blurs the continuities that Péguy himself wished to emphasize. His socialism, as he understood it in 1910, had always essentially been an engaged, Christian mysticism, similar to that of Jeanne d'Arc. Likening his involvement in the Dreyfus Affair to going off to war, Péguy writes that he and his comrades were motivated "by a need for war, for *military* war and for military glory, by a need of sacrifice and even martyrdom, perhaps (no doubt), by a need of sanctity" (p. 107): "par un besoin de guerre, de guerre *militaire,* et de gloire militaire, par un besoin de sacrifice et jusque de martyre, peut-être (sans doute), par un besoin de sainteté" (p. 106).

Always a child of Orléans, always the son of peasants, Péguy identified so closely with the Maid of Orléans that, as M. Adereth writes, "in his last years, she became his model in all things."[8] Saint Joan was Péguy's spiritual exemplar, but Péguy's own image appears in the Jeanne of his plays. "In many ways," Joy Nachod Humes remarks, "Jeanne represents her creator. . . . Not only did Péguy give Jeanne many of his own memories and childhood joys, but also, on the debit side, his spiritual problems."[9] Péguy's Jeanette gives all that she has to the poor in Domremy, but in her adolescence she is spiritually torn, knowing that there is an infinite neediness, an insatiable hunger in the countless poor people of France, who have been made desolate by the war and by their lack of faith, hope, and charity. Recognizing this excessive poverty, she is willing to give all that she is and has for others. In a speech that Madame Gervaise terms blasphemous, Jeanette declares herself ready to suffer the torments of hell, giving her "body to the eternal flame" and her "soul to eternal Absence," in order to save the bodies and the souls of the damned from their suffering:

> O s'il faut, pour sauver de la flamme éternelle
> Les corps des morts damnés s'affolant de souffrance.
> Abandonner mon corps à la flamme éternelle. . . .
> Et s'il faut, pour sauver de l'Absence éternelle

Les âmes des damnés s'affolant de l'Absence,
Abandonner mon âme à l'Absence éternelle.[10]

Péguy is fascinated by the new type of sanctity that Jeanne d'Arc embodied in her own time; in Jeanne's daring response to an unprecedented vocation, he finds an existential model for his own way of life. In his *Mystery of the Charity,* he puts Jeanette in dialogue with another, more traditional seeker after holiness, Madame Gervaise, a cloistered nun. Péguy juxtaposes the two to emphasize the troubling uniqueness of Jeanette's calling. What sort of holiness can be found on a batttlefield? What kind of charity can be practiced in war? What sort of mysticism shows itself in a tireless effort to feed the hungry, to bandage the bleeding, to put an end to human suffering? Jeanette muses aloud in her prayer to God: "Perhaps we need something new, something no one has ever seen. . . . What we need, God, what we finally need is a woman who would also be a saint . . . and who would succeed" (p. 14): "Il nous faudrait peut-être quelque chose de nouveau, quelque chose qu'on n'aurait encore jamais vu. . . . Enfin ce qu'il nous faudrait, mon Dieu, il faudrait nous envoyer une sainte . . . qui réussisse" (p. 372).

The novel vocation from God to which Jeanette responds corresponds to the inspired longings first expressed in her fervent petitions to God on behalf of the suffering people of France. As the play opens, Jeanette is alone. She prays the traditional Lord's Prayer, but then she speaks in a Judaic spirit of longing for the Messiah: "Our father, our father who art in heaven, how far is your name from being hallowed; how far is your kingdom from coming" (p. 10): "Notre père, notre père, qui êtes aux cieux, de combien il s'en faut que votre nom soit sanctifié; de combien il s'en faut que votre règne arrive" (p. 370). Distressed in soul by the warfare among Christians and by the hunger of orphans, Jeanette is, as her friend Hauviette observes, constantly praying. In her longing for peace, she imagines a peace that wages war on war, that kills war. Hauviette objects: "But in order to kill war, you have to make war" (p. 40): "Mais pour tuer la guerre, il faut faire la guerre" (p. 393).

What Jeanette comes to recognize is that in order for God's kingdom to come to France, Christ must come again in his saints, indeed, in her. What is needed is human total self-surrender to God and a mundane, instrumental cooperation with him. Hers is to be a radically secular vocation. Because Jeanette allows God to do "something new" through her, she becomes a new incarnation of Christ. As Péguy writes of Jeanne d'Arc in an essay published in *Nouveau Théologien* in 1911, "[O]f all the saints, she it was to whom certainly it was given that her life and her Passion and her death should most closely imitate the life and the Passion and the death of Jesus": "De toutes les saintes elle fut celle à qui certainement il fut donné que sa vie et sa Passion et sa mort fut imitée au plus près de la vie et de la Passion et de la mort de Jésus."[11] Joan was given a divine vocation, counsel, and the strength to fulfill her mission, but she remained utterly human, vulnerable, and mortal, like Jesus, the Son of Man. Referring to Matthew 26:53, Péguy writes: "*Twelve legions of angels.* She did not ask for them any more than he did. She never asked for them": "*Douze légions d'anges.* Elle ne les demanda pas non plus. Elle ne les demanda jamais."[12]

Anticipating Simone Weil (1909–1943)—albeit with less ambivalence—Péguy seems to have recognized a Jewish quality in Joan's belief in a strong God, the mighty Lord of hosts, who is ready and able to intervene in history.[13] In Joan's spirituality he senses an ardent, Judaic longing for the coming not only of the Father's kingdom in justice and peace but also of the promised Messiah. Like the prophet Simeon in the Temple, Péguy's Joan in *The Mystery of Charity* is "*waiting for the consolation of Israel; of the kingdom of Israel*" (p. 59): "*Attendant la consolation d'Israël; du royaume d'Israël*" (p. 407). She understands that if God's kingdom is to come to earth, the Messiah must come not in Jesus alone but also again and again in his saints, all of whom are and must be suffering servants. Joan's Jesus, moreover, is emphatically Jewish: "He was a Jew, a simple Jew, a Jew like yourselves, a Jew among you" (p. 64): "C'était un Juif, un simple Juif, un Juif comme vous, un Juif parmi vous" (p. 411).

Recognizing the Jewish Jesus, loving him, and following him, Péguy's Joan is a spiritual Semite, specially chosen by God and consecrated to him to be his witness in the world.[14] Is it any wonder, then, that Péguy would have seen a Joan of Arc in Bernard-Lazare, coming to the aid of Dreyfus? A martyred Joan of Arc in Dreyfus, suffering because he was a Jew? A Joan of Arc in himself, because he fought for Dreyfus and for France? For Péguy, who had so many close Jewish friends, Joan of Arc combined in her person the whole world of the Judeo-Christian tradition. Péguy's confession of faith as a Catholic in 1908 coincides with the personal crisis he endured when he, a married man, first fell in love with a young Jewish woman, Blanche Raphaël.[15]

Perhaps in part as a rejoinder to fellow Dreyfusard Anatole France (1844–1924), whose skeptical *Vie de Jeanne d'Arc* appeared in 1908, Péguy wrote *Le Mystère de la charité de Jeanne d'Arc*, his second play about Joan of Arc, in 1909–1910 at the suggestion of his friend, the Jewish actress Simone Casimir-Périer.[16] A peasant in Paris, a Catholic in socialist circles, Péguy endured the traditionally Jewish fate of an outsider. He loved the Jewish people, he defended them, and he identified with them.

Paul Claudel and the Jewish Joan of Arc

The Dreyfus Affair and, more generally, the Jewish question initially put Péguy at odds with Paul Claudel, to whom André Gide had enthusiastically sent a copy of *Le Mystère de charité*. Claudel was moved by the profound beauty and religious depth of Péguy's *Mystère*, but when Péguy responded to his wish for a closer acquaintance with his work by sending him *Notre Jeunesse*, Claudel, an anti-Dreyfusard, wrote to him directly to voice his objections. Referring to Matthew 27:25 as a divine curse on the Jewish people ("la malédiction de Dieu"), Claudel goes so far in his letter as to call the Jews "ces punaises à face humaine."[17] Affronted, Péguy did not reply to Claudel's plea for an explanation of his position. In 1911 and 1912 Claudel and Péguy, the two great founders of the Catholic literary renaissance in France, made renewed efforts to establish a friendly relationship, exchanging expressions of mutual admiration, but they never met face-to-face.[18]

Claudel's troubled reading of *Notre Jeunesse* in 1910 was one factor among the many that contributed to a gradual evolution in his attitude toward Jews and Judaism. As Emmanuel Levinas remarks, that "remarkable evolution," which began with "a very crude anti-Semitism," was "long, . . . painful and uncertain," but it ended in Claudel's deeply respectful recognition of Judaism.[19] In an hour of grace during the Vespers service he attended in the Cathedral of Notre Dame in Paris at Christmastime in 1886, Claudel first became a believer. His philosophic tenets and his prejudices, however, remained intact and only gradually changed through decades of spiritual reading, prayer, and transformative experiences. Over a period of sixty years, Claudel studied the Bible, devoting particular attention to the Old Testament, on which he wrote commentaries. That study, Levinas suggests, begins

"Claudel's discovery of Judaism."[20] Claudel lived to acknowledge publicly his error in the Dreyfus Affair.[21] In 1936 a still wavering Claudel signed a document produced by the World Jewish Congress denouncing German anti-Semitism but refused to allow his signature to be published.[22] On August 1, 1939, on the eve of the Holocaust, Claudel wrote: "All the sacred writers call Israel a witness, but the Greek word 'witness' means 'martyr.' "[23] In the end, it was Auschwitz that completed Claudel's conversion as a Christian, making him truly a brother to the Jew. "It took no less than *that*," Levinas writes, "for him to arrive at a definite reassessment," and with that Claudel passed "the decisive test of the spirituality of the spiritual."[24]

Claudel portrayed Saint Joan of Arc only once, supplying the poetic text for Arthur Honneger's dramatic oratorio, *Jeanne d'Arc au bûcher* (*Joan of Arc at the Stake*). Commissioned by the famous ballerina and mime, Ida Rubinstein (1885–1960), and dedicated to her, it was performed for the first time in Basel, Switzerland, in 1938 and in Paris in 1939. A Russian Jew, Rubinstein played the stunning part of Jeanne d'Arc. It was her last appearance onstage, the last word she spoke to the world before her flight to England, where she survived the ravages of World War II and the flames of the Holocaust.[25]

Rubinstein's commission in 1938 gave Claudel the opportunity to resume the meditations on the Jewish Joan of Arc that he had begun in 1910 with his reading of Péguy's twinned works, *Notre Jeunesse* and *Le Mystère de la charité de Jeanne d'Arc*. The opening words of Claudel's text evoke the story of the Creation in Genesis 1:2, even as they comment on the horror of war in the late Middle Ages and the Nazi threat facing Europe: "Great darkness! Great darkness! / And a great darkness was upon the face of the whole kingdom" ("Ténèbres! Ténèbres! Et les ténèbres couvraient la face du royaume").[26] Invoking the Lord with a plea for salvation from the bestial powers of a watery chaos, Claudel unites the Jewish name for God with the Christian symbol of the fish: "Save us all, Eli Fortis Ischyros." The psalmlike prayer that cries out for help from the deep ("De profundis clamavi ad te Domine") is punctuated by the refrain indicating God's answer: "There was a maid whose name was Joan" ("Il y eut une vierge appelèe Jeanne"). Jeanne, consumed in flames at the end, is to be the light shining into the darkness (cf. Genesis 1:3; John 1:5).

Throughout the oratorio Jeanne's pure, unlettered devotion is contrasted with the artful, allegorical shape-changing of those who conspire against her and who bring charges against her in a language that she does not understand. She stands as the archetypal victim of ecclesiastical inquisition, political intrigue, and literary manipulation, but she rises above a victim's fate. Bound by "the chains of perfect love" ("les chaînes de l'amour"),[27] Jeanne refuses to recant in denial of her mission. When she shrinks in fear before the painful fires of execution, the "blazing flame so hideous" (p. 1225: "cette grande flamme / horrible") that is to be her "bridal garment" (p. 1225: "vêtement de noces"), the chorus sees her momentarily as a mere victim: "She says she's afraid. She's but a poor child after all" (p. 1224: "Elle dit qu'elle a peur! Ce n'est qu'une enfant après tout!").

At that crucial juncture, the Virgin Mary asks: "But cannot Joan herself become a glorious flame in the darkness?" (p. 1225: "Mais ést-ce que Jeanne n'ést pas une grande flamme elle-même?"). The question opens up an infinite realm of ethical possibility, and the frightened Maid finds an existential path of love and freedom for herself, even in the midst of terrible, constraining bondage. The country girl of Lorraine, who had lit candles at Mary's May altar, becomes herself a living candle, freely giving her life, even as it is being taken from her. She conquers her own fear and the fire of death with the stronger fire of her love for God and others: "Flame is now from flame arising" (p. 1225: "Flamme au-dessus de la flamme!"). The Franciscan hymn in praise of Brother Fire, sung by the chorus, becomes a praise of "our sister Saint Joan" (p. 1225: "notre sœur Jeanne / qui ést Sainte").

The final words of *Jeanne d'Arc au bûcher* echo John 15:12: "Greater love hath no man than this—to give his life for those whom he loves" (p. 1226: "Personne n'a un plus grand amour que de donner sa vie pour ceux qu'il aime"). Thus Claudel's Jeanne answers to the charity of Péguy's. The implicit hope is that the saint whose warfare against war eventually brought about peace between two Christian countries, England and France, might also triumph in twentieth-century Europe, winning the greater victory of a unity between persecuted Jews and Christians, the common targets of Hitler's idolatrous Reich. Reinterpreting Romans 8:38, Claudel's prologue asks: "This love uniting us all to our brethren—Who! Who! Who can be so strong as to tear it from our hearts?" ("Cet amour qui nous unit à nos frères. Qui! Qui! Qui sera capable de nous en séparer?").

"Dear Sisters": Saint Joan, Saint Thérèse, and Georges Bernanos

In his focus on the charity of Joan of Arc, Claudel may also have been inspired by the well-known example of Saint Thérèse of Lisieux (1873–1897), the young Carmelite who had been canonized on May 17, 1925, only five years after the canonization of her "dear sister," Saint Joan.[28] In her *Story of a Soul* (*Histoire d'une âme*), Thérèse relates that she had first sensed she was destined to become a "great saint" like "the Venerable Joan of Arc" while a student in boarding school.[29] She composed the "Prayer of France to Jeanne d'Arc," in which she prays on behalf of her much afflicted country for the return of the Maid: "Return, great-hearted daughter, / Liberating angel, / I trust in you" ("Reviens, fille au grand cœur, / Ange libérateur, / l'espère en toi").[30] Later, while a novice, Thérèse played the part of Jeanne d'Arc in a convent play.[31]

Ill with the tuberculosis that would take her life at the age of twenty-four, Thérèse wrote a letter to her sister Marie in which she confided: "*Martyrdom* was the dream of my youth, and this dream has grown within me within Carmel's cloisters." Desiring more than one kind of martyrdom, Thérèse imagines her own death: "With St. Agnes and St. Cecelia, I would present my neck to the sword, and like Joan of Arc, my dear sister, I would whisper at the stake Your Name, O JESUS."[32] In that same letter, Thérèse confesses that she is moved by infinite desires and concludes that her "follies" can only find their meaning in a single vocation, the calling to be the heart of the Church, which is "BURNING WITH LOVE": "I understood that LOVE COMPRISED ALL VOCATIONS, THAT LOVE WAS EVERYTHING, THAT IT EMBRACED ALL TIMES AND PLACES . . . IN A WORD, THAT IT WAS ETERNAL!"[33] Offering herself as a "victim of love" rather than of justice, she begs the saints and angels, as the prophet Eliseus had petitioned Elias (2 Kings 2:9) for a double portion of their spirit.[34] Later, on May 3, 1944, in the midst of World War II, Pope Pius XII named her an equal to Saint Joan of Arc as secondary patroness of France.

Placing the emphasis not on charity but on innocence and child-likeness, Georges Bernanos associates Jeanne d'Arc with Thérèse in his "Sermon of an Agnostic on the Feast of St. Thérèse," published in 1938, the same year that saw the first performance of the Claudel-Honegger oratorio, *Jeanne d'Arc au bûcher*. According to Bernanos, "The advent

of Joan of Arc in the twentieth century has the character of a solemn
warning. The remarkable fate of an obscure little Carmelite girl seems
to me an even more serious sign."[35] The message of both saints, Bernanos insists, is the same: "Christians, hurry up and become children
again, that we may become children too."[36] Using the blustery persona
of "a decent agnostic of average intelligence," Bernanos chastises the
bourgeois churches for their "spirit of resignation to injustice," their
willingness to submit to fascist dictators, their lack of heroic virtue,
their loss of the childlikeness that is eternally young and capable of a
boldly naive opposition to evil.[37]

In his fiction, notably *Journal d'un curé de campagne* (*The Diary of
a Country Priest*), published in 1937, Bernanos focuses repeatedly on
the problem of the modern priest, who is challenged to set an uncom-
promising example of holiness in a culture shaped by bourgeois values. For Bernanos, as for the enemies of the Church, the fall of the best
is the worst. Speaking in the immediate context of the Spanish Civil
War, Bernanos's agnostic persona declares: "Had you followed that
saint [Francis of Assisi] instead of applauding, Europe would never
have known the Reformation, nor the religious wars, nor this horrible
Spanish crusade."[38] Confronted with the fascist outcome of modernity, Bernanos speaks like a prophet of doom to the Church: "I cannot
help feeling that this is your last chance. Your last chance—and ours.
Are you capable of rejuvenating our world or not?"[39]

The imagination of Bernanos sets the New Testament and the
rejuvenating saints of childlikeness—Francis, Joan of Arc, and Thérèse
of Lisieux—against the Old Testament and the bourgeois "spirit of old
age," which continually orients itself toward the status quo, materialism, and the temporal values of this present world.[40] Not unlike Carl-
Theodore Dreyer, the Danish filmmaker whose *Passion de Jeanne d'Arc*
(1928) likens Joan's Catholic judges at Rouen to the Jewish elders who
condemned Christ,[41] Bernanos in *Jeanne, relapse et sainte* (1929) depicts the young Joan of Arc standing trial as a personification of childhood before an aged tribunal of the Church: "All these old men, many
of them under thirty, look enviously at this young France who is so
fresh, so mischievous, who is awfully afraid of being burnt, but still
more afraid of telling a lie."[42] Similarly, in his "Sermon of an Agnostic," Bernanos protests against the "decrepit scruple" of the bourgeoisie, which sits back, refraining from any action against Fascism and
Communism in the vain hope of "preserving an order which no longer

spares itself, which is destroying itself."[43] "The New Testament is eternally young, it is you who are old," the agnostic preacher observes. "And your 'old men' are even older than the oldest of you."[44]

In his criticism of the modern clergy, whom he charges with accommodation to bourgeois values, Bernanos's fictive agnostic (not unlike Nietzsche's Zarathustra, who bespeaks the death of God) revives the charge of deicide traditionally leveled against the Jews. The same class of people that condemned Christ and Joan of Arc is responsible, says Bernanos's preacher, for the killing of God in the present: "Deicide can never again be regarded as a crime for the rabble. It is a most distinguished, a very unusual crime reserved for opulent priests, sanctioned by the powerful middle class and the intellectuals. (In those days they were called scribes.)"[45]

After World War II Jules Isaac, a Jewish survivor of the Holocaust, was to make a similar argument, albeit with a very different motivation. In his influential study, *The Teaching of Contempt*, Isaac refers to the historic trial of Joan of Arc at Rouen, during which a jury of priests and theologians condemned to death a saint of God, as a proof by analogy that the Jewish people as a whole cannot be held accountable for the death of Christ.[46] Partly as a response to Isaac's book, which exposes a long history of anti-Judaic and anti-Semitic teaching by Christian theologians, Vatican II officially rejected in an epochal document entitled *Nostra aetate* (1965) the doctrine of deicide on which Bernanos's agnostic relies.[47]

An anti-Semite, Bernanos associated a mythic conspiracy of rich Jewish bankers with the overweening influence of the bourgeoisie, but he recoiled with horror from Hitler's persecution of the Jews. He was also paradoxically aware of the Old Testament resonance in his own prophetic outcry on behalf of the "humiliated" poor.[48] Speaking in his agnostic voice, Bernanos admits: "If you will give the matter thought, I think you will agree that we are rather like the men of the Old Testament. The modern world is as harsh as the Jewish world, and its incessant clamor is the same as that heard by the Prophets, thrown up to the skies from the huge cities along the waterside. The silence of death is haunting us also."[49] In his own struggle in 1938 with a Joban despair, Bernanos joins his voice with that of a world "awaiting the Messiah" but without a vibrant hope, because its spirit has been "corroded by the same leprosy of which the Semitic imagination bears the hideous wound throughout the centuries: the obsession of nothingness, the impotence—almost physical impotence—to conceive of the Resurrection."[50]

From the point of view of sacrificial authorship, Bernanos is the most disturbing figure of the Catholic renaissance in France, because of his anti-Semitism. Married to Jeanne Talbert d'Arc, a direct descendant of a brother of Jeanne d'Arc, Bernanos worked in 1913–1914 as a journalist in Rouen, writing for the notorious *Action Française,* the newspaper of the royalist party first founded in 1898 during the Dreyfus Affair by Henri Vaugeois and Charles Maurras.[51] At the prompting of Pope Pius XI (1922–1939), the archbishop of Bordeaux publicly condemned the Action Française on August 25, 1926. Shortly thereafter the Holy Office published its earlier decree of January 26, 1914, wherein it prohibited seven books by Maurras, as well as the Action Française periodicals, and specified disciplinary measures. When Action Française responded with an outburst of anticlerical propaganda, Bernanos broke all ties with the organization, which had increasingly allied itself with the Nazis, and he became its outspoken critic. A "reactionary without a party" (as W. M. Frohock styles him), Bernanos withdrew to Brazil in 1938, where he lent his pen to the cause of the French Resistance, until Charles de Gaulle called for his return in 1945.[52]

It would be easy to characterize the leading French Catholic writers of the period under discussion as follows: "Bernanos antisémite, Péguy à l'opposé, Bloy et Claudel dépassant leur antisémitisme," but that would be, as Jacques Petit admits, too easy.[53] What is interesting in each case is the evolution in thought and attitude and, from the point of view of this study, the emergence of a Jewish Joan of Arc. Péguy and Claudel both give Joan a Jewish face and resist her victimization by focusing attention on her agency on behalf of others; her luminous, all-consuming charity. Bernanos, by contrast, attempts to forestall victimization through a radical, artistic opposition of the victim's innocence to the oppressor's guilt. Bernanos understands that the mythic lie attributes guilt to the victim and exonerates the community, and he counters that myth. In his novels and essays, the heroes and heroines suffer as victims precisely because of their innocence. Like René Girard, who describes the single victim mechanism as a relationship of all against one, Bernanos writes in "Joan, Heretic and Saint": "Childhood is alone against everyone."[54]

What troubles the reader of Bernanos is his blindness to his own scapegoating. Frohock rightly observes: "To make [Gustave Flaubert] responsible for everything that has gone wrong in France for a century, as Bernanos does, testifies less to respect for historical truth than to a need for scapegoats. So does his antisemitism."[55] In a universe such as Bernanos paints—a world of age and youth, corruption and inno- cence, black and white—the place of the victim remains forever open. The victimizer in one instance can substitute for the victim in the next, and vice versa. Bernanos witnessed the European catastrophe that pro- duced a sea of victims. To his credit, he always took the part of the one he *saw* in need (however limited his perception), and he endured an ever-increasing isolation as a result of his concern for victims. "The spirit of Childhood is capable of both good and evil," Bernanos recog- nized, sometimes to his own shame, but "it is not the spirit of resigna- tion to injustice."[56]

Bernanos's last work, *Dialogues des Carmélites (The Dialogues of the Carmelites)*, was completed in Tunisia in the months before his death in 1948. It offers a fictional account of the true story of the six- teen Carmelite nuns who were guillotined in Paris on July 17, 1794. The nuns were arrested by the French revolutionaries in their convent at Compiègne, the same city where Joan of Arc had been captured in 1430. Bernanos surely recognized a parallel that had escaped Robert Southey in 1793–1795, when he, then anti-Catholic and fervently republican, was portraying Joan of Arc as a Jacobin.

Franz Werfel's (Re)Incarnation of Joan in Bernadette

A reactionary whose anachronistic, visionary politics resist a com- monplace definition, Bernanos frequently had to react against his own positions over the course of time—so much so that, as Frohock notes, "he later abandoned or contradicted himself about" most of the "spe- cific stands" he had taken earlier.[57] Sensing the dialectical structure of politically engaged ideologies, Bernanos's contemporary, the Jewish, Expressionist poet, dramatist, and novelist Franz Werfel (1890–1945), had consciously rejected political activism early in his career for philo- sophical reasons to which he gave expression in his 1916 essay, "The Christian Mission" ("Die christliche Sendung"). There he argues that every action (*Tat*) has opposite effects, helping one individual and harm- ing another. Political activism depends, he argues, on an ideological "abstraction" that allows one to disregard the effect of one's actions on concrete individuals. Interpreting Christianity through a Hebraic lens, Werfel sees the Christian mission, grounded in the Incarnation and the face-to-face encounters it presupposes and requires, as an embodied opposition to Hellenistic abstraction.[58]

At the end of his "Sermon of an Agnostic," Bernanos's persona, who has been exhorting the Christian laity and clergy to put the gospel into practice and thus embody the Word, closes with a reference to the physical cures wrought at Lourdes in France: "Supposing, my brothers, that I were consumptive, and I wished to drink the waters of Lourdes."[59] Fleeing from the Nazis, Franz Werfel took refuge in Lourdes for seven weeks in summer 1940, before continuing the dangerous journey that brought him and his companions to Spain and, from there, to the United States.[60] While in Lourdes, the Jewish Werfel, who had been educated as a boy in a Catholic school in Prague, familiarized himself with the story of Saint Bernadette Soubirous (1844–1879), to whom the Virgin Mary had appeared in a series of visions, beginning on February 11, 1858. In Lourdes, too, he made a vow that he would tell Bernadette's story, if he managed to escape to America. In fulfillment of his vow, Werfel wrote *Das Lied von Bernadette* (1941; *The Song of Bernadette*, 1942), which was read by millions worldwide.[61] In that novel Werfel gives Joan of Arc the face of Bernadette. Even as Joan of Arc returns for Bernanos in Saint Thérèse, so too she appears anew in Werfel's visionary of Lourdes.

Vita Sackville-West had earlier raised the question of a possible connection between the two girl-saints, Joan and Bernadette:

> What connexion, we may ask again, exists between such mundane warlike admonitions as were received by Jeanne and such admonitions as were received by, say, Bernadette of Lourdes— Bernadette, another peasant girl of thirteen, going out to gather sticks for the fire, and being confronted by an apparition whom she, during a fortnight, was able to identify as the Virgin Mary, and under whose directions she discovered a spring so miraculous as still to draw thousands of pilgrims from all parts of Europe yearly in hopes of a cure?[62]

That Werfel's novel is an extended answer to the question posed by Sackville-West becomes apparent from Bernadette's first appearance. Questioned by Father Pomian about her age, Bernadette replies that she was born on January 7, 1844. The priest calls Bernadette's attention to the importance of that date, which falls within the octave of the Feast of the Epiphany. Turning to the whole class, Father Pomian continues: "And the seventh of January is an important feast day in France, for on that day one was born who rescued our country from deepest disgrace" ("Da wurde jemand geboren, der das Vaterland aus der tiefsten Schande gerettet hat").[63] When the children fail to guess whose birthday coincides with Bernadette's (one student wrongly proposes "The Emperor Napoléon Bonaparte!"), he writes on the chalkboard the words: "Jeanne d'Arc, the Maid of Orléans, born on the seventh of January 1412 at Domrémy" (p. 17): "Jeanne d'Arc, die Jungfrau von Orléans, geboren am 7. Januar 1412 in Domrémy" (p. 33).[64]

In his *Song of Bernadette* Werfel does not explicitly extend this initial point of identification between Saints Bernadette and Joan, but he relates Bernadette's story in such a way that anyone familiar with Joan's will notice multiple parallels. The German tradition to which Werfel fell heir had, via Schiller, attributed to the Virgin Mary (rather than to Saints Catherine, Margaret, and Michael) the role of calling Joan of Arc. The grotto of Massabielle is, in the popular imagination, a haunted, quasi-pagan place, possessing connotations similar to those of Joan's oak woods and fairy tree. Bernadette, like Joan, is poor, young, uneducated, a child of the common people; like Joan, too, she hears voices and sees visions; she is suspected of madness; accused of illicit gain; physically put to the flame.[65] Both saints are put to a severe test by their parents and by Church authorities, who are slow to give credence to their stories. Both affect French rulers. Both establish their credentials through the working of miracles. Even as Joan of Arc was famous for her spirited replies to her judges, Werfel's Bernadette silences the learned sages who question her. Both suffer cruel deaths at a young age but benefit thousands of others through their lives. Joan of Arc dies crying out the name of Jesus; Werfel's Bernadette, dying of bone cancer, exclaims, "J'aime. . . . I love" (p. 397).

Werfel treats Bernadette (as other authors in this book have treated Joan of Arc) as an artist-figure and incorporates into the telling of her story a variety of commentaries on art and artists, especially through the character of the agnostic poet Hyacinthe Lafite. Bernadette's contemplative stance before the Virgin whom she alone can see is, for Werfel, an image of the artist, who communicates an inexpressible reality to others indirectly, through his or her own dialogue with it. In the later chapters of the novel, after Bernadette has joined the convent of the Sisters of Nevers, she exercises her talent for drawing and embroidery, producing original "designs . . . so out of the ordinary, so highly individual in fact, that it took the delighted appreciation of sundry connoisseurs of art among the clergy to soothe the anxious fright" (p. 342) of Bernadette's religious superiors: "Diese freilich sind äußerst ungewöhnlich, ja so eigenartig, daß erst das Entzücken einiger kunstverständiger Kleriker, denen man sie vorlegte, den ängstlichen Schreck Mutter Imberts und die frostige Verwunderung Mutter Vazous beschwichtigen konnte" (p. 505). Even as Bernadette's visions at Lourdes had led to the discovery through her hands of a healing spring, so in the convent the forms of her artistic expression shift, as she turns from embroidery work in the sacristy to the art of healing in the military hospitals of the Franco-Prussian War.

Between 1941, when *Das Lied von Bernadette* first appeared, and 1945, when he died suddenly of a heart attack in Los Angeles, Werfel endured much criticism as a German Jew because of the Catholicity of the novel and because its subject matter seemed to some escapist in view of the horrors of the death camps. (Bertolt Brecht, at work on his own saint play, referred to Werfel pejoratively as "saint frunzis of hollywood, gschweifel of that ilk.")[66] Werfel, however, establishes the Holocaust as the immediate context for his writing of the novel in a personal preface: "Providence brought me to Lourdes. . . . We hid for several weeks in the Pyrenean city. It was a time of great dread. The British radio announced that I had been murdered by the National Socialists. Nor did I doubt that such would be my fate, were I to fall into the hands of the enemy" (p. vii): "Auf diese Weise führte mich die Vorsehung nach Lourdes. . . . Wir verbargen uns mehrere Wochen in der Pyrenäenstadt. Es war eine angstvolle Zeit" (p. 8).[67]

In the chapters entitled "The Hell of the Flesh," "The Lightning Strikes," and "I Never Loved," Werfel describes the throngs of desperately suffering people—crippled, cancerous, maimed, blind, leprous, afflicted with every conceivable disease of body and soul—who have made their way to Lourdes. In these descriptions he clearly means to represent anachronistically the refugees, the wounded soldiers, and the prisoners of the death camps. Dr. Dozous tells Lafite: "You have seen but a small section of the suffering that fills the world. . . . Tomorrow we expect five more trainloads[,] . . . not only Catholics even, but also Protestants and Jews. . . . They are the despairing who come, those who have no way left but this" (p. 379): "Sie haben nur einen winzigen Ausschnitt des Leidens gesehen, von dem die Welt voll ist. . . . Morgen erwarten wir wieder fünf neue Züge mit Kranken[,] . . . nicht einmal nur Katholiken, . . . sondern auch Protestanten und Juden. Es sind die Verzweifelten, die keinen aundern Ausweg mehr haben als diesen" (p. 558).

The account of Bernadette's canonization in 1933 in the last chapter of the novel is deliberately topical. Werfel summarizes the speech of Pope Pius XI, who refers to the "confusion of demonic voices which had accompanied the visions of Bernadette" (p. 403): "das dämonische Stimmengewirre, das Bernadette während ihrer Erscheinungen hörte" (p. 594). "This tumult," declares the pope, "[has] increased immeasurably since her time. It [is] filling the world. . . . The fever of maniacal false doctrines [is] threatening to plunge the human spirit into bloody madness" (p. 403): "Dieses Stimmengewirre habe sich unfaßbar vermehrt seitdem. Die Welt sei voll davon. . . . Das Fieber der rasenden Irrlehren drohe den menschlichen Geist in blutigen Wahnsinn zu stürzen" (pp. 594–595). The allusion to Nazism and Hitler's Third Reich cannot be mistaken. Werfel seals it with an ominous reference to a "military plane" (p. 596: "ein Militärflugzeug") flying in the sky over Rome (p. 404).

As a latter-day Joan of Arc, Werfel's Bernadette Soubirous endures a destiny that replicates the pattern of the sacrificial scapegoat but with the crucial differences of innocence, charity, and a manifest humanity, even after her canonization. Hyacinth Lafite's vain efforts throughout the novel to understand Bernadette's story in mythic terms—as a modern-day worship of the goddess Diana, for example—thematize the opposition between the Judeo-Christian experience and the Hellenic. Werfel's Bernadette is definitely blessed and cursed, in the sense that her visionary experience sets her apart from everyone else, awakens hostility and division, and eventually necessitates her removal from the community, for which the healing stream, opened by Bernadette, has finally become a means of unity.

Werfel's Bernadette is consecrated, however, not sacrificed, nor does she sacrifice herself. She simply loves and heroically suffers, in the manner of a pure child and a mature woman, the consequences of her love and obedience. Throughout *The Song of Bernadette*, Bernadette's genuine, natural holiness is contrasted with the rule-bound, self-sacrificing asceticism of the nun Marie Thérèse Vazous. Insisting on the antisacrificial nature of "the true spirit of the gospel text," Girard has warned that "self-sacrifice can serve to camouflage the forms of slavery brought into being by mimetic desire. . . . What might be concealed here is the desire to sacralize *oneself* and to make *oneself* godlike—which quite clearly harks back to the illusion traditionally produced by sacrifice."[68] A passage in Werfel's novel illustrates precisely this distinction:

> The nun Vazous, had she ever been ill—only she never was—would have uttered no lament amidst bitterest suffering but, rigid and pallid as a medieval queen, would have made a silent sacrifice of her torments. Not so Bernadette. She never thought of making a sacrifice of the inevitable. She had no stealthy eye on some reward. She had kept the tumor on her knee a secret only because she did not want to be relieved of her duties as a nurse. (Pp. 363–364)

> Die Nonne Vazous, wäre sie jemals krank—aber sie ist es nicht— würde im bittersten Leiden keinen Klagelaut von sich geben, son- dern starr und bleich wie eine mittelalterliche Königin ihre Qualen verschweigen und aufopfern. Nicht so Bernadette. Sie denkt nicht daran, das Unabwendbare aufzuopfern. Sie schielt nach keinem Lohn. Sie hat die furchtbare Geschwulst am Knie nur deshalb ver- heimlicht, um von ihrer Arbeit nicht abberufen zu werden. (P. 536)

Vazous sacrifices herself because she desires the crown of sanctity. She imitates the ascetic practices of the saints of old, and she enters into an envious competition with Bernadette, whose grace surpasses hers. Bernadette, by contrast, does not sacrifice herself as an object, nor does she sacrifice anyone else. Instead, she is the chosen instru- ment of love and healing for a diseased world. No one is excluded from the waters that flow at Lourdes, except for Bernadette herself. Dying of bone cancer, Bernadette remains at Nevers in the simple knowledge "The spring is not for me" (p. 365): "für mich ist die Quelle nicht da" (p. 539). Bernadette's role, as Vazous comes to understand it, is to be "the protagonist of all the ailing in the world" (p. 362), in imi- tation of Christ: "die Protagonistin aller Kranken der Welt" (p. 534). For her part, Bernadette "yielded herself to her illness even as she had always been obedient to all that life had brought her," allowing her- self to feel the pain and not denying what she felt (p. 363): "Bernadette gibt sich der Krankheit hin, wie sie sich allem hingegeben hat, was das Leben brachte" (p. 535).

Bernadette, like Joan of Arc, has her covetous imitators and would-be look-alikes. Werfel devotes a whole chapter to "Apes of the Miracle" (p. 318: "Nachbeben oder Affen des Mirakels"), which records "rival phenomena" (p. 213), much of it Satanic in its mimesis. Werfel's story-telling exemplifies the principle spelled out by Girard: "God and Satan are the two supreme models. . . . If we do not imitate Jesus, our models become the [scandalous] living obstacles that we also become for them."[69] Bernadette herself, by contrast, imitates no one except the heavenly Lady whom she loves. In her face-to-face dialogue with the Lady of the visions, the rapt girl responds to her every gesture— "the nodding, the smiling, the beckoning, the folding or outspreading of the lady's hands" (p. 102): "diese Nicken, dieses Lächeln, dieses Winken, dieses Händefalten, dieses Händebreiten der Dame" (p. 157). Thus she presents a lively "image in a mirror" (p. 157: "einem Spiegel-bild"), so that the crowd glimpses the invisible lady in Bernadette's attentiveness to her: "Bernadette was, as it were, the photographic negative of the invisible" (p. 102): "Bernadette ist gewissermaßen das vollkommene Negativ der Unsichtbaren" (p. 157). If Bernadette became a latter-day Joan of Arc, it was, Werfel suggests, because both saints listened obediently to the same Voices. Those Voices always create what is new, unique, and original, the "new kind of sanctity" for which Péguy was longing.

Playing Joan: Leonard Cohen and Erik Ehn

Saints Bernadette and Joan of Arc appear together in the hagiographic imaginary of two contemporary artists: Leonard Cohen, the award-winning Jewish Canadian poet and folk-rock star, and the Catholic playwright Erik Ehn. For both of them, treating the subject of Saint Joan provides an opportunity for reflection on the work of art and artists. Their portrayals of Joan employ marked, antisacrificial strategies as a way of avoiding closure and thus of sustaining the artistic process as an ongoing work of creation. Dark and brooding, Cohen mourns the tragic necessity of the repeated Jehannine sacrifices he makes as a seasonal condition for an ever renewed creativity. Ehn, by contrast, evokes the Divine Comedy in his "Big Cheap Theater" through plays as short as possible, whose very brevity forces a lyric sense of the eternal present (and Presence).

Cohen's "Joan of Arc" dates from his residence in 1966–1967 in New York's Chelsea Hotel, a favorite haunt of recording artists of the sixties.[70] The album *Songs of Leonard Cohen,* unofficially released on December 26, 1967, shows on the back a Joan of Arc figure engulfed by flames, her enchained hands raised upward. Cohen's biographer, Ira B. Nadel, reports that the "unattributed image was actually a widely available Mexican postcard of a saint Cohen found in a Mexican magic store."[71] Representing "the *anima sola,* the lonely soul seeking release from the chains of materiality," the image, which was to reappear on his 1995 album, *Tower of Song,* was for Cohen a self-image: "I sort of felt I was this woman."[72]

The song "Joan of Arc" is reminiscent of a medieval *pastourelle,* for it records the dialogue in a woods between the warrior-shepherdess Joan of Arc, who is riding alone, and a masculine figure, who declares his love for her and identifies himself as "Fire." Tired of fighting, Cohen's Joan is longing to wear a wedding dress. She accepts the embrace of Fire, only to discover that she must be wood. Her wedding dress reduced to ashes, her body to dust, Joan celebrates a painful and destructive marriage with Fire that is nonetheless life-giving and freeing, a mystical loss of the self into the poet's erotic song, sung for the wedding guests.

In his various renditions of this song, Cohen tried different experiments. In the 1971 album, *Songs of Love and Hate,* Cohen both sings and speaks the lines of "Joan of Arc," using two different tracks. The effect of a double voicing was, according to Cohen, inspired by the medieval palimpsest, a manuscript with lines written over lines,[73] but it also evokes Joan's plural Voices.[74] In his 1986 album, *Famous Blue Raincoat,* he emphasizes the dialogic and seductive quality of "Joan of Arc," singing the part of Fire in a duet with Jennifer Warnes, who sings the part of Joan.[75] Drawing on the resources of an anonymous literary tradition, the medieval *pastourelle* of the lyric poets, and evoking the prayer-poetry of the mystics, Cohen manages to find a place where (in Warnes's words) "God and sex and literature meet."[76]

Saint Joan of Arc makes an appearance in another lyric of Cohen's, "Last Year's Man," which was included in *Songs of Love and Hate,* as well as *The Best of Leonard Cohen* (1976). One of his personal favorites, a song he revised over a period of five years, "Last Year's Man," like

"Joan of Arc," is a self-portrait of the artist.[77] In that lyric the motion-less "last year's man" on whom the rain falls down is an artist-figure whose creativity in various media has been depleted. His motionless hand does not reach for the Jew's harp, does not draw with the crayon, and his architectural design remains unrealized: the paper corners on the blueprint on the table are ruined. The rolled out blueprint, held in place with thumbtacks, doubles the tightly stretched skin of a drum that is unplayed by him and in need of mending.

The rain, however, beats on the drumlike skylight above him. The beating of that drum summons him to move on, to let go of his former self, and let that despairing detachment nourish his creativity: "But everything will happen if he only gives the word," the creative word that is alpha and omega. "The lovers will rise up and the mountains touch the ground," he declares, paraphrasing the prophet Isaiah. In the present moment, however, that creative word cannot be spoken by last year's man, who remains sitting paralyzed, perhaps dead, at the table, the rain falling down on his works. The rain is at once a winter rain and a rain in springtime. Winterlike, it offers an objective correlative for last year's man's barrenness, despair, and tears; springlike, it cleanses, purifies, and prepares for the new life that "will happen." The creative word must be spoken, not by last year's old man, but by another self, the new man who can say "amen" to detachment from self and to ar-tistic self-discipline. To make this point, Cohen puns on the words "Amen" and "man," the last words in the final couplet of the first and last stanzas.

Perhaps the sound of the drumbeat, which is also a heartbeat, evokes the martial, marching imagery of the second stanza, where Joan of Arc appears, "playing / with her soldiers in the dark." Cohen's imagery am-biguously recalls the medieval charges against Joan, which insinuated that the Maid of Orléans, whom the French revered as a virgin-saint, was really a whore and camp follower. Cohen, however, reverses that charge. His "I" first encounters the lady as a prostitute and only later discovers that her love is the charity of Joan of Arc. The speaker thanks Joan for having treated him well, for having comforted and healed him, like the other "wounded boys" who remain, albeit temporarily, in her army. Because of her love, his departure is purer than his arrival. Cohen's Joan in this stanza thus resembles Saint Bernadette and the Sisters of Mercy in other lyrics of his, for she enables him to move on, wearing the uniform of his calling as a poet.

The third stanza, the center of the lyric, closes with the archetypal image of the serpent eating its tail, an image that duplicates at the structural center of the poem its larger circular pattern. It shows the opposites of head and tail joining in a marriage that proves both darkly destructive of innocence and fertile for redemption. Once again, the speaker is both an outside observer and a participant in what he sees. An accidental guest at a wedding between two allegorical cities, Babylon and Bethlehem, he joins his flesh with theirs in an orgy. Only when the speaker pulls back the veil of his own flesh and theirs does he see the serpent and realize his own participation in an ageless, repetitive, universal story of sin: Gentile and Jew, "we fell together."

In the fourth stanza, the speaker expresses the longing for redemption in erotic terms: "Some women wait for Jesus / and some women wait for Cain." Ready to play both parts in order to satisfy their desire, the speaker becomes the original fratricide, Cain, and Jesus, the "first-born of many brothers" (Romans 8:29). Cain was "just the man"—last year's man but also the killer with the ax that marks an ending. Jesus was and is the honeymoon, the beginning. And the speaker identifies with both.

In the dynamic of the poem as a narrative of the creative process, both Cain and Jesus are necessary. Indeed, the pairing of Cain and Jesus duplicates the previous pairings of opposites in the poem: Babylon and Bethlehem, Joan of Arc as whore and virgin. As Cain, the speaker must "hoist his ax" to detach himself from his own past, last year's man, his failed works, and all his amorous attachments. As Jesus, he must "hang upon [the] altar" to accept the blow and to begin the honeymoon anew. Both Cain and Jesus are "children of the wilderness," a desert wasteland that, in keeping with Isaiah's prophecy, will blossom in the messianic age: "The lovers will rise up and the mountains touch the ground." In performance this hope of a new period of artistic creativity gains expression in the singing of children's voices.

Cohen's lyric portrait of the artist represents the pattern of his own life, in which the Bethlehem of a priestly and prophetic Judaism has mingled with the Babylon of hedonism and despair. As Cohen's biography shows, a series of love affairs has fueled his art, and each broken relationship has meant an end and a beginning for him. A self-proclaimed lady's man, Cohen was always leaving "last year's man" and "last year's (or last month's) woman" behind. In part, this is what being in Joan of Arc's army symbolizes for him. An erotic symbol, Cohen's Joan is also the ever virginal, because ever free and detached, artist. Whatever sacrificial structures may be in place in Cohen's personal life, in his lyrics he strives for a paradoxical cohesion of opposites. In Joan's double identity, Cohen sees his own mixture of things, the peculiar combination that the critic Anjelica Huston has dubbed "part wolf and part angel."[78]

A Jewish poet of protest whose parents belonged to what he calls "the Dachau generation,"[79] Cohen has regarded the Spanish martyr-poet, Federico García Lorca (1898–1936), murdered during the Spanish Civil War by the Granadian Falangists, as his most important artistic model.[80] Lorca is also an important influence for Erik Ehn. In the preface to *The Saint Plays,* Ehn quotes Lorca to explain what he means when he calls the "saint" a "human mandala—a life in ritual shape held up as a focus for contemplation": "The symbolic and the literal are conflated to produce what Lorca calls the *hecho poetico*—the poetic fact—an irreducible image that is a source of meaning rather than a restatement of it. Saints make autobiography out of conundrum, and practice right conduct on a field occupied simultaneously by the impossible and the ethical (by that which cannot be comprehended yet compels choice)."[81]

The contemplative focus on the life of the saint as a work of art explains the brief, lyric quality of each of Ehn's collected *Saint Plays,* which are staged to arrest the audience's attention on the saint's person and action in the present moment, *sub specie aeternitatis,* while at the same time radically opposing "idolatry" through "definitionally incomplete and inconsistent" set designs and stage directions; an accentuated fragmentariness of plot; a minimalist script that verges on anti-script; and a refusal to offer narrative closure (p. ix).

The first play in Ehn's collection of *Saint Plays* is *Wholly Joan's,* a play in three brief scenes: "The Capture," "The Defense," "The Burning." The title of the play and its placement at the start of the collection suggests a dedication of the whole to Saint Joan of Arc. The title includes an obvious wordplay (holy/wholly) that signals Ehn's characteristically deconstructive, anti-idolatrous, linguistic practice. The words *Wholly Joan's* also allusively recall to a contemporary Catholic audience the motto of Pope John Paul II, who dedicated himself to the Blessed Virgin Mary, Mother of God, with the Latin words: "Totus tua,"

"Totally yours." It thus links Ehn's vocation as a poet and playwright with that of the priest, who serves as a bridge ("pontus") and sacramental mediator "in persona Christi" between God and his people.

As the first play in the collection, *Wholly Joan's* also exemplifies best the artistic principles enunciated in Ehn's preface. All of the *Saint Plays* are short, but *Wholly Joan's* is among the briefest, a bare four pages. Ehn explains that his hagiographic theater attempts to represent the peculiar temporal modality in which saints live their lives: "They move not so as to be endless (extensive through time) but with intensity, to become instant, infinitely attractive, anomalous in time. And so the plays are short. They want to be over before they start" (p. x).[82] Surely few of the saints illustrate this principle better than Joan of Arc, who died at the age of nineteen; who accomplished her historical, military mission for France in the brief, impatient, impetuous term of a year; and who knew by prophecy that her time for action would be extremely limited.

Ehn's play about Joan of Arc includes an internal comment on temporality that marks the distinction between this kind of intense, saintly use of time and hedonistic *carpe diem*. One of Joan's guards tells her: "Love everything you're ever going to love all of a sudden, honey, because you've come to the end of the line" (p. 4). Responding with a pun that blunts the force of his seduction, Joan declares: "That's the old line" (p. 4).

In *Wholly Joan's*, initially performed under Ehn's direction at the Manhattan Class Company on September 8, 1988, the audience first sees Joan of Arc in a circle of light on a dark stage. The light falls "like plate steel," and Joan "delivers and retrieves weight, resisting the circle's physical pull" (p. 3). The vision of Joan in a circle of light recalls Ehn's fundamental dictum that "a saint is a human mandala — a life in ritual shape held up as a focus for contemplation" (p. x). The literal impossibility of a heavy, steellike light, against which Joan must exercise herself, lifting its weight, suggests what Ehn calls in his preface an "esthetic physics," a metaphoric system that expresses the patterns of Christian mysticism in sensual images and bodily gestures (p. ix).

The guards who enter, looking for Joan, interrupt her at prayer. Her words, startling in their metaphoric combination of sexuality and mysticism, give meaning to the gesture of wrestling in the circle of light: "You want me to love to hear you, but you can't make me. . . . I know what it feels like to be in the dead center with you" (p. 3). Joan is in a resistant dialogue with God, who wants to draw her into his "pure center," because she knows "that the center is a target," and God does not work "with guarantees" (p. 3). For her to step into the center of God's love and light is to become a target for attack by others. Joan's capitulation—"Okay. My God, I'm a lover. Jesus, I love you"—draws a triform angel on stage. The angel, who "is three women," represents Joan's traditional Voices (Saints Michael the Archangel, Catherine, and Margaret). She tells Joan, "Jumpin Jesus says to fight" (p. 4). The angel then vanishes as "red police lights flash" (p. 4).

The second and third scenes continue the exploration of love and sacrifice begun in the first. In "The Defense" Joan converses with her guards about their reasons for killing her. The accusation of witchcraft is, they agree, a mere excuse. About the real reasons, though, they disagree. The first guard tells her, "We're killing you because you're a nuisance, and because we feel like it, and because daddy always liked us better" (p. 5). Joan points to a different reason, the mimetic desire that puts the world and the devil in jealous competition with God: "You're killing me because something loves me more than you know how" (p. 5). In another evocation of "esthetic physics," Joan compares the divine love possessing her to "all those distant natural mysteries you're afraid of"—the energy sources of rivers, steam, electricity (p. 5).

When the guards try to stop Joan, they fight her fire with fire. Scene iii opens with Joan tied to the stake in an iconographic pose, "wearing full armor, in a volume of severe light" (p. 6). She is alone, as she was in the opening scene of circled light, and she prays to God in a way that redefines the fire of torture as the fire of his love: "You are always moving towards me, and are moving me towards you, and you are always clear light, with the feel of cool water" (p. 6). Ehn's Joan overmasters her self as she dies through an act of faith that is simultaneously an "act of imagination" (p. ix). She dies smiling, having given God her full surrender: "Happy Valentine's day, God Almighty. You get my heart" (p. 6). God himself is "wholly Joan's," because she is completely his, in the "pure center" of his love (p. 3).

Ehn's *Wholly Joan's* locates historic action in one place while suggesting that it is really happening in a different place altogether, because the saint lives and acts in an altered space and time, a different dimension of reality. Joan approaches the center. Similarly, Ehn writes, "we are all charged with the task of turning into saints ourselves, with a responsibility to lose location and enter into a love so radical that identity surrenders to the condition of metaphor" (p. ix). To live constantly in relation to the Other, out of responsibility for the Other, is to live in the I-and-Thou that is a "poetic oscillation with God" (p. ix), the both-and of metaphor.

The guards enter, only to discover nothing left of Joan of Arc but a large cloth cherry red heart. When the first guard wonders aloud why the fire did not consume her heart, the second replies: "BECAUSE HER HEART IS HOTTER THAN FIRE" (p. 6). The use of the present tense in this final sentence leaves the story without an end, open, even as Joan is still active, still loving. Ehn's "exploded biography" (p. ix) of Saint Joan includes the fragmentation of her body, but it implies the powerful transformation of her life rather than its sacrificial loss.

The authors I have discussed in this concluding chapter all employ anti-sacrificial strategies in order to avert the figural scapegoating of Joan of Arc, whom they view as a representative of themselves and others. They emphasize her innocence. They stress her charitable agency. Her story becomes for them a way of voicing their own prophetic concern for the victims of injustice. Rather than use her death as a symbolic means of distancing themselves from their literary precursors, they employ her life as a means of drawing closer to God, the author of the Bible and the creator of the universe. They find in the biblical word that inspired Joan's life a vital source for their own original speaking in plays, poetry, novels, and songs.

Some of them are, to be sure, more successful than others. None of them completely avoids sacrifice. There are, as Sandor Goodhart remarks in another context, "no non-sacrificial readings" of Joan's story.[83] How could there be? The historic Joan of Arc died at the stake, alone and unsupported, condemned as the guiltiest of the guilty. The covetous, competitive, mimetic tendencies that led to her death remain alive in all of us today. The Catholic and the Jewish authors surveyed here, however, are grounded in a Judeo-Christian tradition that stands directly opposed to the mythic values that endorse the blaming of others, their expulsion, and killing. Their fictions about Joan of Arc speak to us in the age after Auschwitz because they allow us (in Goodhart's words) "to recognize the possibilities for survival in a 'post-sacrificial' universe, a universe in which the expulsion of scapegoats has become confused irretrievably with violence itself, to imagine, that is, if only hypothetically, the possibilities for an anti-sacrificial position."[84] That antisacrificial position is prophetic, endlessly creative, and authorizing, because it speaks "with authority" (Mark 1:28; Matthew 7:29).

The Maiden of Orleans
By Friedrich von Schiller
Translated by Ingeborg Maria Hinderschiedt

To mock man's lofty image in disdain,
Contempt immersed you in the depths of slime.
Was ever Reason not at war with Beauty,
Regarding neither Angel nor the God?
Nor loath to rob the Heart of its abundance,
At all times battling dreams and wounding Faith?

But Poesy—like you of pure descent—,
A valiant shepherdess Herself, like you,
Is reaching out to you, with hand divine,
To soar with you up high to yonder stars,
Embracing with an aureole your being:
Your life, engendered by the Heart, will never
Succumb to death, your fate not be oblivion.

The world is bent on blackening what is bright,
On dragging what is sublime into the mud.
Yet fear not! For there still live valiant hearts
To burn with love of things profound and wondrous.
Let censors run the marketplace, divert
Contemptuously the boisterous crowds, to boot!

A noble spirit loves a nobler cast.

Joan of Arc: A Dramatic Monologue
By Ann W. Astell

They would not let me come to you!
They said it would defile the place
For one on trial for heresy
To enter it, to sue for grace—
And so I knelt outside the church
And sighed for all that was denied:
The Mass, the sacraments—and you!
Until the soldiers at my side
Took hold of me and hauled me up.
They bruised me, gripping to the bone,
And dragged me down indifferent streets,
No echo sounding from the stone,
No sign of recognition in
The silent, staring people passed—
As if I were already dead,

A memory, a shadow cast
One sunless day beneath a cloud—
Perhaps a name that once was heard,
That faintly stirred with fear and fame—
As if all loss could be regained
By simply crossing out my name.

A heretic, perhaps a witch,
But surely England's enemy—
It hardly matters what the charge:
The sentence will be death for me.
A bishop bribed to barb the hook,
My enemies are bold and free—
And no one's here to take my part.
Not even Charles remembers me.
So I must be my own defense.
I hardly know what words I say.
They question me repeatedly
For endless hours every day.
I only tell them what I know:
The little truths like polished stone,
The smooth white pebbles water-worn
One gathers when the waves are blown
Across your ankles on the shore,
The rounded stones that fit so well
Inside the hollow of your hand,
The simple truths that one can tell
Because you've carried them along,
Like skipping stones weighed in the palm,
Held to the light and pocketed,
Familiar, fingered, felt, and warm.

They never let me be alone—
No privacy, no woman near,
Men guarding me both day and night,
No refuge from the look, the leer
That pricks the flesh into a sweat.
Heart beating hollow, cold with fear,
I enter my own emptiness

And here, at last, I find you near.
You are my passion, you—my Love!
A dark love like a velvet rose,
The red bled purple on the stem,
The darker color still enclosed—

They want to burn me at the stake,
To blacken flesh, turn blood to flame,
And die I will, but out of love!
My dying words shall be your name!
You and you alone I love!
O let me only kiss your cross.
Then like a phoenix I shall fly
Up through the flames that wave and toss,
That fire-flare into the air,
Explode in color, crest, and fall,
That rise and writhe and surge above
Until pain peaks—my God! My All!

Notes to Introduction

1. Paul Claudel, *Jeanne d'Arc au bûcher*, in *Théâtre de Paul Claudel* (Paris: Gallimard, 1956), vol. 2, pp. 1202–1203. For the English translation, I consulted the libretto of the 1948 performance by the Philadelphia Orchestra, edited by Beatrice Baron, who used the English translation by Dennis Arundell.

2. Ibid., p. 1203.

3. Christine de Pizan, *Le Ditié de Jehanne d'Arc*, ed. and trans. Angus J. Kennedy and Kenneth Varty, *Nottingham Medieval Studies* 18 (1974): 29–55; 19 (1975): 53–76. Subsequent citations, by stanza and line number, appear in parentheses in the text.

4. Kevin Brownlee, "Structures of Authority in Christine de Pizan's *Ditié de Jehanne d'Arc*," in *Discourses of Authority in Medieval and Renaissance Literature*, ed. Kevin Brownlee and Walter Stephens (Hanover, N.H.: University Press of New England, 1989), p. 150.

5. Deborah A. Fraioli, *Joan of Arc: The Early Debate* (Rochester, N.Y.: Boydell, 2000), p. 103.

6. It is this thesis, among other things, that distinguishes this book from the previous surveys by Charles Wayland Lightbody (*The Judgements of Joan: Joan of Arc, a Study in Cultural History* [Cambridge, Mass.: Harvard University Press, 1961]), Ingvald Raknem (*Joan of Arc in History, Legend and*

Literature, Scandinavian University Books [Oslo: Universitetsforlaget, 1971]), and Hans Mayer ("The Scandal of Joan of Arc: Schiller, Shaw, Brecht, Vishnevskii," in his *Outsiders,* trans. Denis M. Sweet [Cambridge, Mass.: MIT Press, 1982], pp. 29–51).

7. See Michel Foucault, "What Is an Author?" in *Language, Counter-Memory, Practice,* ed. Donald F. Bouchard, trans. Donald F. Bouchard and Sherry Simon (Ithaca: Cornell University Press, 1977), pp. 113–138.

8. Molly Nesbit, "What Was an Author?" *Yale French Studies* 73 (1987): 229–230.

9. Ibid., p. 234.

10. Ibid., p. 233.

11. Ibid.

12. Ibid., p. 234.

13. Roland Barthes, "Authors and Writers," in *A Barthes Reader,* ed. Susan Sontag (New York: Hill and Wang, 1982), p. 190.

14. Ibid., pp. 192–193.

15. Paul Bénichou, *The Consecration of the Writer, 1750–1830,* trans. Mark K. Jensen (Lincoln: University of Nebraska Press, 1999), pp. 341, 339.

16. Ibid., pp. 342.

17. See Walter Benjamin, "The Work of Art in the Age of Mechanical Reproduction," in Walter Benjamin, *Illuminations: Essays and Reflections,* ed. Hannah Arendt, trans. Harry Zohn (New York: Schocken, 1969), pp. 217–251.

18. Harold Bloom, *The Anxiety of Influence: A Theory of Poetry,* 2d ed. (Oxford: Oxford University Press, 1997), p. 88.

19. Ibid., p. xxiv.

20. Ibid., p. 88.

21. Ibid., p. 120.

22. Ibid., p. 10.

23. Ibid., p. xxiv.

24. Ibid., p. 11.

25. René Girard, *Things Hidden since the Foundation of the World,* trans. Stephen Bann and Michael Metteer (Stanford: Stanford University Press, 1987), p. 18.

26. The question of the degree of literacy of the historical Joan of Arc is debated among scholars. She dictated many letters and signed her name to some of them; three signed letters are extant. See Régine Pernoud and Marie-Véronique Clin, *Joan of Arc: Her Story,* trans. and rev. Jeremy duQuesnay Adams, ed. Bonnie Wheeler (New York: St. Martin's, 1998), pp. 246–264.

27. Roland Barthes, "The Death of the Author," in *Authorship from Plato to the Postmodern: A Reader,* ed. Seán Burke (Edinburgh: Edinburgh University Press, 1995), p. 126. Emphasis added.

28. Ibid.

29. Seán Burke, "The Ethics of Signature," in *Authorship from Plato to the Postmodern,* p. 289.

30. Ibid.

31. On the questions surrounding Joan's historic signing of the letter of abjuration, see Pernoud and Clin, *Joan of Arc: Her Story*, pp. 130–131.

32. Bloom, *Anxiety of Influence*, p. xxvi.

33. Edith Wyschogrod, *Saints and Postmodernism: Revisioning Moral Philosophy* (Chicago: University of Chicago Press, 1990), pp. 28–29.

34. Ibid., p. 10.

35. Ibid., p. 13.

36. Benjamin, "Work of Art in the Age of Mechanical Reproduction," pp. 222–223.

37. Ibid., p. 224.

38. I use here the classical terms of Marxist analysis, as explained by Jean Baudrillard in *For a Critique of the Political Economy of the Sign*, trans. Charles Levin (St. Louis: Telos Press, 1981), pp. 123–142.

39. As René Girard emphasizes, multiple charges like these belong to the stereotypes of persecution. See *The Scapegoat*, trans. Yvonne Freccero (Baltimore: Johns Hopkins University Press, 1986).

40. Roger B. Salomon, *Twain and the Image of History* (New Haven: Yale University Press, 1961), pp. 168–169.

Notes to Chapter One

1. Samuel Taylor Coleridge, *Biographia Literaria*, 2 vols., ed. J. Shawcross (Oxford: Clarendon Press, 1907), Vol. 1, p. 50.

2. William Hazlitt, *Lectures on the English Poets* (London: J.M. Dent, 1910, rpt. 1955), p. 161.

3. See Benjamin W. Early, "Southey's *Joan of Arc*: The Unpublished Manuscript, the First Edition, and a Study of the Later Revisions," 2 vols. (Ph.D. dissertation, Duke University, 1951); Arnold R. Beath, "Robert Southey's *Joan of Arc*: A Critical Edition of the First Edition (1796)" (Ph.D. dissertation, Kansas State University, 1974). I use Beath's edition throughout, unless otherwise cited, giving citations in parentheses.

4. Southey was actually named Poet Laureate of England in 1813.

5. James Darmesteter, "Joan of Arc in England," in *English Studies*, trans. Mary Darmesteter (London: T. Fisher Unwin, 1896), p. 57.

6. *Robert Southey: The Critical Heritage*, ed. Lionel Madden (London: Routledge and Kegan Paul, 1972), p. 43. Hereafter all references to original reviews are cited from this edition parenthetically by page and abbreviated title (*CH*).

7. John Milton, *Paradise Lost*, in *Complete Poems and Major Prose*, ed. Merritt Y. Hughes (Indianapolis: Bobbs-Merrill, 1957, rpt. 1980), VII.31. Subsequent references to this edition are cited parenthetically by book and line number.

8. See *British War Poetry in the Age of Romanticism, 1793–1815*, ed. Betty T. Bennett (New York: Garland, 1976), pp. 198–199.

9. Robert Southey, *The Life and Correspondence of Robert Southey,* ed. Reverend Charles Cuthbert Southey (New York: Harper, 1851), p. 73. Emphasis added.

10. René Girard, *Things Hidden since the Foundation of the World,* trans. Stephen Bann and Michael Metteer (Stanford: Stanford University Press, 1987), p. 53.

11. Ibid.

12. Ibid., p. 236.

13. Joseph A. Wittreich Jr., "Introduction," *The Romantics on Milton: Formal Essays and Critical Asides,* ed. Joseph A. Wittreich Jr. (Cleveland: Case Western Reserve University Press, 1970), p. 12.

14. William Wordsworth, *The Poetical Works of William Wordsworth,* 5 vols., ed. Ernest De Selincourt, rev. Helen Darbishire (Oxford: Clarendon Press, 1952–1959), vol. 3, p.116.

15. Quoted in *The Romantics on Milton,* p. 189.

16. Coleridge, *Biographia Literaria,* I:47.

17. Greg Kucich, *Keats, Shelley, and Romantic Spenseriansim* (University Park: Pennsylvania State University Press, 1991), p. 108.

18. Ibid.

19. Ibid., p. 100.

20. Ibid., p. 101. See also Robert F. Gleckner, *Blake and Spenser* (Baltimore: Johns Hopkins University Press, 1985).

21. On Spenser's political allegory, see A. C. Hamilton, *The Structure of Allegory in "The Faerie Queene"* (Oxford: Oxford University Press, 1961); Michael O'Connell, *Mirror and Veil: The Historical Dimension of Spenser's "Faerie Queene"* (Chapel Hill: University of North Carolina Press, 1977); James Nohrnberg, *The Analogy of "The Faerie Queene"* (Princeton: Princeton University Press, 1976); Isabel G. Maccaffrey, *Spenser's Allegory: The Anatomy of Imagination* (Princeton: Princeton University Press, 1976); Nancy P. Pope, *National History in the Heroic Poem* (New York: Garland, 1990); Susanne L. Wofford, *The Choice of Achilles: The Ideology of Figure in the Epic* (Stanford: Stanford University Press, 1992); and David Quint, *Epic and Empire: Politics and Generic Form from Virgil to Milton* (Princeton: Princeton University Press, 1993).

22. Samuel Taylor Coleridge, *Collected Letters of Samuel Taylor Coleridge,* 6 vols, ed. Earl Leslie Griggs (Oxford: Clarendon Press, 1956), I.156, p. 258. Subsequent citations are given parenthetically by abbreviated title (*CL*), volume, letter, and page numbers.

23. Robert Southey, "Original Preface," in *The Poetical Works (1844–1849),* 10 vols. (Hildesheim: Georg Olms Verlag, 1977), vol. 1, p. xxvii.

24. Edmund Spenser, *The Faerie Queene,* ed. Thomas P. Roche Jr., with the assistance of C. Patrick O'Donnell Jr. (New York: Penguin, 1978, rpt. 1979), Preface, Book I.i. Hereafter all citations from this edition are given parenthetically by book, canto, and stanza numbers.

25. In *Paradise Lost* Milton famously rejects chivalric subject matter— "fabl'd Knights / In Battles feign'd"—in favor of a "higher Argument" and "Subject for Heroic Song," that of "Heroic Martyrdom" (IX.30–31, 42, 25, 32).

26. Compare *Paradise Lost* I.63.

27. Arnold Ray Beath, ed., *Robert Southey's "Joan of Arc": A Critical Edition of the First Edition (1796)*, unpublished dissertation, Kansas State University, 1974, p. 316. I use this edition throughout, giving citations parenthetically by book and line numbers.

28. Greg Kucich, *Keats, Shelley, and Romantic Spenserianism* (University Park: Pennsylvania State University Press, 1991), p. 1. See also Frederick Hard, "Lamb on Spenser," in *Royster Memorial Studies* (Chapel Hill: University of North Carolina Press, 1931), pp. 124–138. Hard quotes lines from Southey's "The Ruined Cottage" (1798), which he composed as a compliment to Charles Lamb: "The Spenser allusions in the passage . . . are perhaps worth noting as a reflection of their common interest in the poet at this time" (p. 130).

29. *Selections from the Letters of Robert Southey*, ed. John Wood Warter, 4 vols. (London: Longman, 1856), I.5.

30. For invocations of Joan and George as competing saints, see William Shakespeare, *King Henry VI, Part 1*, Arden edition, ed. Andrew S. Cairncross (London: Methuen, 1962), I.i.153–54; I.vi.28–29; IV.ii.55–56.

31. Edmund Spenser, "A Letter of the Authors Expounding his Whole Intention in the Course of this Worke," in *The Faerie Queene*, p. 15.

32. Beath, ed., *Southey's Joan of Arc*, p. 305; *Life and Correspondence*, I.279.

33. Kucich, *Romantic Spenserianism*, p. 260.

34. Edward Meachen, "History and Transcendence in Robert Southey's Epic Poems," *Studies in English Literature* 19 (1979): 592.

35. Robert Southey, *New Letters of Robert Southey*, ed. Kenneth Curry, 2 vols. (New York: Columbia University Press, 1965), vol. 1, pp. 131, 136.

36. Harold Bloom, *The Anxiety of Influence: A Theory of Poetry*, 2d ed. (Oxford: Oxford University Press, 1997), pp. 88, 13.

37. Ibid., p. 15.

38. In 1796 Coleridge composed "Lines in the Manner of Spenser," a love lyric honoring his wife, Sara Fricker Coleridge. See Samuel T. Coleridge, *The Poems of Samuel Taylor Coleridge*, ed. Ernest Hartley Coleridge (London: Humphrey Milford, 1917), pp. 94–96.

39. The distinction between the allegorical and the symbolic is, of course, a major theme in Coleridge's literary theory. He rejected a broad definition of allegory ("to talk of one thing and thereby convey another") and held that there was an evolution in generic forms from pagan myth to Platonic and Christian allegory and, finally, to symbolism. According to Coleridge, in allegorical writings there is always an "obvious and intentional distinction of the sense from the symbol," so that "the difference" between them "is everywhere presented to the mind or imagination while the likeness is suggested to the mind." Allegory presumes a "disjunction of faculties," which are then united in a polarity to form a homogeneous whole. In contrast, in symbolic writing, the "difference" between an object and its meaning is a matter of degree, not of kind, for the symbol actually participates in "the whole of which it is a representative." Symbolizing, therefore, requires "no disjunction of faculties, but [rather the] simple predominance" of the imagination. Whereas the

construction of an allegory requires the writer's conscious awareness and outward observation, the production of a symbol can be spontaneous and "out
of his own mind": "It is very possible that the general truth represented may
be working unconsciously in the writer's mind during the construction of a
symbol" (Samuel T. Coleridge, *Coleridge's Miscellaneous Criticism*, ed. Thomas
Middleton Raysor [London: Constable, 1936], pp. 30–31, 33, 99).

40. Ernest Bernhardt-Kabisch compares "Joan's prophetic authority . . .
to that of Wordsworth's Poet and Wanderer." See his *Robert Southey* (Boston:
Twayne, 1977), p. 32.

41. Quoted in Beath, "Southey's *Joan of Arc*," notes, p. 299. Coleridge
wrote this sentence in the margin of a page in his copy of Southey's epic.

42. Lynda Pratt, "Coleridge, Wordsworth, and Joan of Arc," *Notes and
Queries* 239.3, n.s. 41 (1994): 336.

43. Southey, *Life and Correspondence*, p. 94.

44. Coleridge, *Poems*, pp. 131–147. See R. R. Dingley, "Joan of Arc and the
Destiny of Nations," *Durham University Journal* 77, n.s. 46 (1985): 203–209.

45. Charles Lamb, *The Works of Charles Lamb*, 5 vols. (New York: A. C.
Armstrong, 1880), vol. 1, pp. 60–61.

46. Southey, *Life and Correspondence*, I.279.

47. Alison Hickey, "Coleridge, Southey, 'and Co.': Collaboration and
Authority," *Studies in Romanticism* 37.3 (1998): 320–321.

48. Girard, *Things Hidden since the Foundation of the World*, p. 35.

49. On Shakespeare's presentation of Joan, see Dominique Guy-Blanquet,
Shakespeare et l'invention de l'histoire (Brussels: Le Cri, 1997).

50. Southey refers to Clément de L'Averdy's *Notices et extraits des manuscripts de la Bibliothèque du Roi, lus au comité établi par sa Majesté dans
l'Académie royale des Inscriptions et belles-lettres* (Paris: Imprimerie Royale,
1790), vol. 3. The long-standing, definitive compilation and edition of the
Jehannine historical materials was published almost fifty years after Southey's
Joan of Arc. See Jules-Etienne-Joseph Quicherat, ed., *Procès de condamnation et de réhabilitation de Jeanne d'Arc dite la Pucelle*, 5 vols. (Paris: Jules
Renouard, 1841–1849; rpt. New York: Johnson, 1965).

51. Thomas De Quincey, "Charles Lamb," in *De Quincey as Critic*, ed.
John E. Jordan (London: Routledge and Kegan Paul, 1973), p. 453.

52. Southey, "Original Preface," in *The Poetical Works*, vol. 1, p. xxii.

53. Ibid., p. xxii.

54. Ibid.

55. Ibid., pp. xxii–xxiii.

56. Southey, "Preface to *Joan of Arc*," in *The Poetical Works*, vol. 1,
pp. xxxi–xxxii.

57. Ibid., p. xxxiii.

58. Robert Southey, *Sir Thomas More: Or, Colloquies on the Progress and
Prospects of Society*, 2 vols. (London: John Murray, 1829), vol. 1, p. 19. Emphasis
added.

59. Ibid.

60. Ibid., p. 38.

61. See Jules Michelet, *Joan of Arc*, trans. Albert Guérard (Ann Arbor: University of Michigan Press, 1957, rpt. 1967), esp. pp. 105–107.

62. Thomas De Quincey, "Joan of Arc," in *De Quincey's Essays: Joan of Arc, the English Mail-Coach, and the Spanish Military Nun*, ed. Carol M. Newman (New York: Macmillan, 1909), p. 5. Subsequent citations of this essay are given parenthetically by page number.

63. Thomas De Quincey, "Charles Lamb," in *De Quincey as Critic*, ed. John E. Jordan (London: Routledge and Kegan Paul, 1973), p. 457.

64. On Michelet's romanticized history, see Linda Orr, *Jules Michelet: Nature, History, and Language* (Ithaca: Cornell University Press, 1976); Edward K. Kaplan, *Michelet's Poetic Vision: A Romantic Philosophy of Nature, Man, and Woman* (Amherst: University of Massachusetts Press, 1977); and Arthur Mitzman, *Michelet, Historian: Rebirth and Romanticism in Nineteenth-Century France* (New Haven: Yale University Press, 1990).

65. De Quincey and Southey write their praises of Joan partly as a chivalric response to Voltaire's denigration of her in his burlesque epic, *La Pucelle d'Orléans* (1755). Southey wrote to Grosvenor Bedford on July 17, 1796: "I said, 'I have *never been guilty* of reading the Pucelle of Voltaire.' Report speaks it worthy of its author—a man whose wit and genius could only be equaled by his depravity" (*Life and Correspondence*, p. 90).

66. De Quincey, "Charles Lamb," p. 454.

67. Southey himself may have recognized this problem. In a letter to Grosvenor Bedford, dated January 1, 1797, he reports that he has "sketched out a tragedy on the martyrdom of Joan of Arc" (*Life and Correspondence*, pp. 94–95).

68. Ibid., p. 454.

69. On the retreat from corporeal reality, see Terry Castle, "The Spectralization of the Other in *The Mysteries of Udolpho*," in *The Female Thermometer: Eighteenth-Century Culture and the Invention of the Uncanny* (Oxford: Oxford University Press, 1995), pp. 120–139.

70. Southey, *Life and Correspondence*, p. 66.

71. Ibid., p. 67.

72. René Girard points explicitly to Marie Antoinette in *The Scapegoat*, trans. Yvonne Freccero (Baltimore: Johns Hopkins University Press, 1986), p. 20.

73. Meachen, "History and Transcendence," p. 604.

Notes to Chapter Two

1. Benjamin W. Wells, "Introduction," *Schiller's Jungfrau von Orleans: Eine romantische Tragödie*, rev. ed. Benjamin W. Wells (Boston: D.C. Heath, 1901), p. vi.

2. E. L. Stahl, *Friedrich Schiller's Drama: Theory and Practice* (Oxford: Clarendon Press, 1954), p. 117.

3. Quoted in Thomas Carlyle, *The Life of Friedrich Schiller* (1825; London: Chapman and Hall, 1899), p. 102.

4. Walter Hinderer and Daniel O. Dahlstrom, "Introduction," in Friedrich Schiller, *Essays*, ed. Walter Hinderer and Daniel O. Dahlstrom, the German Library, vol. 17 (New York: Continuum, 1993), p. xix. I use this collection of Schiller's translated essays throughout. For the German text I use Friedrich Schiller, *Philosophische Schriften*, ed. Helmut Koopmann, in *Sämtliche Werke*, Bd. 5 (Munich: Winkler Verlag, 1968).

5. Friedrich Schiller, *Letters on the Aesthetic Education of Man*, trans. Elizabeth M. Wilkinson and L. A. Willoughby, in *Essays*, Fifth Letter, p. 96. "[E]ine physische Möglichkeit scheint gegeben, das Gesetz auf den Thron zu stellen, den Menschen endlich als Selbstzweck zu ehren, und wahre Freiheit zur Grundlage der politischen Verbindung zu machen. . . . Die moralische Möglichkeit fehlt. . . . In seinen Taten malt sich der Mensch, und welche Gestalt ist es, die sich in dem Drama der jetzigen Zeit abbildet! Hier Verwilderung, dort Eschaffung: die zwei Äußersten des menschlichen Verfalls, und beide in einem Zeitraum vereinigt" (*Philosophische Schriften*, pp. 320–321).

6. Schiller, *Aesthetic Education*, Seventh Letter, p. 104. "[S]o muß man jeden Versuch einer solchen Staatsveränderung so lange für unzeitig und jede darauf gegründete Hoffnung so lange für schimärisch erklären, bis die Trennung in dem innern Menschen wiederaufgehoben" (*Philosophische Schriften*, p. 329).

7. Schiller, *Aesthetic Education*, Second Letter, p. 90. "[J]a daß man, um jenes politische Problem in der Erfahrung zu lösen, durch das ästhetische den Weg nehmen muß, weil es die Schönheit ist, durch welche man zu der Freiheit wandert" (*Philosophische Schriften*, p. 314).

8. Lesley Sharpe, for instance, writes: "It is, of course, in any case difficult to find truly tragic feelings and situations, whatever one's interpretation of the play. . . . Perhaps, therefore, it is safest to regard the term 'Tragödie' as denoting nothing more than the fact that the play ends with the death of the heroine, which is a moving spectacle" (*Schiller and the Historical Character: Presentation and Interpretation in the Historiographical Works and in the Historical Dramas* [Oxford: Oxford University Press, 1982], p. 132).

9. Carlyle, *Life of Schiller*, pp. 156–157. On Schiller's reception in England, see Fredric Ewen, *The Prestige of Schiller in England, 1788–1859* (New York: Columbia University Press, 1932).

10. See H. B. Garland, *Schiller, the Dramatic Writer: A Study of Style in the Plays* (Oxford: Clarendon Press, 1969), p. 228.

11. Frank G. Ryder, "Introduction," in Johann Wolfgang von Goethe, *Plays*, ed. and trans. Frank G. Ryder (New York: Continuum, 1993), p. xvi.

12. For a brilliant study of this sort of fratricidal strife between the poets and their critics, see Sandor Goodhart, *Sacrificing Commentary: Reading the End of Literature* (Baltimore: Johns Hopkins University Press, 1996).

13. Friedrich Schiller, "On the Art of Tragedy," trans. Daniel O. Dahlstrom, in Schiller, *Essays*, p. 18. Emphasis added. "[D]ie Tragödie . . . erhält Macht, ja Verbindlichkeit, die historische Wahrheit den Gesetzen der Dichtkunst unterzuordnen, und den gegebenen Stoff nach ihrem Bedürfnisse zu bearbeiten. . . . bei strenger Beobachtung der historische Wahrheit nicht selten die poetische leiden, und umgekehrt bie grober Verletzung der historischen

die poetische nur um so mehr gewinnen kann" (*Philosophische Schriften,* pp. 161–162).

14. Friedrich Schiller, *Schillers Briefe, 1798–1800,* ed. Lieselotte Blumenthal, in *Schillers Werke* (Nationalausgabe), vol. 30 (Weimar: Hermann Böhlaus, 1961), Letter 261, p. 224. Emphasis added.

15. Schiller, *Aesthetic Education,* Twenty-second Letter, p. 151. "In einem wahrhaft schönen Kunstwerk soll der Inhalt nichts, die Form aber alles tun.... Die Inhalt, wie erhaben und weitumfassend er auch sei, wirkt also jederzeit einschränkend auf der Geist, und nur von der Form ist wahre ästhetische Freiheit zu erwarten. Darin also besteht das eigentliche Kunstgeheimnis des Meisters, daß er den Stoff durch die Form vertilgt" (*Philosophische Schriften,* p. 379).

16. Schiller, *Aesthetic Education,* Twenty-sixth Letter, p. 166. "Insofern also das Bedürfnis der Realität und die Anhänglichkeit an das Wirkliche bloße Folgen des Mangels sind, ist die Gleichgültigkeit gegen Realität und das Interesse am Schein eine wahre Erweiterung der Menschheit und ein entschiedener Schritt zur Kultur" (*Philosophische Schriften,* pp. 395–396).

17. Schiller, *Aesthetic Education,* Twenty-sixth Letter, p. 166. "[E]s ist dasselbe bei allen Völkerstämmen, welche der Sklaverei des tierischen Standes entsprungen sind: die Freude am Schein, die Neigung zum Putz und zum Spiele" (*Philosophische Schriften,* p. 395).

18. Schiller, *Aesthetic Education,* Twenty-sixth Letter, p. 168. "Dieses menschliche Herrscherrecht übt er aus in der Kunst des Scheins, und je strenger er hier das Mein und Dein voneinander sondert, je sorgfältiger er die Gestalt von dem Wesen trennt, und je mehr Selbstständigkeit er derselben zu geben weiß" (*Philosophische Schriften,* p. 397).

19. Schiller writes that he first became acquainted with Shakespeare "at a very early age." See "On Naïve and Sentimental Poetry," trans. Daniel O. Dahlstrom, in Schiller, *Essays,* p. 197.

20. Bernard Shaw, *Saint Joan* (Baltimore: Penguin, 1951), preface, p. 31.

21. Sigmund Freud, "Civilization and Its Discontents," in *Civilisation, War and Death,* ed. John Rickman, Psycho-analytical Epitomes No. 4 (1929; London: Hogarth Press, 1968), p. 53.

22. Elizabeth M. Wilkinson, "Reflections after Translating Schiller's *Letters on the Aesthetic Education of Man,*" in *Schiller: Bicentenary Lectures,* ed. F. Norman (London: University of London, Institute of Germanic Languages and Literatures, 1960), p. 80. See *Schillers Briefe, 1801–1802,* ed. Stefan Ormanns, in *Schillers Werke* (Nationalausgabe), vol. 31 (Weimar: Hermann Böhlaus, 1985), Letter 25, p. 25.

23. Freud, "Civilization and Its Discontents," p. 75.

24. Schiller, *Aesthetic Education,* Sixth Letter, p. 103. "Einseitigkeit in Übung der Kräfte führt zwar das Individuum unausbleiblich zum Irrtum, aber die Gattung zur Wahrheit. Dadurch allein, daß wir die ganze Energie unsers Geistes in einem Brennpunkt versammeln, und unser ganzes Wesen in eine einzige Kraft zusammenziehen, setzen wir dieser einzelnen Kraft gleichsam Flügel an, und führen sie künstlicherweise weit über die Schranken hinaus, welche die Natur ihr gesetzt zu haben scheint" (*Philosophische Schriften,* p. 328).

25. Schiller, *Aesthetic Education,* Sixth Letter, p. 102. "Gerne will ich Ihnen eingestehen, daß sowenig es auch den Individuen bei dieser Zerstückelung ihres Wesens wohl werden kann, doch die Gattung auf keine andere Art hätte Fortschritte machen können" (*Philosophische Schriften,* p. 327).

26. Schiller, *Aesthetic Education,* Sixth Letter, p. 103. "Unter dem Fluch dieses Weltweckes" (*Philosophische Schriften,* p. 328).

27. Schiller, *Aesthetic Education,* Sixth Letter, pp. 102, 104. "Dieser Antagonism der Kräfte ist das große Instrument der Kultur. . . . Es muß also falsch sein, daß die Ausbildung der einzelnen Kräfte das Opfer ihrer Totalität notwendig macht; oder wenn auch das Gesetz der Natur noch so sehr dahin strebte, so muß es bei uns stehen, diese Totalität in unsrer Natur, welche die Kunst zerstört hat, durch eine höhere Kunst wiederherzustellen" (*Philosophische Schriften,* pp. 327, 329).

28. Schiller, *Aesthetic Education,* Sixth Letter, p. 99. "Die Kultur selbst war es, welche der neuern Menschheit diese Wunde schlug. Sobald auf der einen Seite die erweiterte Erfahrung und das bestimmtere Denken eine schärfere Scheidung der Wissenschaften, auf der andern das verwickeltere Uhrwerk der Staaten eine strengere Absonderung der Stände und Geschäfte notwendig machte, so zerriß auch der innere Bund der menschlichen Natur, und ein verderblicher Streit entzweite ihre harmonischen Kräfte" (*Philosophische Schriften,* p. 324).

29. Schiller, *Aesthetic Education,* Ninth Letter, p. 108. "[S]o kehre er, eine fremde Gestalt, in sein Jahrhundert zurück; aber nicht, um es mit seiner Erscheinung zu erfreuen, sondern furchtbar wie Agamemnons Sohn, um es zu reinigen" (*Philosophische Schriften,* p. 334).

30. Friedrich Schiller, *The Maiden of Orléans,* trans. John T. Krumpelmann, University of North Carolina Studies in the Germanic Languages and Literatures, No. 24 (Chapel Hill: University of North Carolina Press, 1959), Prologue, scene iii, line 162. I use this translation throughout, giving act, scene, and line numbers parenthetically. For the German text, I use Friedrich Schiller, *Die Jungfrau von Orleans,* ed. Benno von Weise and Lieselotte Blumenthal, in *Schillers Werke* (Nationalausgabe), vol. 9 (Weimar: Hermann Böhlaus, 1948).

31. Sharpe, *Schiller and the Historical Character,* p. 137.

32. René Girard, *Violence and the Sacred,* trans. Patrick Gregory (Baltimore: Johns Hopkins University Press, 1977).

33. *Schillers Briefe,* vol. 30, Letter 252, p. 217.

34. Schiller, *Aesthetic Education,* Eighth Letter, p. 107. "Nicht ohne Bedeutung läßt der alte Mythus die Göttin der Weisheit in voller Rüstung aus Jupiters Haupte steigen; denn schon ihre erste Verrichtung ist kriegerisch. Schon in der Geburt hat sie einen harten Kampf mit den Sinnen zu bestehen, die aus ihrer süßen Ruhe nicht gerissen sein wollen" (*Philosophische Schriften,* p. 332).

35. John D. Simons, *Friedrich Schiller* (Boston: Twayne, 1981), p. 131.

36. E. J. Engel and W. F. Mainland, "Introduction," *Die Jungfrau von Orleans,* ed. E. J. Engel and W. F. Mainland (London: Thomas Nelson, 1963), p. xv.

37. Friedrich Schiller, "Das Mädchen von Orleans," in *Gedichte, Erzählungen, Übersetzungen* (Munich: Artemis and Winkler, 1993), p. 381.

38. *Schillers Briefe*, vol. 31, Letter 117, p. 101. Emphasis added.

39. Garland, *Schiller, the Dramatic Writer*, pp. 227–228.

40. Ibid., p. 228.

41. Schiller, "On Naïve and Sentimental Poetry," pp. 196–197. Emphasis added. "Der Dichter einer naiven und geistreichen Jugendwelt, sowie derjenige, der in den Zeitaltern künstlicher Kultur ihm am nächsten kommt, ist streng und spröde, wie die jungfräuliche Diana in ihren Wäldern, ohne alle Vertraulichkeit entflieht er dem Herzen, das ihn sucht, dem Verlangen, das ihn umfassen will. Die trockene Wahrheit, womit er den Gegenstand behandelt, erscheint nicht selten als Unempfindlichkeit. Das Objekt besitzt ihn gänzlich, sein Herz liegt nicht wie ein schlechtes Metall gleich unter der Oberfläche, sondern will wie das Gold in der Tiefe gesucht sein. Wie die Gottheit hinter dem Weltgebäude, so steht er hinter seinem Werk" (*Philosophische Schriften*, p. 451).

42. *Schillers Briefe*, vol. 30, Letter 261, p. 224.

43. Schiller, "On Naïve and Sentimental Poetry," p. 197. "Homer unter den Alten und Shakespeare unter den Neuern" (*Philosophische Schriften*, p. 451).

44. Schiller, "On Naïve and Sentimental Poetry," p. 202. "Dieser Weg, den die neueren Dichter gehen, ist übrigens derselbe, den der Mensch überhaupt sowohl im Einzelnen als im Ganzen einschlagen muß. Die Natur macht ihn mit sich eins, die Kunst trennt und entzweit ihn, durch das Ideal kehrt er zur Einheit zurück" (*Philosophische Schriften*, p. 456).

45. "Always as a happy and harmonious time . . . 'joined with Paradise and the Golden Age, with an original human equality and freedom'" (my translation). Viola Geyersbach, "Schiller, 1759–1788," in *Friedrich Schiller, 1759–1805: Ausstellung zum 225. Geburtstag des Dichters der deutschen Klassik* (Weimer: Waisenhaus, 1984), p. 31.

46. Heinrich Düntzer, *The Life of Schiller*, trans. Percy E. Pinkerton (London: Macmillan, 1883), p. 95.

47. Quoted in Düntzer, *Life of Schiller*, p. 102.

48. Schiller, "On Naïve and Sentimental Poetry," p. 199. "Dichter von dieser naiven Gattung sind in einem künstlichen Weltalter nicht so recht mehr an ihrer Stelle. Auch sind sie in demselben kaum mehr möglich, wenigstens auf keine andere Weise möglich als daß sie in ihrem Zeitalter wild laufen, und durch ein günstiges Geschick vor dem verstümmelnden Einfluß desselben geborgen werden. Aus der Sozietät selbst können sie nie und nimmer hervorgehen; aber außerhalb derselben erscheinen sie noch zuweilen, doch mehr als Fremdlinge, die man anstaunt" (*Philosophische Schriften*, p. 454).

49. Schiller, "On Naïve and Sentimental Poetry," pp. 199–200. "Von den Kritikern, den eigentlichen Zaunhütern des Geschmacks, werden sie als Grenzstörer gehaßt, die man lieber unterdrücken möchte" (*Philosophische Schriften*, p. 454).

50. Schiller, "On Naïve and Sentimental Poetry," p. 181. "Sie sind, was wir waren; sie sind, was wir wieder werden sollen. Wir waren Natur, wie sie, und unsere Kultur soll uns, auf dem Wege der Vernunft und der Freiheit, zur Natur

zurückführen. Sie sind also zugleich Darstellung unserer verlornen Kindheit. . . . Zugleich sind sie Darstellungen unserer höchsten Vollendung im Ideale" (*Philosophische Schriften*, pp. 436, 434).

51. Schiller, "On Naïve and Sentimental Poetry," p. 182. "Ein heiliger Gegenstand" (*Philosophische Schriften*, p. 436).

52. Schiller, "On Naïve and Sentimental Poetry," p. 180. "[D]ie Natur mit der Kunst im Kontraste stehe und sie beschäme" (*Philosophische Schriften*, p. 433).

53. Schiller, *Aesthetic Education*, Twenty-fifth Letter, p. 162. "[U]nd es erschient ihm eine Welt, weil er aufgehört hat, mit derselben eins auszumachen" (*Philosophische Schriften*, p. 391).

54. On Johanna's clothing, see Gail K. Hart, "Re-dressing History: Mother Nature, Mother Isabeau, the Virgin Mary, and Schiller's *Jungfrau*," *Women in German Yearbook* 14 (1988): 91–107. I thank Beate Allert for this reference.

55. Schiller, "On Naïve and Sentimental Poetry," p. 245. "[S]o ist jede Trennung und Vereinzelung dieser Kräfte ein gewaltsamer Zustand, und das Ideal der Erholung ist die Wiederherstellung unseres Naturganzen nach einseitigen Spannungen" (*Philosophische Schriften*, p. 501).

56. Schiller, "On Naïve and Sentimental Poetry," p. 233. "Dem sentimentalischen hat sie die Macht verliehen oder veilmehr einen lebendigen Trieb eingeprägt, jene Einheit, die durch Abstraktion in ihm aufgehoben worden, aus sich selbst wiederherzustellen" (*Philosophische Schriften*, p. 489).

57. See René Girard, *Things Hidden since the Foundation of the World*, trans. Stephen Bann and Michael Metteer (Stanford: Stanford University Press, 1987), pp. 51–58; *The Scapegoat*, trans. Yvonne Freccero (Baltimore: Johns Hopkins University Press, 1986).

58. On the traits that mark the outsider, see Girard, *Things Hidden since the Foundation of the World*, pp. 122–123.

59. Lesley Sharpe, *Friedrich Schiller: Drama, Thought, and Politics*, Cambridge Studies in German (Cambridge: Cambridge University Press, 1991), p. 276.

60. Girard, *Things Hidden since the Foundation of the World*, p. 78.

61. Ibid., p. 51.

62. On medieval texts of persecution as a partial demystification of the victimage mechanism, see Girard, *Things Hidden since the Foundation of the World*, pp. 126–138.

63. Ibid., p. 170.

64. Ibid., p. 39.

65. Stahl, *Friedrich Schiller's Drama*, p. 107.

66. René Girard, "Are the Gospels Mythical?" *First Things* 62 (April 1996): 31.

67. Edna Purdie, "Schiller," in *Schiller: Bicentenary Lectures*, p. 19.

68. On Satan and *Skandalon*, see Girard, *Things Hidden since the Foundation of the World*, pp. 162, 418–419.

69. Ibid., p. 26.

70. Stahl, *Friedrich Schiller's Drama*, p. 118.

71. W. White, "Schiller: Reflections on a Bicentenary," in *Schiller: Bicentenary Lectures*, p. 167.

72. See Garland, *Schiller, the Dramatic Writer*, pp. 224–225.

73. Schiller's likening of Johanna as a "blind instrument" and warrior to Samson may well have been inspired by Milton's use of the blinded Samson in *Samson Agonistes* as a figure for himself as poet.

74. Quoted in White, "Reflections on a Bicentenary," p. 167.

75. Girard, *Things Hidden since the Foundation of the World*, p. 53.

Notes to Chapter Three

1. Mark Twain, *Life on the Mississippi*, ed. James M. Cox (New York: Penguin Books, 1984), chap. 46, p. 327. See also Twain's disparaging commentary on Sir Walter Scott's *Ivanhoe* at the end of the fourth chapter of *A Connecticut Yankee in King Arthur's Court*, ed. Bernard L. Stein (Berkeley: Iowa Center for Textual Studies and University of California Press, 1979), pp. 79–80.

2. Writing about *A Connecticut Yankee in King Arthur's Court* in his *Autobiography*, Twain describes it as an attempt "to contrast . . . the English life of the whole of the Middle Ages with the life of modern Christendom and modern civilization—to the advantage of the latter, of course." See *The Autobiography of Mark Twain*, ed. Charles Neider (New York: Harper and Row, 1959), p. 271.

3. See Kim Moreland, *The Medievalist Impulse in American Literature: Twain, Adams, Fitzgerald, and Hemingway* (Charlottesville: University Press of Virginia, 1996), pp. 28–76. See also T. J. Jackson Lears, *No Place of Grace: Antimodernism and the Transformation of American Culture, 1880–1920* (New York: Pantheon, 1981).

4. Albert Bigelow Paine, *Mark Twain: A Biography*, 4 vols. (New York: Harper and Brothers, 1912), vol. 3, p. 1034. Hereafter I cite this work by abbreviated title (*MTB*), giving volume and page numbers parenthetically. Note that different printings of Paine's *Biography* divide it differently into volumes, but the pagination remains unchanged and continuous throughout.

5. Mark Twain lived to witness Joan of Arc's beatification in 1909.

6. Walter Benjamin, "The Work of Art in the Age of Mechanical Reproduction," in *Illuminations: Essays and Reflections*, ed. Hannah Arendt, trans. Harry Zohn (New York: Schocken, 1969), p. 220.

7. Ibid., pp. 220, 223, 243 n.5.

8. Ibid., p. 224.

9. On Clemens's involvement with the Paige typesetter, see Justin Kaplan, *Mr. Clemens and Mark Twain: A Biography* (New York: Simon and Schuster, 1966), esp. chap. 14, "The Yankee and the Machine," pp. 280–311. See also Hamlin Hill, "Mark Twain: Texts and Technology," in *Cultural Artifacts and the Production of Meaning: The Page, the Image, and the Body*, ed. Margaret J. M. Ezell and Katherine O'Brien O'Keeffe (Ann Arbor: University of Michigan Press, 1994), pp. 71–84.

10. Moreland, *Medievalist Impulse*, p. 46.

11. Hill, "Texts and Technology," p. 72.

12. Quoted in Kaplan, *Mr. Clemens and Mr. Twain*, p. 284.

13. Mark Twain, *Personal Recollections of Joan of Arc by the Sieur Louis de Conte (Her Page and Secretary)* (San Francisco: Ignatius, 1989), p. 23. This paperback edition conveniently includes as an appendix Twain's 1904 essay, "Joan of Arc." Hereafter citations are parenthetical by page.

14. Mark Twain, "What Is Man?" in *What Is Man? and Other Philosophical Writings*, in *The Works of Mark Twain*, ed. Paul Baender (Berkeley: Iowa Center for Textual Studies and the University of California Press, 1973), vol. 19, p. 128.

15. See Hill, "Texts and Technology," esp. pp. 71, 81–82.

16. Mark Twain, *Mark Twain's Letters*, ed. Albert Bigelow Paine, 2 vols. (New York: Harper and Brothers, 1917), vol. 2, pp. 506, 508; quoted in Hill, "Texts and Technology," p. 72.

17. Using an amount of printed material as a standard of measurement for humans, Twain puns on the word "page" in *A Connecticut Yankee in King Arthur's Court*. When Clarence informs Hank that he is a page, Hank replies, "You ain't more than a paragraph" (p. 61).

18. Mark Twain, "The Turning Point of My Life," in *What is Man? And Other Philosophical Writings*, p. 458.

19. Twain describes his contraction of the disease as a suicide attempt. Having decided at the age of twelve, shortly after his father's death, that "life on these miserable terms was not worth living," he crept into the bed of a playmate who was seriously ill "to get the disease and have it over" ("The Turning Point," p. 458).

20. Susan K. Harris, *Mark Twain's Escape from Time: A Study of Patterns and Images* (Columbus: University of Missouri Press, 1982), p. 17.

21. Joseph C. Jurick, "Mark Twain's *Joan of Arc*: Origins, Purposes and Accomplishments" (Ph.D. dissertation, University of Illinois, 1962), p. 23; quoted in Lionel Carl Nadeau, "Mark Twain's *Joan of Arc*: An Analysis of the Background and Original Sources" (Ph.D. dissertation, Ball State University, 1979), p. 77.

22. Nadeau, "Mark Twain's *Joan of Arc*"; Alan Gribben, "The Library and Reading of Samuel L. Clemens," 5 vols. (Ph.D. dissertation, University of California, Berkeley, 1974); Ruth Mary Bradley, "The Making of Mark Twain's *Personal Recollections of Joan of Arc*" (Ph.D. dissertation, University of California, Los Angeles, 1970).

23. Twain's anti-Catholicism is a complex matter, full of ambivalence, as is his attitude toward religion in general. See James D. Wilson, "In Quest of Redemptive Vision: Mark Twain's *Joan of Arc*," *Texas Studies in Literature and Language* 20.2 (1978): 181–198.

24. Harris, *Mark Twain's Escape from Time*, pp. 25–26; William Searle, *The Saint and the Skeptics: Joan of Arc in the Work of Mark Twain, Anatole France, and Bernard Shaw* (Detroit: Wayne State University Press, 1976), pp. 15–55.

25. Nadeau, "Mark Twain's *Joan of Arc*," pp. 34–41, 82, 85, 356–404.

26. Searle, *The Saint and the Skeptics*, p. 38.

27. Roger B. Salomon, *Twain and the Image of History* (New Haven: Yale University Press, 1961), p. 185.

28. Harris, *Mark Twain's Escape from Time*, p. 22.

29. Ibid., p. 18.

30. Moreland, *Medievalist Impulse*, p. 42.

31. Benjamin, "Work of Art," p. 226.

32. *The Autobiography of Mark Twain*, p. 226.

33. *Mark Twain's Correspondence with Henry Huddleston Rogers, 1893–1909*, ed. Lewis Leary (Berkeley: University of California Press, 1969), p. 71.

34. Moreland, *Medievalist Impulse*, p. 30.

35. Mark Twain, *The Love Letters of Mark Twain*, ed. Dixon Wecter (New York: Harper and Brothers, 1949), p. 43; quoted in Moreland, *Medievalist Impulse*, p. 30.

36. Peter Stoneley, *Mark Twain and the Feminine Aesthetic*, Cambridge Studies in American Literature and Culture No. 54 (Cambridge: Cambridge University Press, 1992), p. 94.

37. See Giraud Chester, *Embattled Maiden: The Life of Anna Dickinson* (New York: Putnam, 1951); Edward T. James, ed., *Notable American Women, 1607–1950: A Biographical Dictionary*, 3 vols. (Cambridge, Mass.: Belknap Press of Harvard University Press, 1973), vol. 1, pp. 475–476.

38. Laura E. Skandera-Trombley, *Mark Twain in the Company of Women* (Philadelphia: University of Pennsylvania Press, 1994), p. 147.

39. Quoted in Skandera-Trombley, *Mark Twain in the Company of Women*, p. 149.

40. Quoted in Everett Emerson, *The Authentic Mark Twain: A Literary Biography of Samuel L. Clemens* (Philadelphia: University of Pennsylvania Press, 1984), p. 200.

41. Quoted in Edith Colgate Salsbury, *Susy and Mark Twain: Family Dialogues* (New York: Harper and Row, 1965), p. 315.

42. Ibid., p. 356.

43. *Mark Twain's Notebook*, ed. Albert Bigelow Paine (New York: Harper and Brothers, 1935), p. 318; quoted in Searle, *The Saint and the Skeptics*, pp. 33–34.

44. Searle, *The Saint and the Skeptics*, p. 33.

45. Nadeau, "Mark Twain's *Joan of Arc*," pp. 2–3, 231–233.

46. See Arthur Mitzman, *Michelet, Historian: Rebirth and Romanticism in Nineteenth-Century France* (New Haven: Yale University Press, 1990), pp. 32–37. On the relationship between Joan of Arc and Michelet's second wife, Athénaïs, see Linda Orr, *Jules Michelet: Nature, History, and Language* (Ithaca: Cornell University Press, 1976), pp. 12–13, 90–91; Stephen A. Kippur, *Jules Michelet: A Study of Mind and Sensibility* (Albany: State University of New York Press, 1981), pp. 204–209.

47. *Correspondence with Henry Huddleston Rogers*, p. 125.

48. *Mark Twain to Mrs. Fairbanks*, ed. Dixon Wecter (San Marino, Calif.: Huntington Library Publications, 1949), p. 269; quoted in Moreland, *Medievalist Impulse*, p. 56.

49. Mark Twain, "The Turning Point of My Life," in *What Is Man? And Other Philosophical Writings,* p. 458. Subsequent citations are parenthetical by page.

50. Searle, *The Saint and the Skeptics,* p. 149.

51. Twain actually begins with one earlier link in the chain, his nearly fatal bout with measles as a child.

52. Hamlin Hill, *Mark Twain, God's Fool* (New York: Harper and Row, 1973), p. xv.

53. Robert Paul Lamb, Note to Ann Astell, June 1999; quoted with permission.

54. Some scholars regard the account of the chance discovery of a page from a history book as apocryphal, merely a part of Twain's (and Paine's) authorial self-fashioning. James Cox, for instance, calls it a "fabrication" intended "to present the emergence of literary ambition in the untutored but sensitive boy" (*Mark Twain: The Fate of Humor* [Princeton: Princeton University Press, 1966], p. 248).

55. My colleague, Robert Paul Lamb, finds a psychological basis for this image pattern in Clemens's guilt feelings over the death by fire of a drunk to whom Clemens had lent some matches and over the death of his brother Henry, which resulted from a boiler explosion on the Mississippi. That fatal steamboat accident on June 13, 1858, left Henry and hundreds of other victims horribly burned. See chapter 20 of *Life on the Mississippi.* See also *Mark Twain's Letters, 1853–1866,* ed. Edgar Marquess Branch, Michael B. Frank, and Kenneth M. Sanderson (Berkeley: University of California Press, 1988), pp. 80–86.

56. See Yvonne A. Amar, "Mark Twain's Joan of Arc: An 'Asbestos' Character Rising from the Ashes," *Mark Twain Journal* 19.3 (1978–1979): 13–19.

57. On this topic, see Albert E. Stone Jr., *The Innocent Eye: Childhood in Mark Twain's Imagination* (New Haven: Yale University Press, 1961), esp. pp. 221–224.

58. Searle, *The Saint and the Skeptics,* p. 23.

59. Skandera-Trombley, *Mark Twain in the Company of Women,* p. 161.

60. Ibid., pp. 160–161.

61. *Mark Twain's Letters to His Publishers, 1867–1894,* ed. Hamlin Hill (Berkeley: University of California Press, 1967), p. 336.

62. *Correspondence with Henry Huddleston Rogers,* p. 111.

63. See Twain's February 3, 1893, letter to Fred J. Hall, in *Mark Twain's Letters to His Publishers,* p. 336.

64. According to Dixon Wecter, it was Susy's wish to stay in Hartford. See *Love Letters of Mark Twain,* pp. 315, 320.

65. *Correspondence with Henry Huddleston Rogers,* p. 143.

66. Albert Bigelow Paine, "Introduction," *Mark Twain's Letters,* 1:14.

67. *Mark Twain–Howells Letters: The Correspondence of Samuel L. Clemens and William D. Howells, 1872–1910,* ed. Frederick Anderson, William M. Gibson, and Henry Nash Smith, 2 vols. (Cambridge, Mass.: Harvard University Press, 1960), vol. 2, pp. 708–710.

68. *Mark Twain's Letters,* 2:624. In a note, Paine indicates that Twain closed the first half of *Personal Recollections,* written in Florence in 1892–1893, with Joan's Victory at Orléans "and was by no means sure that he would continue the story beyond that point." At the time of his bankruptcy in 1894, "he was determined to reach the tale's tragic conclusion" (2:615).

69. *Love Letters of Mark Twain,* p. 320.

70. Ibid., p. 322.

71. Ibid., p. 333.

72. Frank V. Du Mond (1865–1951) of New York studied under Gustave Boulanger, Jules Lefebre, and Benjamin Constant at the Académie Julian in Paris. He exhibited in the Paris Salon in 1890. See *Who Was Who in American Art,* ed. Peter Hastings Falk (Madison, Conn.: Sound View Press, 1985), pp. xxxiii–xxxv, 175.

73. Benjamin, "Work of Art," p. 223.

74. Paine notes, however, that sales increased after the publication of Twain's essay "Joan of Arc" in *Harper's Magazine* in 1904, as Joan's beatification approached. There were 1,726 copies sold in America in 1904, 2,445 copies in 1905, 5,381 in 1906, and 6,574 in 1907. See *MTB* 3:1226.

75. Paine himself seems to have been infected with Twain's enthusiasm for Joan. He wrote his own two-volume biography, *Joan of Arc: Maid of France* (New York: Macmillan, 1925), and a shorter, popular biography, *The Girl in White Armor: The True Story of Joan of Arc* (New York: Macmillan, 1927). For these biographies, Paine was named a chevalier in the French Legion of Honor.

76. Twain, "What Is Man?" p. 166.

77. Ibid., pp. 183, 189.

78. Ibid., 190.

79. *Mark Twain's Letters,* 2:508.

80. In Florence in 1892–1893, when Twain was writing the first half of *Personal Recollections,* he was also at work on "Those Extraordinary Twins" and *Pudd'nhead Wilson.* James Cox sees all three works as Twain's "valiant attempt to secure enough capital to float his foundering business" (p. 257). According to Cox, "The Extraordinary Twins" is the seminal piece that gave rise to the sentimental *Joan,* on the one hand, and the darkly ironic world of *Pudd'nhead,* on the other. See *Mark Twain: The Fate of Humor,* esp. pp. 255–266.

81. William Dean Howells, *My Mark Twain: Reminiscences and Criticisms,* ed. Marilyn Austin Baldwin (Baton Rouge: Louisiana State University Press, 1967), p. 134.

82. For a letter from Alfred C. Clark, dated August 24, 1895, ordering costumes for Edison's *Joan of Arc,* see Gordon Hendricks, *Origins of the American Film* (New York: Arno Press and the New York Times, 1972), pp. 139–140. See also Charles Musser, *Edison Motion Pictures, 1890–1900: An Annotated Filmography* (New York: Smithsonian Institution Press, 1997), p. 190. I thank my colleague, Marshall Deutlebaum, for this reference.

83. See Paul Schrader, *Transcendental Style in Film: Ozu, Bresson, Dreyer* (Berkeley: University of California Press, 1972). See also Robin Blaetz, *Visions*

of the Maid: Joan of Arc in American Film and Culture (Charlottesville: University Press of Virginia, 2002).

84. Benjamin, "Work of Art," p. 246 n.11.

85. Ibid., p. 221.

Notes to Chapter Four

1. John McMurtry, *The Structure of Marx's World-View* (Princeton: Princeton University Press, 1978), p. 128n.6.

2. Karl Marx, "The Eighteenth Brumaire of Louis Bonaparte," in *On Historical Materialism,* ed. T. Borodulina (Moscow: Progress Publishers, 1972), p. 120.

3. Robert Tucker, *Philosophy and Myth in Karl Marx,* 2d ed. (Cambridge: Cambridge University Press, 1972), p. 122.

4. Ibid., p. 219.

5. Karl Marx, "Speech at the Anniversary of *The People's Paper,*" in *On Historical Materialism,* p. 135. My learned colleague Ingeborg Hinderschiedt informs me that the etymology of *Vehm* is uncertain but that scholars have hypothesized a relationship to the Latin word *poena,* meaning "penalty, punishment."

6. On Hegel and the Jews, see Emmanuel Levinas, *Difficult Freedom: Essays on Judaism,* trans. Séan Hand (Baltimore: Johns Hopkins University Press, 1990), pp. 235–238.

7. Karl Marx, "On the Jewish Question," in *The Marx-Engels Reader,* 2d ed., ed. Robert C. Tucker (New York: W. W. Norton, 1978), p. 49.

8. Karl Marx, *Capital: A Critique of Political Economy,* ed. Frederick Engels (New York: Modern Library, 1906), 1:315.

9. Ibid., note 3.

10. Amy Newman, "Feminist Social Criticism and Marx's Theory of Religion," *Hypatia* 9.4 (1994): 23–25.

11. Sergei Bulgakov, *Karl Marx as a Religious Type,* trans. Luba Barna, ed. Virgil Lang (Belmont, Mass.: Nordland, 1979), p. 76.

12. Tucker, *Philosophy and Myth,* p. 22.

13. Karl Marx, "Theses on Feuerbach," in *On Historical Materialism,* p. 12.

14. Tucker, *Philosophy and Myth,* p. 227.

15. Karl Marx and Friedrich Engels, *On Religion* (New York: Schocken, 1964), pp. 85, 83, 84.

16. Ibid., p. 42.

17. Ibid.

18. Tucker, *Philosophy and Myth,* p. 224.

19. Karl Marx, *Economic and Philosophic Manuscripts of 1844,* trans. Martin Milligan (Moscow: Progress Publishers, 1974), p. 102.

20. Ibid.

21. Tucker, *Philosophy and Myth,* p. 225.

22. Quoted in McMurtry, *Structure of Marx's World-View*, p. 143.

23. Georges Sorel, *Reflections on Violence*, trans. T. E. Hulme and J. Roth (New York: Collier, 1974), p. 50. Subsequent citations are given parenthetically by page.

24. Sorel's comment that the example of Joan of Arc is likely to inspire "literary types" of Socialists may be a veiled allusion to Charles Péguy (1873–1914), whose *Jeanne d'Arc* was published in 1897 and dedicated to all those who had fought against "the universal human evil" ("mal universel humain") and "for the establishment of the universal socialist republic": "pour l'établissement de la République socialiste universelle" (*Œuvres poétiques completes*, ed. Pierre Pèguy [Paris: Gallimard, 1957], p. 27).

25. Bertolt Brecht, *Brecht on Theatre*, ed. and trans. John Willett (London: Methuen, 1978), p. 24.

26. Ibid., p. 25.

27. Ibid., p. 28.

28. Ibid., p. 189.

29. Ibid., p. 87.

30. Ibid.

31. Ibid., p. 80.

32. Ibid., p. 24.

33. Ibid., p. 210.

34. Ibid., p. 30.

35. Bertolt Brecht, *Saint Joan of the Stockyards*, trans. Frank Jones (Bloomington: Indiana University Press, 1969), p. 75. I use this translation throughout, giving page citations parenthetically. For the German text I use Bertolt Brecht, *Die heilige Johanna der Schlachthöfe*, ed. Gisela E. Bahr (Frankfurt am Main: Suhrkamp, 1971).

36. René Girard, *Things Hidden since the Foundation of the World*, trans. Stephen Bann and Michael Metteer (Stanford: Stanford University Press, 1987), pp. 126–138.

37. Theodor W. Adorno, *Notes to Literature*, ed. Rolf Tiedemann, trans. Shierry Weber Nicholsen (New York: Columbia University Press, 1991), vol. 2, pp. 82, 87. Quotes immediately following are from this source and are cited parenthetically by page.

38. *Brecht on Theatre*, p. 24.

39. Ibid., pp. 74–75.

40. See, for example, Martin Esslin's comment that Brecht's *Saint Joan of the Stockyards* parodies "one of the silliest plays in the German classical canon, Schiller's *Maid of Orléans*" (Esslin, *Brecht: The Man and His Work* [Garden City, N. Y.: Doubleday, 1971], p. 55).

41. Walter H. Sokel argues that "Die theoretischen Äußerungen Brecht zur selben Zeit zeigen aber, daß er damit nicht mehr wie in den zwanziger Jahren die Klassiker selbst, sondern ihre Funktion in der modernen Kapitalistischen Gesellschaft angreift. Das Prestige der Klassiker wird systematisch dazu benützt, die aufstrebende Arbeitklasse einzuschüchtern und nieder zu

halten" ("Brechts Marxistischer Weg zur Klassik," in *Die Klassik-Legende,* ed. Reinhold Grimm and Jost Hermand, Schriften zur Literatur 18 [Frankfurt am Main: Anthenaum, 1971], p. 178).

42. Siegfried B. Puknat, "Brecht and Schiller: Nonelective Affinities," *Modern Language Quarterly* 26 (1965): 559 n.2. On the many parallels between Schiller and Brecht, see Walter Hinderer, "Ist das epische Theater etwa eine 'moralische Anstalt'? Bemerkungen zu Brechts Kritischer Aneignung von Schillers Dramaturgie," in *Probleme der Moderne: Studien zur deutschen Literatur von Nietzsche bis Brecht,* ed. Benjamin Bennett, Anton Kaes, William J. Lillyman [Tübingen: Max Niemeyer, 1983], pp. 459–475.

43. Peter Thomson, "Brecht's Lives," in *The Cambridge Companion to Brecht,* ed. Peter Thomson and Glendyr Sacks (Cambridge: Cambridge University Press, 1994), p. 25.

44. *Brecht on Theatre,* p. 224.

45. Ibid., p. 225.

46. Ibid., p. 224.

47. John Fuegi, "The Zelda Syndrome: Brecht and Elisabeth Hauptmann," in *The Cambridge Companion to Brecht,* p. 113.

48. Klaus Völker, *Brecht: A Biography,* trans. John Nowell (London: Marion Boyars, 1979), p. 129.

49. *Brecht on Theatre,* p. 13. For a general study of Shaw and Marx, see Paul A. Hummert, *Bernard Shaw's Marxian Romance* (Lincoln: University of Nebraska Press, 1973).

50. *Brecht on Theatre,* pp. 13, 10, 11.

51. Bernard Shaw, *Collected Letters, 1911–1925,* ed. Dan H. Laurence (New York: Viking, 1985), p. 867.

52. Ibid., pp. 875–876.

53. Quoted in Stanley Weintraub, "Introduction," *"Saint Joan" Fifty Years After,* ed. Stanley Weintraub (Baton Rouge: Louisiana State University Press, 1973), p. 4.

54. Bernard Shaw, *Saint Joan,* ed. Dan H. Laurence (New York: Penguin, 1957), p. 23. Hereafter all quotes from this edition of the "Preface" and play are cited parenthetically by page.

55. Shaw, *Collected Letters,* p. 870.

56. Ibid., p. 380.

57. Ibid., p. 777.

58. Benjamin Bennett, *Modern Drama and German Classicism: Renaissance from Lessing to Brecht* (Ithaca: Cornell University Press, 1979), p. 281. J.L. Wisenthal has argued for an indirect connection between Shaw and Schiller, via Thomas Carlyle's *Life of Schiller* and Carlyle's interpretation of *Die Jungfrau von Orleans.* See Wisenthal, *Shaw's Sense of History* (Oxford: Clarendon Press, 1988), pp. 72–75. Martin Meisel argues that Shaw's *Saint Joan* was partially inspired by Schiller's *Maria Stuart.* See Meisel, *Shaw and the Nineteenth-Century Theater* (Westport, Conn.: Greenwood Press, 1976), p. 366.

59. Marx and Engels, *On Religion,* p. 99.

60. Ibid.

61. Shaw characteristically refers to the Joan of his interpretation as "the real Joan." See James Graham, "Shaw on *Saint Joan*," in *"Saint Joan" Fifty Years After,* p. 17.

62. On the theme of Joan's loneliness, see A. Obraztsova, "A People's Heroine," in *"Saint Joan" Fifty Years After,* pp. 220–229.

63. *The Religious Speeches of Bernard Shaw,* ed. Warren Sylvester Smith (University Park: Pennsylvania State University Press, 1963), pp. 43, 38.

64. Bernard Shaw, "The Quintessence of Ibsenism," in *Selected Non-Dramatic Writings of Bernard Shaw,* ed. Dan H. Laurence (Boston: Houghton Mifflin, 1965), p. 220.

65. Ibid.

66. Shaw, *Religious Speeches,* p. 56.

67. Bennett, *Modern Drama and German Classicism,* p. 272.

68. Alick West, "*Saint Joan:* A Marxist View," in *"Saint Joan" Fifty Years After,* p. 112.

69. Glenn R. Cuomo, "'*Saint Joan* before the Cannibals': George Bernard Shaw in the Third Reich," *German Studies Review* 16.3 (1993): 436. Quotes immediately following are from this article and are cited parenthetically by page.

70. Goebbels collaborated with Gustav Ucicky on the screenplay for *Das Mädchen Johanna* in 1935. See Kevin J. Harty, "The Nazis, Joan of Arc, and Medievalism Gone Awry: Gustav Ucicky's 1935 Film, *Das Mädchen Johanna,*" in *Rationality and the Liberal Arts: A Festschrift Honoring Ira Lee Morgan* (Shreveport, La.: Centenary College, 1997), pp. 122–133.

71. See Hannah Arendt, *Eichmann in Jerusalem: A Report on the Banality of Evil* (New York: Viking, 1963).

72. Thomson, "Brecht's Lives," in *The Cambridge Companion to Brecht,* p. 35.

73. Bertolt Brecht, *Journals, 1934–1955,* trans. Hugh Rorrison, ed. John Willett (New York: Routledge, 1993), p. 279.

74. Bertolt Brecht, *The Visions of Simone Machard,* in *Collected Plays,* ed. John Willett and Ralph Manheim (London: Eyre Methuen, 1976), vol. 7. Subsequent citations are given parenthetically by page. For the German text, I use Bertolt Brecht, *Die Gesichte der Simone Machard,* in *Gesammelte Werke* (Frankfurt am Main: Suhrkamp, 1967), vol. 2, pp. 1841–1911, giving page number parenthetically.

75. Brecht, *Journals, 1934–1955,* p. 183. Brecht regularly uses lower case in his notebook entries.

76. On this point, see Jürgen Albers, "Die Gesichte der Simone Machard: Eine zarte Traumerei nach Motiven von Marx, Lenin, Schiller," *Brecht-Jahrbuch* (1978): 78.

77. Brecht, *Journals, 1934–1955,* p. 272.

78. Ibid.

79. Ibid., p. 270. In his journal Brecht generally avoids capitalizing names.

80. Ibid., p. 271.

81. Ibid., p. 272.

82. James K. Lyon, *Bertolt Brecht in America* (Princeton: Princeton University Press, 1980), p. 106.

83. I owe this suggestion to a conversation with Robert Chenavier, editor of *Cahiers Simone Weil.*

84. Simone Pétrement, *Simone Weil: A Life,* trans. Raymond Rosenthal (New York: Pantheon, 1976), p. 129.

85. To her parents she wrote: "I continue to run about Berlin in diverse directions. One of these days I shall go to the opera" (Pétrement, *Simone Weil,* p. 134).

86. Völker, *Brecht: A Biography,* p. 233.

87. Pétrement, *Simone Weil,* pp. 208–209. See also Michel Surya, *Georges Bataille: La mort a l'oeuvre* (Paris: Frédéric Birr, 1987), pp. 175–180, 193–194, 219–221.

88. For a study of Simone Weil's attitude toward Joan of Arc, see Ann Pirrucello, "Force or Fragility? Simone Weil and Two Faces of Joan of Arc," forthcoming in *Joan of Arc and Spirituality,* ed. Bonnie Wheeler and Ann W. Astell (Palgrave Press).

89. Brecht, *Journals, 1934–1955,* p. 183.

90. Ibid., p. 183.

91. See Lyon, *Bertolt Brecht in America,* p. 78.

92. Russell Janney, *The Miracle of the Bells* (New York: Prentice-Hall, 1946), p. 295.

93. Ibid., p. 260.

94. Ibid., p. 300.

95. The cult of the actress who plays Joan of Arc stands behind the director Otto Preminger's review of applications from eighteen thousand girls for the part eventually played by seventeen-year-old Jean Seberg in the 1957 Hollywood movie, *Saint Joan.*

96. Lyon, *Bertolt Brecht in America,* p. 318.

97. Ibid., p. 326.

98. Ibid., p. 332.

99. Janney, *The Miracle of the Bells,* p. 19. Citations immediately following are from Janney's novel and are given parenthetically by page.

100. Lillian Hellman, *Scoundrel Time* (Boston: Little, Brown, 1976), pp. 93–94. Immediately following citations from *Scoundrel Time* are given parenthetically in the text.

101. On the irregularities in the transcript of Joan's trial, see Régine Pernoud and Marie-Véronique Clin, *Joan of Arc: Her Story,* trans. and rev. Jeremy du Quesnay Adams, ed. Bonnie Wheeler (New York: St. Martin's, 1998), p. 112. In his testimony during the Rehabilitation Trial of 1455–1456, Isambart de la Pierre reports Joan's complaint: "'Oh, you write down everything that is against me all right, but you will not record anything in my favor'" (Régine Pernoud, *The Retrial of Joan of Arc,* trans. J.M. Cohen [New York: Harcourt, Brace, 1955], p. 202). The testimonies of Richard du Grouchet, Jean Fabri, and Pierre Daron similarly point to misreporting and omissions by the scribes and to the control exerted by Cauchon over the trial record. See *Retrial,* pp. 193, 194, 201.

102. Pernoud and Clin, *Joan of Arc: Her Story,* p. 113.

103. William Wright, *Lillian Hellman: The Image, the Woman* (New York: Simon and Schuster, 1986), p. 263.

104. Carl Rollyson, *Lillian Hellman: Her Legend and Her Legacy* (New York: St. Martin's, 1988), p. 355. Immediately following quotes are cited parenthetically by page.

105. Lillian Hellman, *The Lark*, in *The Collected Plays* (Boston: Little, Brown, 1972), p. 559. Subsequent citations of *The Lark* are given parenthetically by title and page.

106. Hellman, *Scoundrel Time*, p. 92.

107. Ibid., p. 109.

108. Ibid., p. 108. See H. Ansgar Kelly, "The Right to Remain Silent: Before and after Joan of Arc," *Speculum* 68.4 (1993): 992–1026.

109. Janney, *Miracle of the Bells*, p. 497.

Notes to Chapter Five

1. Susan Crane, "Clothing and Gender Definition: Joan of Arc," *Journal of Medieval and Early Modern Studies* 26.2 (1996): 297–320; Valerie R. Hotchkiss, "Chapter 4: Transvestism on Trial: The Case of Jeanne d'Arc," in *Clothes Make the Man: Female Cross-Dressing in Medieval Europe*, the New Middle Ages 1 (New York: Garland, 1996), pp. 49–68; Susan Schibanoff, "True Lies: Transvestism and Idolatry in the Trial of Joan of Arc," in *Fresh Verdicts on Joan of Arc*, ed. Bonnie Wheeler and Charles T. Wood (New York: Garland, 1996), pp. 31–61.

2. Hotchkiss, *Clothes Make the Man*, p. 51.

3. Ibid.

4. Crane, "Clothing and Gender Definition," p. 297.

5. Schibanoff, "True Lies," p. 37.

6. George Bernard Shaw, *Saint Joan: A Chronicle Play in Six Scenes and an Epilogue*, ed. Dan H. Laurence (London: Penguin, 1957), p. 1. Hereafter citations are given parenthetically in the text.

7. J. Ellen Gainor, *Shaw's Daughters: Dramatic and Narrative Constructions of Gender* (Ann Arbor: University of Michigan Press, 1991), p. 148.

8. Vita Sackville-West, *Saint Joan of Arc* (New York: Doubleday, 1991), p. 12. Hereafter citations are given parenthetically by abbreviated title (*SJA*) and page.

9. See Shaw, *Saint Joan*, pp. 24–25.

10. Nadia Margolis, *Joan of Arc in History, Literature, and Film: A Select, Annotated Bibliography* (New York: Garland, 1990), p. 132.

11. Karyn Z. Sproles, "Cross-Dressing for (Imaginary) Battle: Vita Sackville-West's Biography of Joan of Arc," *Biography* 19.2 (1996): 158–177.

12. Karyn Z. Sproles also advances this thesis, albeit much more briefly, in her essay, "Virginia Woolf Writes to Vita Sackville-West (and Receives a Reply): *Aphra Behn, Orlando, Saint Joan of Arc*, and Revolutionary Biography," in *Virginia Woolf: Texts and Contexts*, ed. Beth Rigel Daugherty and

Eileen Barrett (New York: Pace University Press, 1996), pp. 189–193. I extend Sproles's insightful argument about the ways that Sackville-West and Woolf influenced each other as biographers, reaching different conclusions in the process.

13. For an excellent study of the pattern of mutual literary influence between Woolf and Sackville-West, see Louise A. DeSalvo, "Lighting the Cave: The Relationship between Vita Sackville-West and Virginia Woolf," *Signs: A Journal of Women in Culture and Society* 8.2 (1982): 195–214. DeSalvo does not discuss *Saint Joan of Arc* and *Roger Fry*. Like most Woolf scholars, she focuses on the period of strong friendship between the two women, which ended in 1934.

14. Thomas S. W. Lewis, "Combining 'the Advantages of Fact and Fiction': Virginia Woolf's Biographies of Vita Sackville-West, Flush, and Roger Fry," in *Virginia Woolf: Centennial Essays*, ed. Elaine K. Ginsberg and Laura Moss Gottlieb (Troy, N. Y.: Whitson, 1983), p. 298.

15. Virginia Woolf, "The New Biography," in *Collected Essays*, ed. Leonard Woolf (London: Chatto and Windus, 1969), vol. 4, p. 234.

16. Ibid.

17. Ibid., p. 233.

18. Ibid.

19. Vita Sackville-West, *The Letters of Vita Sackville-West to Virginia Woolf*, ed. Louise DeSalvo and Mitchell A. Leaska (New York: William Morrow, 1985), p. 238.

20. Ibid., pp. 288–289.

21. Virginia Woolf, *Orlando: A Biography* (New York: Harcourt, 1956), p. 148. Hereafter citations are parenthetical by abbreviated title (*O*) and page.

22. Sproles, "Cross-Dressing for (Imaginary) Battle," p. 162.

23. See Nigel Nicolson, *Portrait of a Marriage: V. Sackville-West and Harold Nicolson* (New York: Atheneum, 1987), pp. 103, 110–111, 116, 133, 152–153, 164.

24. Sackville-West names the saint "Joan" in the title of the book but refers to her as "Jeanne" throughout the text. Accordingly, I use "Jeanne" to name Sackville-West's heroine and "Joan" to refer to the historical saint, but the distinction is occasionally hard to make.

25. See Sackville-West, *Saint Joan of Arc*, pp. 8, 80, 84–86.

26. Nicolson, *Portrait of a Marriage*, p. 105.

27. Charles T. Wood notes that Saint Margaret (alias "Pelagius") also dressed as a man (a monk) and passed for a man, but Wood is misleading here, because Joan's patroness was probably not this Saint Margaret but rather Saint Margaret of Antioch, a popular medieval saint and the patroness of childbirth. See Charles T. Wood, *Joan of Arc and Richard III: Sex, Saints, and Government in the Middle Ages* (New York: Oxford University Press, 1988), pp. 134–135.

28. Agnes Sorel became the mistress of Charles VII in 1444, thirteen years after the death of Joan of Arc.

29. Victoria Glendinning, *Vita: The Life of V. Sackville-West* (New York: Alfred A. Knopf, 1983), p. 285.

30. Sproles, "Cross-Dressing for (Imaginary) Battle," p. 170.

31. Sproles, "Virginia Woolf Writes to Sackville-West," p. 190.

32. Ibid., p. 192.

33. Virginia Woolf, *Congenial Spirits: The Selected Letters of Virginia Woolf*, ed. Joanne Trautmann Banks (New York: Harcourt Brace Jovanovich, 1989), Letter 3325, p. 393. Woolf frequently omits apostrophes in her letters and journals.

34. Ibid., Letter 3146a, p. 377.

35. *Letters of Vita Sackville-West to Virginia Woolf*, p. 394. Ethel Smyth's response to Vita Sackville-West's *Saint Joan of Arc* may be complicated by the fact that George Bernard Shaw had credited Smyth, a composer, with inspiring his portrayal of Joan. On March 9, 1924, Shaw wrote to Smyth: "But for you I might not have been able to tackle St. Joan, who has floored every previous playwright. Your music is more masculine than Handel's" (Bernard Shaw, *Collected Letters, 1911–1925*, ed. Dan H. Laurence [New York: Viking, 1985], p. 868).

36. Glendinning, *Vita*, p. 284.

37. Woolf, *Congenial Spirits*, Letter 3147, pp. 377–378.

38. Ibid., p. 377.

39. Ibid., p. 378.

40. Glendinning, *Vita*, p. 277.

41. James King, *Virginia Woolf* (New York: W. W. Norton, 1995), p. 107.

42. Virginia Woolf, *The Diary of Virginia Woolf*, 4 vols., ed. Anne Olivier Bell, assisted by Andrew McNellie (New York: Harcourt Brace Jovanovich, 1982), vol. 4, p. 23.

43. Ibid. I have expanded Virginia's abbreviations.

44. King, *Virginia Woolf*, p. 91. For studies of Woolf's "madness," see Roger Poole, *The Unknown Virginia Woolf* (Cambridge: Cambridge University Press, 1978); and Allie Glenny, *Ravenous Identity: Eating and Eating Distress in the Life and Work of Virginia Woolf* (New York: St. Martin's, 1999).

45. Virginia Woolf, *A Room of One's Own* (New York: Harcourt, Brace and World, 1957), p. 47.

46. Ibid., p. 51.

47. Ibid., p. 102.

48. Suzanne Raitt, *Vita and Virginia: The Work and Friendship of V. Sackville-West and Virginia Woolf* (Oxford: Clarendon Press, 1993), p. 134.

49. Ibid., p. 133.

50. Virginia Woolf, "A Sketch of the Past," in *Moments of Being: Unpublished Autobiographical Writings*, ed. Jeanne Schulkind (London: Sussex University Press, 1976), p. 66.

51. Ibid., p. 68.

52. Ibid., p. 69.

53. Ibid.

54. Ibid., p. 68.

55. Raitt, *Vita and Virginia*, p. 131.

56. Woolf, "A Sketch of the Past," in *Moments of Being,* p. 69.

57. Woolf, *Congenial Spirits,* Letter 3147, p. 377.

58. Woolf, "A Sketch of the Past," in *Moments of Being,* p. 72.

59. Ibid.

60. *The Diary of Virginia Woolf,* vol. 4, p. 306.

61. Woolf's intermittent work on Fry's biography was combined with other projects. Between 1935 and 1940 she also wrote *The Years, Three Guineas,* and "Pointz Hall" (the first draft of *Between the Acts*).

62. King, *Virginia Woolf,* p. 579.

63. Quoted in Herbert Marder, *The Measure of Life: Virginia Woolf's Last Years* (Ithaca: Cornell University Press, 2000), p. 300.

64. Virginia Woolf, "The Art of Biography," in *Collected Essays,* vol. 4, p. 223.

65. Ibid., p. 221.

66. Ibid., pp. 227–228.

67. Marder, *Measure of Life,* p. 357.

68. King, *Virginia Woolf,* p. 622.

69. Marder, *Measure of Life,* p. 295.

70. Ibid., p. 299.

71. Woolf, *Congenial Spirits,* Letter 740, pp. 89–90.

72. Marder, *Measure of Life,* p. 342.

73. Ibid., p. 343.

74. Ibid.

75. Sandra M. Gilbert and Susan Gubar, *The Madwoman in the Attic: The Woman Writer and the Nineteenth-Century Literary Imagination* (New Haven: Yale University Press, 1979), p. 51.

76. DeSalvo, "Lighting the Cave," p. 199.

77. *The Diary of Virginia Woolf,* vol. 3, 1925–1930, p. 187.

78. Ibid., p. 50.

79. Ibid., vol. 2, 1920–1924, p. 226.

80. Ibid., vol. 4, 1930–1935, p. 287.

81. Woolf, *Congenial Spirits,* Letter 3147, p. 377.

82. See Virginia's letter to Ethel Smith in *Congenial Spirits,* Letter 3481, p. 419.

83. Woolf, *Congenial Spirits,* note 2, p. 419.

84. Sigmund Freud, *Totem and Taboo: Resemblances between the Psychic Lives of Savages and Neurotics,* trans. A. A. Brill (New York: Random House, 1946), p. 116. I take this paragraph from a longer discussion of narcissism in my "Telling Tales of Love: Julia Kristeva and Bernard of Clairvaux," *Christianity and Literature* 50.1 (2000): 125–148.

85. René Girard, "Are the Gospels Mythical?" *First Things* 62 (April 1996): 31.

86. On this subject, see Dawn Perlmutter, "The Sacrificial Aesthetic: Blood Rituals from Art to Murder," *Anthropoetics* 5.2 (Fall 1999–Winter 2000): www.anthropoetics.ucla.edu.

87. Tournier originally studied to become a philosopher. Although Spinoza is the philosopher whom he most admires, his use of binary and tertiary struc-

tures is grounded in Hegelian thought. On Tournier's debt to Hegel, see David Platten, *Michel Tournier and the Metaphor of Fiction* (New York: St. Martin's, 1999), esp. pp. 72, 115, 120, 122–124.

88. On the question of Tournier's status as a Christian writer, see John M. Dunaway, "Michel Tournier: Christian Writer?" *Christianity and Literature* 49 (2000): 357–370; and the response to Dunaway's essay by Susan Petit, "Michel Tournier: *Ecrivain Croyant?*" *Christianity and Literature* 50.2 (2001): 313–326. See also Karen D. Levy, "Tournier's Ultimate Perversion: The Historical Manipulation of *Gilles et Jeanne*," *Papers on Language and Literature* 28 (1992): 72–88.

89. Michel Tournier, *Gilles and Jeanne: A Novel,* trans. Alan Sheridan (New York: Grove Weidenfeld, 1987), p. 10. Subsequent citations are given parenthetically by page. For the French text, I use Michel Tournier, *Gilles et Jeanne: Récit* (Paris: Gallimard, 1983).

90. Edith Wyschogrod, *Saints and Postmodernism: Revisioning Moral Philosophy* (Chicago: University of Chicago Press, 1990), p. 200.

91. Ibid., pp. 218, 221.

92. Ibid., p. 226.

93. Ibid., p. 227.

94. René Girard, *I See Satan Fall Like Lightning,* trans. James G. Williams (Maryknoll, N.Y.: Orbis, 2001), p. 35.

95. René Girard, *Things Hidden since the Foundation of the World,* trans. Stephen Bann and Michael Metteer (Stanford: Stanford University Press, 1987), p. 21.

96. Wyschogrod, *Saints and Postmodernism,* p. 222.

97. David Gascoigne, *Michel Tournier,* New Directions in European Writing (Oxford: Berg, 1996), p. 204.

98. Ibid., p. 203.

99. Girard, *I See Satan Fall,* p. 42.

100. Ibid., p. 38.

101. Ibid., p. 75.

102. Georges Bataille, *The Trial of Gilles de Rais,* trans. Richard Robinson (Los Angeles: Amok, 1991), pp. 61–62.

103. See Régine Pernoud and Marie-Véronique Clin, *Joan of Arc: Her Story,* trans. and rev. Jeremy duQuesnay Adams, ed. Bonnie Wheeler (New York: St. Martin's, 1998), pp. 136–137.

104. Bataille, *Trial of Gilles de Rais,* p. 62.

105. Interview with Yvonne Chauffin in *Le Pélerin,* December 21, 1980; quoted in William Cloonan, *Michel Tournier* (Boston: Twayne, 1985), p. 96.

106. On "mystical naturalism" and Tournier's claim to follow in the decadent tradition of Joris-Karl Huysmans (1848–1902), see Cloonan, *Michel Tournier,* pp. 95–98. Nadia Margolis discusses the "realized mysticism" of Carl-Theodore Dreyer in "Trial by Passion: Philology, Film, and Ideology in the Portrayal of Joan of Arc (1900–1930)," *Journal of Medieval and Early Modern Studies* 27.3 (1997): 469.

Notes to Chapter Six

1. I. C. D'Israeli, *Curiosities of Literature and the Literary Character Illustrated* (New York: D. Appleton, 1846), p. 50. I thank my colleague, Dino Felluga, for this reference.

2. Nadia Margolis, *Joan of Arc in History, Literature, and Film: A Select, Annotated Bibliography* (New York: Garland, 1990), p. 329.

3. Marjorie Villiers, *Charles Péguy: A Study in Integrity* (Westport, Conn.: Greenwood Press, 1975), p. 48.

4. Ibid., p. 55.

5. Charles Péguy, *Men and Saints: Prose and Poetry*, trans. Anne Green and Julian Green (New York: Pantheon, 1944), p. 100. This volume is a facing page edition, which includes *Notre Jeunesse*. Hereafter I cite this work parenthetically by page, giving the French text and English translation.

6. René Girard, *I See Satan Fall Like Lightning*, trans. James G. Williams (Maryknoll, N.Y.: Orbis, 2001), p. 146. In an interview reported in *Figaro* in March 1899, Pope Leo XIII also likened the ordeal of Dreyfus to the martyrdom of Christ. See Joy Nachod Humes, *Two against Time: A Study of the Very Present Worlds of Paul Claudel and Charles Péguy*, North Carolina Studies in the Romance Languages and Literatures, No. 200 (Chapel Hill: University of North Carolina at Chapel Hill, 1978), p. 16.

7. Villiers, *Charles Péguy*, p. 59.

8. M. Adereth, *Commitment in Modern French Literature: Politics and Society in Péguy, Aragon, and Sartre* (New York: Schocken, 1968), p. 61.

9. Humes, *Two against Time*, p. 55.

10. Charles Péguy, *The Mystery of the Charity of Joan of Arc*, trans. Julian Green (New York: Pantheon, 1950), pp. 83–84; Charles Péguy, *Le Mystère de la charité de Jeanne d'Arc*, in *Œuvres poétiques complètes* (Paris: Gallimard, 1957), p. 426. Subsequent quotes from this translation and edition are cited parenthetically by page.

11. Péguy, *Men and Saints*, pp. 172–173.

12. Ibid.

13. On Weil's attitude toward Joan of Arc, see Ann Pirrucello's essay in *Joan of Arc and Spirituality*, ed. Bonnie Wheeler and Ann W. Astell (forthcoming).

14. Pope Pius XII declared that "it is impossible for a Catholic to be an anti-Semite; spiritually all of us are Semites" (quoted in Pinchas E. Lapide, *The Last Three Popes and the Jews*, [London: Souvenir, 1967], p. 118).

15. See Adereth, *Commitment in Modern French Literature*, pp. 74–79; Villiers, *Charles Péguy*, pp. 237–242; Humes, *Two against Time*, p. 159.

16. Villiers, *Charles Péguy*, p. 302.

17. Quoted in Humes, *Two against Time*, p. 21.

18. See Humes, *Two against Time*, pp. 21–23.

19. Emmanuel Levinas, *Difficult Freedom: Essays on Judaism*, trans. Seán Hand (Baltimore: Johns Hopkins University Press, 1990), pp. 127, 128, 130.

20. Ibid., p. 127. In a letter to the organizer of the 1936 World Jewish Congress, Claudel mentions that his study of the Bible has awakened his appre-

ciative understanding of Israel's importance in the plan of salvation: "D'autre part, l'etude continuelle que je fais de la Bible m'a pénétré de l'importance prédominante d'Israël au point de vue de Dieu et de l'humanité." He points to the historic role that the Jewish people have played in their witness to God in the face of Greek paganism: "C'est Israël, avec un courage héroïque et une audace intellectuelle qui serait inexplicable sans une vocation d'en haut, qui a toujours maintenu, contre les séductions de la Grèce, l'idée d'un Dieu person-nel et transcendant, supérieur à toutes les superstitions du paganisme." Hitler's hatred of the Jews is, Claudel suggests, an indication of the paganism of Na-tional Socialism: "Et c'est précisément le paganisme renaissant sous la forme la plus basse et la plus hideuse qui vient, une fois de plus, se heurter à cette pierre inébranlable." See Paul Claudel, "Trois lettres sur Israël," in *Les Juifs* (Paris: Librairie Plon, 1937), pp. v–ix.

21. Humes, *Two against Time,* p. 21.

22. Levinas, *Difficult Freedom,* p. 128.

23. Quoted by Levinas, *Difficult Freedom,* p. 128.

24. Levinas, *Difficult Freedom,* pp. 128, 130.

25. On the life of this fascinating woman, see Vicki Woolf, *Dancing in the Vortex: The Story of Ida Rubinstein,* Choreography and Dance Studies 20 (Amsterdam: Harwood Academic Publishers, 2000).

26. For the words of the Prologue I rely on the libretto edited by Beatrice Baron for the performance by the Philadelphia Orchestra in 1948. Baron reproduces the Salabert edition of Claudel's text. The English translation is by Dennis Arundell.

27. Paul Claudel, *Jeanne d'Arc au bûcher,* in *Théâtre de Paul Claudel,* 2 vols., ed. Jacques Madaule (Paris: Gallimard, 1956), vol. 2, p. 1225. Subsequent cita-tions of the text from this edition are given parenthetically by page.

28. Saint Thérèse of Lisieux, *Story of a Soul: The Autobiography of St. Thé-rèse of Lisieux,* 2d ed., trans. John Clarke, O.C.D. (Washington, D.C.: Institute of Carmelite Studies, 1976), p. 193.

29. Ibid., p. 72.

30. Quoted by Vita Sackville-West and translated by her in *The Eagle and the Dove: A Study in Contrasts: St. Teresa of Avila, St. Thérèse of Lisieux* (Garden City, N.Y.: Doubleday, Doran & Co., 1944), pp. 138–139, 175.

31. On the place of Joan of Arc in the spirituality of St. Thérèse, see Denise Despres, "Le Triomphe de L'Humilite: Thérèse of Lisieux and 'Une Nouvelle Jeanne,'" in *Joan of Arc and Spirituality,* ed. Bonnie Wheeler and Ann W. Astell (forthcoming).

32. Saint Thérèse of Lisieux, *Story of a Soul,* p. 193.

33. Ibid., p. 194. The capitals and italics are in the original.

34. Ibid., p. 195.

35. Georges Bernanos, "Sermon of an Agnostic on the Feast of St. Thérèse," trans. Pamela Morris and David Louis Schindler Jr., in *The Heroic Face of In-nocence: Three Stories by Georges Bernanos* (Grand Rapids, Mich.: William B. Eerdmans, 1999), p. 36.

36. Ibid., p. 36.

37. Ibid., pp. 23, 33.

38. Bernanos, "Sermon of an Agnostic," p. 35.

39. Ibid.

40. Georges Bernanos, "Joan, Heretic and Saint," trans. R. Batchelor, in *The Heroic Face of Innocence: Three Stories by Georges Bernanos* (Grand Rapids, Mich.: William B. Eerdmans, 1999), p. 2.

41. Dreyer's film was censured by the archbishop of Paris in 1928 for its villainous depiction of Church officials. See Richard Abel, *French Cinema: The First Wave, 1915–1929* (Princeton: Princeton University Press, 1984), pp. 196–199, 486–500.

42. Bernanos, "Joan, Heretic and Saint," p. 2.

43. Bernanos, "Sermon of an Agnostic," p. 35.

44. Ibid.

45. Ibid., p. 27.

46. Jules Isaac, *The Teaching of Contempt: Christian Roots of Anti-Semitism,* trans. Helen Weaver (New York: Holt, Rinehart and Winston, 1964), pp. 129, 146. It is worth noting that Joseph and Augustin Lémann, Jewish converts to Catholicism, played an enthusiastic role in promoting the canonization of Joan of Arc, whom they compared to Jewish heroines. See Joseph Lémann, *Jeanne d'Arc et les héroïnes juives, panégyrique prononcé dans la cathédrale d'Orléans le 8 mai 1873* (Orléans: Chenu, 1873). I thank Nadia Margolis for this reference.

47. For studies reviewing the tremendous changes in Jewish-Christian relations, see Jack Bemporad and Michael Shevack, *Our Age: The Historic New Era of Christian-Jewish Understanding* (New York: New City Press, 1996); *John Paul II on Jews and Judaism, 1979–1986,* ed. Eugene J. Fisher and Leon Klenicki (Washington, D.C.: United States Catholic Conference, 1987).

48. W.M. Frohock observes that "one factor remains constant" in Bernanos's politics—his "hatred of the injustice he called 'humiliation,'" which he defined as "taking criminal advantage of those unable to defend themselves—like the Mallorcan peasants herded into trucks and taken to be shot." See W.M. Frohock, "Georges Bernanos (1888–1948)," in *The Politics of Twentieth-Century Novelists,* ed. George A. Panchas (New York: Hawthorn, 1971), p. 162.

49. Bernanos, "Sermon of an Agnostic," p. 26.

50. Ibid.

51. On the complex relationship of the Action Française to the cult of Jeanne d'Arc, see Nadia Margolis, "Trial by Passion: Philology, Film, and Ideology in the Portrayal of Joan of Arc (1900–1930)," *Journal of Medieval and Early Modern Studies* 27.3 (1997): 445–493. See also Michel Winock, "Jeanne d'Arc et les Juifs," *H-Histoire* 3 (1979): 227–238.

52. Frohlick, "Georges Bernanos," p. 170.

53. Jacques Petit, *Bernanos, Bloy, Claudel, Péguy: Quatre écrivains catholiques face à Israël* (Paris: Calmann-Lévy, 1972), p. 11.

54. Bernanos, "Joan, Heretic and Saint," p. 19.

55. Frohock, "Georges Bernanos," p. 166.

56. Bernanos, "Sermon of an Agnostic," p. 33.

57. Frohock, "Georges Bernanos," p. 162.

58. For a divergent interpretation of this essay, see Hans Wagener, *Understanding Franz Werfel* (Columbia: University of South Carolina Press, 1993), pp. 17–18.

59. Bernanos, "Sermon of an Agnostic," p. 38.

60. On Werfel's life, see Peter Stephan Jungk, *Franz Werfel: A Life in Prague, Vienna, and Hollywood,* trans. Anselm Hollo (New York: Grove Weidenfeld, 1990).

61. The critically acclaimed Hollywood film version, starring Jennifer Jones, was released in 1943.

62. Vita Sackville-West, *Saint Joan of Arc* (New York: Doubleday, 1991), p. 333.

63. Franz Werfel, *The Song of Bernadette,* trans. Ludwig Lewisohn (New York: Viking, 1943), p. 17; *Das Lied von Bernadette* (Wein: Bermann-Fischer, 1949), p. 32. Hereafter quotations are cited parenthetically by page.

64. Werfel, *The Song of Bernadette,* p. 17. Subsequent citations are given parenthetically by page.

65. In the chapter entitled "The Fire Plays with You, O Bernadette," Werfel gives prominence to a historical episode during which Bernadette's unharmed fingers were licked by the flame of the candle she was holding, while in ecstasy. An earlier chapter, entitled "You Are Playing with Fire, O Bernadette," highlights the personal risk Bernadette is taking by maintaining the truth of her visions.

66. Bertolt Brecht, *Journals, 1934–1955,* trans. Hugh Rorrison, ed. John Willett (New York: Routledge, 1993), p. 321.

67. The German edition, published in Vienna, does not include the sentence about the British report of his murder.

68. René Girard, *Things Hidden since the Foundation of the World,* trans. Stephen Bann and Michael Metteer (Stanford: Stanford University Press, 1987), pp. 236–237.

69. Girard, *I See Satan Fall Like Lightning,* p. 40.

70. David Sheppard indicates that Cohen wrote "Joan of Arc" as a "love token" to the singer Nico. See David Sheppard, *Leonard Cohen* (New York: Thunder's Mouth Press, 2000), p. 70.

71. Ira B. Nadel, *Various Positions: A Life of Leonard Cohen* (New York: Pantheon, 1996), p. 155.

72. Ibid.

73. Ibid., p. 182.

74. The composer Richard Einhorn (b. 1952) uses a similar technique in his 1994 oratorio, *Voices of Light,* wherein Joan's voice is not a solo but a quartet (sung by Anonymous Four in a 1996 recording), to signify that she speaks not on her own authority but as inspired by her Voices. Einhorn's oratorio was inspired by Carl-Theodore Dreyer's silent film, *The Passion of Joan of Arc* (1928) and has been performed and recorded in combination with a showing of that film.

75. That album includes Cohen's "Song of Bernadette."

76. Quoted in Nadel, *Various Positions,* p. 245.

77. For Cohen's "personal critique" of "Last Year's Man," see Nadel, *Various Positions,* p. 212. I quote from a transcription of the recording.

78. Quoted in Nadel, *Various Positions,* p. 1.

79. Ibid., p. 120.

80. On Cohen's regard for Lorca, after whom he named his daughter, see Nadel, *Various Positions,* pp. 23–24, 51, 92, 206, 213, 246, 249.

81. Erik Ehn, *The Saint Plays* (Baltimore: Johns Hopkins University Press, 2000), p. x. Subsequent quotations are given parenthetically by page.

82. Compare Edith Wyschogrod's comments on the temporality of saints' lives in *Saints and Postmodernism: Revisioning Moral Philosophy* (Chicago: University of Chicago Press, 1990), pp. 61–86.

83. Sandor Goodhart, *Sacrificing Commentary: Reading the End of Literature* (Baltimore: Johns Hopkins University Press, 1996), p. 258.

84. Ibid., p. 40.

Primary Sources

Anouilh, Jean. *L'Alouette.* Paris: La Table Ronde, 1953.

Bataille, Georges. *The Trial of Gilles de Rais.* Trans. Richard Robinson. Los Angeles: Amok, 1991.

Bernanos, Georges. *Dialogues des carmélites.* Ed. Yvonne Guers. Modern French Literature. New York: Macmillan, 1965.

———. "Dialogues of the Carmelites." Trans. Michael Legat. In *The Heroic Face of Innocence: Three Stories by Georges Bernanos,* pp. 39–150. Grand Rapids, Mich.: William B. Eerdmans, 1999.

———. *Jeanne, relapse et sainte.* Paris: Plon, 1929.

———. "Joan, Heretic and Saint." Trans. R. Batchelor. In *The Heroic Face of Innocence: Three Stories by Georges Bernanos,* pp. 1–22. Grand Rapids, Mich.: William B. Eerdmans, 1999.

———. "Sermon of an Agnostic on the Feast of St. Thérèse." Trans. Pamela Morris and David Louis Schindler Jr. In *The Heroic Face of Innocence: Three Stories by Georges Bernanos,* pp. 23–38. Grand Rapids, Mich.: William B. Eerdmans, 1999.

Brecht, Bertolt. *Arbeitsjournal.* 2 vols. Ed. Werner Hecht. Frankfurt am Main: Suhrkamp, 1973.

———. *Brecht on Theatre.* Ed. and trans. John Willett. London: Methuen, 1978.

————. *Die Gesichte der Simone Machard.* In *Gesammelte Werke,* 8 vols., vol. 2: 1841–1911. Frankfurt am Main: Suhrkamp, 1967.

————. *Die heilige Johanna der Schlachthöfe.* Ed. Gisela E. Bahr. Frankfurt am Main: Suhrkamp, 1971.

————. *Journals, 1934–1955.* Trans. Hugh Rorrison. Ed. John Willett. New York: Routledge, 1993.

————. *Saint Joan of the Stockyards.* Trans. Frank Jones. Bloomington: Indiana University Press, 1969.

————. *Schriften zum Theater: Über eine nicht-aristotelische Dramatik.* Ed. Siegfried Unseld. Frankfurt am Main: Suhrkamp, 1957. Rpt. 1969.

————. *The Visions of Simone Machard.* In *Collected Plays,* vol. 7, pp. 1–64. Ed. John Willett and Ralph Manheim. London: Eyre Methuen, 1976.

British War Poetry in the Age of Romanticism, 1793–1815. Ed. Betty T. Bennett. New York: Garland, 1976.

Christine de Pizan. *Le Ditié de Jehanne d'Arc.* Ed. and trans. Angus J. Kennedy and Kenneth Varty. *Nottingham Medieval Studies* 18 (1974): 29–55; 19 (1975): 53–76.

————. *Ditié de Jehanne d'Arc.* Ed. and trans. Angus J. Kennedy and Kenneth Varty. Oxford: Society for Medieval Languages and Literature Monographs, 1977.

Claudel, Paul. *Jeanne d'Arc au bûcher.* In *Théâtre de Paul Claudel,* 2 vols., vol. 2, 1199–1226. Ed. Jacques Madaule. Paris: Gallimard, 1956.

————. *Jeanne d'Arc au bûcher.* Libretto of 1948 performance by the Philadelphia Orchestra. Ed. Beatrice Baron. Trans. Dennis Arundell.

————. "Trois lettres sur Israël." In *Les Juifs,* pp. v–ix. Ed. Daniel-Rops. Paris: Librairie Plon, 1937.

Cohen, Leonard. "Joan of Arc." "Last Year's Man." As recorded in *Songs of Love and Hate.* Produced by Bob Johnston. Columbia Records.

Coleridge, Samuel T. *Biographia Literaria.* 2 vols. Ed. J. Shawcross. Oxford: Clarendon Press, 1907.

————. *Collected Letters of Samuel Taylor Coleridge.* 6 vols. Ed. Earl Leslie Griggs. Oxford: Clarendon Press, 1956–1971.

————. *Coleridge's Miscellaneous Criticism.* Ed. Thomas Middleton Raysor. London: Constable, 1936.

————. *The Poems of Samuel Taylor Coleridge.* Ed. Ernest Hartley Coleridge. Oxford: Humphrey Milford, 1917.

De Quincey, Thomas. "Charles Lamb." In *De Quincey as Critic,* pp. 448–457. Ed. John E. Jordan. London: Routledge and Kegan Paul, 1973.

————. "Joan of Arc." In *De Quincey's Essays: Joan of Arc, the English Mail-Coach, and the Spanish Military Nun,* pp. 1–35. Ed. Carol M. Newman. New York: Macmillan, 1909.

Ehn, Erik. *The Saint Plays.* Baltimore: Johns Hopkins University Press, 2000.

Freud, Sigmund. "Civilization and Its Discontents." In *Civilisation, War and Death,* pp. 26–81. Ed. John Rickman. Psycho-analytical Epitomes No. 4. 1929; London: Hogarth Press, 1968.

————. *Totem and Taboo: Resemblances between the Psychic Lives of Savages and Neurotics.* Trans. A. A. Brill. New York: Random House, 1946.

————. *Totem und Tabu: Einge ubereinstimmungen im seelenleben der wilden und der neurotiker.* Frankfurt am Main: Fischer Taschenbuch Verlag, 1976.

Goethe, Johann Wolfgang von. *Iphigenia in Tauris.* In *Plays,* pp. 81–143. Ed. and trans. Frank G. Ryder. German Library, vol. 20. New York: Continuum, 1993.

————. *Iphigenie auf Tauris.* Ed. Joachim Angst and Fritz Hackert. Stuttgart: Reclam, 1969.

Hazlitt, William. *Lectures on the English Poets.* London: J. M. Dent, 1910. Rpt. 1955.

Hellman, Lillian. *The Lark.* In *The Collected Plays,* pp. 547–602. Boston: Little, Brown, 1971.

————. *Scoundrel Time.* Boston: Little, Brown, 1976.

Janney, Russell. *The Miracle of the Bells.* New York: Prentice Hall, 1946.

Lamb, Charles. *The Works of Charles Lamb.* 5 vols. New York: A. C. Armstrong, 1880.

L'Averdy, Clément de. *Notices et extraits des manuscrits de la Bibliothèque du Roi, lus au comité établi par sa Majesté dans l'Académie royale des Inscriptions et belles-lettres.* Paris: Imprimerie Royale, 1790.

Lémann, Joseph. *Jeanne d'Arc et les héroïnes juives, panégyrique prononcé dans la cathédrale d'Orléans le 8 mai 1873.* Orléans: Chenu, 1873.

Marx, Karl. *Capital: A Critique of Political Economy,* vol. 1. Ed. Frederick Engels. New York: Modern Library, 1906.

————. *Das Kapital: Kritik der politischen Oekonomie.* 2 vols. Ed. Friedrich Engels. Hamburg: O. Meissner, 1883–1885.

————. *Economic and Philosophic Manuscripts of 1844.* Trans. Martin Milligan. Moscow: Progress Publishers, 1974.

————. "The Eighteenth Brumaire of Louis Bonaparte." In *On Historical Materialism,* pp. 120–133. Ed. T. Borodulina. Moscow: Progress Publishers, 1972.

————. *Manifesto of the Communist Party.* Ed. Frederick Engels. Moscow: Progress Publishers, 1977.

————. "On the Jewish Question." In *The Marx-Engels Reader,* 2d ed., pp. 26–52. Ed. Robert C. Tucker. New York: W. W. Norton, 1978.

————. "Speech at the Anniversary of *The People's Paper.*" In *On Historical Materialism,* pp. 134–135. Ed. T. Borodulina. Moscow: Progress Publishers, 1972.

————. "Theses on Feuerbach." In *On Historical Materialism,* pp. 11–13. Ed. T. Borodulina. Moscow: Progress Publishers, 1972.

Marx, Karl, and Friedrich Engels. *On Religion.* New York: Schocken Books, 1964.

Michelet, Jules. *Joan of Arc.* Trans. Albert Guérard. Ann Arbor: University of Michigan Press, 1967.

Milton, John. *Paradise Lost.* In *Complete Poems and Major Prose,* pp. 173–469. Ed. Merritt Y. Hughes. Indianapolis: Bobbs-Merrill, 1957. Rpt. 1980.

Nicolson, Nigel. *Portrait of a Marriage: V. Sackville-West and Harold Nicolson.* New York: Atheneum, 1987.

Paine, Albert Bigelow. *The Girl in White Armor: The True Story of Joan of Arc.* New York: Macmillan, 1927.

————. *Joan of Arc: Maid of France*. 2 vols. New York: Macmillan, 1925.

————. *Mark Twain: A Biography*. 4 vols. New York: Harper and Brothers, 1912.

Péguy, Charles. *Men and Saints: Prose and Poetry*. Trans. Anne and Julian Green. New York: Pantheon, 1944.

————. *The Mystery of the Charity of Joan of Arc*. Trans. Julian Green. New York: Pantheon, 1950.

————. *Œuvres poétiques complètes*. Ed. Pierre Péguy. Paris: Gallimard, 1957.

Pernoud, Régine. *Joan of Arc by Herself and Her Witnesses*. Trans. Edward Hyams. Lanham, Md.: Scarborough, 1994.

————. *The Retrial of Joan of Arc*. Trans. J. M. Cohen. New York: Harcourt, Brace and Co., 1955.

Pernoud, Régine, and Marie-Véronique Clin. *Joan of Arc: Her Story*. Trans. Jeremy duQuesnay Adams. Ed. Bonnie Wheeler. New York: St. Martin's, 1998.

Quicherat, Jules-Etienne-Joseph, ed. *Procès de condamnation et de réhabilitation de Jeanne d'Arc dite la Pucelle*. 5 vols. Paris: Jules Renouard, 1841–1849. Rpt. New York: Johnson, 1965.

The Romantics on Milton: Formal Essays and Critical Asides. Ed. Joseph A. Wittreich Jr. Cleveland: Case Western Reserve University Press, 1970.

Sackville-West, Vita. *The Eagle and the Dove: A Study of Contrasts. St. Teresa of Avila, St. Thérèse of Lisieux*. Garden City, N. Y.: Doubleday, Doran & Co., 1944.

————. *Letters of Vita Sackville-West to Virginia Woolf*. Ed. Louise DeSalvo and Mitchell A. Leaska. New York: William Morrow, 1985.

————. *Saint Joan of Arc*. New York: Doubleday, 1991.

Schiller, Friedrich. "Das Mädchen von Orleans." In *Gedichte, Erzählungen, Übersetzungen*, p. 381. Munich: Artemis and Winkler, 1993.

————. *Die Jungfrau von Orleans*. Ed. Benno von Weise and Lieselotte Blumenthal. In *Schillers Werke* (Nationalausgabe). Vol. 9. Weimar: Hermann Böhlaus, 1948.

————. *Essays*. Ed. Walter Hinderer and Daniel O. Dahlstrom. German Library, vol. 17. New York: Continuum, 1993.

————. *Historische Schriften*. Ed. Karl-Heinz Hahn. In *Schillers Werke*. Vol. 17. Weimar: Hermann Böhlaus, 1970.

————. *Letters on the Aesthetic Education of Man*. Trans. Elizabeth M. Wilkinson and L. A. Willoughby. In *Essays*, pp. 86–178. Ed. Walter Hinderer and Daniel O. Dahlstrom. German Library, vol. 17. New York: Continuum, 1993.

————. *The Maiden of Orléans*. Trans. John T. Krumpelmann. University of North Carolina Studies in the Germanic Languages and Literatures, No. 24. Chapel Hill: University of North Carolina Press, 1959.

————. "On the Art of Tragedy." Trans. Daniel O. Dahstrom. In *Essays*, pp. 1–21. Ed. Walter Hinderer and Daniel O. Dahlstrom. German Library, vol. 17. New York: Continuum, 1993.

————. "On Naïve and Sentimental Poetry." Trans. Daniel O. Dahlstrom. In *Essays*, pp. 179–260. Ed. Walter Hinderer and Daniel O. Dahlstrom. German Library, vol. 17. New York: Continuum, 1993.

————. *Philosophische Shriften*. Ed. Helmut Koopmann. In *Sämtliche Werke*. Vol. 5. Munich: Winkler Verlag, 1968.

————. *Schillers Briefe, 1798–1800*. Ed. Lieselotte Blumenthal. In *Schillers Werke* (Nationalausgabe). Vol. 30. Weimar: Hermann Böhlaus, 1961.

————. *Schillers Briefe, 1801–1802*. Ed. Stefan Ormanns. In *Schillers Werke* (Nationalausgabe). Vol. 31. Weimar: Hermann Böhlaus, 1985.

Shakespeare, William. *King Henry VI, Part 1*. Ed. Andrew S. Cairncross. Arden edition. London: Methuen, 1962.

Shaw, [George] Bernard. *Collected Letters, 1911–1925*. Ed. Dan H. Laurence. New York: Viking, 1985.

————. "The Quintessence of Ibsenism." In *Selected Non-Dramatic Writings of Bernard Shaw*, pp. 205–306. Ed. Dan H. Laurence. Boston: Houghton Mifflin, 1965.

————. *The Religious Speeches of Bernard Shaw*. Ed. Warren Sylvester Smith. University Park: Pennsylvania State University Press, 1963.

————. *Saint Joan: A Chronicle Play in Six Scenes and an Epilogue*. Ed. Dan H. Laurence. New York: Penguin, 1957.

Robert Southey: The Critical Heritage. Ed. Lionel Madden. London: Routledge and Kegan Paul, 1972.

Southey, Robert. *The Life and Correspondence of Robert Southey*. Ed. Reverend Charles Cuthbert Southey. New York: Harper, 1851.

————. *New Letters of Robert Southey*. 2 vols. Ed. Kenneth Curry. New York: Columbia University Press, 1965.

————. *The Poetical Works (1844–1849)*. 10 vols. Hildesheim: Georg Olms Verlag, 1977.

————. "Robert Southey's Joan of Arc: A Critical Edition of the First Edition (1796)." Ed. Arnold R. Beath. Ph. D. dissertation, Kansas State University, 1974.

————. *Selections from the Letters of Robert Southey*. 4 vols. Ed. John Wood Warter. London: Longman, 1856.

————. *Sir Thomas More: Or, Colloquies on the Progress and Prospects of Society*. 2 vols. London: John Murray, 1829.

Spenser, Edmund. *The Faerie Queene*. Ed. Thomas P. Roche Jr., with the assistance of C. Patrick O'Donnell Jr. New York: Penguin, 1978. Rpt. 1979.

Thérèse of Lisieux, Saint. *Story of a Soul: The Autobiography of St. Thérèse of Lisieux*. 2d ed. Trans. John Clark, O. C. D. Washington, D. C.: Institute of Carmelite Studies, 1976.

Tournier, Michel. *Gilles and Jeanne: A Novel*. Trans. Alan Sheridan. New York: Grove Weidenfeld, 1987.

————. *Gilles et Jeanne: Récit*. Paris: Gallimard, 1983.

Twain, Mark. *The Autobiography of Mark Twain*. Ed. Charles Neider. New York: Harper and Row, 1959.

————. *A Connecticut Yankee in King Arthur's Court.* Ed. Bernard L. Stein. In *The Works of Mark Twain,* vol. 9. Berkeley: Iowa Center for Textual Studies and University of California Press, 1979.

————. *Life on the Mississippi.* Ed. James M. Cox. New York: Penguin Books, 1984.

————. *The Love Letters of Mark Twain.* Ed. Dixon Wecter. New York: Harper and Brothers, 1949.

————. *Mark Twain to Mrs. Fairbanks.* Ed. Dixon Wecter. San Marino, Calif.: Huntington Library Publications, 1949.

————. *Mark Twain–Howells Letters: The Correspondence of Samuel L. Clemens and William D. Howells, 1872–1910.* 2 vols. Ed. Frederick Anderson, William M. Gibson, and Henry Nash Smith. Cambridge, Mass.: Harvard University Press, 1960.

————. *Mark Twain's Correspondence with Henry Huddleston Rogers, 1893–1909.* Ed. Lewis Leary. Berkeley: University of California Press, 1969.

————. *Mark Twain's Letters.* 2 vols. Ed. Albert Bigelow Paine. New York: Harper and Brothers, 1917.

————. *Mark Twain's Letters, 1853–1866.* Ed. Edgar Marquess Branch, Michael B. Frank, and Kenneth M. Sanderson. Berkeley: University of California Press, 1988.

————. *Mark Twain's Letters to His Publishers, 1867–1894.* Ed. Hamlin Hill. Berkeley: University of California Press, 1967.

————. *Mark Twain's Notebook.* Ed. Albert Bigelow Paine. New York: Harper and Brothers, 1935.

————. *Personal Recollections of Joan of Arc by the Sieur Louis de Conte (Her Page and Secretary).* New York: Harper and Brothers, 1896; San Francisco: Ignatius, 1989.

————. "The Turning Point of My Life." In *"What Is Man?" and Other Philosophical Writings,* pp. 455–464. Ed. Paul Baender. In *The Works of Mark Twain,* vol. 19. Berkeley: Iowa Center for Textual Studies and University of California Press, 1973.

————. "What Is Man?" In *"What Is Man?" and Other Philosophical Writings,* pp. 125–214. Ed. Paul Baender. In *The Works of Mark Twain,* vol. 19. Berkeley: Iowa Center for Textual Studies and University of California Press, 1973.

Werfel, Franz. *Das Lied von Bernadette: Roman.* Wein: Bermann-Fischer, 1949.

————. *The Song of Bernadette.* Trans. Ludwig Lewisohn. New York: Viking, 1943.

Woolf, Virginia. "The Art of Biography." In *Collected Essays,* vol. 4, pp. 221–228. New York: Harcourt, Brace and World, 1967.

————. *Collected Essays.* 4 vols. Ed. Leonard Woolf. London: Chatto and Windus, 1969.

————. *Congenial Spirits: The Selected Letters of Virginia Woolf.* Ed. Joanne Trautmann Banks. New York: Harcourt Brace Jovanovich, 1989.

————. *The Diary of Virginia Woolf.* 4 vols. Ed. Anne Olivier Bell, assisted by Andrew McNellie. New York: Harcourt Brace Jovanovich, 1982.

————. "The New Biography." In *Collected Essays,* vol. 4, pp. 229–235. Ed. Leonard Woolf. London: Chatto and Windus, 1969.

————. *Orlando: A Biography.* New York: Harcourt, 1956.

————. *A Room of One's Own.* New York: Harcourt, Brace and World, 1957.

————. "A Sketch of the Past." In *Moments of Being: Unpublished Autobiographical Writing,* pp. 64–137. Ed. Jeanne Schulkind. London: Sussex University Press, 1976.

Wordsworth, William. *The Poetical Works of William Wordsworth.* 5 vols. Ed. Ernest De Selincourt. Rev. Helen Darbishire. Oxford: Clarendon Press, 1940–1959.

Secondary Sources

Abel, Richard. *French Cinema: The First Wave, 1915–1929.* Princeton: Princeton University Press, 1984.

Adereth, M. *Commitment in Modern French Literature: Politics and Society in Péguy, Aragon and Sartre.* New York: Schocken Books, 1968.

Adorno, Theodor W. *Notes to Literature.* Vol. 2. Trans. Shierry Weber Nicholsen. Ed. Rolf Tiedemann. New York: Columbia University Press, 1991.

Albers, Jürgen. "Die Geschichte der Simone Machard: Eine zarte Traumerei nach Motiven von Marx, Lenin, Schiller." *Brecht-Jahrbuch* (1978): 66–86.

Amar, Yvonne A. "Mark Twain's Joan of Arc: An 'Asbestos' Character Rising from the Ashes." *Mark Twain Journal* 19.3 (1978–1979): 13–19.

Arendt, Hannah. *Eichmann in Jerusalem: A Report on the Banality of Evil.* New York: Viking, 1963.

Astell, Ann W. "Joan." In *The Saints in Soliloquy: A Collection of Dramatic Monologues,* pp. 39–41. Notre Dame, Ind.: Foundations Press, 1984.

————. "Telling Tales of Love: Julia Kristeva and Bernard of Clairvaux." *Christianity and Literature* 50.1 (2000): 125–148.

Barthes, Roland. "Authors and Writers." In *A Barthes Reader,* pp. 185–193. Ed. Susan Sontag. New York: Hill and Wang, 1982.

————. "The Death of the Author." In *Authorship from Plato to the Postmodern: A Reader,* pp. 125–130. Ed. Seán Burke. Edinburgh: Edinburgh University Press, 1995.

Baudrillard, Jean. *For a Critique of the Political Economy of the Sign.* Trans. Charles Levin. St. Louis: Telos Press, 1981.

Bemporad, Jack, and Michael Shevack. *Our Age: The Historic New Era of Christian-Jewish Understanding.* New York: New City Press, 1996.

Bénichou, Paul. *The Consecration of the Writer, 1750–1830.* Trans. Mark K. Jensen. Lincoln: University of Nebraska Press, 1999.

Benjamin, Walter. "The Work of Art in the Age of Its Mechanical Reproduction." In *Illuminations: Essays and Reflections,* pp. 217–251. Trans. Harry Zohn. Ed. Hannah Arendt. New York: Schocken Books, 1969.

Bennett, Benjamin. *Modern Drama and German Classicism: Renaissance from Lessing to Brecht.* Ithaca: Cornell University Press, 1979.

Bernhardt-Kabisch, Ernest. *Robert Southey.* Boston: Twayne, 1977.

Blaetz, Robin. *Visions of the Maid: Joan of Arc in American Film and Culture.* Charlottesville: University Press of Virginia, 2002.

Bloom, Harold. *The Anxiety of Influence: A Theory of Poetry.* 2d ed. Oxford: Oxford University Press, 1997.

Bradley, Ruth Mary. "The Making of Mark Twain's *Personal Recollections of Joan of Arc.*" Ph.D. dissertation, University of California, Los Angeles, 1970.

Brownlee, Kevin. "Structures of Authority in Christine de Pizan's *Ditié de Jehanne d'Arc.*" In *Discourses of Authority in Medieval and Renaissance Literature,* pp. 131–150. Ed. Kevin Brownlee and Walter Stephens. Hanover, N.H.: University Press of New England, 1989.

Bulgakov, Sergei. *Karl Marx as a Religious Type.* Trans. Luba Barna. Ed. Virgil Lang. Belmont, Mass.: Nordland, 1979.

Burke, Seán. "The Ethics of Signature." In *Authorship from Plato to the Postmodern: A Reader,* pp. 285–291. Ed. Seán Burke. Edinburgh: Edinburgh University Press, 1995.

Carlyle, Thomas. *The Life of Friedrich Schiller.* Vol. 25 in *The Works of Thomas Carlyle,* 30 vols. 1825. London: Chapman and Hall, 1899.

Castle, Terry. "The Spectralization of the Other in *The Mysteries of Udolpho.*" In *The Female Thermometer: Eighteenth-Century Culture and the Invention of the Uncanny,* pp. 120–139. Oxford: Oxford University Press, 1995.

Chester, Giraud. *Embattled Maiden: The Life of Anna Dickinson.* New York: Pantheon, 1951.

Cloonan, William. *Michel Tournier.* Boston: Twayne, 1985.

Cox, James. *Mark Twain: The Fate of Humor.* Princeton: Princeton University Press, 1966.

Crane, Susan. "Clothing and Gender Definition: Joan of Arc." *Journal of Medieval and Early Modern Studies* 26.2 (1996): 297–320.

Cuomo, Glenn R. "'*Saint Joan* before the Cannibals': George Bernard Shaw in the Third Reich." *German Studies Review* 16.3 (1993): 435–461.

Curry, Kenneth. *Southey.* London: Routledge and Kegan Paul, 1975.

Darmesteter, James. "Joan of Arc in England." In *English Studies,* pp. 3–71. Trans. Mary Darmesteter. London: T. Fisher Unwin, 1896.

Despres, Denise. "Le Triomphe de L'Humilite: Thérèse of Lisieux and 'Une Nouvelle Jeanne.'" In *Joan of Arc and Spirituality.* Ed. Bonnie Wheeler and Ann W. Astell. Forthcoming.

DeSalvo, Louise A. "Lighting the Cave: The Relationship between Vita Sackville-West and Virginia Woolf." *Signs: A Journal of Women in Culture and Society* 8.2 (1982): 195–214.

D'Israeli, I.C. *Curiosities of Literature and the Literary Character Illustrated.* New York: D. Appleton, 1846.

Dingley, R.R. "Joan of Arc and the *Destiny of Nations.*" *Durham University Journal* 77, n.s. 46 (1985): 203–209.

Dunaway, John M. "Michel Tournier: Christian Writer?" *Christianity and Literature* 49 (2000): 357–370.

Düntzer, Heinrich. *The Life of Schiller.* Trans. Percy E. Pinkerton. London: Macmillan, 1883.

Early, Benjamin W. "Southey's 'Joan of Arc': The Unpublished Manuscript, the First Edition, and a Study of the Later Revisions." 2 vols. Ph. D. dissertation, Duke University, 1951.

Emerson, Everett. *The Authentic Mark Twain: A Literary Biography of Samuel L. Clemens.* Philadelphia: University of Pennsylvania Press, 1984.

Engel, E. J., and W. F. Mainland. "Introduction." In Friedrich Schiller, *Die Jungfrau von Orleans,* pp. vii–xxvii. Ed. E. J. Engel and W. F. Mainland. London: Thomas Nelson, 1963.

Esslin, Martin. *Brecht: The Man and His Work.* Garden City, N. Y.: Doubleday, 1971.

Ewen, Frederic. *The Prestige of Schiller in England, 1788–1859.* New York: Columbia University Press, 1932.

Foucault, Michel. "What Is an Author?" In *Language, Counter-Memory, Practice,* pp. 113–138. Ed. Donald F. Bouchard. Trans. Donald F. Bouchard and Sherry Simon. Ithaca: Cornell University Press, 1977.

Fraioli, Deborah A. *Joan of Arc: The Early Debate.* Rochester, N. Y.: Boydell, 2000.

Frohock, W. M. "Georges Bernanos (1888–1948)." In *The Politics of Twentieth-Century Novelists,* pp. 160–173. Ed. George A. Panchas. New York: Hawthorn, 1971.

Fuegi, John. "The Zelda Syndrome: Brecht and Elisabeth Hauptmann." In *The Cambridge Companion to Brecht,* pp. 104–116. Ed. Peter Thomson and Glendyr Sacks. Cambridge: Cambridge University Press, 1994.

Gainor, J. Ellen. *Shaw's Daughters: Dramatic and Narrative Constructions of Gender.* Ann Arbor: University of Michigan Press, 1991.

Garland, H. B. *Schiller, the Dramatic Writer: A Study of Style in the Plays.* Oxford: Clarendon Press, 1969.

Gascoigne, David. *Michel Tournier.* New Directions in European Writing. Oxford: Berg, 1996.

Geyersbach, Viola. "Schiller, 1759–1788." In *Friedrich Schiller, 1759–1805. Austellung zum 225 Geburtstag des Dichters der deutschen Klassik,* pp. 31–66. Weimar: Waisenhaus, 1984.

Gilbert, Sandra M., and Susan Gubar. *The Madwoman in the Attic: The Woman Writer and the Nineteenth-Century Literary Imagination.* New Haven: Yale University Press, 1979.

Girard, René. "Are the Gospels Mythical?" *First Things* 62 (April 1996): 27–31.

———. *Le Bouc émissaire.* Paris: Bernard Grasset, 1982.

———. *Des Choses caches depuis la fondation du monde.* Paris: Bernard Grasset, 1978.

———. *I See Satan Fall Like Lightning.* Trans. James G. Williams. Maryknoll, N. Y.: Orbis, 2001.

———. *The Scapegoat.* Trans. Yvonne Freccero. Baltimore: Johns Hopkins University Press, 1986.

———. *Things Hidden since the Foundation of the World.* Trans. Stephen Bann and Michael Metteer. Stanford: Stanford University Press, 1987.

———. *Violence and the Sacred.* Trans. Patrick Gregory. Baltimore: Johns Hopkins University Press, 1977.

———. *La Violence et la sacré.* Paris: Bernard Grasset, 1972.

Gleckner, Robert F. *Blake and Spenser.* Baltimore: Johns Hopkins University Press, 1985.

Glendinning, Victoria. *Vita: The Life of V. Sackville-West.* New York: Alfred A. Knopf, 1983.

Glenny, Allie. *Ravenous Identity: Eating and Eating Distress in the Life and Work of Virginia Woolf.* New York: St. Martin's, 1999.

Goodhart, Sandor. *Sacrificing Commentary: Reading the End of Literature.* Baltimore: Johns Hopkins University Press, 1996.

Gordon, Mary. *Joan of Arc.* New York: Viking Penguin, 2000.

Graham, Ilse Appelbaum. "The Structure of the Personality in Schiller's Tragic Poetry." In *Schiller: Bicentenary Lectures,* pp. 104–144. Ed. F. Norman. London: University of London Institute of Germanic Languages and Literatures, 1960.

Graham, James. "Shaw on *Saint Joan.*" In *"Saint Joan" Fifty Years After,* pp. 15–22. Ed. Stanley Weintraub. Baton Rouge: Louisiana State University Press, 1973.

Gribben, Alan. "The Library and Reading of Samuel L. Clemens." 5 vols. Ph.D. dissertation, University of California, Berkeley, 1974.

Guy-Blanquet, Dominique. *Shakespeare et l'invention de l'histoire.* Brussels: Le Cri, 1997.

Hamilton, A.C. *The Structure of Allegory in "The Faerie Queene."* Oxford: Oxford University Press, 1961.

Hard, Frederick. "Lamb on Spenser." In *Royston Memorial Studies,* pp. 124–138. Chapel Hill: University of North Carolina Press, 1931.

Harris, Susan K. *Mark Twain's Escape from Time: A Study of Patterns and Images.* Columbus: University of Missouri Press, 1982.

Hart, Gail K. "Re-dressing History: Mother Nature, Mother Isabeau, the Virgin Mary, and Schiller's *Jungfrau.*" *Women in German Yearbook* 14 (1988): 91–107.

Harty, Kevin J. "The Nazis, Joan of Arc, and Medievalism Gone Awry: Gustav Ucicky's 1935 Film, *Das Mädchen Johanna.*" In *Rationality and the Liberal Arts: A Festchrift Honoring Ira Lee Morgan,* pp. 122–133. Ed. Willie Cavett and Paul M. Brown Jr. Shreveport, La.: Centenary College, 1997.

Hendricks, Gordon. *Origins of the American Film.* New York: Arno Press and the New York Times, 1972.

Hickey, Alison. "Coleridge, Southey, 'and Co.': Collaboration and Authority." *Studies in Romanticism* 37.3 (1998): 305–349.

Hill, Hamlin. *Mark Twain, God's Fool.* New York: Harper and Row, 1973.

———. "Mark Twain: Texts and Technology." In *Cultural Artifacts and the Production of Meaning: The Page, the Image, and the Body,* pp. 71–84. Ed. Margaret J.M. Ezell and Katherine O'Brien O'Keeffe. Ann Arbor: University of Michigan Press, 1994.

Hinderer, Walter. "Ist das epische Theater etwa eine 'moralische Anstalt'? Bemerkungen zu Brechts Kritischer Aneignung von Schillers Dramaturgie." In *Probleme der Moderne: Studien zur deutschen Literatur von Nietzsche bis Brecht,* pp. 459–475. Ed. Benjamin Bennett, Anton Kaes, and William J. Lillyman. Tübingen: Max Niemeyer, 1983.

Hinderer, Walter, and Daniel O. Dahlstrom. "Introduction." In Friedrich Schiller, *Essays,* pp. vii–xxv. German Library, vol. 17. New York: Continuum, 1993.

Hotchkiss, Valerie R. "Chapter 4: Transvestism on Trial: The Case of Jeanne d'Arc." In *Clothes Make the Man: Female Cross-Dressing in Medieval Europe,* pp. 49–68. New Middle Ages, No. 1. New York: Garland, 1996.

Howells, William Dean. *My Mark Twain: Reminiscences and Criticisms.* Ed. Marilyn Austin Baldwin. Baton Rouge: Louisiana State University Press, 1967.

Humes, Joy Nachod. *Two against Time: A Study of the Very Present Worlds of Paul Claudel and Charles Péguy.* North Carolina Studies in the Romance Languages and Literatures, No. 200. Chapel Hill: University of North Carolina Press, 1978.

Hummert, Paul A. *Bernard Shaw's Marxian Romance.* Lincoln: University of Nebraska Press, 1973.

Isaac, Jules. *The Teaching of Contempt: Christian Roots of Anti-Semitism.* Trans. Helen Weaver. New York: Holt, Rinehart and Winston, 1964.

John Paul II on Jews and Judaism. Ed. Eugene J. Fischer and Leon Klenicki. Washington, D.C.: United States Catholic Conference, 1987.

Jungk, Peter Stephan. *Franz Werfel: A Life in Prague, Vienna, and Hollywood.* Trans. Anselm Hollo. New York: Grove Weidenfeld, 1990.

Jurick, Joseph C. "Mark Twain's *Joan of Arc:* Origins, Purposes and Accomplishments." Ph.D. dissertation, University of Illinois, 1962.

Kaplan, Edward K. *Michelet's Poetic Vision: A Romantic Philosophy of Nature, Man, and Woman.* Amherst: University of Massachusetts Press, 1977.

Kaplan, Justin. *Mr. Clemens and Mark Twain: A Biography.* New York: Simon and Schuster, 1966.

Kelly, H. Ansgar. "The Right to Remain Silent: Before and After Joan of Arc." *Speculum* 68.4 (1993): 992–1026.

King, James. *Virginia Woolf.* New York: W. W. Norton, 1995.

Kippur, Stephen A. *Jules Michelet: A Study of Mind and Sensibility.* Albany: State University of New York Press, 1981.

Kucich, Greg. *Keats, Shelley, and Romantic Spenserianism.* University Park: Pennsylvania State University Press, 1991.

Lapide, Pinchas E. *The Last Three Popes and the Jews.* London: Souvenir, 1967.

Lears, T. J. Jackson. *No Place of Grace: Antimodernism and the Transformation of American Culture, 1880–1920.* New York: Pantheon, 1981.

Levinas, Emmanuel. *Difficult Freedom: Essays on Judaism.* Trans. Seán Hand. Baltimore: Johns Hopkins University Press, 1990.

Levy, Karen D. "Tournier's Ultimate Perversion: The Historical Manipulation of *Gilles et Jeanne.*" *Papers on Language and Literature* 28 (1992): 72–88.

Lewis, Thomas S. W. "Combining 'the Advantage of Fact and Fiction': Virginia Woolf's Biographies of Vita Sackville-West, Flush, and Roger Fry." In *Virginia Woolf: Centennial Essays,* pp. 295–324. Ed. Elaine K. Ginsberg and Laura Moss Gottlieb. Troy, N. Y.: Whitson, 1983.

Lightbody, Charles Wayland. *The Judgements of Joan: Joan of Arc, a Study in Cultural History.* Cambridge, Mass.: Harvard University Press, 1961.

Lyon, James K. *Bertolt Brecht in America.* Princeton: Princeton University Press, 1980.

Maccaffrey, Isabel G. *Spenser's Allegory: The Anatomy of Imagination.* Princeton: Princeton University Press, 1976.

Marder, Herbert. *The Measure of Life: Virginia Woolf's Last Years.* Ithaca: Cornell University Press, 2000.

Margolis, Nadia. *Joan of Arc in History, Literature, and Film: A Select, Annotated Bibliography.* New York: Garland, 1990.

———. "Trial by Passion: Philology, Film, and Ideology in the Portrayal of Joan of Arc (1900–1930)." *Journal of Medieval and Early Modern Studies* 27.3 (1997): 445–493.

Mayer, Hans. "The Scandal of Joan of Arc: Schiller, Shaw, Brecht, Vishnevskii." In *Outsiders,* pp. 29–51. Trans. Denis M. Sweet. Cambridge, Mass.: MIT Press, 1982.

McCullough, Christopher. "*Saint Joan of the Stockyards.*" In *The Cambridge Companion to Brecht,* pp. 96–103. Ed. Peter Thomson and Glendyr Sacks. Cambridge: Cambridge University Press, 1994.

McMurtry, John. *The Structure of Marx's World-View.* Princeton: Princeton University Press, 1978.

Meachen, Edward. "History and Transcendence in Robert Southey's Epic Poems." *Studies in English Literature* 19 (1979): 589–608.

Medievalism in the Modern World: Essays in Honor of Leslie Workman. Ed. Richard Utz and Tom Shippey. Turnhout: Brepols, 1998.

Meisel, Martin. *Shaw and the Nineteenth-Century Theater.* Westport, Conn.: Greenwood Press, 1976.

Mitzman, Arthur. *Michelet, Historian: Rebirth and Romanticism in Nineteenth-Century France.* New Haven: Yale University Press, 1990.

Moreland, Kim. *The Medievalist Impulse in American Literature: Twain, Adams, Fitzgerald, and Hemingway.* Charlottesville: University Press of Virginia, 1996.

Musser, Charles. *Edison Motion Pictures, 1890–1900: An Annotated Filmography.* New York: Smithsonian Institution Press, 1997.

Nadeau, Lionel Carl. "Mark Twain's *Joan of Arc:* An Analysis of the Background and Original Sources." Ph. D. dissertation, Ball State University, 1979.

Nadel, Ira B. *Various Positions: A Life of Leonard Cohen.* New York: Pantheon, 1996.

Nesbit, Molly. "What Was an Author?" *Yale French Studies* 73 (1987): 229–257.

Newman, Amy. "Feminist Social Criticism and Marx's Theory of Religion." *Hypatia* 9.4 (1994): 15–37.

Nohrnberg, James. *The Analogy of "The Faerie Queen."* Princeton: Princeton University Press, 1976.

Notable American Women, 1607–1950: A Biographical Dictionary. 3 vols. Ed. Edward T. James. Cambridge, Mass.: Belknap Press, 1973.

Obraztsova, A. "A People's Heroine." In *"Saint Joan" Fifty Years After,* pp. 220–229. Ed. Stanley Weintraub. Baton Rouge: Louisiana State University Press, 1973.

O'Connell, Michael. *Mirror and Veil: The Historical Dimension of Spenser's "Faerie Queene."* Chapel Hill: University of North Carolina Press, 1977.

Orr, Linda. *Jules Michelet: Nature, History, and Language.* Ithaca: Cornell University Press, 1976.

Perlmutter, Dawn. "The Sacrificial Aesthetic: Blood Rituals from Art to Murder." *Anthropoetics* 5.2 (Fall 1999–Winter 2000): www.anthropoetics.ucla.edu.

Petit, Jacques. *Bernanos, Bloy, Claudel, Péguy: Quatre ecrivains catholiques face á Israël.* Paris: Calmann-Lévy, 1972.

Petit, Susan. "Michel Tournier: *Ecrivain Croyant?" Christianity and Literature* 50.2 (2001): 313–326.

Pétrement, Simone. *Simone Weil: A Life.* Trans. Raymond Rosenthal. New York: Pantheon, 1976.

Pirrucello, Ann. "Force or Fragility? Simone Weil and Two Faces of Joan of Arc." In *Joan of Arc and Spirituality.* Ed. Bonnie Wheeler and Ann W. Astell. Forthcoming.

Platten, David. *Michel Tournier and the Metaphor of Fiction.* New York: St. Martin's, 1999.

Poole, Roger. *The Unknown Virginia Woolf.* Cambridge: Cambridge University Press, 1978.

Pope, Nancy P. *National History in the Heroic Poem.* New York: Garland, 1990.

Pratt, Lynda. "Coleridge, Wordsworth, and Joan of Arc." *Notes and Queries* 239.3, n.s. 41 (1994): 335–336.

Puknat, Siegfried B. "Brecht and Schiller: Nonelective Affinities." *Modern Language Quarterly* 26 (1965): 558–570.

Purdie, Edna. "Schiller." In *Schiller: Bicentenary Lectures,* pp. 1–23. Ed. F. Norman. London: University of London, Institute of Germanic Languages and Literatures, 1960.

Quint, David. *Epic and Empire: Politics and Generic Form from Virgil to Milton.* Princeton: Princeton University Press, 1993.

Raitt, Suzanne. *Vita and Virginia: The Work and Friendship of V. Sackville-West and Virginia Woolf.* Oxford: Clarendon Press, 1993.

Raknem, Ingvald. *Joan of Arc in History, Legend and Literature.* Scandinavian University Books. Oslo: Universitetsforlaget, 1971.

Rollyson, Carl. *Lillian Hellman: Her Legend and Her Legacy.* New York: St. Martin's, 1988.

Ryder, Frank G. "Introduction." In Johann Wolfgang von Goethe, *Plays,* pp. vii–xxviii. Ed. Frank G. Ryder. German Library, vol. 20. New York: Continuum, 1993.

Salomon, Roger B. *Twain and the Image of History.* New Haven: Yale University Press, 1961.

Salsbury, Edith Colgate. *Susy and Mark Twain: Family Dialogues.* New York: Harper and Row, 1965.

Schibanoff, Susan. "True Lies: Transvestism and Idolatry in the Trial of Joan of Arc." In *Fresh Verdicts on Joan of Arc,* pp. 31–61. Ed. Bonnie Wheeler and Charles T. Wood. New York: Garland, 1996.

Schrader, Paul. *Transcendental Style in Film: Ozu, Bresson, Dreyer.* Berkeley: University of California Press, 1972.

Searle, William. *The Saint and the Skeptics: Joan of Arc in the Work of Mark Twain, Anatole France, and Bernard Shaw.* Detroit: Wayne State University Press, 1976.

Sharpe, Lesley. *Friedrich Schiller: Drama, Thought and Politics.* Cambridge Studies in German. Cambridge: Cambridge University Press, 1991.

———. *Schiller and the Historical Character: Presentation and Interpretation in the Historiographical Works and in the Historical Dramas.* Oxford: Oxford University Press, 1982.

Sheppard, David. *Leonard Cohen.* New York: Thunder's Mouth Press, 2000.

Simons, John D. *Friedrich Schiller.* Boston: Twayne, 1981.

Skandera-Trombley, Laura E. *Mark Twain in the Company of Women.* Philadelphia: University of Pennsylvania Press, 1994.

Sokel, Walter H. "Brechts Marxisticher Weg zur Klassik." In *Die Klassik-Legende,* pp. 176–199. Ed. Reinhold Grimm and Jost Hermand. Schriften zur Literatur 18. Frankfurt am Main: Athenaeum, 1971.

Sorel, Georges. *Reflections on Violence.* Trans. T. E. Hulme and J. Roth. New York: Collier, 1974.

Sproles, Karyn Z. "Cross-Dressing for (Imaginary) Battle: Vita Sackville-West's Biography of Joan of Arc." *Biography* 19.2 (1996): 158–177.

———. "Virginia Woolf Writes to Vita Sackville-West (and Receives a Reply): *Aphra Behn, Orlando, Saint Joan of Arc,* and Revolutionary Biography." In *Virginia Woolf: Texts and Contexts,* pp. 189–193. Ed. Beth Rigel Daugherty and Eileen Barrett. New York: Pace University Press, 1996.

Stahl, E. L. *Friedrich Schiller's Drama: Theory and Practice.* Oxford: Clarendon Press, 1954.

Stone, Albert E., Jr. *The Innocent Eye: Childhood in Mark Twain's Imagination.* New Haven: Yale University Press, 1961.

Stoneley, Peter. *Mark Twain and the Feminine Aesthetic.* Cambridge Studies in American Literature and Culture, No. 54. Cambridge: Cambridge University Press, 1992.

Surya, Michel. *Georges Bataille: La mort a l'oeuvre.* Paris: Frédéric Birr, 1987.

Thomson, Peter. "Brecht's Lives." In *The Cambridge Companion to Brecht,* pp. 22–42. Ed. Peter Thomson and Glendyr Sacks. Cambridge: Cambridge University Press, 1994.

Tucker, Robert. *Philosophy and Myth in Karl Marx.* 2d ed. Cambridge: Cambridge University Press, 1972.

Villiers, Marjorie. *Charles Péguy: A Study in Integrity.* Westport, Conn.: Greenwood Press, 1965.

Völker, Klaus. *Brecht: A Biography.* Trans. John Nowell. London: Marion Boyars, 1979.

Wagener, Hans. *Understanding Franz Werfel.* Columbia: University of South Carolina Press, 1993.

Weintraub, Stanley. "Introduction." In *"Saint Joan" Fifty Years After,* pp. 3–7. Ed. Stanley Weintraub. Baton Rouge: Louisiana State University Press, 1973.

Wells, Benjamin W. "Introduction." *Schiller's Jungfrau von Orleans: Eine romantische Tragödie,* pp. iii–xviii. Rev. ed. Benjamin W. Wells. Boston: D. C. Heath, 1901.

West, Alick. "*Saint Joan:* A Marxist View." In *"Saint Joan" Fifty Years After,* pp. 106–113. Ed. Stanley Weintraub. Baton Rouge: Louisiana State University Press, 1973.

White, W. "Schiller: Reflections on a Bicentenary." In *Schiller: Bicentenary Lectures,* pp. 145–168. Ed. F. Norman. London: University of London, Institute of Germanic Languages and Literatures, 1960.

Who Was Who in American Art. Ed. Pater Hastings Falk. Madison, Conn.: Sound View Press, 1985.

Wilkinson, Elizabeth M. "Reflections after Translating Schiller's *Letters on the Aesthetic Education of Man.*" In *Schiller: Bicentenary Lectures,* pp. 46–82. Ed. F. Norman. London: University of London, Institute of Germanic Languages and Literatures, 1960.

Wilson, James D. "In Quest of Redemptive Vision: Mark Twain's *Joan of Arc.*" *Texas Studies in Literature and Language* 20.2 (1978): 181–198.

Winock, Michel. "Jeanne d'Arc et les Juifs." *H-Histoire* 3 (1979): 227–238.

Wisenthal, J. L. *Shaw's Sense of History.* Oxford: Clarendon Press, 1988.

Wittreich, Joseph Anthony, Jr. "Introduction." In *The Romantics on Milton: Formal Essays and Critical Asides,* pp. 3–32. Ed. Joseph Anthony Wittreich Jr. Cleveland: Case Western Reserve University Press, 1970.

Wofford, Susanne L. *The Choice of Achilles: The Ideology of Figure in the Epic.* Stanford: Stanford University Press, 1992.

Wood, Charles T. *Joan of Arc and Richard III: Sex, Saints, and Government in the Middle Ages.* New York: Oxford University Press, 1988.

Woolf, Vicki. *Dancing in the Vortex: The Story of Ida Rubinstein.* Choreography and Dance Studies 20. Amsterdam: Harwood Academic Publishers, 2000.

Wright, William. *Lillian Hellman: The Image, the Woman.* New York: Simon and Schuster, 1986.

Wyschogrod, Edith. *Saints and Postmodernism: Revisioning Moral Philosophy.* Chicago: University of Chicago Press, 1990.

ABOUT THE AUTHOR

ANN W. ASTELL is professor of English at Purdue University. She is the author of several books and editor of *Lay Sanctity, Medieval and Modern*, published by the University of Notre Dame Press.